Lecture Notes in Artificial Intelligence 2854

Edited by J. G. Carbonell and J. Siekmann

Subseries of Lecture Notes in Computer Science

Springer
Berlin
Heidelberg
New York
Hong Kong
London
Milan
Paris
Tokyo

Jörg Hoffmann

Utilizing Problem Structure in Planning

A Local Search Approach

 Springer

Series Editors

Jaime G. Carbonell, Carnegie Mellon University, Pittsburgh, PA, USA
Jörg Siekmann, University of Saarland, Saarbrücken, Germany

Author

Jörg Hoffmann
Universität Freiburg, Institut für Informatik
Georges-Köhler-Allee, Geb. 52, 79110 Freiburg, Germany
E-mail: hoffmann@informatik.uni-freiburg.de

Cataloging-in-Publication Data applied for

A catalog record for this book is available from the Library of Congress

Bibliographic information published by Die Deutsche Bibliothek
Die Deutsche Bibliothek lists this publication in the Deutsche Nationalbibliographie;
detailed bibliographic data is available in the Internet at <http://dnd.ddb.de>.

CR Subject Classification (1998): I.2.8, I.2, F.2.2

ISSN 0302-9743
ISBN 3-540-20259-5 Springer-Verlag Berlin Heidelberg New York

Springer-Verlag Berlin Heidelberg New York,
a member of BertelsmannSpringer Science+Business Media GmbH

http://www.springer.de

© Springer-Verlag Berlin Heidelberg 2003
Printed in Germany

Typesetting: Camera-ready by author, data conversion by Christian Grosche, Hamburg
Printed on acid-free paper   SPIN: 10965696   06/3142   5 4 3 2 1 0

Foreword

Planning is a crucial skill for any autonomous agent, be it a physically embedded agent, such as a robot, or a purely simulated, software agent. For this reason, planning is one of the central research areas in Artificial Intelligence. The area is concerned with the automatic construction of plans that map a given initial situation into a target situation that satisfies some given goal conditions. Here, plans are usually sequences of deterministic actions.

While there has been a lot of research in this area since the beginning of the 1970s, only recently has the practical efficiency of planning methods come into the focus of the research community – most probably partially caused by the biennial international competition of planning systems, which started in 1998.

Planning is known to be a computationally quite demanding problem. Even in its simplest form – planning for basic propositional STRIPS – planning is PSPACE-complete. However, the planning problems humans and artificial agents are asked to solve are often much easier than the general problem. Based on this observation, Jörg Hoffmann investigated the structure of such planning tasks. Starting with the planning tasks used in the first planning competition, he developed his planning methodology to be able to cope with these and other problems published in the planning literature. So, instead of developing a new general planning method that might also solve the problems at hand, Jörg developed his planning methodology having in mind the concrete planning tasks.

The main ingredient of Jörg's planning methodology is the view of planning as a heuristic search, as developed by Geffner and Bonet. This approach is based on extracting informative heuristics, i.e., estimations of a search state's goal distance, automatically from the problem encoding.

Based on this work, Jörg develops a new heuristic that takes into account positive interactions between different actions, he designs a new local search technique, and he introduces a new pruning technique. These three techniques are the main methods used in the planning system FF, whose performance, measured on a large range of benchmark problems, is well above most of the other known planning systems. In fact, FF was the clear winner of the international planning competition in 2000 and is now one of the main references in the area of planning.

This success raised the question of what the structural properties of the benchmark problems are that allow us to solve them so easily. Based on earlier work in the area of propositional satisfiability, Jörg analyzes the landscape of the problems that are induced by the heuristic estimate. He is able to show that the empirical hardness is dependent on the number and size of local minima and plateaus and on the number and distance of improved exits for the latter. The analysis is carried out both theoretically and empirically, and divides the current planning benchmarks into a taxonomy of classes that differ in terms of how easily they can be solved using heuristic planners such as FF. These results are very useful for evaluating domains and for improving local search algorithms.

In summary, this work's two contributions to the state of the art in planning are so significant that the dissertation this book is based on received the prestigious ECCAI award for the best European Ph.D. thesis in 2002.

July 2003   Bernhard Nebel

Acknowledgements

This book is a revised version of my doctoral thesis, submitted to the Albert-Ludwigs-Universität Freiburg. It would not have been written without the support, encouragement, and advice of a large number of people, whom I would like to thank.

I am indebted to my thesis advisor Bernhard Nebel, whose advice was crucial for taking all the research decisions necessary to obtain the results contained in this book. I am also thankful to the second reader of my thesis, Héctor Geffner, whose work on the HSP system inspired my work on FF in the first place. I thank Jana Koehler, from whom I learned loads of things while I was a student member of the IPP team under her lead.

I would like to thank the people in the AI planning community at large; meeting them was always interesting, and fun. Special thanks go to Maria Fox, Derek Long, Julie Porteous, Laura Sebastia, Eva Onaindia, Antonio Garrido, Carmel Domshlak, Ronen Brafman, Blai Bonet, Sylvie Thiebaux, Bart Selman, Carla Gomes, Fahiem Bacchus, and many others, for enjoyable visits, fun nights out, inspiring discussions, and/or fruitful collaborative work. A very special mention goes to Eva Onaindia and Carmel Domshlak, who let me stay in the guestrooms of their private apartments during visits to Valencia University in March 2001 and to Cornell University in May 2003, respectively.

I would like to thank my colleagues in the AI research group in Freiburg, for discussions, visiting conferences together, and generally for making working life enjoyable. Special thanks go to Malte Helmert for numerous useful discussions, and to Jussi Rintanen for reading an early version of my thesis. Very special thanks go to my office mate Thilo Weigel, for many humorous comments, for watering the plants, for suggesting to put a new line into the title of this book, and for singing along to Linkin Park and Britney Spears. Sitting in the office would have been boring without him.

I dedicate this book to my family and friends.

July 2003   Jörg Hoffmann

Table of Contents

List of Figures

Part I

Planning: Motivation, Definitions, Methodology

1. Introduction

One of the distinguishing qualities of humans is their pronounced ability to anticipate the effects of their actions, and form plans to achieve their goals. Being capable of keeping pace with a dynamic world, this ability is not restricted to the specific demands of any single environment. Reasoning generally about actions and plans can thus be seen as fundamental to the development of machines that are able to take intelligent action in the real world, and general problem solving, or *planning*, has been one of the central topics in the research field of Artificial Intelligence from the outset.

As is well known, most general reasoning problems are inherently intractable, or even undecidable. The planning formalisms considered in Artificial Intelligence (henceforth AI) are no exception. There does not seem to be a non-trivial planning formalism in which one can reason efficiently. Nevertheless, all living creatures must reason, and act accordingly, in a real-time environment. While for the lower life forms the reasoning often seems to come down to stimulus-response rules, humans are regularly required to reason about much less trivial problems. They usually do so without much difficulty. Our standpoint is that this is possible because the problems one is confronted with in the real world exhibit *structure*. Utilizing this structure is what makes planning, in real life, feasible.

1.1 Planning, Problem Structure, and Local Search

AI Planning, as we know it today, has evolved out of the early ideas on general problem solving [70, 78, 28], where it was tried to develop programs that are not bound to one specific application, but can reason in a general way. During the history of AI planning, many approaches have been considered to formalize this idea. Even in the simplest and most fundamental of these approaches, STRIPS [31], reasoning is still inherently intractable, precisely PSPACE-complete [15]. Furthermore, there does not seem to be a way around this complexity barrier: as an example, one of the problems that occur naturally in real life are problems of the transportation kind, where some "object" must be transported via the means of some "vehicle", in an abstract sense; now, it was recently proved that any transportation problem where there is only a limited amount of "fuel" available is NP-hard to solve [42, 43]. Considering this, it is apparent that any general problem solving formalism of reasonable expressivity will be intractable to reason

J. Hoffmann: Utilizing Problem Structure in Planning, LNAI 2854, pp. 3–10, 2003.

about in general. It is therefore mandatory, from an algorithmic point of view, to make use of *problem structure* whenever this is possible — "'problem structure" being generally any problem-specific property that might be relevant for efficient reasoning.

The need for utilizing problem structure immediately leads us to one of the most fundamental distinctions in the field of AI planning: that between domain-dependent and domain-independent planning systems. The former systems are allowed to make use of knowledge given to them from the outside, i.e., the human user. The latter systems are provided only with "physics, not advice", and must reason fully automatically. While only domain-independent systems are general problem solvers in the classical sense, domain-dependent planners clearly stand a better chance of being competitive with specialized programs. In this book we focus on domain-independent planning. Domain-independent techniques have the advantage of being more broadly applicable, and generalizing above the structure of specific problems can deliver new and interesting insights into the nature of the problems we are trying to solve — as will be exemplified by the results in this book.

Let us get into the more algorithmic issues. Say we have a problem, defining a search space that we need to explore in order to find a solution. How can we make use of problem structure, in a general way? One of the most common approaches, in AI and computer science in general, to inform a search algorithm about the structure of a problem is to supply it with a *heuristic function*. Such a function returns a number indicating the value of a search state. One can then prefer, in search, the states that are better. Usually determining the exact value of a state is intractable so the heuristic returns an estimate of that value (as an example reference to the vast amount of literature on heuristic search, there is a book by Judea Pearl [80]). The main difficulty is to come up with the heuristic function. For individual problems, this is the responsibility of the human developer. A general problem solver, however, has to come up with the heuristic function on its own. Recently, Bonet et al. [13] have invented, in the context of the STRIPS planning framework mentioned above, a domain-independent heuristic function by generalizing from one of the most common techniques used by human developers. The heuristic method we present here is a variation of this seminal idea.

Once a heuristic function has been defined, there is still the question how to utilize the information it provides. A variety of different search schemes have been proposed in the literature. These can, roughly, be classified into *global* vs. *local* (or complete vs. incomplete) search algorithms. In a nutshell, the picture is the following. A global search algorithm explores the whole search space in the sense that it does not exclude any possibility unless it can be proved that the respective path will not lead to a solution. In difference to that, a local search algorithm explores only a fraction of the search space by iteratively trying to make an improvement based upon the local surroundings of the current search state. A global search will eventually find a solution if there is one. A local search does not give this guarantee. The advantage of local search is that it can more aggressively utilize the heuristic function, by not considering regions of the search space that look unpromising though can not be proved to be fruitless. Note that this is quite similar in spirit to what human problem solvers do: one tends to concentrate on those parts of the problem that seem to be most relevant.

With the above, aggressively utilizing problem structure in a domain-independent planning context can be done by defining a general heuristic function and a local search scheme. In the first half of this book, we do exactly that. We start from the above mentioned recent approach formulating planning as heuristic search [13]. Motivated by example observations, we then modify the algorithms to more consequently utilize the example problem's structure. Amongst other things, we adapt the heuristic function to better capture a certain phenomenon, and introduce a novel local search scheme. We end up with a system that, on a broad range of examples, demonstrates drastically better scaling behavior than all previous approaches.

The unmatched performance of the system calls for a more explicit concept of what exactly the structural properties are that the algorithms utilize (as opposed to the intuitive concepts that were obtained by observing examples). This research topic is closely related to work done in the SAT community (the research field concerned with solving boolean satisfiability problems), addressing the connection between problem structure and local search performance. Particularly relevant in our context is the work done by Frank et al. [36]. In the second half of the book, we adapt their techniques to domain-independent planning, plus developing a few techniques of our own. We obtain a clear picture of what, with respect to our heuristic function, the relevant structural properties are that enable the performance of our system. In particular, we identify problem classes where our heuristic function and local search scheme yield an "approximatively polynomial" solving mechanism (this terminology will become clear soon).

1.2 An Illustrative Example

We insert a small, informal example at this point to illustrate the way general problems are formulated in domain-independent planning, and to give the reader an idea of our algorithms and the structural properties that they utilize. Let us first clarify an important notation. We will henceforth refer to the individual problems that planning systems are confronted with as planning *tasks*. This serves to avoid confusion with the complexity-theoretic notion of decision *problems*.

The example task we consider is a simple instance of the transportation problem kind mentioned above. There are two different locations L_1 and L_2, a single vehicle V, and two objects O_1 and O_2 that must be transported. O_1 is initially co-located with the vehicle and shall end up at the other location, O_2 has got to change locations the other way round. One can either move the vehicle, or load respectively unload an object. The general means of formulating such tasks is in terms of an *initial state* — what the world is like in the beginning — a *goal state*

initial state:			
V is at L_1, O_1 is at L_1, O_2 is at L_2			
goal state:			
O_1 is at L_2, O_2 is at L_1			
action set:			
name	precondition	positive effects	negative effects
$move(l, l')$	V is at l	V is at l'	V is at l
$load(o, l)$	V is at l, o is at l	o is in V	o is at l
$unload(o, l)$	V is at l, o is in V	o is at l	o is in V

Fig. 1.1. Informal example of a planning task

— what we want the world to be like in the end — and a set of *actions* — what we can do to change the world. A domain-independent planning system is then supposed to come up, without any further help, with a sequence of actions that transforms the initial state into a goal state. See an (informal) description of our example task in Figure 1.1.

We present the example task in the style of the STRIPS language, which is (the simpler) one of the planning formalisms that we will consider throughout the book. STRIPS is based on propositional logics. We will give the formal definition later. The formulation of the initial- and goal-states in Figure 1.1 should be self-explanatory. Note that the goal does not specify the location of the vehicle: one can leave unimportant aspects of the final state unspecified. In particular, this implies that there is more than just one goal state. As for the actions, note that they are parameterized and make sense only when these parameters are grounded with constants (i.e., in this case locations or objects). The precondition of an action must hold in the current state for the action to be applicable; if the action is applied, then the positive effects become true, while the negative effects become false.

The example is, of course, mundane, and trivial to solve for the reader as well as for a general reasoning mechanism: there are a mere $2 * 3^2 = 18$ different states reachable in the task (2 possible locations for the vehicle, and each 3 for the objects — L_1, L_2, or inside the vehicle). The situation changes, however, as soon as we introduce additional objects $O_3, \ldots, O_n$ and specify that they must all be transported, like O_1, from L_1 to L_2. While the task does not become any more difficult for the average human solver (except that more steps are necessary to reach the goal), it becomes intractable for a naive general problem solver: now there are $2 * 3^n$ different reachable states, and if we wanted to explore them in a, say, breadth first search manner, then we would need to consider at least $4 * 3^{n-1}$ states before reaching the goal.[1] Thus the need, even in this trivial example, to inform the general problem solver about the structure of the problem. We do that, as said, via a heuristic function.

---

[1] The states where at least one object is not at its goal location are all closer to the initial state than the goal states; arbitrarily fixing one such object yields $4 * 3^{n-1}$ different states.

The heuristic method that has been introduced by Bonet et al. [13] is to *relax* the planning task, and take, in each search state, the difficulty of solving the respective relaxed task as a heuristic measure of that state's real difficulty. The relaxation is to assume that everything that was achieved once remains true forever: the negative effects are ignored. This significantly simplifies the task. We will get into the details later. Let us now illustrate the idea by describing how a local search can find a solution path for our example task. To make the following more readable, we assume that the objects $O_3, \ldots, O_n$ are not mentioned in the goal, i.e., that they can remain at their initial location L_1. A naive breadth first search approach would in this case not need to explore exponentially many, but still $\Omega(n^5)$ states before finding a solution.[2] We consider a straightforward search procedure that, starting from the initial state, always looks at all immediate successors of the current search state and tries to pick one with better, i.e., lower, heuristic value. The solution path we find will be the 6-step action sequence $load(O_1, L_1)$, $move(L_1, L_2)$, $unload(O_1, L_2)$, $load(O_2, L_2)$, $move(L_2, L_1)$, $unload(O_2, L_1)$. The heuristic value of the initial state is 5: in the relaxation, one can execute the same action sequence except that one does not need to move the vehicle back from L_2 to L_1, because moving it from L_1 to L_2 does not affect its being at L_1; so 5 relaxed steps suffice. Of all the successors of the initial state, only the one resulting from $load(O_1, L_1)$ has a better heuristic value: in that state, a relaxed plan is the same as before except that one can additionally skip $load(O_1, L_1)$, giving us the heuristic value 4; in all other successors of the initial state one still needs 5 relaxed steps. Our local search algorithm thus chooses to execute the action $load(O_1, L_1)$. In the resulting state, let us name it s, no successor state has a better heuristic estimation: loading any of $O_3, \ldots, O_n$ does not affect the situation; if one executes the necessary move to L_2, then in the resulting state s' the relaxed plan includes the action $move(L_2, L_1)$ to re-achieve the locatedness of the vehicle at L_1, and the heuristic value of s' is still 4. Explicitly, the relaxed plan for s' is to $unload(O_1, L_2)$, $load(O_2, L_2)$, $move(L_2, L_1)$, and $unload(O_2, L_1)$. There is thus no immediate way to improve the heuristic value from s. There is, however, such a way nearby, merely one more step ahead: from s', applying $unload(O_1, L_2)$ yields a state s'' with heuristic value 3, as a relaxed plan for s'' results from skipping $unload(O_1, L_2)$ from the above relaxed plan for s'. Assume our local search scheme (like the specific search scheme that we will introduce later) is designed so that it detects the state s''. From there, finding a solution path is an easy matter: applying the actions $load(O_2, L_2)$, $move(L_2, L_1)$, and $unload(O_2, L_1)$ in turn yields in each step a state with improved heuristic value, hence leading the local search dead straight to a goal state.

As the reader will have noticed, the task did not present much difficulty to our envisioned search mechanism, despite the fact that there are exponentially many reachable states.[3] The performance is made possible by the high quality

---

[2] All states that are reachable within 5 steps from the initial state must be explored. Loading any 5 of the $n - 1$ available objects in the initial state yields $(n - 1)!/(5! * (n - 6)!)$ different states.

[3] When requiring $O_3, \ldots, O_n$ to be transported to L_2, the respective solution path $load(O_1, L_1)$, $load(O_3, L_1)$, $\ldots$, $load(O_n, L_1)$, $move(L_1, L_2)$, $unload(O_1, L_2)$,

of the heuristic function. Let us briefly look behind the scenes and get a glimpse of the structural reasons for this quality. Consider again what happens with the relaxed plans when one executes the sequence $load(O_1, L_1)$, $move(L_1, L_2)$, $unload(O_1, L_2)$, $load(O_2, L_2)$, $move(L_2, L_1)$, $unload(O_2, L_1)$ in the initial state. The relaxed plan is initially the same sequence except the $move(L_2, L_1)$ action. Executing an action, the relaxed plan for the successor state can always be constructed by removing the respective action; in the single case of $move(L_1, L_2)$, one must also re-include $move(L_2, L_1)$. This phenomenon is caused by two tight structural relationships between the real and the relaxed task: first, *any action that is good for solving the real task is also good for solving the relaxed task* — in effect, the heuristic value on the solution path (in fact, on any solution path that does not use superfluous actions) decreases monotonically; second, once a load or unload action is executed, its *negative effects are no longer needed in either the real or the relaxed task* — in effect, the heuristic value on our solution path decreases *strictly* monotonically except after the first moving action. Note that these structural relationships between the real and the relaxed task are properties of the specific example we have looked at. We will see, however, that they generalize far above that.

1.3 Outline

Chapter 2 provides the background in domain-independent planning. Motivation and goals of the field are somewhat more explained, and a quick overview over its history is given. The *STRIPS* and *ADL* planning languages, which are used throughout the book, are formally defined. We then describe the so-called *benchmark domains*, which constitute the range of example problems we will consider throughout the investigation. A domain is essentially a (possibly infinite) set of related planning tasks, which are referred to as *instances* of the domain. The benchmark domains are simplified formal adaptions of real-world problems, and they are the traditional means of evaluation in the AI planning literature. Our background survey finishes with a brief presentation and evaluation of the previously most influential approaches to domain-independent planning.

Containing the first half of this book's technical contributions, Part II gradually introduces and evaluates the algorithms used in our own approach to domain-independent planning. The implemented planning system is named FF (short for Fast-Forward). Chapter 3 describes the algorithmic heart of the system, the *FF base architecture*. We start from the aforementioned heuristic search approach by Blai Bonet and Héctor Geffner [13, 9]. We employ a modified version of their heuristic method, estimating the length of a relaxed solution (a plan that solves the task if the negative effects are ignored) to the search states. We introduce a novel local search scheme, and invent a pruning technique. The resulting system is shown to exhibit, in most of the benchmark domains, drastically better

---

$unload(O_3, L_2)$, ..., $unload(O_n, L_2)$, $load(O_2, L_2)$, $move(L_2, L_1)$, $unload(O_2, L_1)$ is found easily in a manner similar to what is described above.

scaling behavior than the previous approaches. It is empirically investigated in detail where, on the algorithmic path from HSP to FF, the performance boost was obtained.

Chapters 4 and 5 extend the FF base architecture with additional techniques designed to deal with special kinds of structural phenomena: *dead ends* and *goal orderings*, respectively. Each of these phenomena occurs only in a subset of the benchmarks that we use for testing. The techniques that we integrate to deal with the phenomena improve FF's behavior somewhat when the phenomena are present and have, in the phenomena's absence, no (non-marginal) effect on performance. Dead ends are states from which the goal is unreachable. Chapter 4 examines their effect on FF's search algorithm, identifies two situations where dead ends do provably not arise, and introduces a number of algorithms that can be used if they do. The algorithms are evaluated, and one of them is integrated into the system. Goal orderings arise in tasks where it is sometimes wiser to postpone the achievement of one goal until after the achievement of another. Chapter 5 presents two different approaches to define, recognize, and handle goal orderings. The first approach is adapted from work done by Jana Koehler in collaboration with the author [61, 62], and recognizes goal orderings as a pre-process to planning. The second approach is new, and recognizes goal orderings during search as a side effect of our heuristic method. We evaluate the approaches against each other, and decide to use both.

Chapter 6 concludes the algorithmic efforts of Part II by taking a look at an evaluation of FF in a more official setting: that of the *2nd International Planning Systems Competition*. This event took place in April 2000, the collected data providing a snapshot of the state-of-the-art in planning at that time. FF convincingly outperformed the other domain-independent systems, and earned the title of being a "Group A Distinguished Performance Planning System" — it also earned the somewhat more measurable value of two 1st prizes sponsored by Celcorp and Schindler Lifts Inc.

In Part III we turn our attention to the *reasons* for FF's unprecedented efficiency. We concentrate on the dramatic performance of the FF base architecture. While Chapter 3 motivates the algorithms with example observations, these do not provide a coherent explanation as to what enables their performance. What exactly are the structural properties that the FF base architecture utilizes? In Part III we make these properties explicit, through identifying the *local search topology* of the planning benchmarks, i.e., the quality of FF's heuristic function. Chapter 7 starts the investigation by empirically examining small example instances. The heuristic functions we consider are h^+ — the function that returns the length of an *optimal* relaxed plan — as well as h^{FF} — FF's heuristic function, which is an approximation of h^+ (h^+ is NP-hard to compute). We make a number of fascinating observations: in almost all of the benchmark domains, our small examples contain no dead ends that are not recognized by h^+; in the majority of the domains, there are no local minima under h^+; in almost half of the domains, the maximal distance to exits on benches is constant across instance size. These observations largely carry over to h^{FF}. We prove that FF's local search scheme is polynomial in domains where all these properties hold true, and we hypothesize that our observations are true for all — not only the small — instances of the respective domains.

Chapter 8 verifies the hypotheses about the h^+ function. We prove that the topological phenomena we observed in the small examples are in fact common to the respective entire domains, with a single exception. As a side effect of our proofs we also determine what the structural reasons are behind the topological phenomena, on the level of the planning tasks' specifications.

Chapter 9, finally, presents empirical data to support the hypothesis that the quality of h^+ gets largely preserved in the approximation h^{FF}. We take samples from the state spaces of large instances from the respective domains, and visualize the data. Except in two cases, the results strongly support the hypothesis. In particular, there is a number of domains where h^+ provably has the necessary quality to make FF's search scheme polynomial, and h^{FF} largely has that quality according to extensive empirical data. In these domains, FF is thus "largely", or *approximatively*, polynomial.

2. Planning

We say more on the motivation, goals, and history of AI planning (Section 2.1). We define the two planning languages that will be used throughout the book (Section 2.2), and we informally describe the set of example problems, i.e., planning domains we will consider (Section 2.3). We discuss the hitherto most influential approaches to planning (Section 2.4).

2.1 Motivation, Goals, and History

Traditionally, it is tried in AI to model human, or more generally intelligent behavior. From this point of view domain-independent planning, or general problem solving, is interesting because as argued before it is a necessary prerequisite for taking intelligent action in a changing world. From a more practical point of view, the strength of domain-independent planning lies in its flexibility. If a problem changes, then any program intended specifically to solve that problem must be updated on the implementation level. After a sufficient number of updates one will end up with what has infamously been termed "spaghetti-code", and had better program the application from scratch. Working with a domain-independent planner, one performs the updates by changing the declarative problem *specification*, while the underlying reasoning mechanism can stay the same. The potential benefits of such a general problem solver are evident. The likewise evident difficulty is that a general program will (presumably) never be as efficient as a specific application. Indeed, the goal in the field of AI planning (more on this below) is somewhat less ambitious than that. Still, even with AI planning technology being not yet practically applicable "as is" to real-world, in particular industrial problems, developing general problem solving techniques has its practical value. A technique that is not specific to any particular problem can, due to its general nature, easily be *made* specific, i.e., adapted to a specific situation. So progress on the side of the general reasoning techniques indirectly translates to the side of the specific ones.

If there is a "goal" that the AI planning community can agree upon, then it is probably best formulated thus: *get general reasoning mechanisms to a point where they are, in real-world applications, within the range of performance of specialized algorithms.* If, in an application, a general planner demonstrates the same asymptotic runtime behavior as the specific program, then the planner

J. Hoffmann: Utilizing Problem Structure in Planning, LNAI 2854, pp. 11–31, 2003.
© Springer-Verlag Berlin Heidelberg 2003

might indeed be the better alternative — as long as the constant performance factor can be made up for by increased computational power.

The roots of AI planning lie in the early ideas on general problem solving [70, 28], particularly in the work on GPS (General Problem Solver) by Allen Newell and others [78, 28]. Various languages have been proposed for formalizing the general problem solving idea. To name a few of the most influential ones: the STRIPS language formulates tasks in terms of propositional logic [31, 66]; the ADL language goes beyond STRIPS through admitting complex condition formulae and conditional effects [81]; the Situation Calculus uses situation variables in a first order language to explicitly refer to different world states [71]; hierarchical approaches, like HTN (Hierarchical Task Network) planning [89, 29], arrange the possible actions in a hierarchy of abstraction levels. As said before, in this book we use the STRIPS and ADL languages which have been by far the most popular — and are therefore the best studied — languages in AI planning research.

Fundamentally connected with the process of developing planning systems, and therefore with AI planning research, are the example problems used for evaluation: the *benchmarks*. These inevitably steer the field into their direction, as the "best" planner at any time is supposed to be the one that solves them most efficiently. So it is crucial to use benchmarks that come close to the envisioned applications. The goal of the field being to efficiently reason about real-world problems, the benchmarks are thus adaptions of such problems. A "problem" here comes in the form of a *domain* which is a (usually infinite) set of semantically related planning tasks (for example, if one wants to control the traffic in a port then one is interested in the family of traffic situations that can arise, not only in the specific situation arising at any point in time). Ideally, the benchmark domains should formulate applications. In reality the benchmarks are (yet) a good deal away from that, being very simplistic formal adaptions of real-world problems. The main reason for that is the prevailing lack of efficiency of planners even in very simplistic situations — which has to some extent been overcome only lately, amongst others by the research that we present in this book. Still, the benchmark domains are logical adaptions of real-world scenarios and, if simplistic, can reasonably be assumed to represent some of the structural phenomena that are relevant in the real world.

Since 1998, a powerful new means of large-scale evaluation has been established in the AI planning community, namely the *international planning systems competitions*. The first such event took place alongside the AIPS-1998 conference, the second one two years later alongside AIPS-2000. Repetition is expected in two-year turns in the future. We will henceforth refer to the past events as the AIPS-1998 respectively AIPS-2000 (planning systems) competitions. The advantage of a competition is that it provides a snapshot of the state of the art, evaluating many planners on many example tasks using exactly the same computational resources. Clearly, such data is a lot more conclusive than the single small-scale experiments reported in individual papers. Also, a competition can establish a data base of commonly used benchmark examples, thereby facilitating empirical comparison between planning systems. In fact, the benchmark domains we consider in this book include all domains used at the competitions, and in the experiments where that is possible we also use the same instances.

It is time we said a few words on the algorithmic approaches that have been tried to tackle domain-independent planning. The most influential ones have been *partial order planning, planning graph analysis, planning as satisfiability,* and *planning as heuristic search.* The approach we present in this book falls into the last category. The algorithmic principles underlying the approaches will be explained later. Let us make some historical remarks at this point. From the outset (around 1970) until 1995, more or less all proposed algorithms searched in the space of (incomplete) plans, these being either totally or partially ordered. In the form used nowadays, the *partial order* approach has first been proposed 1991 by McAllester and Rosenblitt [69]. Since then numerous researchers have built on that approach (e.g. [82, 39, 79]). In 1995, *planning graph analysis* was proposed by Blum and Furst [7], the (at that time) spectacular performance of the Graphplan system causing nearly everybody in the field to pursue that line of research (e.g. [64, 37, 56, 2, 94]). Kautz and Selman used Graphplan to boost the performance of their earlier invented *planning as satisfiability* framework [59], and topped Graphplan's performance in experiments reported 1996 [60]. The research line has since been pursued in various investigations (e.g. [40, 57, 58]). *Planning as heuristic search,* finally, was pioneered 1996 and 1997 in papers by McDermott [72] and Bonet et al. [13]. The competitive performance of Blai Bonet's and Héctor Geffner's HSP (Heuristic Search Planner) system at the AIPS-1998 competition [9, 73] spawned a whole number of research efforts, amongst others (e.g. [10, 85, 41]) the one that we describe in this book. Nowadays the most efficient systems known are heuristic search planners. Such planners, in particular the FF system we propose here, were extremely successful in the AIPS-2000 competition [3, 45, 11, 35, 27].

2.2 STRIPS and ADL

We will now define the STRIPS and ADL languages. As said, these form the framework that we will be looking at throughout the book. We slightly extend the original definitions [31, 81] in that we give a formal framework for planning *domains* rather than only for single planning *tasks*. This provides a better background for talking about domains, which we will frequently do in the context of the benchmarks mentioned earlier. In Chapter 8 we will *prove* properties of domains, so there the formal background is essential.

Our definitions are straightforward formalizations of the way in which STRIPS and ADL domains are usually used within the planning community. We start by defining the STRIPS language, then explain how it is extended to ADL. When we talk about sets, we always mean *finite* sets unless we explicitly say otherwise.

2.2.1 Predicates, Facts, and Groundings

The base entity in both STRIPS and ADL are facts, i.e., predicates whose arguments are constants or variables. We take a strictly syntactical point of view, talking about strings which are sequences of symbols over the alphabet $\Sigma = \{a, \ldots, z, A, \ldots, Z, 0, \ldots, 9, \text{-}\}$.[1] *Predicates* are pairs (prd, ar), $prd \in \Sigma^+$ being a string — the name of the predicate — and $ar \in \mathbf{N}_0$ being the arity of the predicate. *Constants* are strings, *variables* are abstract entities different from the constants. Given a predicate (prd, ar), a *fact* is a tuple $(prd, arg_1, \ldots, arg_{ar})$, where all *arguments* arg_i are either constants or variables. We say that the fact is *based on* (prd, ar). One important concept is that of grounding (our algorithms all work on grounded task representations, which we define below). A fact is *grounded in variable v with a constant c* by replacing all occurrences of v with c. If all arguments of a fact are constants, then the fact is a *ground fact*, or *proposition*. The (infinite) set of all ground facts is denoted as F.

For sets of entities where that makes sense, we allow subscripts to indicate the predicates, variables, and/or constants which (the facts in) the entities make use of. If there is a subscript to an entity then all its facts are based on one of the given predicates, and/or the arguments are all taken from the respective sets. The first set where we allow subscripts is that of all ground facts F. Let us use the set to exemplify the notation. Given a set of predicates $\mathcal{P}$, a set of variables V, and/or a set of constants C, the ground facts that can be built when restricting oneself to the respective sets are denoted by $F^{\mathcal{P}}$ (all ground facts using only predicates in $\mathcal{P}$), $F^{\mathcal{P},C}$ (all ground facts using only predicates in $\mathcal{P}$ and only constants in C), or $F^{\mathcal{P},V,C}$ (all ground facts using only predicates in $\mathcal{P}$, only variables in V, and only constants in C), etc. The ordering of the subscripts is always that in the third example. Alternatively, we say that a set of entities is *based on* $\mathcal{P}$, V, and/or C.

2.2.2 States, Actions, and Tasks

A grounded STRIPS task representation consists of two states (the initial state and the goal state) as well as a set of actions. A *state* is a set of ground facts $s \subseteq F$ — the propositions that are true in the state. An *action* is a triple $a = (pre(a), add(a), del(a))$ of sets of ground facts: the *precondition* $pre(a) \subseteq F$, the *add list* $add(a) \subseteq F$, and the *delete list* $del(a) \subseteq F$ of the action. The (infinite) set of all STRIPS actions is denoted as $\mathcal{A}$. A *STRIPS task* is a triple (A, I, G) of *action set* $A \subseteq \mathcal{A}$, *initial state* $I \subseteq F$, and *goal state* $G \subseteq F$. The semantics will be defined below. Let us first define in which way tasks are instances of domains.

2.2.3 Operators, Instances, and Domains

As said, a domains is essentially a (possibly infinite) set of planning tasks. This set is defined in terms of the predicates used, a set of operators (functions into the

---

[1] As long as the alphabet contains at least two symbols, it does not matter at all for the subsequent investigation what exactly it is. We use the standard alphabet.

set of actions), and a (possibly infinite) set of instances. Applying the operators to sets of constants given by the instances yields the tasks that belong to the domain. The definitions are as follows. A *STRIPS operator with p parameters* is a tuple $o = (V(o), pre(o), add(o), del(o))$, where $V(o) = (v_1, \dots, v_p)$ is a p-tuple of variables, the *operator parameters* (we use $V(o)$ also to denote the set $\{v_1, \dots, v_p\}$ of these parameters), $pre(o) \subseteq F^{V(o),\emptyset}$, $add(o) \subseteq F^{V(o),\emptyset}$, and $del(o) \subseteq F^{V(o),\emptyset}$ are sets of facts. Note that the only variables are operator parameters, and that the operator is not allowed to use constants. We identify o with a function $o :$ $(\Sigma^+)^p \mapsto \mathcal{A}$ from the set of all p-tuples of constants to the set of all STRIPS actions. The image of a constant tuple under o is the result of grounding (the facts in) $pre(o)$, $add(o)$, and $del(o)$ in the operator parameters with the respective constants. Let us focus on the instances. A *STRIPS instance* is a triple (C, I, G) of *constants* $C \subseteq \Sigma^+$, initial state $I \subseteq F^C$, and goal state $G \subseteq F^C$ (the states use only the available constants). Domains, finally, are these. A *STRIPS domain* is a triple $\mathcal{D} = (\mathcal{P}, \mathcal{O}, \mathcal{I})$: a set of predicates $\mathcal{P}$, a set $\mathcal{O}$ of STRIPS operators based on $\mathcal{P}$, and a possibly infinite set $\mathcal{I}$ of STRIPS instances based on $\mathcal{P}$. For $(C, I, G) \in \mathcal{I}$, we say that (C, I, G) is an *instance of $\mathcal{D}$*.

Instances (C, I, G) of a domain $(\mathcal{P}, \mathcal{O}, \mathcal{I})$ are directly associated with (ground) tasks (A, I, G), namely by applying all operators in $\mathcal{O}$ with p parameters to all p-tuples of constants in C to obtain the action set A (this is the process of *grounding*, which is done as a pre-process in many planning systems, including the one we propose in this book; we will talk about the process in detail in Section 3.1).

Often, we identify instances of a domain with the respective tasks. Also, in line with the original definition of STRIPS tasks [31], we will regularly abstract the notion of planning tasks from the one of planning domains, i.e., we will talk about arbitrary tasks (A, I, G). Theoretically, an arbitrary task (A, I, G) can be seen as the only instance of a domain where the predicates used are all 0-ary and correspond directly to the propositions in the task, while the operators correspond directly to the actions.

2.2.4 Plans

Let us now define the semantics of STRIPS tasks. We start with the semantics of action applications. These are defined via the *Result* function, mapping states and action sequences to states. An action a is *applicable* to a state s, if $add(a) \cap del(a) = \emptyset$ (it is not self-contradictory) and $pre(a) \subseteq s$ (its preconditions are fulfilled); in that case, applying the (sequence consisting solely of the) action yields the resulting state $Result(s, \langle a \rangle) := s \cup add(a) \setminus del(a)$. If the action is not applicable in s, the result of applying it is undefined. The result of applying sequences of arbitrarily many actions is defined recursively by $Result(s, \langle \rangle) := s$, and $Result(s, \langle a_1, \dots, a_n \rangle) := Result(Result(s, \langle a_1, \dots, a_{n-1} \rangle), \langle a_n \rangle)$.

Note that it does not depend on the state s whether an action is self-contradictory or not. Disallowing such actions is usually not done in the planning literature. Originally, the delete effects were applied before the add effects

[31, 66]; other researchers applied the effects the other way round (e.g. [64]). Postulating an empty intersection between add and delete effects is necessary to legitimate the way in which we compile negative conditions away (negative conditions can appear in ADL syntax of which STRIPS is a subset, see below; we compile them away in a pre-process which will be described in Section 3.1.2). Strangely, while the technique for compiling negations away was first published by Gazen and Knoblock [37], they do not mention that the actions must not be self-contradictory (more on this in Section 3.1.2). Anyway, at no point in the literature (that the author is aware of) has anyone made explicit use of the possibility to include add effects into the delete list. In particular, the results of other authors that we build on remain valid when removing that possibility. In the benchmark domains we consider throughout the book, there are no self-contradictory actions (at least none whose preconditions can ever be fulfilled: when moving from A to B, for example, the precondition postulates that A is different from B).

The semantics of tasks are as follows. Given a STRIPS task (A, I, G), a *plan*, or *solution*, for (A, I, G) is a sequence $P \in A^*$ such that $G \subseteq Result(I, P)$: a sequence of actions that maps the initial state into a state that fulfills all goals. The task is *solvable* if there is at least one plan for it. A plan is *optimal* if there is no plan that contains less actions — the shorter the plan, the better it is considered to be. While the planner we propose here does not guarantee the plans it finds to be optimal, we will need the optimality concept when we derive the principle underlying our heuristic method. We remark that, while our plans are simple sequences of actions, *sequential plans*, there are various other definitions in the literature, like partially ordered plans and parallel plans (the latter play a role in our heuristic function). We will say some more about these concepts when we describe the respective planners — the approaches by which such plans are found — below.

Put briefly, STRIPS planning comes down to finding a plan for, or proving unsolvability of, a given arbitrary STRIPS task. Considering this, a question of particular interest is, how hard is it to do that, i.e., what is the complexity of the corresponding decision problem? As was first proved by Bylander [15], the problem is PSPACE-complete. We will need this theorem for various proofs throughout the book, so we include it with a short proof sketch.

Definition 2.2.1. *Let PLANSAT denote the following problem:*

Given a STRIPS task (A, I, G), is (A, I, G) solvable?

Theorem 2.2.1 (Bylander). *Deciding PLANSAT is PSPACE-complete.*

Proof Sketch. Hardness is proved by a generic reduction: to an input vector for an arbitrary Turing machine with polynomially bounded space, one can polynomially construct a STRIPS task that is solvable if and only if the Turing machine accepts the input. Membership follows by iteratively (i.e., without keeping them in memory) guessing 2^n actions (where n is the number of distinct propositions in the task; no plan is longer than 2^n steps unless it contains loops), and checking whether any of the reached states fulfills the goal. Finished with NPSPACE = PSPACE.

2.2.5 Extension to ADL

In addition to what is possible in STRIPS, there can be complex conditions and conditional effects in ADL, i.e., conditions that are logic formulae and effects that depend on the state of execution. More precisely, the logic formulae are first-order formulae without equality, using the set of predicate symbols of the respective domain (in particular there are no function symbols). The (infinite) set of all formulae is denoted as $\mathcal{L}$, the (infinite) set of all *closed* formulae — the formulae without free variables — is denoted as $\mathcal{L}_0$. We allow subscripts to indicate the used predicates etc. When a formula is based on a set C of constants, the quantifiers $\forall x$ or $\exists x$ are associated with C, i.e., of the form $\forall x \in C$ respectively $\exists x \in C$. Formulae based on constant sets are used in ground tasks, where the range of the quantifiers must be fixed to the respective constants in order to validate the logical semantics. Many definitions for STRIPS, like those of facts and states, remain unmodified in ADL. We extend the other definitions as follows.

In ADL actions and tasks, we fix a set of constants. This is just a formal vehicle to associate the quantifiers in the formulae with a set of constants — in ground tasks, this set of constants is given by the respective instance. The definitions are as follows. Given a set of constants C. An *ADL action* is a pair $a = (pre(a), E(a))$ where $pre(a) \in \mathcal{L}_0^C$ is a closed formula and $E(a)$ is a set of ground effects; *ground effects* are triples $e = (con(e), add(e), del(e))$ where $con(e) \in \mathcal{L}_0^C$, the *effect condition*, is a closed formula and $add(e) \subseteq F^C$ as well as $del(e) \subseteq F^C$ are sets of ground facts (the add list and the delete list). The (infinite) set of all ADL actions is denoted as $\mathcal{A}_{adl}$. ADL tasks are triples (A, I, G) of action set $A \subseteq \mathcal{A}_{adl}^C$, initial state $I \subseteq F^C$, and *goal condition* $G \in \mathcal{L}_0^C$. Roughly, the semantics will be the same as before except that effects are only applied if their conditions hold true, and that a solution plan must reach a state where the goal condition is fulfilled. Note that STRIPS tasks are special cases of ADL tasks by a few trivial transformations: the actions $(pre(a), add(a), del(a))$ can be mapped to actions $(\bigwedge_{p \in pre(a)} p, \{(\top, add(a), del(a))\})$ featuring a single effect with trivially fulfilled effect condition, and the goal state G can be mapped to the goal condition $\bigwedge_{g \in G} g$.

Let us extend the definition of domains. An *ADL operator with p parameters* is a triple $o = (V(o), pre(o), E(o))$, where $V(o) = (v_1, \ldots, v_p)$ are (as before) the parameters, $pre(o) \in \mathcal{L}^{V(o),\emptyset}$ is the precondition, and $E(o)$ is a set of effects. Effects are tuples $e = (V(e), con(e), add(e), del(e))$, where $V(e)$ is a tuple of variables, the *effect parameters* (also used to denote the set of these parameters), with $V(e) \cap V(o) = \emptyset$; $con(e) \in \mathcal{L}^{V(o) \cup V(e),\emptyset}$ is a formula; and $add(e) \subseteq F^{V(o) \cup V(e),\emptyset}$ and $del(e) \subseteq F^{V(o) \cup V(e),\emptyset}$ are sets of facts. Like in STRIPS, the only variables are the parameters, and no constants are used. Given a set of constants C, we identify o with a function $o^C : (\Sigma^+)^p \mapsto \mathcal{A}_{adl}^C$ from p-tuples of constants to

ADL actions. The image of a constant tuple under o^C is the result of: grounding the operator in its parameters with the respective constants; inserting for each effect with p' effect parameters and each p'-tuple in C one copy of the effect grounded in its parameters with the respective constants; associating the quantifiers in all formulae with the set C. An *ADL instance* is a triple (C, I, G) like in STRIPS, except that $G \in \mathcal{L}_0^C$ is a formula. Domains are triples $(\mathcal{P}, \mathcal{O}, \mathcal{I})$ like in the STRIPS case; for syntactical convenience, we allow the set of operators $\mathcal{O}$ to comprise both ADL- and STRIPS-operators (based on $\mathcal{P}$). Instances of domains are associated with tasks by, as before, applying the operators to the respective tuples of constants.

We define the semantics of actions by overloading the *Result* function. The $\models$ relation between states and formulae is defined in the standard inductive manner. The result of applying a sequence consisting solely of one action $a = (pre(a), E(a))$ to a state s is defined as $Result(s, \langle a \rangle) := s \cup A(s, a) \setminus D(s, a)$, where $A(s, a)$ ($D(s, a)$) is the union of the add (delete) lists of the effects $e = (con(e), add(e), del(e)) \in E(a)$ whose effect condition is fulfilled in s, i.e., for which $s \models con(e)$ holds. Prerequisites for applicability are fulfillment of the precondition, $s \models pre(a)$, and non-contradicting effects, $A(s, a) \cap D(s, a) = \emptyset$ (the latter restriction is necessary for the same reason as explained above in the STRIPS case). If an action is not applicable to a state, then the result of applying it is undefined. The result of applying an action sequence is defined exactly as before. A plan for a task (A, I, G) is a sequence $P \in A^*$ of actions for which $Result(I, P) \models G$ holds. Like in the STRIPS case, deciding solvability for arbitrary ADL tasks is PSPACE-complete. This is a simple consequence of Bylander's theorem above.

Definition 2.2.2. *Let ADL-PLANSAT denote the following problem:*

Given an ADL task (A, I, G), is (A, I, G) solvable?

Theorem 2.2.2. *Deciding ADL-PLANSAT is PSPACE-complete.*

Proof. Hardness follows directly from Theorem 2.2.1 as STRIPS is a special case of ADL. Membership can be proved analogously to the STRIPS case: no plan needs to be longer than 2^n steps, with n being the maximal number of different propositions in the task (one can derive n, for example, by calculating the total number of ways in which constant tuples can be used to ground the predicates), so like before one can iteratively guess that many actions and check the reached states for goal satisfaction. Verifying whether a state satisfies a closed formula where all quantifiers range over a finite set of constants (a pre-, effect- or goal-condition) can be done in PSPACE: do a depth-first search in the AND-OR tree that results when one replaces $\forall$ quantifiers by AND nodes and $\exists$ quantifiers by OR nodes, the sons of a node being determined by the respective constants in an arbitrary ordering; satisfaction of a formula without quantifiers in a state can be decided in polynomial time.

Henceforth, if we specifically want to talk about STRIPS or ADL (tasks, or domains, or actions ...), then we say so explicitly. Without an explicit restriction to either language, the discussion is valid for both languages alike.

2.3 The Benchmark Domains

As said above, evaluation of planning systems is traditionally done by running them on certain benchmark tasks, i.e., on tasks that are instances of domains which model (simplified versions of) real-world problems, and which have been established as benchmarks in the literature. The STRIPS and ADL frameworks that we consider in this book have been the most popular formalisms in the planning literature of the past decades, so naturally for these formalisms there is the largest collection of benchmarks available. Throughout the book, we will look at a collection of 20 of the most frequently used domains. Their names are *Assembly, Blocksworld-arm, Blocksworld-no-arm, Briefcaseworld, Ferry, Freecell, Fridge, Grid, Gripper, Hanoi, Logistics, Miconic-ADL, Miconic-SIMPLE, Miconic-STRIPS, Movie, Mprime, Mystery, Schedule, Simple-Tsp,* and *Tireworld.* While this list is not exhaustive (of course, there appear other example domains in the literature), it does contain the domains that are most popular in the AI planning community. In particular, the list contains all 13 STRIPS and ADL domains that were used in the AIPS-1998 and AIPS-2000 competitions: the domains in the AIPS-1998 competition were *Assembly, Grid, Gripper, Logistics, Movie, Mprime,* and *Mystery*; those at AIPS-2000 were *Blocksworld-arm, Freecell, Logistics, Miconic-ADL, Miconic-SIMPLE, Miconic-STRIPS,* and *Schedule* (plus the only non-STRIPS and non-ADL competition domain, a *Miconic* variant with numeric variables).

We now provide the reader with an impression of what these benchmark domains are about. This knowledge will be relevant for understanding the subsequent discussions. From a technical point of view, the questions of interest for each domain are these:

1. What are the predicates, operators, and instances?
2. For various experimental purposes, how can we automatically generate (random) instances?

We briefly overview the answers to the above two questions, grouping together domains that are semantically related. Exact formal answers to the first question are contained in Appendix A (to decide what exactly the infinite sets of instances in the domains are, we have abstracted from the published benchmark collections). We will need these precise formalisms only in Chapter 8, when proving properties of domains. The second question is interesting for various experimental purposes that we will pursue in the book. Our answers to the question are contained in Appendix B, describing for each domain a generation and, if applicable, randomization strategy that we have implemented for automated instance generation. This information supplements, throughout the book, the descriptions of those experimental example collections where we have used automatically generated instances. In experiments where this seemed more appropriate, we have used (parts of) the AIPS-1998 and AIPS-2000 competition collections. We include brief descriptions of these collections in the following.

As indicated, we group related domains together in order to give the overview more structure. There are, roughly, three semantical groups of domains in our collection: the transportation domains, the construction domains, and those that belong to neither group. We start our overview with the transportation domains.

2.3.1 Transportation Domains

In this group of domains, there are a number of locations, a number of objects that must be transported, and a number of vehicles which are the means of transportation. Predicates are *at-* (a location) and *in-* (a vehicle) relations, plus sometimes a few predicates that encode additional functionalities (like object typing, etc.). Operators mostly either move a vehicle, or load (unload) an object onto (from) a vehicle. Our collection contains 10 variations of this theme. Some of these use other names than "locations", "vehicles", and "objects", but the correspondence should be clear. We start our overview with the simpler variations.

Logistics is a STRIPS domain, and the classical example of a transportation domain. Locations are organized in terms of cities, each of which contains a set of them. Trucks can transport objects within cities, airplanes transport them between different cities. Locations are directly accessible from each other, i.e., if a vehicle can move between two locations then this can be done directly. The instances in *Logistics* specify the initial locations of all vehicles and objects, as well as the goal locations of the objects. Talking about automated generation, the instances are determined by the number of cities and their locations, as well as the number of trucks, airplanes, and objects, modulo the distribution of initial and goal locations. Thus, our generator takes in all the numbers as parameters, and randomly distributes the initial and goal locations. The parameters of the generation strategy are *domain parameters* in the sense that instances with the same parameter setting are identical modulo randomization. We use the domain parameter concept in the overview here, and throughout the book in descriptions of experiments; the concept will be especially useful for the investigation in Chapter 9. The *Logistics* domain has been used in the AIPS-1998 and AIPS-2000 competitions. Both collections contain a set of instances that scale in terms of the above domain parameters. The instances in the AIPS-1998 collection are particularly large: one of the largest instances there features 20 cities with 16 locations each, 77 trucks, 5 airplanes, and 42 objects; the largest AIPS-2000 instance features 14 cities with 2 locations each, 14 trucks, 4 airplanes, and 41 objects.

Gripper and *Ferry* are STRIPS domains that vary the transportation theme in that the vehicles have limited transportation capacity. In *Gripper*, there are two rooms A and B and a number of balls that must be transported from A to

B by a robot with two hands, where each of the hands can hold only one ball at a time; the domain parameter is the number of balls, there is no randomization. The AIPS-1998 *Gripper* collection contains the tasks with 4 to 42 balls, in steps of 2. In *Ferry*, there is a number of locations, and a number of cars that must be transported via a ferry that can only transport one car at a time; domain parameters are the numbers of locations and cars, random element is the distribution of initial- and goal-locations.

Briefcaseworld is an ADL domain, making use of conditional effects. There are some locations, and some objects to be transported via a briefcase. One can either put an object into the briefcase, take it out, or move the briefcase. The moving action moves, by a conditional effect, all objects along that are currently inside the briefcase. Domain parameters are the numbers of locations and objects, random element is again the distribution of initial- and goal-locations.

The *Miconic-STRIPS*, *Miconic-SIMPLE*, and *Miconic-ADL* domains formalize different variations of an elevator transportation problem rooted in an industrial application [65] (these domains thus come very close to the ideal situation of benchmarks modeling applications). The first variation is a STRIPS domain, the two latter ones are ADL formulations (*Miconic-SIMPLE* only makes use of conditional effects and negative preconditions). In all three domains, the instances specify a number of floors, a number of passengers with different origin and destination floors, and the initial position of the (single) elevator. The goal is to serve all passengers. Operators move the elevator up or down (each floor being directly accessible), stop the elevator, or, in *Miconic-STRIPS* only, board passengers (or let them depart). In the ADL domains, if the lift stops, then by conditional effects all passengers get out that are at their destination, and all waiting passengers get in (which obviously comes closer to the realistic scenario than the STRIPS formulation). Domain parameters are the numbers of floors and passengers, random element is the distribution of initial and goal locations (respectively floors). In the *Miconic-ADL* variant, there are a lot of additional constraints — formulated in terms of complex preconditions — like VIPs that must be transported first, or passengers in conflict groups A or B that must not be together in the lift at any time. There are a whole number of domain parameters to control these constraints. We do not go into the details here, which can be found in Appendix B. Anyway, we will use the AIPS-2000 competition collection in all but one of our experiments with *Miconic-ADL* (namely the experiment described in Chapter 7, where we need particularly small instances due to computational reasons). The competition collections for all *Miconic* variants contain instances where the passengers scale up from 1 to 30, always featuring twice as many floors as passengers. The collections have been produced with the same generators that we use in this book. For *Miconic-ADL*, the parameters to control the constraints have been used with their default values in the competition; we do the same in the single experiment where we need randomly generated instances of this domain (the default values are listed in the respective section of Appendix B).

Grid is a STRIPS transportation domain where the places are arranged in a grid-like reachability relation, and can be locked; there are keys in different shapes — matching different locks — and the goal is to transport the keys via a robot. Operators move the robot from a place to a connected open place, open a locked place with a matching key, or pick-up (putdown, pickup-and-lose) a key (the robot can hold only one key at a time, pickup-and-lose exchanges the current key for another one). Note that places can only be opened, but not locked. The domain parameters are the size of the grid, as well as the numbers of different key and lock shapes, keys, and locks; random element is the distribution of initial and goal places of keys, the initial place of the robot, and the initial distribution of locked places. The AIPS-1998 competition collection contains 5 scaling instances: the smallest one features 9 keys on a 5×5 grid, the largest one specifies 13 keys on a 9×9 grid.

The final transportation variations we consider here are the *Mprime* and *Mystery* domains. These are STRIPS domains, and transportation variations where vehicles consume fuel; the available amount of fuel decreases monotonically, i.e., there is no refueling action. In both domains, there are a number of locations whose reachability relation forms an arbitrary map, there are vehicles with varying transportation capacity, and a number of objects to be transported. Each location has, initially, a given amount of fuel. Moving a vehicle away from a location consumes one fuel unit. In *Mprime*, there is an additional operator that can transfer fuel between connected locations. The domain parameters in our generation strategy are simplified in that the map is simply a circle (see the details of the strategy in the respective section of Appendix B). Anyway, we will use the AIPS-1998 competition collections in all of our experiments with these domains except the one in Chapter 7 where we need very small instances. The competition collections contain tasks of varying size, featuring roughly between 5 to 20 locations, 1 to 10 vehicles, and 3 to 40 objects to be transported.

2.3.2 Construction Domains

The construction domains in our collection are generally not as closely related as the transportation domains above. What they (i.e., the construction domains) have in common, roughly, is that a complex object must be built out of its individual parts. There are five such domains in our collection. Let's start with the simple ones.

Blocksworld-arm and *Blocksworld-no-arm* are the two most popular STRIPS variations of the well-known Blocks World domain: there is a table and a number of blocks which can be placed either on the table or on another block, and the goal is to achieve a set of *on*-relations, i.e., to arrange the blocks into some given goal stacks. The two domains differ in terms of the operators that are available to achieve the goal. In *Blocksworld-arm* there are four operators to pick up a block from the table, put a block down onto the table, stack a block onto another block, or unstack a block from another block. All these operators assume the existence of a robot arm in the obvious way. Not so in *Blocksworld-no-arm*: three operators directly move a block from the table to another block, move a block from another block to the table, or move a block from some block to another block (the operators moving a block onto some target block are restricted, in our formulation, so that the target block is different from the moved block). The domain parameter in both domains is the number of blocks. For randomization, we use the random Blocksworld state generator developed by John Slaney and Sylvie Thiebaux [93] — this generator outputs each legal Blocksworld state with equal probability. The *Blocksworld-arm* domain was used in the AIPS-2000 competition, instances containing from 4 to 50 blocks. We do not use this collection in our experiments, but rely on the theoretically justified method by Slaney and Thiebaux instead.

The *Hanoi* domain is a STRIPS formulation of the classical Towers of Hanoi problem. There is one operator to move a disc from one disc to another disc (the pegs are encoded as maximally large discs). The domain parameter is the number of discs, there is no randomization.

The *Freecell* domain is a STRIPS formulation of a well-known solitaire card game which comes with Microsoft Windows (the card game, not its STRIPS formulation). A number of cards is initially arranged in stacks over a number of columns, and must be moved to their goal positions in the correct order, obeying certain stacking rules, and making use of a number of free cells. Operators move cards between different kinds of places. Domain parameters are the number of columns, the number of cards (from different suits), and the number of free cells. Random element is the initial arrangement of the cards. Like with *Miconic-ADL*, *Mystery*, and *Mprime*, except in Chapter 7 we will always use the AIPS-2000 competition collection in our experiments with the domain. This collection contains tasks that are derived from the original card game instances: like in the original game, there are always four suits of cards, eight columns, and four free cells; scaling parameter is the number of cards in each suit, which varies between 2 and 13 (the original game always features 13, i.e., all cards from each suit).

The *Assembly* domain, finally, is an ADL domain that fits most literally into the concept of construction domains as described at the beginning of this section. The goal is to assemble a complex object together out of its parts; the parts, in turn, must be assembled together themselves, so that the part-of relation forms a tree with the goal object as root. Operators assemble (remove) a part into (from) the respective higher-level object. There are several additional constraints which are formulated in terms of complex first-order logic preconditions: transient parts that must be incorporated only temporarily, ordering constraints on the order in which parts are assembled, also ordering constraints on the order in which parts can be removed. In addition, assembling or removing a part can require a number of resources (machines) to be committed to the respective higher-level object, which is done via commit and release operators. Domain parameters are the depth of the part-of tree, the maximal number of parts that each higher-level object can have, the number of resources, as well as probabilities determining how frequent ordering constraints and transient parts occur. See the details in Appendix B. Everywhere except in Chapter 7, we will use the AIPS-1998 competition collection for our *Assembly* experiments. The instances in that collection feature between 19 to 72 objects (parts) and 1 to 2 resources. Transient parts and the respective ordering constraints are rather sparse (more on this topic in Sections 7.1 and 8.5).

2.3.3 Other Domains

There are five domains in our collection whose semantics do not exactly fit into either of the above groups.

Simple-Tsp is a trivial STRIPS version of the well-known Tsp problem. There is a number of locations which must be visited. A move operator can be applied to any two different locations, achieving the "visited" relation for the destination location (i.e., in Tsp terms the graph is fully connected and all edge costs are equal). Domain parameter is the number of locations, there is no randomization.

Movie is also a very simple STRIPS domain. The goal is to prepare watching a movie, which involves buying one item each out of five types of snacks, rewinding the tape, and resetting the counter. The only difference between the instances is the number of snacks that there are of each type. Our generation strategy simplifies this slightly in that all types of snacks contain the same number of items, such that the only domain parameter is this number. In fact, the domain parameter does not matter much as any item will do: the effect of buying an item of some type is always to have the respective type of snack, no matter which item one has decided for (note that thus, the set of reachable states is *identical* for all instances). There is no randomization. The AIPS-1998 collection fulfills the simplification that our generation strategy makes, containing the tasks where there are 5 to 34 snacks of each type.

Tireworld is a STRIPS domain where one must replace a number of flat tires. This involves quite a number of working steps, like fetching the appropriate tools out of the boot, inflating the spare tires, loosening the nuts, jacking up the hubs, removing the old wheels, etc. The domain parameter is the number of tires to be replaced, there is no randomization.

In the ADL domain *Fridge*, for a number of fridges the broken compressor must be replaced with a new one. To do that, one must stop the fridges, unfasten all screws that hold the broken compressors, remove the compressors (the number of screws varies between instances, which is formulated in terms of a universally quantified precondition of this operator), attach the spare compressors, fasten the screws again, and start the fridges. The domain parameters are the numbers of fridges and screws per compressor (each compressor within an instance is held by the same number of screws), there is no randomization.

Finally, there is the ADL domain *Schedule* in our collection. Instances are Scheduling tasks, where a number of objects must be processed with a number of machines to change their shape, surface, or color; one can also drill holes in varying orientations and widths. As usual, each machine can only process one object at a time. One can move forward in time by a do-time-step operator (which completes the processes on all machines). Operators make use of conditional effects, for example painting an object has an effect saying "the object is no longer painted in any color it was painted in before". There are rather a lot of domain parameters (details in Appendix B), namely the numbers of objects, different shapes, colors, widths and orientations of holes, and a number of probabilities that a part is required to have some property in the goal. In all experiments but the one described in Chapter 7, we will use the AIPS-2000 competition collection. In that collection, there are scaling instances with 2 to 51 objects to be processed, while there are always 3 different shapes, 4 different colors, 3 different hole widths, and 2 different hole orientations.

2.4 Previous Approaches

We describe the algorithmic principles underlying the previously most influential approaches to planning, and evaluate example planners on a collection of 100 benchmark tasks (5 from each of the above 20 domains). We focus on *partial order planning*, *planning graph analysis*, and *planning as satisfiability* in turn. For simplicity, we describe the algorithms for STRIPS only.

2.4.1 Partial Order Planning

The name of the *partial order planning* approach originates from the kind of plans that is searched for. A partially ordered plan is a set of actions together with a set of ordering relations, specifying which actions must be executed before which other ones. In difference to a sequential plan, such a plan is *partially* ordered in the sense that ordering relations are only imposed where it is necessary. This provides more execution flexibility, and reduces the number of plans (by avoiding arbitrary variation over unnecessary ordering constraints).

Search is done in the space of *incomplete* partially ordered plans. These constitute, in addition to the action and ordering constraint sets, a set of *causal links*. A causal link is a triple (a, p, a'), the semantics being that the action a shall be used to establish the precondition p of the action a'. A partially ordered plan is incomplete if there are *flaws* in it. A flaw is an action a' such that for $p \in pre(a')$ there is no causal link (a, p, a'); or an *unresolved threat*, i.e., an action a'' such that there is a causal link (a, p, a') with $p \in del(a'')$ and neither $a'' < a$ nor $a' < a''$ is contained in the set of ordering constraints. The initial and goal states are encoded as "dummy" actions, constrained before respectively after all other actions, and adding all initial propositions respectively requiring all goal propositions as preconditions. If one replaces, in a partially ordered plan without flaws, the causal links (a, p, a') with ordering constraints $a < a'$, then any topological sorting (a sequential plan respecting all ordering constraints) of the partially ordered plan is a solution for the planning task (note here that partially ordered plans with inconsistent ordering relations have no topological sorting). Search starts with the plan that contains only the initial state and goal state actions. Search options are to remove flaws by adding causal links (and the respective supporting action, if necessary) for unsupported preconditions, or by resolving

domain	task1 t	task1 s	task2 t	task2 s	task3 t	task3 s	task4 t	task4 s	task5 t	task5 s
Assembly										
Bw-arm	2.95	8	-	-	-	-	-	-	-	-
Bw-no-arm	0.04	4	-	-	-	-	-	-	-	-
Briefcase	0.13	5	-	-	-	-	-	-	-	-
Ferry	0.09	6	-	-	-	-	-	-	-	-
Freecell	-	-	-	-	-	-	-	-	-	-
Fridge										
Grid	-	-	-	-	-	-	-	-	-	-
Gripper	-	-	-	-	-	-	-	-	-	-
Hanoi	1.15	7	-	-	-	-	-	-	-	-
Logistics	-	-	-	-	-	-	-	-	-	-
Mic-ADL										
Mic-SIM	0.00	4	-	-	-	-	-	-	-	-
Mic-STR	0.00	4	1.95	30	10.00	49	111.51	85	217.55	102
Movie	0.03	7	0.18	7	0.51	7	1.31	7	2.64	7
Mprime	-	-	-	-	-	-	-	-	-	-
Mystery	0.06	4	0.51	5	8.36	10	-	-	156.58	8
Schedule	0.01	2	-	-	-	-	-	-	-	-
Simple-Tsp	0.01	5	1.14	10	2.57	15	13.20	20	52.22	25
Tireworld	0.49	19	12.77	32	-	-	-	-	-	-

Fig. 2.1. Runtime (t) and solution length (s) results for UCPOP in our benchmark example collection. A dash means that no plan was found after 5 minutes. An empty entry means that the planner could not be run on the respective task. Some domain names are abbreviated in order to fit the figure into the page without making it too tiny to read

threats through inserting (one of the two possible) ordering constraints. Several methods have been proposed in the literature as to which search option should be chosen first [39, 83]. In the experiments we describe below, we have used the ZLIFO (zero-commitment last in first out) strategy [39]. Put briefly, this prefers search options that make no new commitment (like resolving a threat which can only be resolved in one consistent way), and, if there are no such options, works first on those flaws that have appeared last. Note that search proceeds backwards from the goals to the initial state in the sense that, when search starts, the only flaws in the plan are the unsupported preconditions of the goal action.

We evaluate the partial order approach by running an example planner, UCPOP [82], on 5 example tasks from each of our 20 domains. We chose UCPOP because it is the most widely known partial order planner, and it can handle ADL (though we encountered a problem with complex preconditions, see below). The planner is implemented in Lisp (in contrast to the other approaches we are going to see, a partial order planner that is implemented in C does not seem to exist). We use UCPOP version 4.0. The experiments were run, like all experiments about which we report in this book, on a Sun Ultra 10 running at 350 MHz with 256 MByte main memory. See our runtime and solution length data in Figure 2.1. As will be done in all the experiments in the book, runtime is given in seconds and solution length is given in terms of the number of actions in the plan.

Let us briefly describe what the example tasks used in Figure 2.1 are. We will use the same example collection for evaluating the other approaches, i.e., planning graph analysis, planning as satisfiability, HSP, and our own system FF.

In all domains, the tasks grow in size in order to give an indication of the planners' *scaling behavior*, i.e., their asymptotic runtime performance in the domains. In the competition domains except *Blocksworld-arm* and *Gripper*, we have selected 5 instances from the respective competition collections, starting with one of the smallest instances and scaling up, in even steps, to one of the largest instances. In all other domains, we have used the generation strategies described in Appendix B. In *Blocksworld-arm* and in *Blocksworld-no-arm*, the instances are randomly generated ones with 4, 8, 12, 16, and 20 blocks, respectively. In *Briefcaseworld*, there are 2, 4, 6, 8, and 10 portables to be transported, always with one more location than portables. Similarly, the *Ferry* examples contain 2, 4, 6, 8, and 10 cars respectively 3, 5, 7, 9, and 11 locations. In *Fridge*, there are 1, 2, 3, 4, and 5 fridges, the number of screws is constantly 4. In *Gripper* there are 5, 10, 15, 20, and 25 balls to be transported, in *Hanoi* there are 3, 4, 5, 6, and 7 discs to be moved, in *Simple-Tsp* there are 5, 10, 15, 20, and 25 locations to be visited, in *Tireworld* finally there are 1, 2, 3, 4, and 5 tires to be replaced.

Like we will do in the experiments to come, we cut off unsuccessful trials after 5 minutes. UCPOP's runtime performance is very poor in almost all of our domains — we will see below that there are planners that perform much better. In the *Assembly*, *Fridge*, and *Miconic-ADL* domains we could not run UCPOP at all because it complained that the (correctly) quantified variables in complex preconditions were "unbound". This appears to be a bug, but the authors of UCPOP could not locate the problem. The only domains where UCPOP scales up are *Miconic-STRIPS*, *Movie*, *Mystery*, and *Simple-Tsp*. As for *Movie*, we will see that this does not constitute a problem for any of the planners we try (remember that the set of reachable states does not grow with the instances). In the other three domains, apparently the backward search strategy of UCPOP yields a complete plan without too much search.

2.4.2 Planning Graph Analysis

The name of the *planning graph analysis* approach stems from a data structure that is central for all the computations done, the *planning graph*. This is a layered graph structure containing proposition and action nodes. The structure is in essence a succinct encoding of reachability information. This information is useful for avoiding unnecessary effort in a backward search.

The planning graph is built as follows. One starts with the initial propositions, which form the first *proposition layer*, proposition layer number 0. Then the first *action layer*, action layer number 0, is inserted as the set of all actions whose preconditions are contained in proposition layer 0 (i.e., the initial state) plus one "NOOP" action for each proposition p, with p being the sole precondition and (add) effect of the NOOP. An edge is inserted between each proposition p and action a such that $p \in pre(a)$. Also, pairs of actions are marked as *mutually exclusive* if they *interfere*, i.e., if one deletes a precondition or effect of the other or vice versa. Once action layer 0 has been built, one proceeds to proposition layer 1. This contains all add effects of the actions in layer 0, and edges are inserted between the actions and their effects (note that the propositions from layer 0 are propagated upwards by their respective NOOPs). A pair of propositions p and p' in layer 1 is marked mutually exclusive if all actions in layer 0 that achieve a are exclusive of all actions in layer 0 that achieve a'. Action layer 1 is made up out of all actions whose preconditions are contained in proposition layer 1, no pair of preconditions being mutually exclusive. The NOOPs for the propositions in layer 1 are inserted. Pairs of actions a and a' are marked exclusive if they interfere, or if they have *competing needs*, i.e., if there are $p \in pre(a)$ and $p' \in pre(a')$ such that p and p' are marked exclusive at layer 1. Subsequently, proposition layer 2 is built as the union of the add effects of all actions in layer 1, and so forth. The process is iterated until either a proposition layer is reached that contains all goals non-exclusively, or a fix point is reached (i.e., the new proposition layer is identical to the previous one).

The planning graph encodes reachability information in the following sense: if a pair of propositions is marked exclusive at a proposition layer i, then there is no parallel plan with i time steps that achieves both propositions together. A *parallel plan with i time steps* is a sequence $\langle A_0, \ldots, A_{i-1} \rangle$ of non-interfering action sets, i.e., a sequence of action sets where in each set no action deletes a precondition or add effect of any other action. A parallel plan *achieves* a set of facts if, after executing any linearization of the plan in the initial state, the set of facts is true. Note that it does not make a difference in which order one linearizes the non-interfering action sets. Graphplan searches for parallel plans achieving the goals by doing a backward search from the goals to the initial state. Search starts once the planning graph has reached all goals non-exclusively in some layer — note that, because the graph encodes reachability as said above, the task is proved unsolvable if a fix point occurs before the goals are reached. Say the goals are contained in layer m. Graphplan tries to achieve them by selecting a set of non-exclusive actions at layer $m-1$ whose add effects support all goals. The union of these actions' preconditions then forms a new *sub*-goal set at proposition layer $m-1$, and search continues. If at some point there is no non-exclusive supporting set of actions for a set of sub-goals, then search backtracks. The backtracking procedure succeeds if it reaches the initial state — in which case the selected action sets form a parallel plan for the task — and the procedure fails if all possibilities have been explored. In the latter case, the planning graph is extended to layer $m+1$, and search continues from there. This way, it is guaranteed that the first found plan is optimal in the sense that there is no parallel plan that achieves the goals with fewer time steps.

We evaluate the planning graph analysis approach by running an example planner on the same benchmark collection as used above. The planner is IPP [64] version 4.0, which we chose because it is a very efficient implementation of Graphplan, and can deal with ADL. The planner is implemented in C. See the data in Figure 2.2.

Evidently, the runtime performance of IPP is much better than that of UCPOP, c.f. Figure 2.1. Solution length on the examples that both planners solve is roughly similar (Graphplan guarantees the minimal number of time steps but

domain	task1		task2		task3		task4		task5	
	t	s	t	s	t	s	t	s	t	s
Assembly	-	-	-	-	-	-	-	-	-	-
Bw-arm	0.03	8	0.19	14	-	-	-	-	-	-
Bw-no-arm	0.04	4	0.44	11	64.83	20	-	-	-	-
Briefcase	0.02	5	0.05	13	2.24	14	-	-	-	-
Ferry	0.02	6	0.07	10	92.59	22	-	-	-	-
Freecell	-	-	-	-	-	-	-	-	-	-
Fridge	0.01	12	0.05	24	0.08	36	0.15	48	0.30	60
Grid	2.32	14	-	-	-	-	-	-	-	-
Gripper	0.17	15	53.44	29	-	-	-	-	-	-
Hanoi	0.04	7	0.04	15	0.15	31	0.43	63	1.84	127
Logistics	0.06	20	-	-	-	-	-	-	-	-
Mic-ADL	0.00	4	144.19	20	-	-	-	-	-	-
Mic-SIM	0.00	4	79.10	22	-	-	-	-	-	-
Mic-STR	0.01	4	55.68	27	-	-	-	-	-	-
Movie	0.00	7	0.02	7	0.03	7	0.04	7	0.04	7
Mprime	3.24	11	20.91	9	-	-	-	-	-	-
Mystery	0.10	6	0.12	5	11.84	13	2.11	8	112.13	17
Schedule	0.07	2	-	-	-	-	-	-	-	-
Simple-Tsp	0.02	5	4.92	10	-	-	-	-	-	-
Tireworld	0.04	19	10.22	30	-	-	-	-	-	-

Fig. 2.2. Runtime (t) and solution length (s) results for IPP in our benchmark example collection. A dash means that no plan was found after 5 minutes

not the minimal number of actions). UCPOP outperforms IPP only in *Miconic-STRIPS* and *Simple-Tsp* (in the latter domain, Graphplan is inadequate due to the huge amount of symmetrical options while trying to prove that there is no plan with less than n time steps for n locations [33]). In almost all other domains, IPP scales better — though mostly it can still only solve the smaller examples in our collection.

2.4.3 Planning as Satisfiability

A planning task can be translated into SAT by various encoding methods so that satisfying truth assignments correspond to solutions for the planning task. One can then use an arbitrary SAT solver to find a satisfying assignment to the propositional variables, and thus a plan for the task. The advantage of this is that search is not necessarily focussed into any particular direction — the variables in the encoding can be worked on in an arbitrary order — and that the fast advance of the state of the art in SAT solving systems carries directly over to the planner.

We describe the specific algorithms that are used in the Blackbox system [60]. Encoding the planning task proceeds by a direct translation from the planning graph structure we have described in Section 2.4.2. A planning graph with m layers, such that layer m contains the goals non-exclusively, is translated into a SAT instance as follows. There are variables p_i for each proposition at a layer i, and variables a_i for each action at a layer i. The variables p_0 — the initial state propositions — are constrained to be true, likewise for the goals in layer m. Each proposition variable p_i implies the disjunction of the actions in layer $i - 1$ that can achieve it, i.e., a clause $\neg p_i \vee a_{i-1}^1 \vee \ldots \vee a_{i-1}^n$ is included in the SAT instance,

domain	task1 t	s	task2 t	s	task3 t	s	task4 t	s	task5 t	s
Assembly										
Bw-arm	0.14	8	1.17	14	-	-	-	-	-	-
Bw-no-arm	0.05	4	2.93	10	-	-	-	-	-	-
Briefcase										
Ferry	0.11	6	0.46	10	-	-	-	-	-	-
Freecell	-	-	-	-	-	-	-	-	-	-
Fridge										
Grid	14.23	14	-	-	-	-	-	-	-	-
Gripper	2.88	15	-	-	-	-	-	-	-	-
Hanoi	0.22	7	1.77	15	-	-	-	-	-	-
Logistics	0.29	20	-	-	-	-	-	-	-	-
Mic-ADL										
Mic-SIM										
Mic-STR	0.01	4	-	-	-	-	-	-	-	-
Movie	0.02	7	0.11	7	0.08	7	0.17	7	0.19	7
Mprime	1.16	9	3.63	7	-	-	-	-	-	-
Mystery	0.17	4	0.17	4	8.65	12	1.98	8	58.54	6
Schedule										
Simple-Tsp	0.10	5	27.72	10	-	-	-	-	-	-
Tireworld	0.35	19	78.94	30	-	-	-	-	-	-

Fig. 2.3. Runtime (t) and solution length (s) results for Blackbox in our benchmark example collection. A dash means that no plan was found after 5 minutes. An empty entry means that the planner could not be run on the respective task

where $a^1 \ldots a^n$ are the achievers of p in layer $i-1$. In a similar fashion, an action implies its preconditions, i.e., the clauses $\neg a_i \vee p_{i-1}^1, \ldots, \neg a_i \vee p_{i-1}^n$ are included for each action a at a layer i, with $pre(a) = \{p^1, \ldots, p^n\}$. The exclusion relations are simply encoded by specifying $\neg a_i \vee \neg a_i'$ for each pair of actions a and a' (at all layers i where both actions occur) that interfere — the other exclusion relations that Graphplan infers are logical consequences of these constraints, and would therefore be redundant in the SAT encoding.

The overall search for a plan in Blackbox proceeds in a fashion similar to what is done in Graphplan. A planning graph is built until a layer is reached that contains all goals. The graph is translated to a SAT encoding. One can then choose from a collection of SAT solvers, both complete ones like Tableau [21] and incomplete stochastic ones like Walksat [90]. If a satisfying truth assignment is found, it is translated into a plan. Complete search fails when it has proven the SAT instance to be unsolvable (or, if specified, when an upper time limit is reached), incomplete search is cut off (and restarted, if the maximum number of trials is not yet reached) after a given maximal number of unsuccessful variable flips. Upon failure, the planning graph is extended by one layer, and the same process is iterated. Note that using a complete solver (without time limit) at each step guarantees, like Graphplan, parallel optimality, while using an incomplete solver does not.

We evaluate the approach by running Blackbox, version 3.5. This can not deal with ADL so we can run it only on part of our examples. There is no planning as satisfiability system in existence that can deal with ADL, at least none that the author is aware of. Blackbox is implemented in C. There are rather a lot of command line options, which makes evaluation a bit tricky. We have decided to use the default options. With these options, in each iteration a complete search mechanism is tried for 30 seconds; if that produces no solution then a series of stochastic searches is tried with various cut-off and restart parameters. In a few tests we have run, the default system performed consistently a lot better than the other options we tried. See the data for the default system in Figure 2.3.

Concerning solution length, these results are roughly similar to what we have seen before. As for runtime, Blackbox is faster than UCPOP almost everywhere except in *Miconic-STRIPS* and *Simple-Tsp*. Compared to IPP, however, Blackbox demonstrates inferior runtime behavior, being outperformed to some extent in most domains, and drastically outperformed in *Hanoi*.

A bit odd here is that Kautz and Selman [60] have reported Blackbox to outperform Graphplan. The differences to our experiment lie in the Graphplan implementation compared to (IPP4.0 is a very efficient implementation), and in the computational resources available (Blackbox often ran out of memory in the experiment). We do not invest further effort in investigating the performance of Blackbox, but assert that the system achieves performance competitive with that of modern Graphplan implementations. The runtime performance that we obtain in the next part of the book is far beyond this.

3. Base Architecture

This part of the book describes and evaluates the algorithmic concepts used in our own approach to planning. The approach is implemented in the FF planning system (short for Fast-Forward). The chapter at hand introduces the basic techniques used in FF (which we will henceforth refer to as the *FF base architecture*). The two subsequent chapters describe additional techniques that are integrated on top of the base architecture in order to deal with special kinds of structural phenomena (dead ends and goal orderings). The last chapter of the part gives an account of the events in the AIPS-2000 competition, where the FF system participated very successfully.

FF belongs to the family of planners that approach planning by heuristic search. The heuristic search approach in the form we use it has been introduced by Bonet et al. [13], and was first implemented in Blai Bonet's and Héctor Geffner's HSP system [9, 12]. The approach proves to be efficient: in the benchmark example collection we use for evaluation, our implementation of (the first version of) HSP scales far better than the planners we have seen so far. The FF base architecture, in turn, scales still far better than HSP.

The chapter is organized as follows. FF's implementation works on grounded task representations; we describe how the action set is computed as a pre-process, and how complex ADL tasks are compiled into a better manageable normal format (Section 3.1). We review the algorithms used in the HSP system, precisely the first version of that system because it was this version that inspired the development of FF; the approach is evaluated by running our own implementation, which makes the comparison to FF more fair (Section 3.2). We then motivate and introduce FF's main algorithmic techniques in turn: the heuristic function (Section 3.3), the local search scheme (Section 3.4), and a pruning technique (Section 3.5). All algorithms are introduced with simple STRIPS notations, their extension to ADL is summarized separately (Section 3.6). We evaluate the resulting planning system (Section 3.7), demonstrating that on almost all of our benchmarks it outperforms HSP, being many orders of magnitude faster than the systems we have seen previously. The chapter finally features a detailed investigation of which algorithmic differences between FF and HSP have which effects on runtime and solution length performance (Section 3.8).

As a preface, we define the base concepts which the FF and the HSP system have in common. These are the definitions that form the core of our local search approach, and that underlie our subsequent investigation of local search topology.

J. Hoffmann: Utilizing Problem Structure in Planning, LNAI 2854, pp. 35–73, 2003.
© Springer-Verlag Berlin Heidelberg 2003

The search space in our framework is the space of all states that are reachable from the initial state: the so-called *state space*.

Definition 3.0.1. *Given a task* (A, I, G)*. The set* S *of reachable states is*

$$S := \{s \mid \exists\, P \in A^* : Result(I, P) = s\}$$

The state space *to* (A, I, G) *is the directed graph* (S, E) *where the nodes are the reachable states, and the edge set is*

$$E := \{(s, s') \mid s, s' \in S,\ \exists\, a \in A : Result(s, \langle a \rangle) = s'\}$$

The state space defined above is sometimes referred to as the *forward state space* in the planning literature, and search in this space as *forward search* (as opposed to the *backward search* done, e.g., by Graphplan). This terminology, together with the system's efficiency, has given FF its name.

As one would expect, the size of the state space usually grows exponentially in the size of the planning task (in particular, this is true for all our benchmark domains except *Movie*). So uninformed search is unlikely to be manageable, and the idea is to use informed, or *heuristic*, search instead.[1] That is, during search one wants to focus on the "good" states. A state is the better the closer it is to the goal.

Definition 3.0.2. *Given a task* (A, I, G)*, with state space* (S, E)*. The* goal distance *of* $s \in S$ *is the length of an optimal plan for* (A, s, G)*, or* ∞ *if there is no such plan:*

$$gd(s) := min\{n \mid P = \langle a_1, \ldots, a_n \rangle \in A^*, P \text{ is plan for } (A, s, G)\}$$

where the minimum over an empty set is ∞*.*

A state s has zero goal distance $gd(s) = 0$ if and only if s fulfills the goal condition. We refer to such states as *goal states*. If, starting from a state s, the goal can not be reached anymore then the set in the above definition is empty, resulting in $gd(s) = \infty$. We will discuss such "dead end" states in detail in Chapter 4.

Computing the goal distance of a state is of course as hard as planning itself (in particular, the goal distance of the initial state of an arbitrary task is ∞ if and only if the task is unsolvable). So one needs a function that approximates gd: a heuristic.

Definition 3.0.3. *Given a task* (A, I, G)*, with state space* (S, E)*. A* heuristic *is a function* $h : S \mapsto \mathbf{N}_0 \cup \{\infty\}$*, such that* $h(s) = 0 \Leftrightarrow gd(s) = 0$*.*

---

[1] There has also been some success for approaches that realize uninformed search via a symbolic representation of (parts of) the state space, in particular using BDDs [26, 50, 5].

Note that we make no assumptions about the quality of the approximation, except that the heuristic returns 0 exactly on the goal states. We restrict the heuristic to be a function into the natural numbers. This serves to reflect the intuition that the heuristic returns a value estimating the number of steps we still need to do before we can reach the goal. The heuristics that we will consider in this book are all functions into the natural numbers. As an exception, a heuristic can return ∞ to indicate that the state at hand might be a dead end. This will be discussed in Chapter 4.

The main problem now is, how can we come up with a heuristic function? While in specific applications the human designer can supply the system with an appropriate function, a general problem solver has to come up with the function all on its own. An approach that often works well for the human heuristic function designer is the following: simplify, or *relax*, the problem at hand into a simpler problem that can be solved efficiently; then, in any search state, solve the simpler problem and take the difficulty of doing that as an estimate of the state's real difficulty (an example reference to the field of heuristic search is the book by Judea Pearl [80]). This approach has first been applied to planning by Bonet et al. [13]. The idea is to relax the planning task by ignoring the delete lists.

Definition 3.0.4. *Given a STRIPS action* $a = (pre(a), add(a), del(a))$, *the re-laxation* a^+ *of* a *is defined as*

$$a^+ := (pre(a), add(a), \emptyset).$$

Given an ADL action $a = (pre(a), E(a))$, *the* relaxation a^+ *of* a *is defined as*

$$a^+ := (pre(a), \{(con(e), add(e), \emptyset) \mid e = (con(e), add(e), del(e)) \in E(a)\}).$$

For a set A *of actions, the* relaxation A^+ *of* A *is* $A^+ := \{a^+ \mid a \in A\}$. *The relaxation of a planning task* (A, I, G) *is* (A^+, I, G). *An action sequence* $P = \langle a_1, \ldots, a_n \rangle \in A^*$ *is a relaxed plan for* (A, I, G) *if* $\langle a_1^+, \ldots, a_n^+ \rangle$ *is a plan for* (A^+, I, G).

Definition 3.0.4 stands at the very center of our investigation, and its terminology will be used throughout the book which is why we introduce the rather many abbreviations. Our heuristic function, described in Section 3.3 for STRIPS and in Section 3.6.1 for ADL, works by solving the relaxed task (A^+, s, G) for every single search state s during a forward search.

Executing a relaxed action, all add effects become true but no propositions are made false, i.e., the set of true propositions increases monotonically. We need to take some time to explain the consequences that this has in the STRIPS, and especially in the ADL framework. In the STRIPS language, the relaxation reduces the complexity of the problem dramatically, as has first been proven by Bylander [15]. The complexity of deciding plan existence for a STRIPS task goes down from PSPACE-completeness for the general case to P for the relaxed case. Relaxed solvability can be decided as follows. Start with $s := I$; then iteratively (at most $|A|$ times) include (into s) the add effects of all actions whose preconditions are contained in s, until a fix point occurs; the relaxed task is solvable if and only if the goals are contained in the fix point of s. The solution algorithm which we introduce in Section 3.3 is an efficient variation of this idea.

In the ADL language, matters are more complicated. Let us examine the situation. Quite to the contrary of the STRIPS case, deciding plan existence for relaxed ADL tasks is still PSPACE-complete. This is due to the need for checking satisfaction of first-order formulae in states. We do not include a full formal proof. Membership follows with Theorem 2.2.2. Hardness follows by a straightforward reduction from the problem of deciding truth of an arbitrary QBF formula [96]. Briefly, the QBF formula $Q_1 p_1 : \ldots Q_n p_n : \phi$ quantifies via $Q_i \in \{\forall, \exists\}$ the n propositional variables $p_1 \ldots p_n$; create an ADL task using n predicates $P_1, \ldots, P_n$, and two constants T and F; the action set is empty, the initial state is $I := \{(P_1, T), \ldots, (P_n, T)\}$, and the goal formula is $G := Q_1 x_1 \in \{T, F\} : \ldots Q_n x_n \in \{T, F\} : \phi'$ where ϕ' results from ϕ by replacing all sub-expressions p_i with (P_i, x_i). With this construction, $I \models G$ and thus solvability of (A, I, G) holds if and only if the QBF formula is valid.[2]

In our algorithmic framework, we deal with this complexity problem by transferring all the hard computations into a pre-processing phase. The pre-processing is of course exponentially costly in the worst case. If the formulae used in the task at hand are however not exceedingly complex, then the pre-processing is manageable. After all, the formulae are supposed to be execution conditions of actions in a real-world problem. In particular, in all of our 20 benchmark domains the runtime taken for pre-processing is negligible compared to overall solution time. The formulae in ADL tasks are pre-processed in terms of three main steps: the quantifiers are compiled away; the negations are translated; the formulae are brought into DNF. Algorithmic and theoretical details about these processes are in Section 3.1.2. Here, we explain their relevance with respect to the relaxation of ADL tasks.

We first say some words on the quantifiers. Note that in the above the complexity of deciding relaxed plan existence in ADL stems entirely from evaluating the goal condition, the actions being ignored. The complexity of evaluating a first-order formula in a state, in turn, stems entirely from the quantification. For a closed quantifier free formula, it is trivial to evaluate whether or not the formula holds in any given state. Compiling away the quantifiers (replacing them with conjunctions or disjunctions, respectively) thus results in a (possibly large) formula that can be tested in polynomial time.

---

[2] We remark that the same decision problem (checking satisfaction of first-order formulae in states) appears in data base theory [17, 98]. The state corresponds to a relational database, the formula corresponds to a query expressed in the relational calculus. The question is whether the relations in the database fulfill the query. While in data base theory usually either *data complexity* (the query is fixed) or *expression complexity* (the data base is fixed) are considered, in our case we consider *combined complexity* where both inputs are variable. If we fix the planning domain, then checking satisfaction of operator preconditions corresponds to the data complexity case. More on this in Section 3.1.

Negations constitute another important complication with relaxed ADL tasks. The complication does not stem from the complexity of deciding formula satisfaction, but from the semantics that arise in the presence of negations. If there are negations, then it is not always preferable to have more propositions true. This has consequences concerning solution mechanisms for relaxed solvability, and for the semantics of relaxed plans. We first focus on the latter.

In the STRIPS case, there are no negations at all. In effect, a relaxed STRIPS task is simpler than the original task in the formal sense that *any plan for the original task is (in its relaxed version) also a plan for the relaxed task.* This is a desirable property. For one thing, it implies that the relaxed task can — in principle — be used to extract an admissible heuristic (some more on this topic below). For another thing, the property prevents the heuristic function from mistaking a state for a dead end: it can not happen that there is no relaxed plan for a task that is solvable (more details about this are given in Chapter 4).

In the presence of negations, it does *not* hold that all plans for the original task also solve the relaxed task. Consider the example ADL task where the initial state is $I = \{g_1\}$, the goal condition is $G = \neg g_1 \wedge g_2$, and the action set A comprises one action a with empty precondition and a single effect $(\top, \{g_2\}, \{g_1\})$. Applying the action in the initial state yields a goal state: g_2 is added, and g_1 is deleted. The relaxed task, however, is unsolvable: without delete lists there is no way of making g_1 false so there is no plan for (A^+, I, G). Explicitly, our desired property is violated because the action sequence $\langle a \rangle$ is a plan for (A, I, G) but $\langle a^+ \rangle$ is no plan for (A^+, I, G). For the relaxation to make sense in ADL, we must therefore postulate that there are no negations.

Definition 3.0.5. *Given an ADL task (A, I, G). A formula is* negation free *if it does not contain any negations. (A, I, G) is* negation free *if G and the preconditions and effect conditions of all actions in A are negation free.*

In a negation-free ADL task, as well as in STRIPS tasks, our desired property is true.

Proposition 3.0.1. *Let (A, I, G) be a STRIPS task or a negation-free ADL task. Then any plan for (A, I, G) is also a relaxed plan for (A, I, G).*

Proof. In a relaxed plan, propositions that have been made true once remain true. Now, in a STRIPS or negation-free ADL task having more propositions true never does any harm because no precondition or effect condition nor the goal requires a proposition to be false.

We will see in Section 3.1.2 how an arbitrary ADL task can be compiled into a task that is negation free. For the moment, let us get back to the topic of deciding relaxed solvability. We first remark that deciding solvability of a negation-free relaxed ADL task is still PSPACE-complete. This can be proved by a straightforward extension of the proof for the general case above: an arbitrary QBF formula $Q_1 p_1 : \ldots Q_n p_n : \phi$ can be translated by bringing ϕ into negation normal form, then using the same ADL task as above except that there are additional predicates not-$P_1, \ldots,$ not-P_n with $I := \{(P_1, T), \ldots, (P_n, T), (\text{not-}P_1, F), \ldots, (\text{not-}P_n, F)\}$ and ϕ' in G being created from ϕ by replacing p_i with (P_i, x_i) and $\neg p_i$ with $(\text{not-}P_i, x_i)$.

With the above, it does not help us to only compile the negations away. Neither is it sufficient to only compile the quantifiers away: for a quantifier free ADL task with negations, deciding relaxed solvability is still NP-hard (which follows directly from results by Bylander [15]). If we have a task that neither contains quantifiers nor negations, however, the following method decides relaxed solvability in polynomial time. Start with $s := I$; then iteratively (until a fix point occurs, or at most as many times as there are effects with distinct add lists) include (into s) the add lists of all effects such that $s \models con(e)$ holds for the effect condition and $s \models pre(a)$ holds for the corresponding action precondition; the relaxed task is solvable if and only if $s \models G$ holds in the fix point. The satisfaction of formulae can be tested efficiently because they do not contain quantifiers. The method is equivalent to solvability of the relaxed task because the formulae do not contain negations. The solution algorithm which we introduce in Section 3.6.1 is an efficient variation of this method. As said, our pre-processing procedures go beyond the above by transforming all formulae into DNF: for this normal form our algorithms can be implemented very efficiently.

We now get back to the more general — less ADL-specific — issues. After we have decided solvability of a relaxed task, the length of a respective relaxed plan (if there is one) will be our heuristic value to a state. As a measure of goal distance, we are obviously not interested in *any* relaxed plan: these plans might contain arbitrarily many superfluous actions that have nothing to do with how difficult it really is to solve the state at hand. We rather want to know how many relaxed actions we *at least* need to execute, i.e., we want to know the length of an *optimal* relaxed plan. We define this for STRIPS and negation-free ADL tasks only, as we have seen above that the relaxation does not make much sense in the presence of negations.

Definition 3.0.6. *Let (A, I, G) be a STRIPS task or a negation-free ADL task, with state space (S, E). The relaxed distance of $s \in S$ is the length of an optimal relaxed plan for (A, s, G), or ∞ if there is no such plan:*

$$h^+(s) := min\{n \mid P = \langle a_1, \ldots, a_n \rangle \in A^*, P \text{ is relaxed plan for } (A, s, G)\}$$

where the minimum over an empty set is ∞.

A heuristic function is called *admissible* if its value is always an underestimation of the real value of a state. Admissible heuristic functions are very useful for optimization problems because using them in certain standard search schemes guarantees that the first found solution is optimal [80]. The h^+ function is an admissible heuristic function because any real plan is also a relaxed plan, c.f. Proposition 3.0.1. So h^+ could be used to find optimal plans. However, computing h^+ is still NP-complete in the STRIPS case (as was proved by Bylander [15]) and thus also in the ADL case even if all formulae are in quantifier-free and negation-free DNF. The approach that has first been taken in HSP, and that we adopt in the FF system, is to approximate h^+.

3.1 Grounding

All algorithms we are going to describe in the rest of the book are defined for grounded planning tasks. In contrast to that, the input for a planning system is an instance of a domain, i.e., the sets of predicates and operators used in the domain as well as the set of constants and the initial and goal states of the specific instance. From that high-level description, the grounded task is obtained by applying the operator functions to the objects, yielding the action set. As was mentioned above, for ADL tasks the pre-processing procedures go beyond grounding in the sense that the task is compiled into a simple propositional normal form. We briefly describe the algorithms, and add in some detail about the relevant theoretical properties of the processes, concerning various issues that will be important for what is to come. First we say some words on STRIPS, then we focus on ADL.

3.1.1 STRIPS

The naive way of computing the action set to an instance is to simply apply all operators with k parameters to all k-tuples of constants, and collect the results. Within a fixed domain this process is polynomial because the maximal number of parameters is fixed.

Proposition 3.1.1. *Given a fixed STRIPS domain $\mathcal{D} = (\mathcal{P}, \mathcal{O}, \mathcal{I})$. For an instance (C, I, G) of the domain, let (A, I, G) be the task to (C, I, G). Then $|A|$ is polynomial in C.*

Proof. Follows from the fact that the finite operator set is fixed for the given domain: $|A| \in O(|C|^{maxp})$ where $maxp$ is the maximal number of parameters of any operator in $\mathcal{O}$.

One can utilize simple knowledge about the domain to speed up the action set computation and at the same time shorten the grounded task description. An observation that can often be made at least in the benchmarks is that some of the predicates are static in the following sense.

Definition 3.1.1. *Given a STRIPS domain $\mathcal{D} = (\mathcal{P}, \mathcal{O}, \mathcal{I})$. A predicate $(prd, ar) \in \mathcal{P}$ is static if it does not appear in any add- or delete-list of any operator $o \in \mathcal{O}$.*

Static predicates can be used to encode properties that do not change over time, like the types of the objects or the linked locations on a road map. If a predicate is static then it can be removed entirely from the grounded task description: say p is a proposition — a grounded fact — based on the predicate. If p is contained in the initial state then it is permanently true, if it is not contained in the initial state then it is permanently false. So in the former case p can be left out of preconditions and in the latter case an action using p will never become applicable and can be skipped.

An effective way to take account of, and remove, static predicates is the following. First, match the static preconditions of the operators to the initial state, generating all and only constant tuples for which these preconditions are fulfilled. Parameters that are not constrained by a static precondition are naively multiplied out. The static preconditions can be left out of the final actions. Static propositions can be left out of the initial and the goal state. More on static predicates and how to deal with them can be found in work done by Koehler and Hoffmann [63]. Note that removing static predicates does not change the semantics of a task. We state that formally — together with ADL — shortly below.

3.1.2 ADL

Naive computation of action sets in ADL instances is the same as in STRIPS except that one also needs to ground the effect parameters, as described in Section 2.2.5. Because in a fixed domain the maximal number of (effect) parameters is fixed, the naive process is polynomial.

Proposition 3.1.2. *Given a fixed ADL domain $\mathcal{D} = (\mathcal{P}, \mathcal{O}, \mathcal{I})$. For an instance (C, I, G) of the domain, let (A, I, G) be the task to (C, I, G). Then $|A|$ and $|E(a)|$ for all $a \in A$ are polynomial in $|C|$.*

Proof. Follows directly from the operator set being fixed for the given domain: $|A| \in O(|C|^{maxp})$ where $maxp$ is the maximal number of parameters of any operator in $\mathcal{O}$; $|E(a)| \in O(|C|^{maxp'})$ for all actions a produced by an operator o, where $maxp'$ is the maximal number of effect parameters of any effect of any operator in $\mathcal{O}$.

Dealing with static predicates in ADL is more involved than in STRIPS. While their definition remains almost the same (except that they are now not to appear in the add or delete list of any *effect*), one can not simply match them against the initial state: preconditions and effect conditions as well as the goal condition are arbitrary formulae, not conjunctions of propositions. The idea is still to replace static propositions by *true* or *false*. More generally, if p is never added and not in the initial state then all its occurrences are false; if p is never deleted and in the initial state then all its occurrences are true. Inserting the truth value of a proposition can lead to simplifying updates of the formula. If the precondition of an action simplifies to false then the action can be removed, similar for an effect; if the goal condition simplifies to false then the task is proved unsolvable. More details on this process are described by Koehler and Hoffmann [63]. Again, removing static predicates does not change the semantics of a task at all. We include this simple observation, for both STRIPS and ADL tasks, as a formal statement that we will refer to in Chapters 4 and 8, in the context of proving properties of planning tasks by looking at them after static predicates removal.

Proposition 3.1.3. *Given a (STRIPS or ADL) task (A, I, G). Let (A', I', G') be the task that results from removing static predicates. The following holds.*

1. *Both tasks share the same state space (S, E) in the sense that there is a bijection π between states under which the respective graphs are identical; and*
2. *both tasks share the same relaxed distances, i.e., $\forall s \in S : h^+(s) = h^+(\pi(s))$.*

Proof. Obvious: only actions or effects are skipped that never become applicable anyway, and only conditions are skipped that are always true anyway.

The only difference between the state spaces is that, without removing static predicates, each state contains a number of static propositions that are not contained in the corresponding state after removing static predicates.

Negation-Free Compilation. As was said before, ignoring delete lists makes sense as a relaxation only if the formulae in the task are negation free — otherwise the "relaxation" might even render a solvable task unsolvable. We will now describe how an arbitrary ADL task can be compiled into a negation-free ADL task. First we need to fix the notion of "compilation". By a compilation we mean a task that is solvable iff the original task is solvable, such that from a solution for the compiled task we can easily construct a solution for the original task. Formally this reads as follows.

Definition 3.1.2. *Given a task (A, I, G). A task (A', I', G') together with a surjective function $\pi : (A')^* \mapsto A^*$ is a compilation of (A, I, G) if:*

1. *any sequence $P' \in (A')^*$ is a plan for (A', I', G') if and only if $\pi(P')$ is a plan for (A, I, G);*
2. *π is computable in time linear in $|P'|$ for $P' \in (A')^*$;*
3. *there is a constant $c \in \mathbf{N}_0$ such that $|P'| = |\pi(P')| + c$ for all $P' \in (A')^*$ that are plans for (A', I', G').*

With the first condition in Definition 3.1.2 any plan for (A', I', G') yields a plan for (A, I, G), with surjectivity of π and the first condition to any plan for (A, I, G) there is a plan for (A', I', G'). By the second condition, any plan for (A', I', G') can be easily transformed into a plan for (A, I, G). By the third condition, relative plan length is preserved (in particular, if P' is an optimal plan for (A', I', G') then $\pi(P')$ is an optimal plan for (A, I, G)).

Fundamental work on compilations, or *compilation schemes*, between planning formalisms has been done by Bernhard Nebel [76]. We introduce the rather specialized notion in Definition 3.1.2 only to make the properties of the compilation methods in this and the following section precise. Briefly, our definition is stricter than Nebel's definition in that we explicitly postulate the linear time plan translation function π preserving plan length modulo a constant — after all, we want to use the compiled task only to solve the original task. On the other hand the definition is more generous than Nebel's in that we make no restrictions on how large the compiled task is — in Nebel's work it is postulated that the compilation size is polynomial in the original size. In fact the compilation that we describe in the next section can cause an exponential blow up in the task description (by compiling away quantifiers, as discussed earlier).

The following process computes, to any ADL task (A, I, G), a negation-free compilation (A', I', G') and π. Initialize (A', I', G') as (A, I, G). If (A, I, G) is already negation free then stop. Otherwise:

1. put all preconditions and effect conditions as well as the goal condition into negation normal form where negations are only in front of propositions;
2. step through all preconditions and effect conditions as well as the goal condition; if you come across a negated proposition $\neg p$ then:
   a) introduce a new proposition p^-;
   b) set $p^- \in I \Leftrightarrow p \notin I$;
   c) in all effects $(con(e), add(e), del(e))$ of an action, set $del(e) := del(e) \cup \{p^-\}$ if $p \in add(e)$ and $add(e) := add(e) \cup \{p^-\}$ if $p \in del(e)$;
   d) in all preconditions and effect conditions as well as the goal condition, replace $\neg p$ with p^-.

Details on the implementation of the compilation process, which follows Gazen and Knoblock [37], are described by Koehler and Hoffmann [63]. Note that the propositions p^- really always have the inverse truth value of p only if it can never happen that an action application adds and deletes p at the same time: in that case, also p^- would be added and deleted, so either way of assigning priority between adding and deleting (c.f. Section 2.2.4) would result in a state where p and p^- have the same truth value. This technical subtlety was not mentioned (overlooked, probably) by either Gazen and Knoblock or Koehler and Hoffmann. We deal with the problem by disallowing action applications that add and delete the same proposition, c.f. Sections 2.2.4 and 2.2.5.

The compilation process affects only condition formulae and the add and delete lists of effects. The π function simply maps sequences of modified actions to the same sequence of the original actions. The new task and π fulfill the requirements for a compilation, preserving plan length exactly. The process obviously takes time polynomial in the size of the original task. The following simple property holds for the effect and action sets.

Proposition 3.1.4. *Given a fixed ADL domain $\mathcal{D} = (\mathcal{P}, \mathcal{O}, \mathcal{I})$. For an instance (C, I, G) of the domain, the above described process computes a compilation (A', I', G') and π of the task to (C, I, G) such that (A', I', G') is negation free, and $|A'|$ as well as $|E(a')|$ for all $a' \in A'$ are polynomial in $|C|$.*

Proof. Follows with Proposition 3.1.2 because only the condition formulae, add- and delete-lists of the actions are modified.

Propositional Compilation. As we will see later in this chapter, in our algorithmic setting computing the heuristic value of a state involves repeated application of all actions. As planning tasks often contain thousands of actions, checking action applicability and fulfillment of effect conditions is therefore extremely time critical. We have seen at the beginning of this chapter that evaluating (negation-free) formulae in states is PSPACE-hard in general. As said before, we deal with the problem by doing all the hard computations in a pre-processing phase, leaving us with easily manageable classes of formulae during planning (the formulae being exponential in size at worst, but of moderate size in practice, i.e., in particular in the benchmarks). We compile all formulae into a simple propositional normal format, namely STRIPS-like conjunctions of propositions. For that format, the heuristic algorithms can be implemented very efficiently.

Definition 3.1.3. *Given an ADL task* (A, I, G). *A formula is* propositional *if it is a conjunction of propositions.* (A, I, G) *is* propositional *if G and the preconditions and effect conditions of all actions in A are propositional.*

The process for compiling the formulae away follows, again, Gazen and Knoblock [37] and the implementation techniques described by Koehler and Hoffmann [63]. Briefly, the method works as follows. Initialize (A', I', G') as (A, I, G). If (A, I, G) is already propositional then stop. Otherwise:

1. compile the negations away as described above;
2. expand the quantifiers in all formulae, i.e., replace $\forall x \in C : \phi$ with $\bigwedge_{c \in C} \phi\frac{c}{x}$ and $\exists x \in C : \phi$ with $\bigvee_{c \in C} \phi\frac{c}{x}$ (by $\phi\frac{c}{x}$ we denote the substitution of x with c in ϕ);
3. put all formulae into DNF by moving conjunctions below disjunctions;
4. if the precondition of an action a consists of more than one disjunct then remove a and create one new action for each disjunct, with the disjunct as precondition and the same effects as a; if an effect condition consists of more than one disjunct then remove the effect and create, for each disjunct, one new effect with the same add and delete lists;
5. if the goal condition has more than one disjunct then introduce new propositions g and s; set $G := \{g\}$ and insert s into the initial state and into the preconditions of all actions; create one artificial action for each disjunct where the precondition is the disjunct plus s and the only effects are to add g and to delete s.

The π function here maps single actions to the actions they originated from (i.e., the new actions for precondition disjuncts inherit the "name" of the original action), and entirely skips artificial actions that achieve a goal disjunct. Note that either no plan for (A', I', G') contains such an action — if the goal has not been split up — or that all plans for (A', I', G') contain exactly one such action. So plan length in the compiled task is either preserved exactly or increased constantly by $c = 1$.

The first algorithmic step of the process is polynomial in the size of the task. The second step is exponential in general; concerning precondition and effect condition formulae, the process is polynomial within a fixed domain as the maximal nesting of quantifiers is restricted (which it is not for the goals).[3] The third step, transformation into DNF, can again be exponential. We remark that

---

[3] As mentioned before, within a fixed domain checking satisfaction of precondition or effect condition formulae corresponds to the data complexity problem considered in data base theory [17, 98]. Expanding the quantifiers prior to checking satisfaction is one polynomial method to solve this problem.

this step is not necessary from a complexity theoretic point of view: we have seen before that in a quantifier-free and negation-free task relaxed solvability can be decided in polynomial time. Computing the DNF enables a very efficient implementation of the heuristic function (as will be described in Section 3.6.1); more on that topic is said directly below. The fourth and fifth steps are obviously linear in the size of their input.

Let us remark once again that the possibly exponential blow-up inherent in our pre-processing techniques, while it can easily be provoked by abstract examples, does not constitute a problem in the benchmarks, in fact in no planning task we tried so far. If the formulae — which are after all meant to be applicability conditions of planning operators and effects in real-world problems — are not exceedingly complex, then the compilation process uses negligible runtime and memory. Nevertheless it is an interesting open research direction to (efficiently) implement algorithms that avoid grounding or at least compilation of formulae into DNF.

In the propositional compilation there are still only polynomially many *different* actions and effects.

Proposition 3.1.5. *Given a fixed ADL domain $\mathcal{D} = (\mathcal{P}, \mathcal{O}, \mathcal{I})$. For an instance (C, I, G) of the domain, the above described process computes a compilation (A', I', G') and π of the task to (C, I, G) such that: (A', I', G') is propositional; the number of actions in A' with different effect sets is polynomial in $|C|$; for each action $a' \in A$ the number of effects with different add- and delete-lists in $E(a')$ is polynomial in $|C|$.*

Proof. Follows from the above description and the fact that the sets of predicates and operators are fixed for the given domain: if an action a is split into a set of new actions, then all these new actions have exactly the same effects as a; likewise for effects. Polynomiality, before DNF, of action set size and number of effects in $|C|$ for a fixed domain was shown in Proposition 3.1.4.

The only difference between the propositional compilation of an ADL task and a STRIPS task is the possible existence of conditional effects. We will in the rest of the book identify conjunctions of propositions in propositional ADL tasks with *sets* of propositions. If (A', I', G') and π is the compilation of a task (A, I, G) then we also refer to (A', I', G') alone as the compilation of (A, I, G).

Let us remark that the original task and its propositional compilation are connected more closely than is required by the definition of a compilation, at least if the goal is not split up in which case the following strong property holds.

Proposition 3.1.6. *Given a negation-free ADL task (A, I, G) with state space (S, E). Let (A', I', G') (and π) be the propositional compilation of (A, I, G) computed by the above described process, with state space (S', E'). If the compilation process does not split up the goal condition, then the following holds.*

1. *There is a graph isomorphism between the state spaces, i.e., a bijection $\sigma : S \mapsto S'$ such that $(s, s') \in E$ iff $(\sigma(s), \sigma(s')) \in E'$; and*
2. *the relaxed distances are identical, i.e., $\forall s \in S : h^+(s) = h^+(\sigma(s))$.*

Proof. All compilation steps are equivalence transformations on logical formulae, except splitting conditions up when their DNF has more than one disjunct. Splitting up action preconditions replaces one action with several parts that induce exactly the same state transitions, whether in the relaxed or the real task. The same holds for splitting up effect conditions.

We will need the above property in Chapters 7 and 8 to justify the way in which we measure h^+ values in propositional compilations of planning tasks, and verify the results by looking at their negation free formulations. The tasks we will consider there are taken from our benchmark domains and have therefore in particular no disjunctive goal conditions, which is why we do not elaborate in detail on what exactly the situation would be if the goal condition was split up.

The reader is advised to keep in mind what the differences between (full) ADL tasks, negation-free ADL tasks, and propositional ADL tasks are. We will stick to this hierarchy throughout the book, discussing matters on the respectively most general level that is appropriate. In connection with the relaxation, only negation-free ADL is appropriate as in the presence of negations ignoring delete lists does not necessarily simplify the task. In connection with (most of) our algorithms, only propositional ADL is appropriate as this is the format which the implementation is based on. To avoid the clumsiness of language, we will sometimes allow statements about negation-free or propositional compilations of STRIPS tasks. These are, naturally, identical to the original tasks.

3.2 HSP

Let us get into the algorithmical part of the book. Planning as heuristic search has first been implemented in Blai Bonet's and Héctor Geffner's HSP system [9, 12]. As said at the beginning of the chapter, FF shares the main algorithmic concepts with HSP.

There are nowadays several different versions of HSP, integrated into a hybrid system that can be configured by a number of search options, including forward or regression search and optimal search with admissible heuristics [9, 10, 41, 12, 11]. The system we describe in this section is the very first version of HSP: HSP1 as it was used in the AIPS-1998 planning systems competition [9]. HSP1 is the closest relative to FF. More importantly, the development of FF was essentially a process of modifying, motivated by example observations, the algorithms used in HSP1.

3.2.1 Heuristic

As explained earlier, the approach taken in HSP is to perform search in the state space, guided by a heuristic function that results from relaxing the task in the sense that all delete lists are ignored. For any search state s, the length $h^+(s)$ of an optimal relaxed plan for s can give an estimate of the state's goal distance. However, computing h^+ is still NP-hard. Considering this, Bonet et al. [13] make, on top of ignoring all delete lists, another simplifying assumption: that all propositions in the task must be achieved separately. The resulting computation can be done in polynomial time.

Assuming that all propositions must be achieved separately, i.e., ignoring possible positive interactions, the cost of achieving a set of propositions is exactly the sum of the individual costs. More precisely, Bonet et al. [13] define the cost of a proposition p in a reachable state s of a STRIPS task (A, I, G) as follows.

$$cost_s(p) := \begin{cases} 0 & \text{if } p \in s \\ c+1 & \text{if } [min_{a \in A, p \in add(a)} \sum_{p' \in pre(a)} cost_s(p')] = c \\ \infty & \text{otherwise} \end{cases} \quad (3.1)$$

The costs are computed in a simple forward chaining way where all values are initialized to 0 if $p \in s$ and to ∞ otherwise. Then, every time an action a is applicable in s, each $p \in add(a)$ is put into s (if it's not already in there) and $cost_s(p)$ is updated to $min(cost_s(p), 1 + \sum_{p' \in pre(a)} cost_s(p'))$. These updates are continued until the cost values do not change anymore. The heuristic value of a state is defined as follows.

$$h^{HSP}(s) := \sum_{g \in G} cost_s(g) \quad (3.2)$$

If the cost of one goal is ∞ then this implies that (A^+, I, G) is unsolvable, which means that s is a dead end; as said before, dead ends will be discussed in Chapter 4. For propositional ADL tasks the cost values are defined similar to Equation 3.1; for effects that achieve a proposition the cost of all effect conditions plus the respective action's preconditions is summed up.

We remark that the h^{HSP} function is not admissible, because ignoring positive interactions can result in overestimation. Consider the following example, where the initial state is empty $I = \emptyset$, the goals are $\{g_1, g_2\}$, and there are the following three actions:

name		(pre,	add,	del)
actg_1	=	({p},	{g_1},	$\emptyset$)
actg_2	=	({p},	{g_2},	$\emptyset$)
act$p$	=	($\emptyset$,	{p},	$\emptyset$)

The cost of p is 1, the cost of each of the goals is 2. Assuming propositions to be achieved independently, HSP therefore estimates the distance of the initial state to a goal state to $h^{HSP}(I) = 4$. The task is however solvable in only three steps, as actg_1 and actg_2 share the precondition p.

3.2.2 Search

While HSP's heuristic function can be computed in polynomial time, the computation is still costly because a single state evaluation involves repeated application of all actions [10, 12]. In the hope to reach the goal with as few state evaluations as possible, the search scheme in HSP1 was therefore chosen to be a local one, more precisely a variation of hill-climbing [9]. In hill-climbing, search always evaluates all direct successors of a state, and randomly chooses one with best evaluation. This process iterates until a goal state is reached. The search algorithm implemented in HSP1 extends this basic algorithm by a number of restarting techniques: if a search path looks unpromising in the sense that it contains many non-improving steps, then the path is cut off and search starts from scratch, i.e., from the initial state. Due to the random element in the algorithm, the next search path will be a different one.

One investigation that will be described later in this chapter is a precise evaluation of FF in comparison to its relative HSP1, i.e., an investigation of which algorithmic differences have which effect on performance. For this investigation, we needed to implement our own version of HSP1. In personal communication with Blai Bonet and Héctor Geffner, we implemented the following search algorithm.

- Start in the initial state; in any state s, evaluate all direct successors of s and randomly select one successor with best (least) h^{HSP} value.
- Store the states on the current search path, and disallow cycles.
- Count the number of consecutive times in which the best successor of a state does not improve the heuristic value. If that counter exceeds $2 * h^{HSP}(I)$, then restart.
- Across restart trials, keep visited states s and their heuristic value $h^{HSP}(s)$ in memory; before evaluating a state, see if its value is already stored.

In HSP1, some more variations of restarts are implemented. The algorithms behave roughly similar in terms of scaling behavior: in the majority of the benchmark domains we tried, the solved instances were the same for both planners (though the original implementation was usually slower). We say more on the comparison with HSP1 below.

3.2.3 Evaluation

For evaluating HSP, or rather the approach that is used in HSP1, we give data collected by running our own implementation. This makes the comparison with FF, which uses the same data structures and pre-processing, more fair. Figure 3.1 shows runtime and solution length values on the benchmark example collection we have seen before. To take account of the random element in the algorithm we have run the planner five times on each task, and averaged the values. If one trial did not solve a task then we set the runtime to the time limit of 300 seconds. Solution length is averaged (and rounded to the next lower integer) only over those trials that succeeded. A dash means that no trial solved the respective task. We remark that five trials seemed to be enough because the variance that we found between different trials was usually low; this might be due to the fact that each hill-climbing trial starts out from the same state — the initial state. For

domain	task1 t	task1 s	task2 t	task2 s	task3 t	task3 s	task4 t	task4 s	task5 t	task5 s
Assembly	1.19	215	2.50	348	-	-	-	-	-	-
Bw-arm	0.02	18	0.05	19	0.20	65	2.84	530	5.07	484
Bw-noarm	0.02	7	0.07	20	1.68	23	7.34	20	26.18	31
Briefcase	0.02	15	0.05	21	0.07	17	0.43	57	2.30	85
Ferry	0.03	9	0.02	15	-	-	-	-	-	-
Freecell	2.11	23	6.17	44	10.12	60	86.96	165	-	-
Fridge	0.01	12	0.05	24	0.17	36	0.43	48	1.01	60
Grid	0.52	20	3.45	101	-	-	189.08	1498	-	-
Gripper	0.03	17	0.08	37	0.22	59	0.43	79	0.80	98
Hanoi	0.02	14	0.03	36	0.07	72	-	-	-	-
Logistics	0.05	25	2.08	91	16.94	187	117.47	297	-	-
Mic-ADL	0.02	4	-	-	-	-	-	-	-	-
Mic-SIM	0.01	4	0.08	27	0.73	54	4.12	84	11.44	124
Mic-STR	0.02	4	0.11	33	1.07	75	4.93	98	15.26	167
Movie	0.02	7	0.02	7	0.03	7	0.04	7	0.04	7
Mprime	0.14	5	4.38	13	79.47	6	188.73	56	256.26	56
Mystery	0.04	4	0.05	5	2.11	15	1.12	8	9.72	6
Schedule	0.09	2	-	-	-	-	-	-	-	-
SimpleTsp	0.01	5	0.03	10	0.11	15	0.25	20	0.50	25
Tireworld	0.06	32	0.29	262	6.10	2859	-	-	-	-

Fig. 3.1. Runtime (t) and solution length (s) results of our HSP1 implementation, averaged over five trials. A dash means that no trial found a plan after 5 minutes

example, solving the first *Assembly* task took 0.89, 1.14, 1.45, 1.11, respectively 1.39 seconds in our five trials.

The best data we have seen so far for this example collection is that of IPP in Figure 2.2. The runtime performance of our HSP1 implementation is far beyond that. The new planner outperforms IPP in all but the *Miconic-ADL* and *Schedule* domains — where neither planner does particularly well — as well as in the *Fridge* and *Hanoi* domains — where IPP scales better. The runtime performance is often bought at the cost of bad solution quality: from the 40 tasks that both planners solve, HSP's plans are longer than IPP's in 24 cases, and (slightly) shorter in only 2 cases; sometimes the plans are rather unnecessarily long, like in the *Tireworld* instance with 2 wheels where IPP needs 30 actions and our planner here 262 (we will say more on the reasons for this behavior in Section 3.8).

It should be noted here that these results differ from the behavior that HSP1 showed in the AIPS-1998 competition where it competed against Graphplan-based and SAT-based planners. There, HSP1's runtime was competitive with, but not superior to, that of the other planners (solving more tasks but being somewhat slower on those examples that the others could solve). Also, in the AIPS-1998 competition HSP1 did generally not find significantly longer solutions than the other planners. Speculating where the differences of HSP1 to our implementation here stem from, the search strategy obviously plays a role, and so probably do (at least concerning runtime behavior) implementation details concerning the pre-processing, and the data structures used.

3.3 Heuristic

We now introduce the heuristic function used in FF. Our idea is to approximate h^+ by extracting *one*, not necessarily optimal, relaxed solution to the tasks (A^+, s, G) for search states s: while computing an optimal relaxed solution is NP-hard, deciding relaxed solvability can be done in polynomial time. If such a polynomial decision procedure constructs a witness for solvability then we can use that witness for heuristic evaluation. We will see that the Graphplan system, as we described in Section 2.4.2, is such a polynomial decision procedure.

The advantage of explicitly extracting a relaxed plan is that it can, unlike HSP's heuristic function, take account of positive interactions. We will exemplify this below. Furthermore, we describe a few techniques to extract as short relaxed plans as easily possible. Finally we explain how the algorithms can be implemented efficiently. We first concentrate on simple STRIPS notations. The extension to (propositional) ADL tasks is described afterwards in Section 3.6.

3.3.1 Planning Graphs for Relaxed Tasks

Let us examine how Graphplan behaves when it is started on a planning task that does not contain any delete lists. As we have described in Section 2.4.2, a planning graph is a directed layered graph that alternates between proposition and action layers, starting with the initial state (proposition layer 0) and extending the graph from any proposition layer i by the applicable actions (action layer i) and their respective effects (proposition layer $i + 1$). A pair of propositions within a layer is marked as exclusive if all pairs of actions achieving the propositions are exclusive; a pair of actions within a layer is marked as exclusive if they interfere (if one action deletes a precondition or an add effect of the other) or if they have competing needs (some of their preconditions are exclusive). The planning graph of a relaxed task does not contain any exclusion relations.

Proposition 3.3.1. *Let (A^+, I, G) be a relaxed STRIPS task. Started on (A^+, I, G), Graphplan will not mark any pair of propositions or actions as mutually exclusive.*

Proof. By induction on the depth of the planning graph.

Base case: time step 0. Only interfering actions are marked mutual exclusive at time step 0. As there are no delete effects, no pair of actions interferes.

Inductive case: time step i → time step $i + 1$. Per induction hypothesis, the propositions are not exclusive as their achievers one time step ahead are not. From this it follows that no pair of actions has competing needs. They do not interfere either.

The planning graph is built until a proposition layer is reached that contains all goals, or until the graph has reached a fix point without reaching the goals. In the latter case, the task is proved unsolvable [8]. In the former case, a recursive backward search algorithm tries to extract a solution subgraph by selecting a set of achieving actions at each layer and propagating those action's preconditions into the next lower layer. The algorithm backtracks when there is no non-exclusive set of achievers to select. On relaxed tasks, search never has to backtrack.

Proposition 3.3.2. *Let (A^+, I, G) be a relaxed STRIPS task. Started on (A^+, I, G), Graphplan will never backtrack.*

Proof. Backtracking only occurs if all achievers for a proposition p are exclusive of some already selected action. With Proposition 3.3.1, no exclusions exist so this does not happen. Also, if p is in graph layer i, then there is at least one achiever in layer $i - 1$ supporting it.

With the above argumentation, Graphplan's search in a relaxed task performs only a single sweep over the graph, starting from the top layer going down to the initial layer, and collects a relaxed plan on its way. In particular, the procedure takes only polynomial time in the size of the task.

Theorem 3.3.1. *Let (A^+, I, G) be a relaxed STRIPS task where the length of the longest add list of any action is l. Then Graphplan will, in time polynomial in l, $|A^+|$ and $|I|$, either find a solution to (A^+, I, G) or report that (A^+, I, G) is unsolvable.*

Proof. Building the planning graph is polynomial in l, $|A^+|$, $|I|$ and t, where t is the number of time steps built [8]. Now, in our case the total number $|A^+|$ of actions is an upper bound to the number of time steps. This is just because after this number of time steps has been built, all actions appear at some layer in the graph. Otherwise, there is a layer i where no new action appears, i.e., action layer $i - 1$ is identical to action layer i. If the task is unsolvable this implies that the process stops and reports unsolvability. If the task is solvable then this implies that all goals are contained in proposition layer i, causing the process to stop and start extracting a plan. Similarly, action layer $|A^+|$ would be identical to action layer $|A^+| - 1$, implying termination. The graph building phase is thus polynomial in l, $|A^+|$ and $|I|$.

Concerning the plan extraction phase: with Proposition 3.3.2, search traverses the graph from top to bottom, collecting a set of achieving actions at each layer. Selecting achievers for a set of propositions is $O(l*|A^+|+|I|)$: A set of propositions has at most size $l*|A^+|+|I|$, the maximal number of distinct propositions in the graph. An achieving action can be found for each proposition in constant time using the planning graph. As the number of layers to be looked at is $O(|A^+|)$, search is polynomial in the desired parameters.

Starting Graphplan on a task (A^+, s, G) yields — in polynomial time, with Theorem 3.3.1 — either the answer that (A^+, s, G) is unsolvable, or a relaxed solution $\langle A_0, \ldots, A_{m-1} \rangle$ where each A_i is the set of actions selected in parallel at time step i and m is the number of the first proposition layer containing all goals. We define our heuristic as follows.

Definition 3.3.1. *Given a STRIPS task (A, I, G), a reachable state s, and the answer that Graphplan returns when started on (A^+, s, G). The FF heuristic value to s is*

$$h^{FF}(s) := \begin{cases} \sum_{i=0,\ldots,m-1} |A_i| & \text{answer is solution } \langle A_0, \ldots, A_{m-1} \rangle \\ \infty & \text{answer is unsolvability of } (A^+, s, G) \end{cases}$$

In the second case, (A^+, s, G) is proved to be a dead end (which will be discussed in Chapter 4). We remark that one could in principle also, in the above setting, use m as the heuristic value. It is easy to see that this is an admissible heuristic. However m is usually *a lot* lower than the true goal distance so it is not an informative heuristic. Using it on the benchmarks in a few experiments did not produce much better results than searching the state space without any heuristic at all.

Extracting a plan can take account of positive interactions between propositions. Consider again the example from Section 3.2.1, empty initial state $I = \emptyset$, two goals $\{g_1, g_2\}$, and three actions:

name		(pre,	add,	del)
$actg_1$	$=$	$(\{p\},$	$\{g_1\},$	$\emptyset)$
$actg_2$	$=$	$(\{p\},$	$\{g_2\},$	$\emptyset)$
$actp$	$=$	$(\emptyset,$	$\{p\},$	$\emptyset)$

Starting Graphplan on the initial state, the goals are contained in proposition layer two, causing selection of $actg_1$ and $actg_2$ in action layer one. This yields the new goal p at proposition layer one, which is achieved with $actp$. The resulting plan is $\langle \{actp\}, \{actg_1, actg_2\} \rangle$, giving us the correct goal distance estimate $h^{FF}(I) = 3$, as distinct from HSP's estimate $h^{HSP}(I) = 4$.

Positive interactions can be a structural property important to take account of. The way in which HSP's heuristic ignores them sometimes results in considerable overestimation of the goal distance. Using Graphplan to explicitly extract relaxed plans successfully overcomes this weakness, at least in the cases we considered. Extreme examples are the *Assembly* and *Tireworld* domains. Let us consider two example state evaluations. For the largest *Assembly* task in the AIPS-1998 competition collection, the goal distance of the initial state is $gd(I) \leq 112$ (FF's solution plan length); HSP's heuristic function dramatically overestimates this to $h^{HSP}(I) = 472$, while FF's heuristic function estimates $h^{FF}(I) = 89$. For the *Tireworld* task with three tires to be replaced, the goal distance of the initial state is $gd(I) \leq 41$; the HSP estimate is $h^{HSP}(I) = 138$ while the h^{FF} estimate is $h^{FF} = 28$. Other domains where we observed overestimation are *Freecell*, and to some extent *Miconic-STRIPS*. We will show in Section 3.8 that in all these domains using h^{FF} significantly improves runtime behavior compared to using h^{HSP}.

3.3.2 Solution Length Optimization

While the heuristic function h^{FF} is in terms of possible overestimation more cautious than HSP's heuristic, h^{FF} is still not underestimating in general and can not be made so at polynomial costs. One can however apply techniques to make Graphplan return as short relaxed solutions as easily possible. This section describes some such techniques. The first technique is a built-in feature of Graphplan and ensures a minimality criterion for the relaxed plan. The two other techniques are heuristic optimizations.

NOOPs-First. As described in Section 2.4.2, the original Graphplan algorithm makes use of so-called NOOPs, which propagate propositions from one proposition layer to the next. When performing backward search, the NOOPs are considered just like any other achieving action, i.e., one way of making a proposition true at time $i > 0$ is to simply keep it true from time $i - 1$. As a NOOP is merely a way of saying "do nothing at this point" the NOOPs are not included into the final plan.

In Graphplan, the implementation uses as a default the *NOOPs-first* heuristic, i.e., if there is a NOOP present for achieving a proposition p, then this NOOP is considered first, before the planner tries selecting other "real" actions that achieve p. On relaxed tasks, the NOOPs-first heuristic results in a plan that is minimal in the following sense.

Proposition 3.3.3. *Let (A^+, I, G) be a relaxed STRIPS task, which is solvable. Using the NOOPs first strategy, the plan that Graphplan returns will contain each action at most once.*

Proof. Let us assume the opposite, i.e., one action a occurs twice in the plan $\langle A_0, \ldots, A_{m-1} \rangle$ that Graphplan finds. We have $a \in A_i$ and $a \in A_j$ for some layers i, j with $i < j$.

Now, the action a has been selected at layer j to achieve some proposition p at layer $j + 1$. As the algorithm is using the NOOPs-first strategy, this implies that there is no NOOP for proposition p contained in action layer j: otherwise, the NOOP—not action a—would have been selected for achieving p.

In contradiction to this, action layer j does indeed contain a NOOP for proposition p. This is because action a already appears in action layer $i < j$. As p gets added by a, it appears in proposition layer $i + 1 \leq j$. Therefore, a NOOP for p is inserted in action layer $i + 1 \leq j$, and, in turn, will be inserted into each action layer $i' \geq i + 1$.

Difficulty Heuristic. With the above argumentation, if we can achieve a proposition by using a NOOP, we should do that. The question is, which action should we choose when no NOOP is available? It is certainly a good idea to select an action whose preconditions seem to be "easy". From the graph building phase, we can obtain a simple measure for the difficulty of an action's preconditions as follows.

$$\text{difficulty}(a) := \sum_{p \in pre(a)} min\{i \mid p \text{ is in proposition layer } i\} \qquad (3.3)$$

The difficulty of each action can be set when it is first inserted into the graph. During plan extraction, facing a proposition for which no NOOP is available, we then simply select an achieving action with minimal difficulty. This heuristic works well in situations where there are several ways to achieve one proposition, but some ways need less effort than others. An example is the *Grid* domain, where one can either pick up a key k if the hand is free, or — simultaneously with picking up the new key — drop the key k' one is currently holding. We observed that Graphplan, when extracting the relaxed plans, often chose the latter option yielding as a sub-goal to get hold of k' — such that k' often was picked up for no reason other than to drop it again when picking up k. This phenomenon is overcome by the difficulty heuristic, improving the behavior of FF in *Grid* considerably.

Action Set Linearization. Assume Graphplan has selected a parallel set A_i of actions at a time step i, i.e., achieving actions have been selected for all goals at time step $i+1$. As we are only interested in sequential solution length, we still have a choice on how to linearize the actions. Some linearizations can lead to shorter plans than others. If an action $a \in A_i$ adds a precondition p of another action $a' \in A_i$, then we do not need to include p in the new set of propositions to be achieved one time step earlier, given that we restrict ourselves to execute a before a'. The question now is, how do we find a linearization of the actions that minimizes our new proposition set? The corresponding decision problem is NP-complete.

Definition 3.3.2. *Let* OPTIMAL ACTION LINEARIZATION *denote the following problem.*

Given a set A of relaxed STRIPS actions and a positive integer K. Is there a one-to-one function $f : A \mapsto \{1, 2, \ldots, |A|\}$ such that the number of unsatisfied preconditions when executing the sequence $\langle f^{-1}(1), \ldots, f^{-1}(|A|) \rangle$ is at most K?

Theorem 3.3.2. *Deciding* OPTIMAL ACTION LINEARIZATION *is NP-complete.*

Proof. Membership is obvious: guess the one-to-one function and count the number of unsatisfied preconditions. Hardness is proved by transformation from DIRECTED OPTIMAL LINEAR ARRANGEMENT [30]. Given a directed graph $G = (V, E)$ and a positive integer K, the question is, is there a one-to-one function $f : V \mapsto \{1, 2, \ldots, |V|\}$ such that $f(u) < f(v)$ whenever $(u, v) \in E$ and such that $\sum_{(u,v) \in E} (f(v) - f(u)) \leq K$?

Given a directed graph, we define a set of actions as follows. For each node w in the graph, we define an action in our set A. For simplicity of notation, we identify the actions with their corresponding nodes. To begin with, we set $pre(w) = add(w) = \emptyset$ for all $w \in V$. Then, for each edge $(u, v) \in E$, we create new propositions $p_w^{(u,v)}$ and $r_w^{(u,v)}$ for each $w \in V$.

Using these new propositions, we now adjust all precondition and add lists to express the constraint that is given by the edge (u, v). Say action u is ordered before action v in a linearization. We need to simulate the difference between the positions of u and v. To do this, we define our actions so that the bigger this difference is, the more unsatisfied preconditions there are when executing the linearization. First, we punish all actions that are ordered before v, by giving them an unsatisfied precondition.

$$pre(w) := pre(w) \cup \{p_w^{(u,v)}\} \text{ for } w \in V, \ add(v) := add(v) \cup \{p_w^{(u,v)} \mid w \in V\}$$

With this definition, the actions w ordered before v—and v itself—will have the unsatisfied precondition $p_w^{(u,v)}$, while those ordered after will get this precondition added by v. Thus, the number of unsatisfied preconditions we get here is exactly $f(v)$.

Secondly, we give a reward to each action that is ordered *before* u. We simply do this by letting those actions add a precondition of u, which would otherwise go unsatisfied.

$$add(w) := add(w) \cup \{r_w^{(u,v)}\} \text{ for } w \in V, \ pre(u) := pre(u) \cup \{r_w^{(u,v)} \mid w \in V\}$$

That way, we will have exactly $|V| - (f(u) - 1)$ unsatisfied preconditions, namely the $r_w^{(u,v)}$ propositions for all actions except those that are ordered before u.

The number of unsatisfied preconditions we get for a linearization f is

$$\sum_{(u,v)\in E} (f(v) + |V| - (f(u) - 1)) = \sum_{(u,v)\in E} (f(v) - f(u)) + |E| * (|V| + 1)$$

We thus define our new positive integer $K' := K + |E| * (|V| + 1)$.

Finally, we make sure that actions u get ordered before actions v for $(u, v) \in A$. We do this by inserting new logical "safety" propositions $s_1^{(u,v)}, \ldots, s_{K'+1}^{(u,v)}$ into v's precondition and u's add list.

$$pre(v) := pre(v) \cup \{s_1^{(u,v)}, \ldots, s_{K'+1}^{(u,v)}\}, \ add(u) := add(u) \cup \{s_1^{(u,v)}, \ldots, s_{K'+1}^{(u,v)}\}$$

Altogether, a linearization f of our actions leads to at most K' unsatisfied preconditions if and only if f satisfies the requirements for a directed optimal linear arrangement. Obviously, the action set and K' can be computed in polynomial time.

Our purpose with linearizing an action set in a certain order is to achieve a smaller number of unsatisfied preconditions, which in turn might lead to a shorter relaxed solution. Thus we are not willing to pay the price that finding an optimal linearization of the actions is likely to cost. There are a few methods how one can approximate such a linearization, like introducing an ordering constraint $a < a'$ for each action a that adds a precondition of another action a', and trying to linearize the actions such that many of these constraints are met. During experimentation in the benchmark domains, parallel actions adding each other's preconditions occured so rarely that even approximating seemed not worth the effort. We thus simply linearize all actions in the order they get selected, causing almost no computational overhead.

3.3.3 Efficient Implementation

There is of course no point in running the original Graphplan implementation on each search state in a forward search. For a specialized implementation within our context, one can exploit the fact that there are no exclusion relations at all, and that the implementation is repeatedly called on planning tasks that all share the same set of actions — the tasks (A^+, s, G) for reachable states s.

After grounding, we build what we call the *connectivity graph*. This graph consists of two layers, one containing all actions, and the other all propositions. From each action, there are edges to all preconditions, add effects and delete effects. Other way round, from each proposition there are pointers to all actions that add it, that delete it, or that it is precondition of. All of FF's computations are efficiently implemented using this graph structure (for ADL, there is an additional layer representing, in a similar fashion, the effects).

As a relaxed planning graph contains no exclusion relations, the only information one needs to represent the graph is what we call the *level* of the propositions and actions, i.e., for each proposition or action the number of the first layer at which it appears in the graph. Called on a task (A^+, s, G), our version of Graphplan computes these levels by using the following fix point computation. The levels of all propositions and actions are initialized to ∞. For each action there is also a counter, which is initialized to 0. Then, proposition layer 0 is built implicitly by setting the level of all propositions $p \in s$ to 0. Each time when a proposition p gets its level set, all actions of which p is a precondition get their counter incremented. As soon as the counter for an action a reaches the total number of a's preconditions, a is put to a list of scheduled actions for the current layer. After a proposition layer i is finished, all actions scheduled for step i have their level set to i, and their adds, if not already present, are put to the list of scheduled propositions for the next proposition layer at time step $i + 1$. Having finished with action layer i, all scheduled propositions at step $i + 1$ have their level set, and so on. The process continues until all goals have a level lower than ∞, or until no more changes occur. We remark that this view of planning graph building corresponds closely to the computation of the cost values in HSP, where actions are iteratively applied yielding updates of proposition costs.

When the graph building phase stops without reaching the goals, the heuristic value of s is set to $h^{FF}(s) := \infty$, cf. Definition 3.3.1. In the other case, all goals having a level lower than ∞, the relaxed version of Graphplan's solution extraction mechanism is invoked. See Figure 3.2.

Instead of putting all goals into the top layer and then propagating them down by using NOOPs-first, each goal g is simply put into a goal set G_i located at g's first layer i. Then, there is a for-next loop down from the top to the initial layer. At each layer i, an achieving action with level $i - 1$ gets selected for each proposition in the corresponding goal set. If there is more than one such achiever, a best one is picked according to the difficulty heuristic. The preconditions are put into their corresponding goal sets. Each time an action is selected, all of its adds are marked true at times i and $i - 1$. The marker at time i prevents achievers to be selected for propositions that are already true anyway. Marking

for $i := 1, \ldots, m$ **do**
    $G_i := \{g \in G \mid \text{level}(g) = i\}$
endfor
for $i := m, \ldots, 1$ **do**
    for all $g \in G_i$, g not marked true at time i **do**
        select an action a with $g \in add(a)$, level$(a) = i - 1$,
                        and minimal difficulty
        for all $p \in pre(a)$, level$(p) \neq 0$, p not marked true at time $i - 1$ **do**
            $G_{\text{level}(p)} := G_{\text{level}(p)} \cup \{p\}$
        endfor
        for all $p \in add(a)$ **do**
            mark p as true at times $i - 1$ and i
        endfor
    endfor
endfor

Fig. 3.2. Relaxed plan extraction for a task (A^+, s, G)

at time $i - 1$ assumes that actions are linearized in the order they get selected: a precondition that was achieved by an action ahead is not considered as a new goal.

3.4 Search

In this section we briefly introduce the search mechanism that is used in FF. The mechanism is somewhat unusual — not to be found in previous literature to the best of the author's knowledge — in that it combines hill-climbing with systematic search. It is still a local search mechanism in the sense that there is no backtracking: once a decision has been made, that decision is never taken back; the search scheme thus explores only a part of the search space in general, and is not complete.

3.4.1 Enforced Hill-Climbing

Like it is the case for h^{HSP}, computing h^{FF} involves application of all actions. This is costly because action sets are usually large. So with the same motivation as Bonet and Geffner [9] had for HSP1, the first search mechanism we experimented with was hill-climbing. Running the resulting planner on example benchmarks, we made an interesting observation. The reader was given a glimpse of the same observation already during the discussion of the introductory example in Section 1.2, where at one point on the hill-climbing path there is no *immediate* successor with better evaluation, but there *is* such a successor only one more step ahead. This is exactly the phenomenon we observed in instances from, e.g., the *Gripper* and *Logistics* domains. Not looking further than a single step ahead, hill-climbing often wasted a lot of time until its random walk happened to find the correct states which were just beyond its horizon. Similarly, in other domains, like *Tireworld*, we observed that the better states — while not necessarily being merely a single more step ahead — were close by but not being found by random walk until after a rather long time. In Part III, we will make these observations precise in terms of the local search topology of the benchmarks, and explicitly identify the patterns of structure that cause these phenomena. This will explain the superb runtime performance of our search algorithm. Observing that the better states were usually close by, our idea was to perform a complete lookahead for them. See the algorithm in Figure 3.3.

initialize the current plan to the empty plan $<>$
$s := I$
while $h(s) \neq 0$ **do**
        perform breadth first search for a state s' with $h(s') < h(s)$,
                not expanding states s'' where $h(s'') = \infty$
        if no such state can be found **then**
            output "Fail", stop
        endif
        add the actions on the path to s' at the end of the current plan
        $s := s'$
endwhile

Fig. 3.3. The enforced hill-climbing algorithm, for a task with heuristic h

Like hill-climbing, the algorithm starts out in the initial state. Then, facing an intermediate search state s, a complete breadth first search starting out from s is invoked. This finds the closest better successor, i.e., the nearest state s' with strictly better evaluation, or fails. In the latter case, the whole algorithm fails, in the former case, the path from s to s' is added to the current plan, and search is iterated. When a goal state — a state with evaluation 0 — is reached, search stops. States with infinite heuristic value are not expanded, i.e., removed from the search space. These states are interpreted as dead ends. Removing them is justified if the heuristic value is ∞ only in dead ends. We will discuss this in detail in Chapter 4.

Our implementation of breadth first search starting from s is standard, where states are kept in a queue. One search iteration removes the first state s' from the queue, and evaluates it by running relaxed Graphplan. If the evaluation is better than that of s, search succeeds; if the evaluation is ∞ then s' gets removed from the queue. Otherwise, the successors of s' are put to the end of the queue. Repeated states are avoided by keeping a hash table of visited states in memory. If no new states can be reached anymore, breadth first search fails.

3.4.2 Completeness

We postpone the theoretical discussion concerning the completeness of enforced hill-climbing to the chapter about dead ends, i.e., to Chapter 4. Here we give an example of a task where enforced hill-climbing, using the h^{FF} heuristic, stops without finding a solution. Consider the following task, where the initial state is $I = \{g_1, p_1\}$, the goals are $\{g_1, g_2\}$, and there are the following five actions:

name		(*pre*,	*add*,	*del*)
actp_2	=	$(\{p_1\},$	$\{p_2\},$	$\emptyset)$
actp_3	=	$(\{p_2\},$	$\{p_3\},$	$\emptyset)$
actg_2	=	$(\{p_3\},$	$\{g_2\},$	$\emptyset)$
act$p$	=	$(\emptyset,$	$\{p\},$	$\{p_1\})$
actg_2'	=	$(\{p\},$	$\{g_2\},$	$\{g_1\})$

Starting from the initial state there are two ways of achieving the missing goal g_2: one via actp_2, actp_3, and actg_2, the other via act$p$ and actg_2'. The latter way is shorter, but deletes the goal g_1 which can not be re-achieved. Also, act$p$ deletes p_1, which can not be re-achieved and is needed for the first action sequence; so applying act$p$ in the initial state leads into a dead end. From the point of view of h^{FF}, however, applying act$p$ in the initial state is a good choice, and thus enforced hill-climbing gets trapped in that dead end. In more detail: relaxed Graphplan returns the first relaxed plan it finds, so $h^{FF}(I) = 2$ by the plan $\langle\{\text{act}p\}, \{\text{act}g_2'\}\rangle$ (note that this is, in fact, a relaxed plan for the task). Similarly we obtain $h^{FF}(Result(I, \langle\text{act}p_2\rangle)) = 2$ (by the same plan or the plan consisting of actp_3 and actg_2) and $h^{FF}(Result(I, \langle\text{act}p\rangle)) = 1$ (by the single action actg_2'). The algorithm chooses to apply act$p$, and terminates unsuccessfully.

3.5 Pruning

In this section, we present a heuristic technique that identifies a set of promising successors to a state. The idea is to restrict search to this set of successors, i.e., prune the other successors from the search space. The technique can, in principle, be used to prune the search space in any forward state space search planning algorithm. It is obtained as a side effect of using relaxed Graphplan as a heuristic estimator. We motivate and introduce the technique with two examples, then briefly discuss the effect that it has on completeness.

3.5.1 Helpful Actions

Consider the *Gripper* domain. There are two rooms, A and B, and a certain number of balls, which are all in room A initially and shall be moved into room B. The planner controls a robot, which changes rooms via the *move* operator, and which has two grippers to *pick* or *drop* balls. Each gripper can hold only one ball at a time. We look at a small task where 2 balls must be moved into room B. Say the robot has already picked up both balls, i.e., in the current search state the robot is in room A and each gripper holds one ball. There are three applicable actions in this state: move to room B, or drop one of the balls back into room A. The relaxed solution that our heuristic extracts is the following.

$$\langle\{\mathrm{move}(A, B)\}, \{\mathrm{drop}(\mathrm{ball1}, B, \mathrm{left}), \mathrm{drop}(\mathrm{ball2}, B, \mathrm{right})\}\rangle$$

This is a parallel relaxed plan consisting of two time steps. The action set selected at the first time step contains the only action that makes sense in the state at hand, move to room B. We therefore pursue the idea of restricting the action choice in any state to only those actions that are selected in the first time step of the relaxed plan. We call these the *helpful* actions. In the above example state, this strategy cuts down the branching factor from three to one.

Sometimes, considering only the actions that are selected by the relaxed planner is too restrictive. Consider the following *Blocksworld-arm* example, where we got four operators to *stack*, *unstack*, *pickup*, or *putdown* blocks. In our task the arm is initially holding block C, and blocks A and B are on the table. The goal is to stack A onto B. Started on this state, relaxed Graphplan will return one of the following three time step optimal solutions.

$\langle \{\mathrm{putdown}(C)\},$ $\langle \{\mathrm{stack}(C, A)\},$ $\langle \{\mathrm{stack}(C, B)\},$
    $\{\mathrm{pickup}(A)\},$ or $\{\mathrm{pickup}(A)\},$ or $\{\mathrm{pickup}(A)\},$
    $\{\mathrm{stack}(A, B)\}\rangle$ $\{\mathrm{stack}(A, B)\}\rangle$ $\{\mathrm{stack}(A, B)\}\rangle$

All of these are valid relaxed solutions, as in the relaxation it does not matter that stacking C onto A or B deletes facts that we still need. If C is on A, we can not pickup A anymore, and if C is on B, we can not stack A onto B anymore.

The first action in each relaxed plan is only inserted to get rid of C, i.e., free the robot arm, and from the point of view of the relaxed planner, all of the three starting actions do the job. Thus the relaxed solution extracted might be any of the three above. If it happens to be the second or third one, then we lose the path to an optimal solution by restricting ourselves to the corresponding actions, $\mathrm{stack}(C, A)$ or $\mathrm{stack}(C, B)$. Therefore, we define the set $H(s)$ of helpful actions to a state s as follows.

Definition 3.5.1. *Given a STRIPS task* (A, I, G), *a reachable state* s, *and the goal set* $G_1(s)$ *that Graphplan constructs at time step 1 when extracting a plan for* (A^+, s, G). *The set of* helpful actions *to* s *is defined as*

$$H(s) := \{a \in A \mid pre(a) \subseteq s, add(a) \cap G_1(s) \neq \emptyset\}$$

In words, we consider as helpful actions all those applicable ones that add at least one goal at the first time step. In the above *Blocksworld-arm* example, freeing the robot arm is among the goals at step 1. All the three possible starting actions achieve that proposition, so all these actions are helpful. In the above *Gripper* example, the modification does not change anything.

The notion of helpful actions shares some similarities with what Drew McDermott calls the *favored actions* [72, 74], in the context of computing *greedy regression graphs* for heuristic estimation. In a nutshell, greedy regression graphs back chain from the goals until facts are reached that are contained in the current state. Among other things, the graphs provide an estimate of which actions might be useful in getting closer to the goal: those applicable ones which are members of the *effective subgraph*, which is the minimal cost subgraph achieving the goals.

There is also a similarity between the helpful actions heuristic and what is known as *relevance* from the literature [77, 49]. Consider a *Blocksworld-arm* task where hundreds of blocks are on the table initially, but the goal is only to stack one block A on top of another block B. The set $H(I)$ will in this case contain only the single action pickup(A), throwing away all those applicable actions moving around blocks that are not mentioned in the goal. These actions are irrelevant. The main difference between the helpful actions heuristic and the concept of relevance is that relevance in the usual sense refers to what is useful for solving the whole task. Being helpful, on the other hand, refers to something that is useful *in the next step*.

3.5.2 Completeness

The helpful actions heuristic does not preserve completeness. In the following short example, the heuristic prunes all solutions from the state space. Say the initial state is $\{g_1\}$, the goals are $\{g_1, g_2\}$, and there are the following actions:

name		(pre,	add,	del)
$actp_{g_2}$	$=$	$(\emptyset,$	$\{p_{g_2}\},$	$\emptyset)$
$actg_2$	$=$	$(\{p_{g_2}\},$	$\{g_2\},$	$\emptyset)$
$actg_2'$	$=$	$(\emptyset,$	$\{g_2\},$	$\{g_1\})$
$actp_{g_1}$	$=$	$(\emptyset,$	$\{p_{g_1}\},$	$\emptyset)$
$actg_1$	$=$	$(\{p_{g_1}\},$	$\{g_1\},$	$\emptyset)$
$actg_1'$	$=$	$(\emptyset,$	$\{g_1\},$	$\{g_2\})$

In this planning task, there are two possibilities to achieve the missing goal g_2. One of these, $actg_2$, needs the precondition p_{g_2} to be achieved first by $actp_{g_2}$; the other option, $actg_2'$, deletes the goal g_1. The latter option requires one step less than the former option, so relaxed Graphplan chooses the second alternative. The set of goals at the single layer created by graph construction is $G_1(I) = \{g_2\}$ (g_1 is contained in the current state so it is not a goal at layer 1). This gives us one helpful action, $H(I) = \{actg_2'\}$. This action leads to the state where only g_2 is true. To this state, we obtain the set of helpful actions containing only $actg_1'$. That action leads us back to the initial state. Helpful actions thus cuts out the solutions from the state space of this example task. We remark that the task does not contain dead ends: one can always reach g_1 and g_2 by applying $actp_{g_1}$, $actg_1$, $actp_{g_2}$, and $actg_2$.

In STRIPS domains, one could theoretically overcome the incompleteness of helpful actions pruning by considering not only the first relaxed plan that Graphplan finds, but computing a kind of union over all relaxed plans that Graphplan could possibly find. More precisely, in a search state s, consider the relaxed task (A^+, s, G). Extend the relaxed planning graph until fact level $|A^+|$ is reached. Set a goal set $G_{|A^+|}$ at the top fact level to $G_{|A^+|} := G$. Then proceed from fact level $|A^+| - 1$ down to fact level 1, where at each level i a set G_i of goals is generated as the union of G_{i+1} with the preconditions of all actions in level i that add at least one fact in G_{i+1}. Upon termination define as helpful all actions that add at least one fact in G_1. It can be proved that this way the starting actions of all optimal solutions from s are considered helpful. However, in all examples the technique was tried on it always selected all applicable actions as helpful.

3.6 Extension to ADL

Let us briefly explain how FF's algorithms can be extended to ADL. Computing the heuristic value of a state involves, like in the STRIPS case, application of all actions. As said before, we therefore compute the propositional compilation of a given ADL task (c.f. Section 3.1.2) before starting the algorithms. So extension to propositional ADL suffices here.

3.6.1 Heuristic Function

For STRIPS tasks, we have seen that one can run (an efficient implementation of) Graphplan in order to obtain, in polynomial time, a relaxed plan for a given search state. ADL, even propositional ADL, is beyond the expressivity of original Graphplan. We can however use the more expressive IPP system, c.f. Section 2.4.2, which integrates propositional conditional effects directly into its graph construction and search algorithms. Analogous to Graphplan, it is easy to see that IPP's planning graph for a propositional ADL task with empty delete lists does not contain any exclusion relations, and that therefore search never backtracks. So in a propositional ADL task one can obtain a relaxed plan in polynomial time by running IPP.

Definition 3.6.1. *Given a propositional ADL task* (A, I, G), *a reachable state* s, *and the answer that IPP returns when started on* (A^+, s, G). *The FF heuristic value to* s *is*

$$h^{FF}(s) := \begin{cases} \sum_{i=0,\ldots,m-1} |A_i| & \text{answer is solution } \langle A_0, \ldots, A_{m-1} \rangle \\ \infty & \text{answer is unsolvability of } (A^+, s, G) \end{cases}$$

We do not run IPP on all search states during a forward search. Instead, we extend our specialized Graphplan implementation for relaxed STRIPS, c.f. Section 3.3.3, to actions with (propositional) conditional effects. Small changes suffice.

Relaxed Planning Graphs with Conditional Effects. For extending the graph building phase to actions with conditional effects, one simply needs to keep an additional level value for all *effects* of an action. The level of an effect indicates the first layer where all its effect conditions plus the corresponding action's preconditions are present. To compute these integers in an efficient manner we keep a counter for each effect $e \in E(a)$ which gets incremented each time a condition $c \in con(e)$ becomes present and each time a precondition $p \in pre(a)$ of the respective action becomes present. The effect gets its level set as soon as its counter reaches $|con(e)| + |pre(a)|$. The effect's add effects $add(e)$ are then scheduled for the next layer. The process is iterated until all goals are reached the first time, or until a fix point occurs. In the latter case the heuristic value is set to ∞, in the former case relaxed plan extraction is invoked.

Relaxed Plan Extraction with Conditional Effects. The relaxed plan extraction mechanism for propositional ADL differs from its STRIPS counterpart in merely two small details. Instead of selecting achieving actions, the extraction mechanism selects achieving effects. Once an effect $e \in E(a)$ of action a is selected, all of its effect conditions plus a's preconditions need to be put into their corresponding goal sets. Afterwards, not only the effect's own add effects $add(e)$ are marked true at the time being, but also the added facts of all effects $e' \in E(a)$ that are *implied*, i.e., those effects of a with $con(e') \subseteq con(e)$. In particular, this will include the unconditional effects of a, which have an empty effect condition.

3.6.2 Pruning

For STRIPS, we defined as helpful all applicable actions achieving at least one goal at time step 1, c.f. Section 3.5.1. For ADL, we simply change this to *all applicable actions having an appearing effect that achieves a goal at time step* 1, where an appearing effect is an effect whose condition is satisfied in the current state.

Definition 3.6.2. *Given a propositional ADL task* (A, I, G), *a reachable state* s, *and a goal set* $G_1(s)$ *that IPP constructs at time step* 1 *when extracting a plan for* (A^+, s, G). *The set of* helpful *actions to* s *is defined as*

$$H(s) := \{a \in A \mid pre(a) \subseteq s, \exists e \in E(a) : con(e) \subseteq s \wedge add(e) \cap G_1(s) \neq \emptyset\} \ .$$

3.7 Evaluation

We have now finished introducing the algorithms that make up the FF base architecture. Let us see how it behaves. Runtime and solution length results on our benchmark example collection are shown in Figure 3.4.

The runtime performance is way beyond what we have seen so far. The reader can probably best convince herself by making a few quick comparisons with Figures 2.1, 2.2, 2.3, and 3.1, even if that involves some turning of pages. The only planner that is not utterly outpaced by FF is our HSP1 implementation. To name a few facts, the FF base architecture solves 91 out of the 100 benchmark examples in our collection; for HSP1 this number is 78, for Blackbox it is 28, for IPP it is 48, and for UCPOP it is 28. In 73 of the example tasks, the FF base architecture finds a plan faster than any of the other planners, in 9 more tasks

domain	task1 t	task1 s	task2 t	task2 s	task3 t	task3 s	task4 t	task4 s	task5 t	task5 s
Assembly	0.13	28	0.41	51	1.37	68	3.50	99	5.93	112
Bw-arm	0.01	8	0.04	14	0.73	40	9.89	66	-	-
Bw-no-arm	0.01	4	0.04	10	0.28	16	0.72	20	2.46	28
Briefcase	-	-	-	-	-	-	-	-	-	-
Ferry	0.02	6	0.02	10	0.07	23	0.04	30	0.07	33
Freecell	0.48	21	1.95	37	3.65	48	7.49	73	-	-
Fridge	0.01	12	0.08	24	0.27	36	1.29	48	4.61	60
Grid	0.13	14	0.46	39	2.09	58	1.97	49	18.99	149
Gripper	0.01	15	0.04	29	0.03	45	0.05	59	0.09	75
Hanoi	0.01	7	0.01	15	0.03	31	0.08	63	0.31	127
Logistics	0.01	20	0.31	75	1.27	115	5.11	191	17.43	251
Mic-ADL	0.04	4	0.08	21	2.12	52	-	-	36.38	96
Mic-SIM	0.00	4	0.05	24	0.18	34	0.88	65	1.58	73
Mic-STR	0.00	4	0.03	27	0.14	46	0.64	76	1.29	95
Movie	0.01	8	0.02	8	0.02	8	0.03	8	0.04	8
Mprime	0.05	5	0.41	10	3.20	8	3.14	14	1.91	11
Mystery	0.02	4	0.02	5	0.23	11	-	-	0.94	8
Schedule	0.05	2	0.38	21	1.97	36	10.18	66	20.08	79
Simple-Tsp	0.00	5	0.01	10	0.02	15	0.03	20	0.03	25
Tireworld	0.04	19	0.06	30	0.13	41	0.23	52	0.57	63

Fig. 3.4. Runtime (t) and solution length (s) results of the FF base architecture. A dash means that no plan was found after 5 minutes

it is equally fast. Let us concentrate on the scaling behavior of the planners, i.e., their asymptotic runtime performance. This is indicated by the development that the respective results undergo with growing example size. In the following, if we say that planner A *scales better* than planner B in a domain, then we mean that, in the data at hand, the ratio between B's runtime and A's runtime in the domain grows with example size. Planner A scales *drastically* better than B if B cannot solve the largest example task(s) but A can. Let us compare the scaling behavior of FF to that of the other planners. UCPOP, c.f. Figure 2.1, could be run in 17 domains. FF scales better in all of these except *Briefcaseworld* (where helpful actions pruning cuts out the solutions, more on this below), drastically better in 13 of them. Blackbox, c.f. Figure 2.3, could be run in 14 domains. In *Movie* and *Mystery*, neither planner scales better, in the other 12 domains FF scales drastically better. IPP, c.f. Figure 2.2, could be run in all 20 domains. FF scales better in 16 domains, drastically better in 14 of these. The only cases where either UCPOP, Blackbox, or IPP scale better than FF are in the aforementioned *Briefcaseworld* domain, and in *Fridge* (where IPP is more effective). Let us focus on HSP1, c.f. Figure 3.1. There are five domains where FF does *not* scale better than HSP1: in *Briefcaseworld*, where HSP1 finds the plans thanks to not using helpful actions pruning; in *Movie*, where none of the planners has any difficulty; in *Mystery*, where HSP1 solves one more task though FF is faster in the other cases; in *Fridge* and *Blocksworld-arm*, finally, where HSP1 scales better. In all the other 15 domains, FF scales better than our HSP1 implementation. FF scales drastically better in the 7 domains *Assembly*, *Ferry*, *Grid*, *Hanoi*, *Logistics*, *Schedule*, and *Tireworld*.

Focusing on solution quality, it is important to note that FF's performance does *not* suffer from over long plans, in contrast to our HSP1 implementation.

For the 71 tasks that both planners solve, FF's plan is shorter than that of HSP1 in 46 cases, equally long in 18 cases, and longer in only 7 cases. The latter 7 cases are the 5 *Movie* tasks where FF needs 8 instead of 7 actions (this will be explained in the next section), as well as one task each in *Mprime* and *Mystery* for both of which FF needs 8 instead of 6 actions. HSP1's plans, on the other hand, are regularly 1.5 times as long as FF's. Let us also make a quick comparison to the previous planners, of which IPP guarantees a minimal number of time steps. We consider the 44 tasks that are solved by FF and at least one of the previous planners, and compare FF's plan length to the minimum of the lengths found by the others. In 2 cases FF's plan is shorter, in 30 cases it is equally long, and in 12 cases it is longer. Of the 12 "bad" cases, 9 times FF's plan is only a single action longer than the best plan found by the others, 2 times it is 2 actions longer, and a single time (in *Mprime*) the difference amounts to 3 actions.

In summary, the FF base architecture convincingly outperforms the previous approaches in most of the domains. Part III will explain this by investigating the quality of h^{FF}, especially with respect to its use in enforced hill-climbing. The remainder of Part II optimizes the base architecture in cases where it yet has difficulties. These cases are indicated by the unsolved tasks in Figure 3.4: one in *Blocksworld-arm*; the whole *Briefcaseworld* collection; each one task in *Freecell*, *Miconic-ADL*, and *Mystery*. The latter three failures are caused by *dead ends* in the respective tasks. We will focus on dead ends in Chapter 4, and handle them by invoking a safety net algorithm in case FF fails. The failure in *Briefcaseworld* is due to helpful actions pruning. Remember that in this domain portables need to be moved using a briefcase; whenever the briefcase is moved, all portables inside it are moved along by a conditional effect. The delete effects of moving state that a portable is no longer at the start location. Ignoring this, keeping portables inside the briefcase does not hurt, and taking them out is never considered helpful. We will handle this phenomenon with the same safety net technique that handles dead ends, c.f. Chapter 4. The failure in the largest *Blocksworld-arm* example, finally, happens because the FF base architecture exhausts the available memory resources. In Chapter 5 we will see that there are *goal orderings* present in *Blocksworld-arm* (and some other domains); these orderings can cause trouble for a search algorithm that is not aware of them. We will discuss two techniques for informing search about goal orderings, and show that these techniques can be useful.

3.8 What Makes the Difference to HSP?

Considering the performance results we have just seen, one question that immediately springs to mind is this: if FF is so closely related to HSP, then why does it perform so much better? FF's base architecture uses the same basic ideas as HSP1, local search in the state space, and heuristic evaluation by approximating h^+. The differences lie in the way FF approximates h^+, the search strategy, and helpful actions pruning. To obtain a picture of which new technique yields which performance results, we conducted a number of experiments where those techniques could be turned on and off independently of each other. Using all combinations of techniques, we measured runtime and solution length performance on a large example collection.

3.8.1 Experimental Setup

As said, we use experimental code where each of FF's new algorithmic techniques is attached to a switch, turning the technique on or off. The eight different configurations of the switches yield eight different heuristic planners. When all switches are off, the resulting planner is our implementation of HSP1. When all switches are on, the resulting planner is the FF base architecture.

To obtain data, a large example collection was set up, containing a total of 939 planning tasks from our 20 domains. We used 30 to 69 instances per domain (except *Hanoi*, where there were eight). As very small instances are likely to produce noisy data, we tried to avoid those by rejecting tasks that were solved by FF in less than 0.2 seconds. This was possible in all domains but *Movie*, where all tasks in the AIPS-1998 collection get solved in at most 0.03 seconds. The collections were the following. In all the competition domains except *Blocksworld-arm*, *Gripper*, and *Grid*, we used (the larger instances of) the AIPS-1998 and AIPS-2000 competition collections. In all other domains we used the automated (randomized) instance generators described in Appendix B. In *Blocksworld-arm* and *Blocksworld-no-arm*, we generated tasks with 7 to 17 blocks, five per size. In *Gripper*, our tasks where those with 10 to 59 balls. In *Grid*, we used the five AIPS-1998 instances, plus 50 randomly generated ones similar in size to the largest example in the competition collection. In *Fridge*, there were 1 to 14 fridges with 1 to 12 screws each, omitting the over large cases where both values are high. In *Hanoi*, there were 3 to 10 discs, in *Tsp*, there were 10 to 59 locations, in *Tireworld*, there were 1 to 30 wheels. In *Briefcaseworld*, we generated 55 instances with 10 to 20 portables and locations, 5 of each size. In *Ferry*, we generated 50 instances with 5 to 50 (in steps of 5) cars and locations, 5 of each size.

For each of the eight configurations of switches, we ran the respective planner on each of the tasks in our example collection. Configurations using randomized hill-climbing were run five times on each task, and the results averaged (the variance between different trials was usually low, c.f. Section 3.2.3). To complete the experiments in a reasonable time, we restricted memory consumption to 128 MByte and time consumption to 150 seconds — usually, if FF needs more time or memory on a planning task of reasonable size then it doesn't manage to solve it at all.

3.8.2 Runtime

For our runtime investigation, if a configuration did not find a solution plan to a given task, we set the respective runtime value to the time limit of 150 seconds (sometimes a configuration can terminate faster without finding a plan, for example an enforced hill-climbing planner getting trapped in a dead end). In the following we designate each switch configuration by three letters: "H" stands for helpful actions on, "E" stands for enforced hill-climbing on, "F" stands for FF estimates on. If a switch is turned off the respective letter is replaced by a "−": FF is configuration "HEF", our HSP1 implementation is "− − −", and "H−−" for example is hill-climbing with HSP goal distances and helpful actions pruning. For a first impression of our runtime results, see the averaged values per domain in Figure 3.5.

domain	− − −	− −F	−E−	−EF	H−−	H−F	HE−	HEF
Assembly	117.39	31.75	92.95	61.10	47.81	20.25	20.34	16.94
Bw-arm	0.60	8.81	80.02	56.20	1.21	10.13	25.19	40.65
Bw-no-arm	4.06	2.53	8.37	30.11	1.41	0.83	0.27	6.11
Briefcase	16.35	5.84	66.51	116.24	150.00	150.00	150.00	150.00
Ferry	141.00	10.58	86.85	16.22	138.00	5.48	62.47	4.83
Freecell	65.73	46.05	54.15	51.27	57.35	42.68	43.99	41.44
Fridge	28.52	53.58	31.89	52.60	0.85	0.69	1.88	2.77
Grid	138.06	119.53	115.05	99.18	115.00	95.10	18.73	11.73
Gripper	2.75	1.21	15.16	1.00	1.17	0.48	0.17	0.11
Hanoi	93.76	75.05	6.29	3.91	150.00	78.82	4.47	2.70
Logistics	79.27	102.09	79.77	111.47	36.88	39.69	10.18	11.94
Mic-ADL	150.00	150.00	102.54	54.23	142.51	128.28	95.45	59.00
Mic-SIM	2.61	2.01	2.47	1.93	1.35	0.86	0.55	0.56
Mic-STR	2.71	2.32	4.84	1.53	1.44	1.01	0.64	0.36
Movie	0.02	0.02	0.02	0.02	0.02	0.02	0.02	0.02
Mprime	73.09	69.27	82.89	81.43	47.09	58.45	18.56	26.62
Mystery	78.54	90.55	71.60	86.01	75.73	95.24	85.13	86.21
Schedule	135.50	131.12	143.59	141.42	77.58	38.23	12.23	13.77
Simple-Tsp	4.11	0.82	2.45	0.75	2.48	0.57	0.15	0.07
Tireworld	135.30	110.38	119.22	121.34	121.13	105.67	97.41	85.64

Fig. 3.5. Averaged runtime per domain for all eight configurations of switches

Figure 3.5 shows, for each domain and each configuration, the averaged runtime over all instances in that domain. As the instances in each domain are not all of the same size but typically scale from smaller to very large tasks, averaging over all runtimes is a very crude approximation of runtime behavior. The data in Figure 3.5 provides a general impression of our runtime results per domain, and gives a few hints on the phenomena that might be present in the data. Compare, for example, the values on the right hand side — those planners using helpful actions — to those on the left hand side — those planners expanding all sons of search nodes. In *Briefcaseworld* the right hand side values are higher, but in almost all other domains they are considerably lower. This is especially true for the two rightmost columns, showing values for planners using helpful actions and enforced hill-climbing. This indicates that the main sources of performance lie in the pruning technique and the search strategy — looking at the rightmost "HE−" and "HEF" columns, which only differ in the goal distance estimate, those two configuration values are usually close to each other compared to the other configurations in the same domain.

To put our observations on a solid basis we looked, for each domain, at each pair of configurations in turn, amounting to $20 * \frac{8*7}{2} = 560$ pairs of planner performances. For each such pair we decided whether one configuration performed significantly better than the other one. To decide significance we counted the number of tasks that one configuration solved faster. We found this to be a more reliable criterion than things like the difference between runtimes for each task. As tasks grow in size, rather than being taken from a population with finite mean size, parametric statistical procedures like computing confidence intervals for runtime differences make questionable assumptions about the distribution of data. We thus used the following non-parametric statistical test, known as the two-tailed sign test [91]. Assume that both planners, A and B, perform equally on a given domain. Then, given a random instance from the domain, the probability that B is faster than A should be equal to the probability that A is faster than B. Take this as the null hypothesis. Under that hypothesis, if A and B behave differently on an instance, then B is faster than A with probability $\frac{1}{2}$. Thus, the tasks where B is faster are distributed over the tasks with different behavior according to a binomial distribution with $p = \frac{1}{2}$. Compute the probability of the observed outcome under the null hypothesis, i.e., if there are n tasks where A and B behave differently, and k tasks where B is faster, then compute the probability that according to a binomial distribution with $p = \frac{1}{2}$ at least k positive outcomes are obtained in n trials. If that probability is less or equal than .01 then reject the null hypothesis and say that B performs significantly better than A. Symmetrically, decide whether A performs significantly better than B. We remark that in all domains except *Movie* the tasks where two configurations behaved equally were exactly those that could not be solved by either of the configurations. In 60% of the cases where we found that one configuration B performed significantly better than another configuration, B was faster on *all* instances with different behavior. In 71%, B was faster on all but at most one such instance.

We are particularly interested in pairs A and B of configurations where B results from A by turning one of the switches on, leaving the two others unchanged. Deciding about significant improvement in such cases tells us about the effect that the respective technique has on performance in a domain. There are 12 pairs of configurations where one switch is turned on. Figure 3.6 shows our findings in these cases.

The results are shown for the "F", "E", and "H" switches, which become active in turn from left to right. For each of these switches there are four configurations of the two other, background, switches, displayed by four columns in the table. In each column the behavior of the respective background configuration with the active switch turned off is compared to the behavior with the active switch turned on. If performance is improved significantly the table shows a "+", if it is significantly degraded the table shows a "−", and otherwise the respective table entry is empty. For example consider the top left corner, where the "F" switch is active, and the background configuration is "−−", i.e., hill-climbing without helpful actions. Planner A is "− − −", using HSP distances, and planner

domain	F				E				H			
	--	-E	H-	HE	--	-F	H-	HF	--	-F	E-	EF
Assembly	+	+	+	+		-	+	+	+	+	+	+
Blocksworld-arm		+			-		-	-		-	+	+
Blocksworld-no-arm	+		+	-	+	-	+	+	+	+	+	+
Briefcaseworld	+	-			-	-			-	-	-	-
Ferry	+	+	+	+	+	-	+	+		+	+	+
Freecell	+	+	+	+	+	+	+	+	+	+	+	+
Fridge	-				-	-	-	-	+	+	+	+
Grid	+		+	+	+		+	+	+	+	+	+
Gripper	+	+	+	+	-	+	+	+	+	+	+	+
Hanoi		+			+	+	+	+				
Logistics	-	-	+		-	+	+		+	+	+	+
Miconic-ADL		+		+	+	+	+	+		+	+	+
Miconic-SIMPLE	+	+	+		+		+	+		+	+	+
Miconic-STRIPS	+	+	+	+		+	+	+		+	+	+
Movie					+	+	+	+				
Mprime	+	+	+			+	+		+	+	+	+
Mystery					+	+	+	+				
Schedule			+	+		-	+	+	+	+	+	+
Simple-Tsp	+	+	+	+	+	+	+	+	+	+	+	+
Tireworld	+		+	+		-	+	+		+	+	+

Fig. 3.6. The effect of turning on a single switch, keeping the others unchanged. Summarized in terms of significantly improved or degraded running time performance per domain, and per switch configuration

B is "$--F$", using FF distances. B's performance is significantly better than A's, indicated by a "+".

The leftmost four columns in Figure 3.6 show our results for h^{HSP} versus h^{FF}. Clearly, the latter goal distance estimates are superior in our domains in the sense that, for each background configuration, the behavior gets significantly improved in 10 to 13 domains. In contrast there are only 5 cases altogether where performance gets worse. The significances are quite scattered over the domains and background configurations, indicating that a lot of the significances result from interactions between the techniques that occur only in the context of certain domains. For example, performance is degraded in *Logistics* when the background configuration does not use helpful actions, but improved when the background configuration uses hill-climbing with helpful actions. This kind of behavior can not be observed in any other domain. In 6 domains, FF's estimates improve performance consistently over all background configurations, indicating a real advantage of the different distance estimates. As described in Section 3.3, h^{HSP} overestimates the goal distance in *Assembly*, *Freecell*, and *Miconic-STRIPS* (as well as in *Tireworld*, degrading performance in all but one of the cases). In *Gripper*, we found the following. If the robot is in room A and holds only one ball, FF's heuristic prefers picking up another ball over moving to room B, i.e., the picking action leads to a state with better evaluation. Now, if there are n balls left in room A then HSP's heuristic estimate of picking up another ball is $4n-2$, while the estimate of moving to room B is $3n + 1$. Thus if there are at least 4 balls left in room A, moving to room B gets a better evaluation. Ignoring positive interactions, HSP overestimates the usefulness of the moving action.

Comparing hill-climbing versus enforced hill-climbing, i.e., looking at the four columns in the middle of Figure 3.6, the observation is that the performance advantage of enforced hill-climbing is correlated with helpful actions pruning. Without the pruning technique, performance gets improved in 18 cases but degraded in 12 cases; with the technique, enforced hill-climbing improves performance significantly in 17 of our 20 domains (i.e., 34 cases), being degraded only in *Fridge* and one case of *Blocksworld-arm* (i.e., 3 cases). We draw two conclusions. First, whether one or the other search strategy is better depends on the domain. A simple example for that is the *Hanoi* domain, where hill-climbing always restarts before it can reach the goal — on all paths to the goal, there are exponentially many state transitions where the son has no better evaluation than the father. Second, there is an interaction between enforced hill-climbing and helpful actions pruning that occurs consistently across almost all of our domains. This can be explained by the effect that the pruning technique has on the different search strategies. In hill-climbing helpful actions pruning prevents the planner from looking at too many superfluous successors on each single state that a path goes through. This saves time proportional to the length of the path. The effects on enforced hill-climbing are more drastic. The pruning technique removes unnecessary successors of each state during a breadth first search, i.e., it cuts down the branching factor. This yields performance speedups exponential in the depths that are encountered.

We finally compare consideration of all actions versus consideration of only the helpful ones. Look at the rightmost four columns of Figure 3.6. The observation is simply that helpful actions are really helpful — they improve performance significantly in almost all of our planning domains. This is especially true for those background configurations using enforced hill-climbing, due to the same interaction that we have outlined above. In some domains, helpful actions pruning imposes a very rigid restriction on the search space: in *Schedule* we found that states can have hundreds of successors, where only about 2% of those are considered helpful. In other domains only a few actions are pruned: in *Hanoi*, for example, at most three actions are applicable in each state, which are all considered helpful in most of the cases. Even a small degree of restriction usually leads to a significant improvement in performance. In *Briefcaseworld* helpful actions prune out too many possibilities, as described in Section 3.7.

3.8.3 Solution Length

We also investigated which of FF's new techniques serve most to overcome the bad solution quality behavior of our HSP1 implementation. Comparing two configurations A and B, we took as the data set the respective solution length for those tasks that both A and B managed to solve — obviously there is not much point in comparing solution length when one planner can not find a solution at all. We then counted the number n of tasks where A and B behaved differently, and the number k where B's solution was shorter, and decided about significance like described in the last section. Figure 3.7 shows our results in those cases where a single switch is turned.

The data in Figure 3.7 are organized in the obvious manner analogous to Figure 3.6. Let us focus on the leftmost four columns, h^{HSP} versus h^{FF}. The observations are that, with enforced hill-climbing in the background, FF goal

domain	F				E				H			
	--	-E	H-	HE	--	-F	H-	HF	--	-F	E-	EF
Assembly		+	+	+		+	+		+	+		
Blocksworld-arm				+	+	+	+	+	+	+	+	
Blocksworld-no-arm			+	+		+		+		+	+	
Briefcaseworld		+			+	+						
Ferry		+	+		+			+			+	+
Freecell		+	+						+	+		
Fridge	-		-			+	+		+	+	+	
Grid			+	+	+	+	+	+	+	+		
Gripper	+	+	+	+	+			-			-	
Hanoi												
Logistics		+	-	+	+	+	+	+	+		+	
Miconic-ADL		+		+				+				+
Miconic-SIMPLE	-	+	+	+		+	+	+		+	+	+
Miconic-STRIPS	+	+	+	+	+	+	+	+			+	+
Movie					-	-	-	-				
Mprime												
Mystery												
Schedule			+					-	+	+		
Simple-Tsp												
Tireworld				+				+				

Fig. 3.7. The effect of turning on a single switch, keeping the others unchanged. Summarized in terms of significantly improved or degraded solution length performance per domain, and per switch configuration

distance estimates often result in shorter plans, and that there are two domains where solution lengths are improved across all background configurations. Concerning the second observation, this is due to properties of the domain that FF's heuristic does recognize, but HSP's does not. Recall what we observed about the *Gripper* domain in the preceding section. With the robot standing in room A, holding only one ball, the FF heuristic gives picking up the ball a better evaluation than moving to room B. The HSP heuristic does not do this. Therefore using the HSP heuristic results in longer plans, where balls are transported to room B one by one instead of two by two. Concerning the first observation, improved solution lengths when enforced hill-climbing is in the background, we do not have a good explanation for this. It seems that the greedy way in which enforced hill-climbing builds its plans is just better suited when distance estimates are cautious, i.e., low.

Consider the four columns in the middle of Figure 3.7, hill-climbing versus enforced hill-climbing. There are many cases where the different search strategy results in shorter plans. We figure that this is due to the different plateau behavior that the search methods exhibit, i.e., their behavior in flat regions of the search space (we will discuss plateaus in detail when focusing on local search topology in Part III). Enforced hill-climbing enters a plateau somewhere, performs complete search for a state with better evaluation, and adds the shortest path to that state to its current plan prefix. When hill-climbing enters a plateau, it strolls around more or less randomly, until it hits a state with better evaluation or has enough of it and restarts. All the actions on its path to the better state are kept in the final plan.[4]

---

[4] In *Movie*, the phenomenon is this. If a planner chooses to reset the counter on the VCR before it chooses to rewind the movie (initially, neither heuristic makes a distinction between these two actions), then it has to reset the counter again. The enforced hill-climbing planners always reset the counter first. The hill-climbing planners on the other hand randomly choose either ordering with equal probability.

Finally, we compare consideration of all actions versus consideration of only the helpful ones, results depicted in the rightmost four columns of Figure 3.6. There is only one single case where solution length performance is degraded by turning on helpful actions. This indicates that the actions on the shortest path to the goal are in fact usually considered helpful — unless *all* solution paths are thrown away as is sometimes the case only in the *Briefcaseworld* domain. Quite the other way around than one should think, pruning the search space with helpful actions sometimes leads to significantly shorter solution plans. There is a simple explanation to this, at least when the underlying search method is hill-climbing. Consider what we said above about the plateau behavior of hill-climbing, randomly adding actions to the current plan in the search for a better state. If such a search engine uses a pruning technique that successfully steers it into the direction of the goals, it might well take less steps to find the way off a plateau.

As said in Section 3.8.1 hill-climbing was given five tries on each task, and results averaged. In five tries around half of the solutions use the correct ordering, such that for all tasks the average value is lower than the corresponding value for the enforced hill-climbing planners.

4. Dead Ends

Dead ends are a phenomenon that can cause trouble for FF's search algorithm: they are states from which the goal is unreachable. We have already come across dead ends previously, in particular Sections 3.4.2 and 3.7 gave examples where dead ends cause enforced hill-climbing to fail. In this chapter we discuss dead ends in detail, considering a number of possibilities to deal with them. We choose a simple safety net solution that has no effect on FF's performance in case of success, and can often help in case of failure.

The chapter is organized as follows. We first give sufficient (largely syntactical) criteria for recognizing planning tasks that do not contain any dead ends (Section 4.1) — thereby automatically determining "safe" cases. We then describe some algorithmic techniques we have tried for dealing with dead ends, if they arise (Section 4.2). We finally evaluate the algorithmic technique we have chosen to use in FF (Section 4.3). As a preface, we fill in the formal details about dead ends, their relation to FF's heuristic function, and their effects on the completeness of FF's search algorithm. Note that there are actually two sources of incompleteness in the FF base architecture: dead ends, which we discuss here, and the helpful actions pruning technique. For the moment, i.e., the more theoretical part of this chapter up to the end of Section 4.1, we completely ignore the pruning technique. In the more practical Sections 4.2 and 4.3, we include the pruning technique into our considerations.

Definition 4.0.1. *Given a task (A, I, G), with state space (S, E). A state $s \in S$ is a dead end if $gd(s) = \infty$.*

As formalized in Definition 3.0.3, a heuristic function h can return $h(s) = \infty$ for a state s. Taking this as an indication that s is a dead end, the obvious idea for any forward search algorithm is to remove s from the search space. This is exactly what is done in FF's search algorithm, c.f. Section 3.4.1. The technique is only adequate if s is really a dead end, i.e., if h is completeness-preserving in the following sense.

Definition 4.0.2. *Given a task (A, I, G) with state space (S, E) and heuristic h. The heuristic is* completeness preserving, *if $h(s) = \infty \Rightarrow gd(s) = \infty$ for all $s \in S$. With a completeness preserving heuristic, a dead end state s is* recognized *if $h(s) = \infty$ and* unrecognized *otherwise.*

If a heuristic function guarantees to return ∞ only on dead end states, then it makes sense to call these states recognized dead ends as opposed to unrecognized

J. Hoffmann: Utilizing Problem Structure in Planning, LNAI 2854, pp. 75–88, 2003.
© Springer-Verlag Berlin Heidelberg 2003

dead ends where the heuristic returns a finite value. We will see below that only the unrecognized dead ends can cause trouble for FF's search algorithm. Let us first state that FF's heuristic function h^{FF} is, in fact, completeness preserving. This is because of its close relation to the h^+ function.

Proposition 4.0.1. *Let (A, I, G) be a STRIPS task or a negation-free ADL task. The h^+ heuristic is completeness preserving.*

Proof. By Definition 3.0.6, $h^+(s) = \infty$ iff (A^+, s, G) is unsolvable. For STRIPS and negation free ADL tasks any plan for (A, s, G) is also a plan for (A^+, s, G), c.f. Proposition 3.0.1. By contra-position we thus know that (A, s, G) is unsolvable, i.e., s is a dead end.

For ADL, it is a necessary prerequisite here that the task is negation free. We have already seen this in the following example task (described at the beginning of Chapter 3). The initial state is $I = \{g_1\}$, the goal condition is $G = \neg g_1 \wedge g_2$, and the action set A comprises one action with empty precondition and a single effect $(\top, \{g_2\}, \{g_1\})$. Applying the action in the initial state yields a goal state: g_2 is added, and g_1 is deleted. The relaxed task, however, is unsolvable: without delete lists there is no way of making g_1 false so there is no plan for (A^+, I, G). Thus $h^+(I) = \infty$ although $gd(I) = 1$.[1]

The h^{FF} function is only defined for propositional ADL tasks. In this case, $h^{FF} = \infty$ if and only if $h^+ = \infty$.

Proposition 4.0.2. *Let (A, I, G) be a STRIPS task or a propositional ADL task, with state space (S, E). For all $s \in S$, $h^{FF}(s) = \infty \Leftrightarrow h^+(s) = \infty$.*

Proof. By Definitions 3.3.1 and 3.6.1, $h^{FF}(s) = \infty$ if and only if Graphplan respectively IPP terminate without finding a plan for (A^+, s, G). As both these planners are sound and complete [8, 64], this is equivalent to unsolvability of (A^+, s, G). This is, in turn, equivalent to $h^+(s) = \infty$ by Definition 3.0.6.

Recall FF's search algorithm, enforced hill-climbing as described in Section 3.4. Starting from the initial state there is a number of search iterations. In each iteration starting from a state s, a complete breadth first search is performed for a state s' with strictly better heuristic value $h(s') < h(s)$. The next iteration starts out from s'. Search stops when a goal state, $h(s) = 0$, is reached. States s'' with $h(s'') = \infty$ are skipped. This algorithm is complete under the following circumstances.

Theorem 4.0.1. *Given a solvable task (A, I, G) with state space (S, E) and completeness-preserving heuristic h. If no state $s \in S$ is an unrecognized dead end, then enforced hill-climbing will find a solution.*

---

[1] In the negation free compilation of (A, I, G), the goal condition is $g_1^- \wedge g_2$ while the action's effect has the form $(\top, \{g_2, g_1^-\}, \{g_1\})$, so there $h^+(I) = 1$.

Proof. Assume enforced hill-climbing does not reach the goal. Then we have some intermediate state $s = Result(I, P)$, P being the current plan, where breadth-first search can not improve the situation. Now, $h(s) > 0$ as search has not ended yet. If there was a path from s to some goal state s', then breadth first search would find that path — remember that h is completeness preserving so only states are skipped that do not have a path to the goal; thus search would obtain $h(s') = 0 < h(s)$, and terminate positively. A path to a goal state can therefore not exist, showing that s is a dead end state. Furthermore, $h(s) < \infty$ must hold as $h(I) < \infty$ (h is completeness preserving and the task is solvable) and $h(s) \leq h(I)$ (either s is the initial state itself or a state with lower heuristic value).

As for the opposite direction of Theorem 4.0.1, enforced hill-climbing does not necessarily get trapped in an unrecognized dead end if there is one, but we have already seen that this can happen (the dead end encountered in the example from Section 3.4.2 is unrecognized). If there are no unrecognized dead ends then we can use enforced hill-climbing without running the risk of terminating unsuccessfully in spite of the task being solvable (ignoring FF's pruning technique for the moment). We now give two sufficient criteria for recognizing tasks that do not contain any dead ends at all, and thereby automatically determining cases where enforced hill-climbing can safely be applied.

4.1 Dead-End Free Tasks

Naturally, a task is called *dead-end free* if the corresponding state space does not contain dead ends.

Definition 4.1.1. *Given a task* (A, I, G), *with state space* (S, E). *The task is dead-end free if the state space does not contain any dead ends,* $gd(s) < \infty$ *for all* $s \in S$.

Ideally, what one wants to do is decide exactly whether a given planning task contains dead ends or not. This is however not possible at lower cost than the solvability decision itself.

Definition 4.1.2. *Let DEADEND-FREE denote the following problem:*

Given a task (A, I, G), is (A, I, G) dead-end free?

Theorem 4.1.1. *Deciding DEADEND-FREE is PSPACE-complete.*

Proof. We prove hardness for the STRIPS case, and membership for ADL. Hardness follows by polynomially reducing PLANSAT to DEADEND-FREE. Given a STRIPS task (A, I, G), we simply add an action to A that is executable in all states and re-establishes the initial state.

$$A' := A \cup \{(\emptyset, I, \bigcup_{a \in A} add(a) \setminus I)\}$$

Applying the new action to any reachable state leads back to the initial state: all facts that can ever become true are removed, and those in the initial state are added. Now, the modified task (A', I, G) is dead-end free iff (A, I, G) is solvable. From left to right, if (A', I, G) is dead-end free, then it is solvable, which implies that (A, I, G) is solvable, as we have not added any new possibility of reaching the goal. From right to left, if (A, I, G) is solvable, then also is (A', I, G), by the same solution plan P. One can then, from all states in (A', I, G), achieve the goal by going back to the initial state with the new action, and executing P thereafter.

Membership in PSPACE follows from the fact that ADL-PLANSAT and its complement are both in PSPACE, c.f. Theorem 2.2.2. A non-deterministic algorithm that decides the complement of DEADEND-FREE and that needs only polynomial space can be specified as follows. Guess a state s. Verify in polynomial space that s is reachable from the initial state. Further, verify that the goal cannot be reached from s. If this algorithm succeeds, it follows that the instance is not dead-end free — since s constitutes a dead end. This implies that the complement of DEADEND-FREE is in NPSPACE, and hence in PSPACE. Finished with PSPACE = co-PSPACE.

An exact decision about the existence of dead ends is as hard as planning itself. In the remainder of this section we introduce two criteria that are sufficient for a task being dead end free, given it is solvable. The criteria are (for the most part, as discussed below) syntactical restrictions on a planning task's specification. Before we start, we introduce some finer distinctions between the different kinds of behavior that a planning task can exhibit with respect to dead ends. These notations will also be important in Part III.

Definition 4.1.3. *Given a task (A, I, G) with state space (S, E) and completeness-preserving heuristic h. The state space is*

1. *undirected, if $\forall (s, s') \in E : (s', s) \in E$*
2. *harmless, if $\exists (s, s') \in E : (s', s) \notin E$, and $\forall s \in S : gd(s) < \infty$*
3. *recognized, if $\exists s \in S : gd(s) = \infty$, and $\forall s \in S : gd(s) = \infty \Rightarrow h(s) = \infty$*
4. *unrecognized, if $\exists s \in S : gd(s) = \infty \wedge h(s) < \infty$*

We require the heuristic function to be completeness preserving in order to make the notions of *recognized* and *unrecognized* intuitively correct — the heuristic functions we consider in this book are completeness preserving anyway, c.f. Propositions 4.0.1 and 4.0.2. For solvable tasks, the classes are exhaustive and pairwise disjoint. Clearly, any state space falls into at least one of the classes. Likewise clearly the last three classes have an empty intersection. If a planning task is solvable and undirected, then there can be no dead ends because from any state one can get back to the initial state and solve the task from there. [2]

---

[2] If a task is unsolvable then all states are dead ends but the state transitions can still be undirected. Local search can not prove unsolvability anyway, so we are only interested in solvable tasks.

Our criteria are sufficient for the state space of a task being undirected or (at most) harmless, respectively. We need the notion of *inconsistency* at some points.

Definition 4.1.4. *Given a task (A, I, G). Two facts are* inconsistent *if there is no reachable state $s \in S$ that contains both of them. Two sets of facts F and F' are* inconsistent *if each fact in F is inconsistent with at least one fact in F'.*

We restrict ourselves to STRIPS tasks in the following. One can use the same key ideas to define the criteria for propositional ADL tasks, but this makes the notations much more complicated. We remark that the following will also be important in Part III — as it will turn out, the phenomena we identify here form one half of the structural properties that enable the high quality of FF's heuristic function.

4.1.1 Undirected State Spaces

An obvious reason why a state space can be undirected — and why the state spaces in many of our benchmark domains are in fact undirected — is when to each action a there is an inverse action $\bar{a}$ which always undoes exactly a's effects. The following is a summarized version of definitions and results published by Jana Koehler in collaboration with the author [62].

Definition 4.1.5. *Given a STRIPS task (A, I, G). An action $a \in A$ is* invertible, *if:*

1. *there is an action $\bar{a} \in A$ such that*
   a) *$pre(\bar{a}) \subseteq (pre(a) \cup add(a)) \setminus del(a)$,*
   b) *$add(\bar{a}) = del(a)$, and*
   c) *$del(\bar{a}) = add(a)$;*
2. *$add(a)$ is inconsistent with $pre(a)$; and*
3. *$del(a) \subseteq pre(a)$.*

For any state s and applicable action a, $\bar{a}$ is applicable in $Result(s, a)$ due to part 1(a) of Definition 4.1.5. Parts 2 and 3 of that definition make sure that a's effects do in fact appear, and parts 1(b) and (c) make sure that $\bar{a}$ undoes exactly those effects.

Theorem 4.1.2. *Given a STRIPS task (A, I, G). If all actions $a \in A$ are invertible, then the state space to the task is undirected.*

Proof. Assume we have a reachable state $s \in S$, and an action a that is applicable, $pre(a) \subseteq s$, yielding the state $s' := Result(s, \langle a \rangle)$. We need to show that there is an action $\bar{a}$ such that $Result(s', \langle \bar{a} \rangle) = s$. By prerequisite, we can choose an action $\bar{a}$ that inverts a in the sense of Definition 4.1.5. Applying $\bar{a}$ in s' (note here that $pre(\bar{a}) \subseteq s'$ because $s' \supseteq (pre(a) \cup add(a)) \setminus del(a)$) leads us back to s:

$$\begin{aligned}
Result(s', \langle \bar{a} \rangle) &= (s' \cup add(\bar{a})) \setminus del(\bar{a}) \\
&= (((s \cup add(a)) \setminus del(a)) \cup del(a)) \setminus add(a) \\
&= (s \cup add(a)) \setminus add(a) \quad \text{as } del(a) \subseteq pre(a) \subseteq s \\
&= s \quad\quad\quad\quad\quad\quad\quad\quad \text{as } add(a) \cap s = \emptyset
\end{aligned}$$

In the last equation, $add(a) \cap s = \emptyset$ as $add(a)$ is inconsistent with $pre(a) \subseteq s$.

All prerequisites of Theorem 4.1.2 are purely syntactical except inconsistency. Deciding inconsistency is, once again, as hard as planning itself — for an arbitrary task, introduce two new propositions, one being permanently true and one which can only be made true if the original goal is achieved beforehand; the new propositions are inconsistent iff the original task is unsolvable. There are however several polynomial time (incomplete but sufficient) approximation techniques for inconsistency in the literature [8, 32, 38, 87]. Therefore it is feasible to use Theorem 4.1.2 for identifying tasks that are undirected, and thus dead end free in case they are solvable.

4.1.2 Harmless State Spaces

Our second criterion is weaker, and implies only the non-existence of dead ends in the solvable case; that is, if the criterion holds then the state space of the task, if it is solvable, is at most harmless (either undirected or harmless).

Our first key observation is this. For the non-existence of dead ends, it is not necessary that for each action a the inverse action $\bar{a}$ undoes *exactly* a's effects. It is already enough if $\bar{a}$ achieves (at least) all facts that have been true before. Actions for which such a weak form of inverse action exists are called *at least invertible*.

Definition 4.1.6. *Given a STRIPS task (A, I, G). An action $a \in A$ is* at least invertible, *if there is an action $\bar{a} \in A$ such that*

1. $pre(\bar{a}) \subseteq (pre(a) \cup add(a)) \setminus del(a)$,
2. $add(\bar{a}) \supseteq del(a)$, and
3. $del(\bar{a})$ is inconsistent with $pre(a)$.

The first two conditions of the definition are obvious. As for the last point, note that we do not refer to a's add list at all. Inconsistency of $\bar{a}$'s deletes with a's preconditions implies that $\bar{a}$ deletes only facts that have not been true in s (but might have been made true by a's add list). Note also that Definition 4.1.5 is stronger than Definition 4.1.6. If $del(\bar{a}) = add(a)$, and $add(a)$ is inconsistent with $pre(a)$, then, of course, $del(\bar{a})$ is inconsistent with $pre(a)$.

Another situation when an action cannot lead into dead ends is the following: the action's delete effects are irrelevant — they are not important for anything in the task but the action itself; and the action's add effects are static, that is, not deleted by any action. By the latter property applying the action once is enough, and by the former property applying the action does not rule out any possibilities except applying it a second time.

Definition 4.1.7. *Given a STRIPS task* (A, I, G). *An action* $a \in A$ *has* irrelevant delete effects, *if*

$$del(a) \cap (G \cup \bigcup_{a \neq a' \in A} pre(a')) = \emptyset$$

An action has static add effects, *if*

$$add(a) \cap \bigcup_{a' \in A} del(a') = \emptyset$$

If all actions in a solvable task are either at least invertible or have irrelevant delete effects and static add effects, then the state space is at most harmless.

Theorem 4.1.3. *Given a solvable STRIPS task* (A, I, G). *If it holds for all actions* $a \in A$ *that either*

1. *a is at least invertible, or*
2. *a has irrelevant delete effects and static add effects,*

then the task is dead-end free.

Proof. To any reachable state $s = Result(I, \langle a_1, \ldots, a_n \rangle) \in S$, we need to identify a solution P for (A, s, G). Let $\langle p_1, \ldots, p_m \rangle \in A^*$ be a solution for (A, I, G) (which exists as (A, I, G) is solvable by prerequisite). We construct P as follows.

$M := \emptyset$
for $i := n \ldots 1$ **do**
    if a_i is at least invertible by $\overline{a_i}$ **then**
        if $\overline{a_i} \notin M$ apply $\overline{a_i}$ **endif**
    else $M := M \cup \{a_i\}$
    endif
endfor
for $i := 1 \ldots m$ **do**
    if $p_i \notin M$ **then** apply p_i **endif**
endfor

M serves as a kind of memory set for the actions that could not be inverted. We need to prove that the preconditions of all applied actions are fulfilled in the state where they are applied, and that the goals are true upon termination.

Let us start with the first loop. We denote by $s_i := result(I, \langle a_1, \ldots, a_i \rangle)$ the state after executing the ith action on the path to s, and by s'_i the state before the first loop starts with value i. We prove:

$$s'_i \supseteq (s_i \cap (G \cup \bigcup_{a \in A \setminus M_i} pre(a))) \cup \bigcup_{a \in M_i} add(a)$$

M_i here denotes the current state of the set. We proceed by backward induction over i. If $i = n$, we got $s'_i = s_i$ and $M_i = \emptyset$, so the equation is trivially true. Now assume the equation is true for $i \geq 1$. We prove that the equation holds for $i - 1$. If a_i is not at least invertible, then no action is applied, $s'_{i-1} = s'_i$, and

$M_{i-1} = M_i \cup \{a_i\}$. Concerning the left hand side of the equation, we observe that a_i does by prerequisite not delete any fact from $G \cup \bigcup_{a \in A \setminus M_{i-1}} pre(a)$ (M_{i-1} contains a_i), so all relevant facts from s_{i-1} have already been true in s_i'; concerning the right hand side of the equation, we observe that the facts in $add(a_i)$ are never deleted by prerequisite, so $\bigcup_{a \in M_{i-1}} add(a)$ is contained in s_i'. Now assume that a_i is at least invertible by $\overline{a_i}$. We got $M_{i-1} = M_i$. Assume $\overline{a_i}$ is applied. It is applicable because its preconditions are contained in s_i, and it is not an element of M_i. For the resulting state s_{i-1}', all facts that a_i has deleted from s_{i-1} are added, and only facts are deleted that have not been true in s_{i-1} anyway; also, none of the add effects of actions in M_i is deleted, so the equation is fulfilled. Finally, if $\overline{a_i}$ is not applied, then its add effects are already contained in s_i', subsuming the delete effects of a_i.

Inserting $i = 0$ in the equation we have just proven, we get

$$s_0 \supseteq \left(I \cap \left(G \cup \bigcup_{a \in A \setminus M_0} pre(a) \right) \right) \cup \bigcup_{a \in M_0} add(a)$$

The second loop starts from s_0. So we start a solution plan, excluding the actions in a set M_0, from a state including all initial facts that are contained in the goal or in the precondition of any action not in M_0. As the state additionally contains all add effects of all actions in M_0, and those add effects are not deleted by any action, it is clear that we can simply skip the actions in M_0 and achieve the goal.

Like it is the case for Theorem 4.1.2, all prerequisites of Theorem 4.1.3 are purely syntactical except inconsistency.[3] One can thus use Theorem 4.1.3 to identify tasks that are dead end free in case they are solvable, guaranteeing enforced hill-climbing to find a solution.

4.1.3 Practical Implications

The instances of quite a range of our benchmark domains can be classified by the above criteria. Brief descriptions of the domains are in Section 2.3, the formal definitions can be looked up in Appendix A.

Corollary 4.1.1. *Let* (A, I, G) *be an instance of the Blocksworld-arm, Blocksworld-no-arm, Ferry, Gripper, Hanoi, or Logistics domains. Then the state space to* (A, I, G) *is undirected.*

Proof. In all these domains, after removing static predicates (types and non-equality) all actions are invertible in the sense of Definition 4.1.5. In *Blocksworld-arm*, stack(x, y) is undone by unstack(x, y), and pickup(x) is undone by putdown(x); similarly in *Blocksworld-no-arm* and *Hanoi* any block or disc that is moved somewhere can be moved back. In the transportation domains *Ferry*, *Gripper*, and *Logistics*, loading an object onto a vehicle is undone by unloading

---

[3] Note that Theorem 4.1.3 subsumes Theorem 4.1.2 in the sense that all tasks that fulfill the prerequisites of the latter theorem also fulfill the prerequisites of the former.

the object, and moving a vehicle is undone by moving it back. Finished with Proposition 3.1.3 (semantic identity after removing static predicates) and Theorem 4.1.2.

Corollary 4.1.2. *Let* (A, I, G) *be an instance of the Miconic-STRIPS, Movie, Simple-Tsp, or Tireworld domains. Then the state space to* (A, I, G) *is at most harmless.*

Proof. In these domains, after removing static predicates (types and non-equality) all actions are either at least invertible in the sense of Definition 4.1.6 or have irrelevant delete effects and static add effects in the sense of Definition 4.1.7. In *Miconic-STRIPS*, moving the lift is invertible (by moving back), boarding a passenger is at least invertible (by the same action, as its delete list is empty), and letting a passenger depart has irrelevant delete- and static add-effects. In *Movie*, getting some snack fulfills the latter requirements (no deletes at all, static add effects) while rewinding the movie and resetting the counter are at least invertible. In *Simple-Tsp*, moving somewhere is at least invertible by moving back. In *Tireworld*, all actions are invertible except inflating a wheel which has irrelevant delete effects and static add effects. Finished with Proposition 3.1.3, Theorem 4.1.3, and the observation that all instances of these domains are solvable.

Considering these results, a promising approach seems to be the following. Given a (STRIPS) planning task, first evaluate Theorems 4.1.2 and 4.1.3; if one of them holds then use enforced hill-climbing, otherwise employ a complete heuristic search mechanism. For the domains listed in Corollaries 4.1.1 and 4.1.2, this approach would successfully apply enforced hill-climbing. For other domains the approach will prevent us from getting trapped in a dead end. There are however the following difficulties with the approach.

- The criteria are sufficient but not complete and can therefore fail to recognize tasks that are dead-end free, like for example the instances of the *Grid* domain.[4] Apart from that, a task can contain dead ends but still no unrecognized ones.
- Even in the presence of unrecognized dead ends enforced hill-climbing can often be successful, as it does not necessarily get trapped in one; examples for that are contained in the *Mprime* and *Mystery* domains (we will say more about these domains below).
- Finally, we actually want to use helpful actions pruning inside enforced hill-climbing, which renders the algorithm incomplete even on dead-end free tasks, like for example in *Briefcaseworld*, c.f. Sections 3.5.2 and 3.7.

As for the last point, an idea to overcome this is the following: in each breadth first search iteration of enforced hill-climbing, first employ helpful actions pruning; if that fails, then do the same iteration again but this time with the pruning

---

[4] Among other things, a move in *Grid* is not invertible in the strict sense of Definition 4.1.5, because it is not stated in the precondition that the start location must be open; nevertheless, as we will prove in Section 8.3.5, there are no dead ends.

technique turned off. This way, as is easy to see, the algorithm is still complete in the absence of unrecognized dead ends. In fact this method has been used in an earlier version of FF [44]. We do not use the method now. The reason is that, as will be described in Chapter 5, we enhance enforced hill-climbing with two more techniques to deal with goal orderings. Neither of these techniques is completeness preserving in general, so if enforced hill-climbing fails then it is not clear what the reason for that failure is, or which combination of techniques might be more successful. Throughout the rest of the chapter, we assume that helpful actions pruning is used.

As for the first two points, incompleteness of recognizing dead-end free tasks and possible success of enforced hill-climbing on tasks that do contain dead ends, there is not much one can do about this. Thus, considering the excellent results we have obtained with enforced hill-climbing on our benchmarks, c.f. Section 3.7, we definitely at least want to try the algorithm on a given planning task. The question is, what do we do if it fails?

4.2 Handling Dead Ends

In this section, we briefly describe some experimental search techniques with which we have tried to handle dead ends. We evaluate the techniques on an example domain, *Mystery*, and make a decision about which technique to use in FF.

4.2.1 Restarts

An often used idea in hill-climbing is the following. If a hill-climbing trial does not seem to be making any progress, then stop the trial and restart the algorithm, i.e., select a random start position in the search space and perform a new hill-climbing trial from there, in the hope that it is easier to solve the problem starting from the new position.

As we have described in Section 3.2.2, HSP1 applies this idea to planning. A hill-climbing trial is cut off if there are too many consecutive non-improving steps. As all trials must start out in the initial state, there is no random selection of starting states; but action selection is randomized and thus it is to be hoped that the new trial will by chance not do the same mistakes as the previous one.

Obviously the idea to perform restarts can be applied to the problem we are facing right now, what to do if enforced hill-climbing gets trapped in a dead end. We do not need a criterion for cutting off hill-climbing trials as we only want to restart if enforced hill-climbing reports failure. There is no random selection of starting states. The question left to be answered is, how do we randomize enforced hill-climbing? We have experimented with three different answers to the question.

1. An obvious way of randomizing the algorithm is by randomizing the node expansion order during breadth first search. In our implementation, the set

of (helpful) successors to each search node is randomly permuted before it is inserted into the list of nodes that must still be expanded. With d being the shallowest search depth at which a better state can be found, this way any better state at depth d might be chosen as the next starting point.

2. Our second randomization is a somewhat stricter formulation of the above one: once the first better state has been found at depth d, the entire breadth first search space at depth d is looked at, and one best state is randomly chosen. This way, the next starting point will be a *best* state at depth d (as opposed to one state better than the current starting state, like above).

3. Finally, we tried a rather strong randomization where in each iteration of enforced hill-climbing with probability 0.5 the usual breadth first search for a better state is done, but with equal probability a random action is applied.

With each randomization method, our implementation restarts every time enforced hill-climbing reports failure, until either a plan is found or the program is terminated from outside. We ran the FF base architecture and the three restart implementations on the AIPS-1998 competition collection of the *Mystery* domain, this being a collection of tasks where the FF base architecture often stops without finding a plan. The data are shown in Figure 4.1.

task	FF	rnd-1	rnd-2	rnd-3	bfs
prob-01	0.03	0.03	0.03	0.03	0.01
prob-02	0.31	0.18	0.24	0.56	0.25
prob-03	0.09	0.08	0.08	0.27	0.09
prob-06	- (42.06)	-	-	-	-
prob-09	- (0.23)	-	-	1.22	0.33
prob-10	- (81.50)	-	-	-	-
prob-11	0.04	0.04	0.04	0.06	0.03
prob-13	- (2.24)	-	-	-	-
prob-14	33.66	28.03	31.68	32.77	31.59
prob-15	0.93	0.85	0.91	1.13	0.91
prob-17	0.71	0.66	0.68	0.69	0.67
prob-19	- (1.22)	0.39	-	0.40	12.41
prob-20	0.45	0.34	0.42	1.20	0.42
prob-22	-	-	-		-
prob-25	0.02	0.04	0.02	0.03	0.03
prob-26	- (0.77)	-	-	1.86	0.84
prob-27	0.06	0.08	0.07	0.07	0.06
prob-28	0.04	0.03	0.04	0.02	0.02
prob-29	0.07	0.06	0.07	0.09	0.07
prob-30	0.22	0.22	0.23	0.24	0.22

Fig. 4.1. Runtimes for different configurations of FF on the AIPS-1998 *Mystery* collection (instances that can be proved unsolvable by IPP are left out of the table). A dash means that no plan was found after 5 minutes

We have first run IPP on the *Mystery* collection shown in Figure 4.1, and left those instances out that were proved unsolvable — on these tasks, all hill-climbing variations are lost anyway. FF stands for the FF base architecture, rnd-1 to rnd-3 stand for the above listed three different versions of randomized restart implementation. In its rightmost column the figure also shows data for the technique we have actually decided to use, as will be described below; for now, let us ignore this column.

A dash indicates that the respective planner did not find a plan to the respective task after five minutes. For FF, times in parentheses specify the runtime after which enforced hill-climbing reported failure (on task "prob-22" even this had not happened after five minutes). Concerning runtimes on the tasks that FF *can* solve, the runtimes of the restart implementations are roughly similar; rnd-3 sometimes needs somewhat longer, which is easily explained by the way this method inserts random actions with probability 0.5. Concerning the tasks that FF can not solve, the results for the restart techniques are disappointing: out of seven such tasks, rnd-1 solves a single task, rnd-2 solves no task at all, and rnd-3 being the most successful approach here solves three tasks.

Considering these results one might be tempted to use rnd-3 as the method of choice — at least this seems to be successful in *some* cases where plain enforced hill-climbing is lost. We have however decided to use a much simpler technique for dealing with the cases where enforced hill-climbing fails. While this technique behaves as well as rnd-3 in the above *Mystery* collection, it has the advantage that it guarantees completeness.

4.2.2 A Safety Net Solution

Our idea is as simple as this:

1. Do enforced hill-climbing (using helpful actions pruning) until the goal is reached or the algorithm fails.
2. If enforced hill-climbing fails, skip everything done so far and try to solve the task by a complete heuristic search algorithm, precisely what Russel and Norvig [88] term *greedy best-first* search. This strategy simply expands all search nodes by increasing order of goal distance estimation (using no pruning technique).

In short, we use best-first search as a safety net if enforced hill-climbing fails to find a plan. The runtime values for this approach in the *Mystery* collection are given in the rightmost column of Figure 4.1. With the five minute runtime cut off applied, the method solves as many tasks as the most successful randomization technique rnd-3. In contrast to the latter method we do however have completeness and know therefore that eventually a solution will be found to any solvable task, if the algorithm is given enough time (and memory).

Note that the idea is almost the same as we discussed in Section 4.1.3 above (using a complete search mechanism if Theorem 4.1.3 can not be applied). The difference is merely that we employ the complete search if enforced hill-climbing failed, rather than if we were not able to prove that the task at hand is dead-end free. The approach involves the effort to run enforced hill-climbing at least once. However, considering the many cases where enforced hill-climbing performs excellently in spite of the presence of dead ends, this seems to be the smaller sacrifice.

4.3 Evaluation

We evaluated our safety net solution by running it on the same example collections that we used for comparing FF to HSP, c.f. Section 3.8. Obviously this needs only be done in those domains where the FF base architecture sometimes terminates without finding a plan. These are the *Briefcaseworld*, *Freecell*, *Miconic-ADL*, *Mprime*, and *Mystery* domains. [5] The data for *Mystery* has already been shown above. As for the remaining four domains, for ease of presentation we chose, in each domain, 30 example tasks. The data are shown in Figure 4.2.

task	Briefcaseworld	Freecell	Miconic-ADL	Mprime
task1	(0.10) 0.64	9.32	0.11	0.05
task2	(0.10) 0.62	28.33	0.10	0.23
task3	(0.12) 0.62	3.54	0.11	0.10
task4	(0.20) 1.39	42.29	0.52	0.03
task5	(0.12) 0.77	(16.71) 58.53	0.55	
task6	(0.16) 0.86	7.29	0.50	1.81
task7	(0.14) 0.73	5.34	0.83	
task8	(0.18) 0.79	4.42	0.84	0.35
task9	(0.26) 1.16	(9.87) 51.34	(0.88) 2.26	0.16
task10	(0.21) 0.67	12.54	2.09	33.95
task11	(0.27) 1.97	(25.24) 48.78	1.87	0.07
task12	(0.26) 1.06	7.02	(1.11) 6.82	0.17
task13	(0.23) 1.08	7.78	(2.54) 8.52	(2.19) -
task14	(0.20) 1.43	(14.64) 85.72	3.01	-
task15	(0.22) 1.52	(15.97) 90.75	3.41	3.05
task16	(0.24) 2.28	(130.61) -	4.61	0.25
task17	(0.39) 1.60	(6.01) 97.80	9.50	0.88
task18	(0.36) 1.54	9.33	3.36	
task19	(0.38) 2.11	(25.48) -	(7.29) 78.61	0.91
task20	(0.36) 2.23	(216.69) -	5.84	2.87
task21	(0.48) 3.44	(14.56) 88.74	7.44	(0.88) -
task22	(0.55) 3.16	(5.23) 43.63	(5.52) 33.84	-
task23	(0.43) 2.67	(15.56) 82.98	10.24	3.04
task24	(0.39) 2.62	(70.08) -	18.70	2.67
task25	(0.48) 2.17	-	17.53	0.04
task26	(0.66) 5.70	(34.90) -	(9.94) 54.55	0.15
task27	(0.54) 2.98	(10.17) 77.37	(11.61) 50.99	0.78
task28	(0.71) 3.83	29.35	21.28	0.09
task29	(0.46) 4.67	(17.86) -	23.01	0.30
task30	(0.61) 5.45	-	(18.76) 77.92	1.90

Fig. 4.2. Runtime for the FF base architecture, respectively that architecture including safety net, on example collections from domains where the FF base architecture sometimes fails. Times in parentheses specify the time after which failure was reported. A dash means that no plan was found (no failure was reported) after 5 minutes

Figure 4.2 is to be understood as follows. Times in parentheses specify the time after which the FF base architecture reported failure. If that happened, the time not in parentheses specifies the total runtime when using the safety net afterwards. If the FF base architecture succeeded then the time given is simply

---

[5] We will prove in Chapters 7 and 8 that the latter four domains are with one exception the only ones in our collection where unrecognized dead ends can arise.

its total runtime. Runtime cut off was as usual at five minutes, indicated by a dash.

Let us examine the data from left to right. In the leftmost column we have data for the *Briefcaseworld* domain. The instances are randomly generated ones with 10 to 15 objects, 5 tasks of each size. On all tasks, the FF base architecture reports failure, which is due to the helpful actions technique. Time until failure is less than a second, and applying best-first search afterwards reliably yields solutions after a few seconds (in fact, the total runtimes including failure and safety net are still better than the runtimes for HSP1: on the five examples from our benchmark collection, c.f. Section 3.2.3, with 2 to 10 objects in steps of 2, the runtime values are 0.02, 0.05, 0.07, 0.43, 2.30 for HSP1, and 0.02, 0.03, 0.07, 0.20, 0.62 for FF with safety net).

The second column shows data for the *Freecell* domain, precisely for the largest 6 groups of instances that were used in the AIPS-2000 competition, 8 to 13 cards in each of the four suits, 5 tasks per size. In 10 out of 16 cases where enforced hill-climbing fails, best-first search manages to find a plan within five minutes. We also tried the restart methods described above, and none could solve any of the tasks that are not solved by FF with safety net.

Next we have a collection of *Miconic-ADL* examples, also from the AIPS-2000 competition collection. The instances have 9 to 27 passengers (increasing in steps of 2), twice as many floors as passengers, 3 tasks per size. All tasks where enforced hill-climbing fails are solved by the safety net.

Finally we have the AIPS-1998 *Mprime* competition collection. Most of these tasks get solved by the FF base architecture. Task5 and task7 are left out because they are proved unsolvable by IPP. In task14 and task22 no failure was yet reported after five minutes. Started on task13 and task21, FF reports failure very quick, however best-first search fails to find a solution. The restart methods do not succeed in these tasks either.

5. Goal Orderings

Sometimes it is wiser to postpone the achievement of one goal until after the achievement of another: there are cases where two goals g_1 and g_2 are ordered $g_1 \leq g_2$ in the sense that achieving g_2 before g_1 results in unnecessary effort. We will be more precise below. Let us first consider an example. A prototypical domain where goal orderings arise is *Blocksworld-arm*. There are operators to *stack, unstack, pickup* or *putdown* blocks. Say we have three blocks A, B, and C which are all on the table initially, and which we want to arrange into a single stack where A is on top of B, and B is on top of C. The goal set is $G = \{(on, A, B), (on, B, C)\}$. Obviously stacking A onto B first causes unnecessary effort — one has to unstack A again in order to stack B onto C. In other words, there is a goal ordering $(on, B, C) \leq (on, A, B)$ present in the example task. We will use this as a simple illustrative example throughout the chapter.

The FF base architecture sometimes has trouble in the presence of goal orderings, especially in the *Blocksworld-arm* domain. From our benchmark example collection, c.f. Section 3.7, this is the only domain where FF hits the computational border at our largest task: on all other unsolved tasks, FF reports failure within the given runtime and memory resources.

Goal orderings can obviously be problematic for a search algorithm that is not informed about them. Especially the greedy way in which enforced hill-climbing selects actions can be misled when ignoring ordering constraints. Let us quickly consider the above example. In the initial state, h^{FF} is 4: pickup A and B, and stack them onto B and C, respectively. Both picking actions yield a state with h^{FF} value 3: in both cases, the relaxed planner can stack the respective block into its goal position and deal with the other block afterwards. So it is only a matter of chance whether enforced hill-climbing correctly chooses to pickup B first, or whether it decides to start with A.

This chapter discusses two ways of informing search about goal orderings. The first technique approximates goal orderings as a pre-process, and then feeds the goals to the planner in the correct order (a technique that can be applied to any planning mechanism). The second technique approximates goal orderings on the fly during an FF-style forward search, utilizing knowledge that can be extracted from Graphplan's relaxed solutions to the search states. In FF, we use both techniques. The are described in the following two sections (Sections 5.1 and 5.2). Afterwards, we evaluate the effects of the techniques (in all combinations) on FF's performance in domains where goal orderings appear (Section 5.3), showing that

J. Hoffmann: Utilizing Problem Structure in Planning, LNAI 2854, pp. 89–105, 2003.
© Springer-Verlag Berlin Heidelberg 2003

the techniques can often be useful. We introduce our algorithmic techniques for STRIPS, and explain how they can be extended to propositional ADL tasks (only in these cases, the goal being a conjunction of propositions, does it make sense to talk about goal orderings in the way we do).

5.1 Pre-Computing Goal Orderings

The idea to approximate goal orderings as a pre-process, in the hope to avoid unnecessary effort during search, has been pursued by a number of researchers in the past [54, 18, 55]. The specific approach we discuss here originates from work done by Jana Koehler [61], and has been formalized in collaboration with the author [62]. The full investigation forms a long article. We present a brief summary.

The idea is to approximate goal orderings as a pre-process and then feed the goals to the planner in the appropriate order. First we must define what exactly a goal ordering is. We say that there is a goal ordering $g_1 \leq g_2$ if, from any state where g_2 has been achieved (strictly) first, g_2 must be deleted again in order to achieve g_1. The states we are talking about are these.

Definition 5.1.1. *Given a STRIPS or propositional ADL task (A, I, G) with $g_1, g_2 \in G$. By $S_{(g_2, \neg g_1)}$, we denote the set of reachable states in which g_2 is true and g_1 has not yet been true, i.e., the set of states s, $g_2 \in s$ such that there is $P = \langle a_1, \ldots, a_n \rangle \in A^*$ with $s = Result(I, P)$ and $g_1 \notin Result(I, \langle a_1, \ldots, a_i \rangle)$ for $0 \leq i \leq n$.*

As said, we order g_1 before g_2 if from all these states one must delete g_2 in order to achieve g_1.

Definition 5.1.2. *Given a STRIPS or propositional ADL task (A, I, G) with $g_1, g_2 \in G$. We say that there is a goal ordering between g_1 and g_2, written $g_1 \leq g_2$, if*

$$\forall s \in S_{(g_2, \neg g_1)} : \forall P = \langle a_1, \ldots, a_n \rangle \in A^* : g_1 \in Result(s, P) \Rightarrow$$
$$\exists i \in \{1, \ldots, n\} : g_2 \notin Result(s, \langle a_1, \ldots, a_i \rangle)$$

As g_2 is not true at some point on the path defined by P, some action (or some action's effect, in the propositional ADL case) must delete g_2. As an example, reconsider the *Blocksworld-arm* instance described at the beginning of the chapter: there are three blocks A, B, and C which are all on the table initially and shall be stacked so that A is on top of B and B is on top of C, $G = \{(on, A, B), (on, B, C)\}$. We have $(on, B, C) \leq (on, A, B)$ in the sense of Definition 5.1.2: from any state where A is on top of B but B is not on top of C, we must unstack A in order to achieve (on, B, C).

5.1.1 Recognizing Goal Orderings

A precise decision about goal orderings is as hard as planning itself.

Definition 5.1.3. *Let GOAL-ORDER denote the following problem:*

Given a STRIPS or propositional ADL task (A, I, G) with $g_1, g_2 \in G$, does $g_1 \leq g_2$ hold?

Theorem 5.1.1. *Deciding GOAL-ORDER is PSPACE-complete.*

Proof. The hardness proof proceeds for STRIPS (and thereby for propositional ADL) by polynomially reducing the complement of PLANSAT, c.f. Theorem 2.2.1, to GOAL-ORDER. Let (A, I, G) be an arbitrary STRIPS instance. Let g_1, g_2, and p be new propositions. We define the modified action set A' by including the actions

name		(*pre*,	*add*,	*del*)
act$I$	$=$	$(\{g_2, p\},$	$I,$	$\{p\})$
act$G$	$=$	$G,$	$\{g_1\},$	$\emptyset)$

The modified initial state is

$$I' := \{g_2, p\}$$

and the modified goal is

$$G' := G \cup \{g_1, g_2\}$$

In the modified task, $g_1 \leq g_2$ holds if and only if the original task is unsolvable. $g_1 \leq g_2$ holds per Definition 5.1.2 if and only if from all states in $S_{(g_2, \neg g_1)}$ (states where g_2 is true but g_1 has not yet been achieved) any action sequence achieving g_1 must delete g_2. As no action deletes g_2 this means that there is no action sequence achieving g_1. From left to right, the new initial state is in $S_{(g_2, \neg g_1)}$. By construction the non-existence of a sequence achieving g_1 from I' implies the non-existence of a solution for (A, I, G). From right to left, assume (A, I, G) is unsolvable. Assume also we have a state $s \in S_{(g_2, \neg g_1)}$ from which there is a plan P achieving g_1. By construction P must also achieve the original goal G. s is reachable from I', by a sequence P'. Concatenating P' with P, and removing the new actions, yields a plan for (A, I, G) in contradiction.

A non-deterministic algorithm that decides the complement of GOAL-ORDER and that needs only polynomial space is the following. Guess a state s. Test in polynomial space that $s \in S_{(g_2, \neg g_1)}$: this is the case iff $g_2 \in s$, $g_1 \notin I$, and s is reachable from I without adding g_1. Now test whether g_1 can be reached without deleting g_2. This algorithm succeeds if and only if there is no goal ordering $g_1 \leq g_2$. Reachability without adding (deleting) a proposition p can be checked similarly to solvability for ADL: iteratively guess at most 2^n actions, with n being the maximal number of different propositions in the task, failing when p is added (deleted), succeeding when the desired state or fact is reached. It follows that the complement of GOAL-ORDER is in NPSPACE, and hence in PSPACE. Finished with PSPACE = co-PSPACE.

We must approximate goal orderings. In the subsequent discussion, we restrict ourselves to the STRIPS case. The approximation technique we choose to employ will later be extended to propositional ADL. Koehler and Hoffmann [62] describe two goal ordering approximation techniques for STRIPS. The first of these techniques is sufficient: the approximated ordering relations are guaranteed to be goal orderings in the sense of Definition 5.1.2. The second technique is not provably sufficient in general, but works empirically well and has the advantage of being computationally very efficient. We have decided to use the second technique in FF.

The idea behind both techniques is to gather knowledge about $S_{(g_2, \neg g_1)}$ in terms of a set of propositions F (the so-called *false set*) that must be false in any state $s \in S_{(g_2, \neg g_1)}$ (first technique), or of which some approximation method tells us that they are probably false in these states (second technique). We can then order g_1 before g_2 if there does not seem to be a way of achieving g_1 without deleting g_2. Say we already have the set F. The technique we use is the following.

Definition 5.1.4. *Given a STRIPS task (A, I, G) with $g_1, g_2 \in G$, and a set of propositions F. We say that there is an approximative ordering with respect to F between g_1 and g_2, written $g_1 \leq_F g_2$, if for all $a \in A$ with $g_2 \notin del(a)$ and $g_1 \in add(a)$ either*

1. *$pre(a) \cap F \neq \emptyset$, or*
2. *there is $p \in pre(a)$ such that, for all $a' \in A$ with $g_2 \notin del(a')$ and $p \in add(a')$, $pre(a') \cap F \neq \emptyset$ holds.*

We consider g_1 to be ordered before g_2 if all actions that achieve g_1 without deleting g_2 either: have a precondition that is false in the states $S_{(g_2, \neg g_1)}$, according to the underlying set F; or have a precondition for which all achievers that do not delete g_2 have a false precondition in the states $S_{(g_2, \neg g_1)}$, according to F.

Assume the propositions in F are really false in all states $s \in S_{(g_2, \neg g_1)}$. Then any action a that fulfills the first part of Definition 5.1.4 will never become applicable. If the action fulfills the second part of Definition 5.1.4, then there is a precondition $p \in pre(a)$ whose achievers will never become applicable, unless they delete g_2. However, we have no guarantee that the precondition p needs to be achieved at all. The approximation is justified in the following sense.

Theorem 5.1.2. *Given a STRIPS task (A, I, G) with $g_1, g_2 \in G$, and a set of propositions F such that $g_1 \leq_F g_2$ holds. Let $s \in S_{(g_2, \neg g_1)}$ be a state where g_2 has been achieved before g_1. If*

1. *$F \cap s' = \emptyset$ for all $s' \in S_{(g_2, \neg g_1)}$, and*
2. *$pre(a) \cap s = \emptyset$ for all $a \in A$ with $g_2 \notin del(a)$, $g_1 \in add(a)$, and $pre(a) \cap F = \emptyset$,*

then all action sequences achieving g_1 from s contain an action that deletes g_2.

Proof. Assume that there is an action sequence $P = \langle a_1, \ldots, a_n \rangle \in A^*$ that does achieve g_1 from s without deleting g_2: $g_1 \in Result(s, \langle a_1, \ldots, a_n \rangle)$ with $g_2 \notin$

$del(a_i)$ for $1 \leq i \leq n$. Without loss of generality, a_n is the first action in the sequence that achieves g_1. As no action deletes g_2, we have $Result(s, \langle a_1, \ldots, a_i \rangle) \in S_{(g_2, \neg g_1)}$ for $i < n$. By the first prerequisite, $F \cap Result(s, \langle a_1, \ldots, a_i \rangle) = \emptyset$ follows for $i < n$.

With $g_1 \leq_F g_2$ and $g_1 \in add(a_n)$ we have, by Definition 5.1.4, either $pre(a_n) \cap F \neq \emptyset$, or a precondition $p \in pre(a)$ such that all $a' \in A$ with $g_2 \notin del(a')$ and $p \in add(a')$ have $pre(a') \cap F \neq \emptyset$. The former case is a contradiction to applicability of a_n in $Result(s, \langle a_1, \ldots, a_{n-1} \rangle)$ as $F \cap Result(s, \langle a_1, \ldots, a_{n-1} \rangle) = \emptyset$. In the latter case, our second prerequisite tells us that $pre(a_n) \cap s = \emptyset$ and therefore $p \notin s$. So p must be achieved by some action a_i in P. But again this action can not be applicable in $Result(s, \langle a_1, \ldots, a_{i-1} \rangle)$ because a_i adds p and does not delete g_2; so by $g_1 \leq_F g_2$ we have $pre(a_i) \cap F \neq \emptyset$ in contradiction to $F \cap Result(s, \langle a_1, \ldots, a_{i-1} \rangle) = \emptyset$.

If the ordering $g_1 \leq_F g_2$ is based on a set F whose intersection with all $s \in S_{(g_2, \neg g_1)}$ is really empty, and we start out from a state where the preconditions of g_1's appropriate achievers (those that do not delete g_2) are not true, then we are forced to delete g_2 in order to reach g_1. Regarding sufficiency, there thus remain the following questions: how can we compute a set F of propositions that are not true in any state $s \in S_{(g_2, \neg g_1)}$? And how can we guarantee that the preconditions of g_1's appropriate achievers are not true in any state $s \in S_{(g_2, \neg g_1)}$?

As the formulation suggests, both questions basically ask for the same thing: a technique that finds propositions which are never true in a state $s \in S_{(g_2, \neg g_1)}$. A straightforward approach to find such propositions is to exploit the fact that all $s \in S_{(g_2, \neg g_1)}$ contain g_2. Thus, propositions that are inconsistent with g_2 have the desired property. As mentioned earlier, there are several good approximation techniques for inconsistency in the literature [8, 32, 38, 87].

An idea is therefore to compute F using an inconsistency detection mechanism, and, additionally, to postulate that the preconditions of g_1's appropriate achievers are inconsistent with g_2, meaning they got a non-empty intersection with F. Reconsider Definition 5.1.4. With the additional postulation, all the actions a will fulfill the first part of the definition anyway, so the second part can be skipped. This approach is discussed by Koehler and Hoffmann [62], yielding the first technique mentioned above: use Graphplan to find a set of propositions that are inconsistent with g_2 (the propositions that are exclusive of g_2 in the fix point layer of the planning graph), and approximate goal orderings via the first part of Definition 5.1.4. It follows from Theorem 5.1.2 that these approximative orderings are guaranteed to be goal orderings in the sense of Definition 5.1.2.

As said above, we use the second technique discussed by Koehler and Hoffmann [62], approximating goal orderings by Definition 5.1.4 without additional postulations. Concerning the set F, it turns out that one can obtain good results — at least on the benchmarks — without even investing the effort to compute a set of provably inconsistent propositions. The definition we use is as follows.

Definition 5.1.5. *Given a STRIPS task* (A, I, G) *with* $g_1, g_2 \in G$. *The greedy false set to* g_2 *is defined as*

$$F_g := \bigcap_{a \in A,\, g_2 \in add(a)} del(a)$$

We consider as false all propositions that are necessarily deleted when achieving g_2. Of course, these propositions are not necessarily inconsistent with g_2 because it might be possible to re-achieve them without deleting g_2.

Using Definitions 5.1.4 and 5.1.5 does not guarantee that the resulting ordering relations are justified in the sense of Definition 5.1.2. The technique is however still justified in a weaker sense by Theorem 5.1.2, and it yields good results in the benchmark domains: in the STRIPS domains of our collection the goal orderings it derives are exactly the same as those derived by the sufficient technique. The set F_g according to Definition 5.1.5 can be computed by performing a single sweep over the action set. In fact, based upon the connectivity graph as described in Section 3.3.3, the implementation performs a sweep only over the actions that achieve g_2 — the connectivity graph contains pointers from g_2 to all these actions.

Extending the definitions we use to propositional ADL is a trivial matter. Definition 5.1.5 is extended by performing intersection over all effects that can achieve g_2, rather than over all actions. Extending Definition 5.1.4 is likewise done by considering the effects that can achieve g_1: as the preconditions of an effect $e \in E(a)$, consider the union $con(e) \cup pre(a)$ of the effect condition with the precondition of the respective action.

Let us focus on our *Blocksworld-arm* example again, with three blocks A, B, and C that must be stacked so that A is on top of B and B is on top of C. The goal ordering $(on, B, C) \leq_{F_g} (on, A, B)$ is derived as follows. The greedy false set to (on, A, B) is $F_g = \{(holding, A), (clear, B)\}$: the only action that achieves (on, A, B) is stack(A, B). Let us test Definition 5.1.4. The only action that achieves (on, B, C) is stack(B, C). The precondition of this is $\{(holding, B), (clear, C)\}$, which has an empty intersection with F_g. However, all actions that can achieve $(holding, B)$ share the precondition $(clear, B)$ which is contained in F_g. Therefore, the second part of Definition 5.1.4 holds true, and it is correctly concluded that $(on, B, C) \leq (on, A, B)$. On the other hand, $(on, A, B) \leq (on, B, C)$ does not hold because stacking A onto B is not hindered at all by the false set to stack(B, C).

5.1.2 An Agenda-Driven Planning Algorithm

Having dealt with the problem of approximating goal orderings, there is still the question how to utilize these orderings for speeding up the planner. The approach we have integrated in FF is to use a *goal agenda* as proposed by Jana Koehler [61]. This implements a loop around the planner, iteratively invoking the system on a series of tasks with incrementally increasing goal sets, i.e., subsets of the original goal. The subsets and their ordering are based on the set of ordering relations found by approximating goal orderings.[1]

Say we have a (STRIPS or propositional ADL) task (A, I, G). For each pair of goals $(g_1, g_2) \in G \times G$ it is determined by Definitions 5.1.4 and 5.1.5 whether $g_1 \leq_{F_g} g_2$ holds. The resulting information is a directed graph, the *goal graph*, where the nodes are the goals and the edges are those pairs where the ordering approximation succeeded. We want to partition the goal into a *goal agenda*, i.e., into a series of sets (entries) $G_1, \ldots, G_n \subseteq G$ with $\bigcup_{i=1}^{n} G_i = G$ and $G_i \cap G_j = \emptyset$ for $i \neq j$. The goal agenda shall respect all edges in the goal graph. The graph can contain cycles ($g_1 \leq g_2$ does not imply that $g_2 \not\leq g_1$, and apart from that we are using an approximation method) so by respecting the edges in the goal graph we mean the following:

1. goals g_1, g_2 that lie on a cycle in the goal graph belong to the same entry, i.e., $g_1, g_2 \in G_i$;
2. if there is path in the goal graph from g_1 to g_2 but none from g_2 to g_1, then $g_1 \in G_i$ and $g_2 \in G_j$ with $i < j$.

A simple algorithmic method that achieves these properties is the following. First, compute the transitive closure of the goal graph. Then, for each goal $g \in G$, count the number of ingoing edges g_{in} and the number of outgoing edges g_{out}. Move disconnected goals (no ingoing or outgoing edges at all) into a separate set G_{sep}. Set the *degree* of all other goals to $g_{in} - g_{out}$. Merge goals with identical degree into the same entry of the goal agenda, and order the entries by increasing degree. Insert G_{sep} as the last entry of the agenda.

It is clear that the agenda computed by this algorithm does respect the edges of the goal graph: nodes on cycles have the same ingoing and outgoing edges in the transitive closure, and therefore in particular the same degree; if there is a path from g_1 to g_2 but none from g_2 to g_1, then g_1 has more outgoing edges in the transitive closure, and therefore a smaller degree. The agenda is not over-discriminating in the sense that it does not make distinctions where none are imposed by the goal graph — an exception being the set G_{sep} about which the goal graph contains no information at all. It does not theoretically make much difference where we insert G_{sep}. Inserting it at the end seems to make sense considering the way the goal agenda is used for planning.[2]

Once the goal agenda $G_1, \ldots, G_n$ is computed, it is used as follows. First, start the planner on the task (A, I, G_1), i.e., the original initial state but only the first entry of the agenda. Execute the resulting plan in I, yielding a state s_1. Then invoke the planner again, on the task $(A, s_1, G_1 \cup G_2)$. Execute the resulting plan, and so forth. In each iteration i the planner is invoked on the

---

[1] A different idea of how to use an ordering $g_1 \leq g_2$ is to prune, during a forward search, states where g_2 has been achieved before g_1. Such an approach is described by Porteous and Sebastia [84]. We will discuss a stronger technique below in Section 5.2.
[2] Koehler and Hoffmann [62] try to order G_{sep} with respect to the other entries already in the agenda, extending the definition of orderings to *sets* of goals; this does not, however, make much difference in practice (as reflected by the benchmarks).

task $(A, s_{i-1}, G_1 \cup \ldots \cup G_i)$, until the final task is to solve the original goal $G = G_1 \cup \ldots \cup G_n$ starting out from the state s_{n-1} (with G_{sep} as the last entry, we will care about these disconnected goals when we have achieved everything else).

5.1.3 Completeness, and Integration into FF

Obviously, the goal agenda approach is correctness preserving, i.e., if the underlying planner is correct then so will be the planner controlled by the above mechanism. The approach does not preserve optimality.[3] On dead-end free tasks, the goal agenda is completeness preserving, due to the following simple observation.

Proposition 5.1.1. *Given a planning task (A, I, G), and a proposition set $G' \subseteq G$. For a reachable state s, if (A, s, G') is not solvable then s is a dead end.*

Proof. With $G' \subseteq G$ we know that (A, s, G) can not be solvable either.

If one of the subtasks $(A, s_{i-1}, G_1 \cup \ldots \cup G_i)$ is unsolvable then s_{i-1} is a dead end. So in a dead-end free task all subtasks are solvable, and any complete planner will find a plan. If there are dead ends, however, the goal agenda can force a planner to be trapped in one, by forcing an ordering of the goals that is impossible to achieve. An example for that is given in the longer article [62].

As for using the goal agenda in FF, we must decide how exactly to integrate the approach into the search mechanisms. From Chapters 3 and 4, we so far have the following architecture, c.f. Section 4.2.2:

1. Do enforced hill-climbing, using helpful actions pruning, until the goal is reached or the algorithm fails.
2. If enforced hill-climbing fails, solve the task by best-first search.

The first search mechanism performs very well in the benchmarks, but is incomplete in the presence of dead ends (even on dead-end free tasks, due to the pruning technique). The second search mechanism, serving as a safety net, is complete and works empirically well in those cases where the first mechanism fails.

With the goal agenda we have another heuristic technique that preserves completeness only in the absence of dead ends. We have therefore implemented the straightforward idea to use the goal agenda for enforced hill-climbing only — which is not complete anyway — and leave the safety net unchanged. After grounding and pre-compilation, goal orderings are approximated and the goal agenda is derived. Then enforced hill-climbing, using helpful actions pruning, is called on the entries of the goal agenda in the incremental way described above.

---

[3] One might even suspect that calling a planner repeatedly on incremental subgoals can yield highly non-optimal plans. Remember, however, that we have approximated the orderings so that (probably) the earlier goals need not be deleted to achieve the later goals; so a reasonable planning algorithm will not do that unless it is necessary.

If that fails at some point, for whichever reason (a dead end encountered by enforced hill-climbing, important actions pruned by helpful actions, or a dead end forced by the goal agenda), then the complete best-first search phase is invoked on the original task.

In our *Blocksworld-arm* example, we have seen that the only ordering relation derived is $(on, B, C) \leq (on, A, B)$. So the goal agenda there is $G_1 = \{(on, B, C)\}, G_2 = \{(on, A, B)\}$. The first run of enforced hill-climbing only knows about the goal (on, B, C), and is therefore not tempted to stack A onto B first.

5.2 Computing Goal Orderings On-Line

So far we have approached goal orderings by recognizing them as a pre-process, then use the pre-computed information during planning. A different idea is to reason about goal orderings *on-line*, i.e., during (forward) search. The obvious advantage of this is that we got more information available, namely the current search state s and the path on which we reached s from I. The obvious disadvantage is that the reasoning must be done for every single search state and is thus extremely time critical. We will see that in the FF framework we get interesting on-line information for free.

5.2.1 Untimely Goals

Assume we are in a search state s where we have achieved a goal g. The question one can ask is, was it a good idea to achieve g? Or should some other goal be achieved first? Inspired by the definition of goal orderings we have discussed above, we say that achieving g was *untimely* if all plans from s must delete (and re-achieve) g.

Definition 5.2.1. *Given a STRIPS or propositional ADL task (A, I, G), and a reachable state s where some goal $g \in G$ has been achieved, $g \in s$. g is untimely in s if in all plans $P = \langle a_1, \ldots, a_n \rangle$ for (A, s, G) there is an action a_i after the execution of which g is not true, $g \notin Result(s, \langle a_1, \ldots, a_i \rangle)$.*

This definition is stronger than the goal orderings we discussed before (Definition 5.1.2). If there is a goal $g' \in G$ such that $g' \leq g$ holds and g' is not true anywhere on the path to s (and in s itself), then g is untimely — it must be deleted for reaching g'. It can be, however, that there is no such goal g' but g is untimely nevertheless, because achieving the conjunction of the remaining goals can be more difficult than achieving them separately.[4]

In our *Blocksworld-arm* example, stacking A onto B first leads into a state where (on, A, B) is untimely: all plans need to unstack A from B in order to achieve (on, B, C). In general, deciding about untimely goals is PSPACE-complete.

---

[4] As mentioned at the beginning of Section 5.1.2, Porteous and Sebastia [84] use pre-computed orderings to perform the weaker test.

Definition 5.2.2. *Let UNTIMELY-GOAL denote the following problem:*

Given a STRIPS or propositional ADL task (A, I, G), and a reachable state s where some goal $g \in G$ has been achieved, $g \in s$. Is g untimely in s?

Theorem 5.2.1. *Deciding UNTIMELY-GOAL is PSPACE-complete.*

Proof. The hardness proof proceeds by polynomially reducing PLANSAT, c.f. Theorem 2.2.1, to UNTIMELY-GOAL. Let (A, I, G) be an arbitrary STRIPS instance. Let p and g be atomic propositions not contained in the instance so far. We obtain a modified instance by setting $A' := A \cup \{a = (\{p\}, \{g\} \cup I, \{p\})\}$, $I' := \{p\}$, and $G' := G \cup \{g\}$. In the modified instance, g is untimely in $Result(I', \langle a \rangle)$ if and only if there is no solution to the original task: from left to right, if all plans for $(A', \{g\} \cup I, G \cup \{g\})$ delete g then that means that there is no plan — no action deletes g; from right to left, if there is no plan from I to G then there is no plan from $\{g\} \cup I$ to $G \cup \{g\}$.

A non-deterministic algorithm that decides the complement of UNTIMELY-GOAL is this. For a given state s and goal g with $g \in s$ in a propositional ADL task (A, I, G), check whether the goals can be reached from s without deleting g. This can be done by iteratively guessing at most 2^n actions, with n being the maximal number of different propositions in the task, failing when g is deleted, and succeeding when the goals are reached. The algorithm succeeds if and only if g is untimely in s. It follows that the complement of UNTIMELY-GOAL is in NPSPACE, and hence in PSPACE. Finished with PSPACE = co-PSPACE. $\qed$

5.2.2 Approximating Untimely Goals

Again, we must look for approximation techniques. In the STRIPS case, it is trivial to come up with an approximation that is sufficient. For a given state s and goal g with $g \in s$ in a STRIPS task (A, I, G), g is untimely in s if and only if (A_g, s, G) is unsolvable, where A_g are all actions except those that delete g. So the decision about untimely goals can be reduced to a decision about unsolvability. Now, in the context of FF's heuristic function we have already seen a sufficient criterion for unsolvability in STRIPS: by Theorem 3.3.1 Graphplan decides, in polynomial time, solvability of a task when ignoring the delete lists; by contra position to Proposition 3.0.1, unsolvability of a relaxed task implies unsolvability of the real task. So we can start Graphplan, or rather FF's specialized implementation of it, to decide solvability of (A_g^+, s, G). If the task is unsolvable then g is guaranteed to be untimely in s.

The method has two drawbacks. First, it is not clear how to extend it to propositional ADL: while we have the same criterion for unsolvability, we can not say in advance which actions will delete g and which will not. Second, the method involves computing FF's heuristic function two times for each search state where a goal has been achieved — one time to determine whether the goal is untimely in the state, and another time (with different action set, i.e., the original one) to determine the state's heuristic value. One can instead obtain heuristic information in STRIPS and propositional ADL alike simply by having a closer look at the relaxed plan that the heuristic function computes. We first define that technique for STRIPS.

Definition 5.2.3. *Given a STRIPS task (A, I, G), a reachable state s where some goal $g \in G$ has been achieved, $g \in s$, and the plan $\langle A_0, \ldots, A_{m-1} \rangle$ that Graphplan extracts for (A^+, s, G). g is* approximatively untimely *in s if there is an action $a \in A_i$, $0 \leq i < m$ such that $g \in del(a)$.*

We consider a goal g to be untimely in a state s if the relaxed plan for s contains an action a that deletes g. Of course it might be that a has been included per chance, i.e., it might be that there is a relaxed plan for s that does not contain such an action. So the approximation technique is not sufficient. In our experiments on the benchmarks, however, we did not find a single false positive case, a goal being classified untimely though it's not. In the *Blocksworld-arm* example, when s is the state where (on, A, B) is achieved but (on, B, C) is not, then the relaxed plan to s that FF's heuristic extracts is $\langle \{unstack(A, B)\}, \{pickup(B)\}, \{stack(B, C)\} \rangle$. The plan contains the action unstack(A, B) which deletes (on, A, B), so the goal is correctly considered untimely.

Definition 5.2.3 can be extended to propositional ADL simply by requiring that the relaxed plan contains an action with a *selected effect* that deletes g. By selected effect, we mean an effect that was selected to achieve a (sub-) goal during relaxed plan extraction.

5.2.3 Completeness, and Integration into FF

In our implementation, if a state contains an approximatively untimely goal then the state is removed from the search space. This is of course not completeness-preserving in general. Consider the following example. The initial state is empty, the goals are $\{g_1, g_2\}$, and there are the following two actions:

name		(pre,	add,	del)
actg_1	=	$(\emptyset,$	$\{g_1\},$	$\emptyset)$
actg_2	=	$(\{g_1\},$	$\{g_2\},$	$\{g_1\})$

All solutions to this task need to apply actg_1, use actg_2 thereafter, and re-establish g_1. The crucial point here is that g_1 *must* be temporarily destroyed — so though g_1 is untimely in the state s where it is achieved before g_2, it is appropriate to achieve it in this way. FF's relaxed plan for s contains actg_2 so the state is removed. We remark that the example task is dead-end free.

The FF architecture we have so far is this:

1. Use the goal agenda around enforced hill-climbing with helpful actions pruning, until the goal is reached or the algorithm fails.
2. If the algorithm fails, solve the task by best-first search.

As approximating untimely goals is not complete in general, we integrate the technique only into the first part of that search architecture. During enforced hill-climbing, when a state is evaluated it is checked whether the state contains an approximative untimely goal. If so, the state is removed from the search space. If enforced hill-climbing fails — which might be due to the search technique, or helpful actions pruning, or the goal agenda, or approximating untimely goals — then the safety net is invoked.

5.3 Evaluation

We evaluate the two goal ordering techniques (or rather their use within FF) on the example collection used for comparing FF to HSP, c.f. Section 3.8. On each task, we run four planners: FF without goal ordering techniques (−−), FF with goal agenda (G−), FF with approximation of untimely goals (−U), and FF with both techniques (GU). The goal ordering techniques are only used during enforced hill-climbing, and turned off during best-first search if enforced hill-climbing fails. Any run is given 5 minutes runtime and 128 M Byte memory. We show runtime curves for all planners, or, in simple cases, summarize the behavior. In all cases, we summarize the solution length behavior.

For both goal ordering techniques, the overhead is negligible in all our domains: computing the goal agenda is done by a few simple structural checks of the grounded planning task (as described above), and approximating untimely goals is done as a side effect of extracting relaxed plans (when selecting an action or effect, check if it deletes a goal contained in the current state). So we show data only for those domains where the techniques have a non-marginal impact on performance. These domains are *Blocksworld-arm*, *Blocksworld-no-arm*, *Hanoi*, *Miconic-ADL*, *Movie*, *Schedule*, and *Tireworld*.[5] We focus on each domain in turn.

The *Blocksworld-arm* collection contains 55 random tasks, with 7 to 17 blocks, 5 instances per size. The runtime data is shown in (the admittedly hard to read) Figure 5.1. When examining the data in detail, the following can be observed: the planners using the goal agenda are clearly superior to those that are not using it; untimely goals approximation has only a marginal improvement effect when the goal agenda is active; without goal agenda, untimely goals approximation yields significant improvements, though it worsens performance in some cases. To see these observations in Figure 5.1, note that the curves for (G−) and (GU) are generally in the lower part of the figure while those for (−−) and (−U) are generally in the upper part; that the curves for (G−) and (GU) are almost the same, with the latter curve sometimes being somewhat below; that (−U) can solve more instances than (−−), but some instances (of size 16) are only solved by (−−). A bit more precisely, given the data for two planners (A) and (B) we have

---

[5] In *Fridge*, the goal agenda (correctly) constrains the (fridge-on, x) propositions to be achieved last; this has, however, no impact on FF's performance — presumably because FF does not achieve these propositions ahead of time anyway.

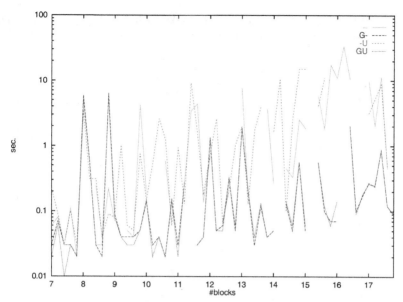

Fig. 5.1. Runtime curves on *Blocksworld-arm* for FF with different goal ordering techniques. Time is shown on a logarithmic scale. If a task could not be solved within the given time and memory then the data point is omitted

measured the following parameter: if a planner can not solve a task then set the runtime to the maximum of 300 seconds; afterwards, compute the ratios of (B)'s runtime divided by (A)'s runtime, and average. In the *Blocksworld-arm* data here, (G−) is on average 1.06 times slower than the fastest planner (GU), (−U) is on average 379.52 times slower than (GU), and (−−) is on average 1374.73 times slower than (GU). Note that there is a lot of variation in the runtimes, so the high average values can stem from a few extreme cases where a task is easy for one planner but unsolvable for another. For example, the maximum ratio for (−−) versus (GU) is 15000.

There are also some interesting observations concerning solution length behavior. As it turns out, (−U) finds the shortest solutions, followed by (G−) and (GU) (which behave roughly the same), while (−−) sometimes returns rather long solutions. We have measured average values of solution length ratios, counting only those tasks that both planners can solve. The results are: the plans found by (GU) are on average 1.15 times longer than those of (−U); the plans of (G−) are on average 1.17 times longer than those of (−U); for (−−), the factor is 1.23. In summary, it seems that in *Blocksworld-arm*, or at least in the randomly generated instances we use here, approximating untimely goals is good for improving FF's runtime performance, though not as good as the goal agenda. On the other hand, the former technique is better at improving solution quality. Combining both techniques behaves very similarly to using only the goal agenda, but is slightly faster and also yields slightly better solutions.

In *Blocksworld-no-arm* (again random tasks with 7 to 17 blocks), the picture we obtain is somewhat different (and in fact more typical). See the runtime curves in Figure 5.2

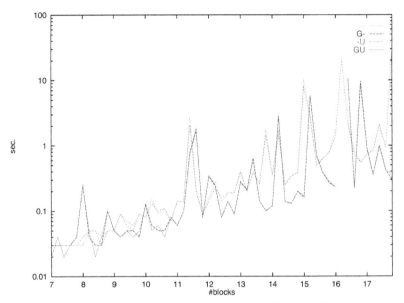

Fig. 5.2. Runtime curves on *Blocksworld-no-arm* for FF with different goal ordering techniques. Time is shown on a logarithmic scale. If a task could not be solved within the given time and memory then the data point is omitted

Again, the planners using the goal agenda have a runtime advantage over those that don't; but this time approximating untimely goals has little effect in either case. Observe that the curves for (GU) and (G−) are very close together, likewise for (−U) and (−−), and that the curves for the former planners are generally below those for the latter. (G−) is on average 1.02 times slower than (GU), and (−−) is on average 1.45 times slower than (−U); on the other hand, (−−) is 17.66 times slower than (GU). Concerning solution quality, we get a different picture: the goal agenda planners are inferior. The plan lengths for (GU) and (G−) are exactly the same, likewise for (−U) and (−−). The plans of the goal agenda planners are on average 1.51 times longer.

For *Hanoi* (3 to 10 discs), we do not show the runtime curves. Each goal ordering technique results in a failure: in *Hanoi* one must repeatedly delete goals along any solution path so approximating untimely goals is inadequate; the goal agenda has an interaction with helpful actions pruning, which excludes important actions when the only goal is to get the bottom disc in place (the first entry of the agenda). So the planners with goal ordering technique(s) solve the tasks by best-first search. This is somewhat slower than enforced hill-climbing, on average 1.31 times. All planners find the optimal solutions.

In *Miconic-ADL*, we look at 60 examples from the AIPS-2000 competition collection, with 8 to 27 passengers to be transported. The results are similar to those for *Blocksworld-no-arm*. See the runtime curves in Figure 5.3.

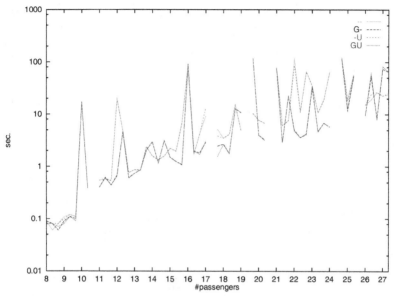

Fig. 5.3. Runtime curves on *Miconic-ADL* for FF with different goal ordering techniques. Time is shown on a logarithmic scale. If a task could not be solved within the given time and memory then the data point is omitted

Again, there is a runtime advantage of goal agenda planners, and approximating untimely goals has only a small effect. Ratio-wise, the data is rather close together: (G−) is on average 1.009 times slower than (GU), (−−) is on average 1.008 times slower than (−U); between the groups, the factor for (−−) versus (GU) is 2.67. Concerning solution quality, the goal agenda planners have exactly the same plan length results, likewise the planners without goal agenda. None of the groups is superior to the other. The average ratio (between non-goal agenda and goal agenda planners) is 1.02.

In *Movie*, where we use the AIPS-1998 collection, the situation is the following. There are no runtime differences worth mentioning — all planners solve these tasks within maximally 0.03 seconds. As for plan length, (−−) solves all the tasks with 8 steps, while the other planners need only 7 steps. To briefly explain this phenomenon: the only mistake one can make in *Movie* is to reset the counter before the tape is rewound. If one resets the counter first then the respective goal is untimely, which is recognized by the approximation. The goal agenda has 3 entries, where the first is to rewind the tape, the second is to reset the counter, and the third is to buy all snacks (this last entry being, in fact, the set of disconnected goals — the only ordering inferred is to rewind the tape before resetting the counter).

In *Schedule*, we use 69 examples from the AIPS-2000 competition collection, with 5 to 49 objects to be processed. The results are similar to those for *Miconic-ADL*. See the runtime curves in Figure 5.4.

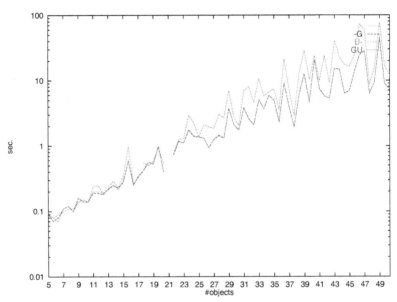

Fig. 5.4. Runtime curves on *Schedule* for FF with different goal ordering techniques. Time is shown on a logarithmic scale. If a task could not be solved within the given time and memory then the data point is omitted

There are again the two groups of planners, with and without goal agenda. The runtime advantage of the goal agenda planners is as follows: (G−) is on average 1.002 times slower than (GU), (−U) versus (−−) is 1.003 on average, and (−−) versus (GU) is 14.73. Concerning solution length, again the goal agenda planners have exactly the same results, likewise for the other group. No group is superior to the other. The average ratio (between non-goal agenda and goal agenda planners) is 0.97.

We finally consider the *Tireworld* domain. Our collection contains the tasks with 1 to 30 wheels to be replaced. Once again, there is a division into groups with respect to using the goal agenda or not. The planners that do not use this technique fail to solve any task with more than 15 tires, solving the 15 tire task in 109.91 (−−) respectively 98.08 (−U) seconds. The other planners easily scale up to 30 wheels, solving the largest task in 13.00 (G−) and 12.68 (GU) seconds. The ratio values are 1.05 for (−−) versus (−U), 1.03 for (G−) versus (GU), and 59.18 for (−−) versus (GU). As for solution length, the goal agenda planners, respectively the non-goal agenda planners, have exactly the same results. The ratio (GU) versus (−−) is 1.12 on average, i.e., using the goal agenda results in somewhat longer plans.

Summing our evaluation up, the most important observations are the following.

— Using the goal agenda often results in improved runtimes; sometimes this is bought at the cost of slightly longer plans.
— Approximating untimely goals has little effect in most of our domains, especially when used in combination with the goal agenda.

One might consider skipping the second technique altogether, and use the goal agenda only. However, in none of our domains does approximating untimely goals do any harm, and it can sometimes help to improve both runtime and solution length performance. So both goal ordering techniques are used in FF.

6. The AIPS-2000 Competition

We close this part of the book with a short chapter showing an evaluation of FF (in its full architecture) that has been compiled in an official setting: the AIPS-2000 planning systems competition. Of course, the competition's focus was not to evaluate FF, but to compare the performance of the planning systems in existence at the time. From our point of view here, the data provides an evaluation of FF against the state-of-the-art in spring 2000.

The competition took place from March to April 2000, organized by Fahiem Bacchus. There were two main tracks, one for fully-automated (i.e., domain-independent) planners, and one for hand-tailored (i.e., domain-dependent) planners. Both tracks were divided into five parts, each one concerned with a different planning domain. The FF system took part in the fully automated track. It demonstrated runtime behavior superior to that of the other domain-independent planners and was therefore entitled "Group A Distinguished Performance Planning System". It also won an award (sponsored by Schindler Lifts Inc.) for the 1st place in the Miconic 10 Elevator domain, ADL track, and a 1st prize (sponsored by Celcorp) for outstanding performance. We briefly present the data collected in the fully automated track. More details about the competition can be found in an article by Fahiem Bacchus [3].

The competition domains where *Logistics*, *Blocksworld-arm*, *Schedule*, *Freecell*, and the *Miconic* variants. We focus on these domains in turn. Let us remark that, while the *Logistics*, *Blocksworld-arm*, and *Miconic* domains were already known at the time when FF was developed, the *Schedule* and *Freecell* domains were first seen in the competition. The planners were run on a 500 MHz Pentium III machine with 1GB main memory (except in *Miconic*, which was run on site at AIPS-2000 using 450 MHz Pentium III machines with 256 MByte main memory). If no solution was found within 30 minutes, the respective planner was declared to have failed on the respective task.

6.1 The *Logistics* Domain

We first look at the *Logistics* domain. The instances were subdivided into two sets, the easy and the harder ones. The planners that did well on all of the easy instances were also run on the harder set. These planners were FF, HSP2 [12, 11], System-R [67], GRT [85, 86], Mips [24, 27], and STAN [34, 35]. Figure 6.1 shows their runtime curves.

J. Hoffmann: Utilizing Problem Structure in Planning, LNAI 2854, pp. 107–112, 2003.
© Springer-Verlag Berlin Heidelberg 2003

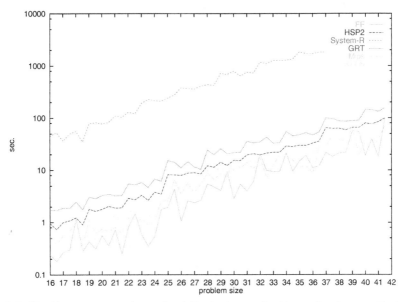

Fig. 6.1. Runtime curves on large *Logistics* instances for those six planners that could scale up to them. Time is shown on a logarithmic scale

System-R does significantly worse than the other planners. The better planners all behave rather similar, FF and Mips tend to be fastest. We remark that the Mips version used in the competition was a hybrid system incorporating among other things an FF implementation [27], which is the mechanism that solved these *Logistics* tasks. Also, the STAN competition version was a hybrid that solved these tasks with a forward heuristic search, the heuristic function being an enhancement of FF's function with automatically extracted domain knowledge [34, 35]. More generally, all of the systems except System-R solved these tasks by heuristic methods which can in one way or the other be seen as descendants of HSP.

None of the shown planners guarantees the returned plans to be optimal. STAN finds the shortest plans on most instances. System-R finds significantly longer plans than the others, ranging from 1.78 to 2.61 times STAN's plan lengths, with an average of 2.24. The lengths of FF's plans are within 0.97 to 1.15 times STAN's plan lengths, with an average of 1.05.

6.2 The *Blocksworld-arm* Domain

Just like the *Logistics* tasks, the competition instances of *Blocksworld-arm* were divided into a set of easier, and of harder ones. Figure 6.2 shows the runtime curves of the planners that scaled to the harder ones.

System-R scales most steadily to the *Blocksworld-arm* tasks used in the competition. In particular, it is the only (fully automated) planner that can solve all

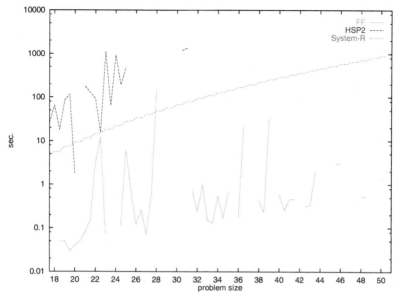

Fig. 6.2. Runtime curves on large *Blocksworld-arm* instances for those three planners that could scale up to them: FF, HSP2, and System-R. Time is shown an a logarithmic scale

of those tasks. HSP2 solves some of the smaller instances, and FF solves about two thirds of the set. If FF succeeds on an instance, then it does so rather fast. For example, FF solves one of the size 50 tasks in 1.27 seconds, where System-R needs 892.31 seconds. None of the three planners finds optimal plans. On the tasks that HSP2 manages to solve, its plans are within 0.97 to 1.77 times System-R's plan lengths, with an average of 1.53. On the tasks that FF manages to solve, its plans are within 0.83 to 1.08 times System-R's plan lengths, average 0.96.

6.3 The *Schedule* Domain

Only a subset of the planners in the competition could handle the kind of conditional effects that are used in *Schedule*. Their runtime curves are shown in Figure 6.3.

Apart from those planners already seen, there are runtime curves for IPP [64], PropPlan, and BDDPlan [50, 97]. FF outperforms the other planners by many orders of magnitude — remember that time is shown on a logarithmic scale. FF's plans tend to be slightly longer than the plans returned by the other planners on the smaller instances. Optimal plans are found by Mips, PropPlan, and BDDPlan. FF's plan lengths are within 1.75 times the optimal lengths, with an average of 1.16. Only HSP sometimes finds longer plans than FF, being in a range from 0.62 to 1.17 times FF's plan lengths, 0.94 on average.

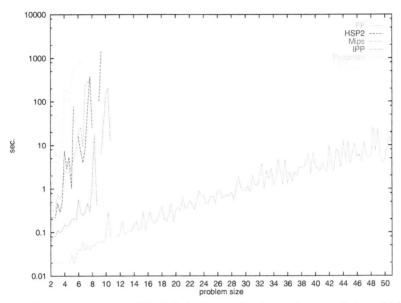

Fig. 6.3. Runtime curves on *Schedule* instances for those planners that could handle conditional effects. Time is shown on a logarithmic scale.

6.4 The *Freecell* Domain

In *Freecell*, as mentioned before, the largest instances in the competition correspond to instances of the real card game that comes with Microsoft windows. Figure 6.4 shows the runtime curves of the four competition participants that scaled best.

From the group of the best-scaling planners, HSP2 is slowest, while STAN is fastest. FF is generally second place, and has a lot of variation in its running times. On the other hand, FF is the only planner that is capable of solving the real-world tasks. It solves four out of five such tasks. We remark that, again, the hybrids Mips and STAN solve these tasks by heuristic search. None of the shown planners guarantees the found plans to be optimal, and none of the shown planners demonstrates superior solution length performance. STAN produces unnecessarily long plans in a few cases. Precisely, on the tasks that both HSP and FF manage to solve, HSP's plan lengths are within a range of 0.74 to 1.26 times FF's plan lengths, average 0.95. On tasks solved by both Mips and FF, plan lengths of Mips are within 0.69 to 1.28 times FF's lengths, average 1.01. For STAN, the range is 0.65 to 3.18, with 1.12 on average.

6.5 The *Miconic* Domain

The final domain used in the competition was the *Miconic* family. As many planners were not capable of handling ADL tasks, the competitors were divided

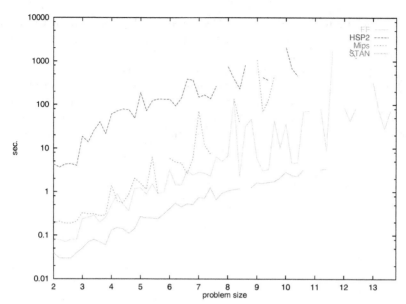

Fig. 6.4. Runtime curves on *Freecell* tasks for those planners that scaled to larger instances. Time is shown on a logarithmic scale

into groups, each group handling only a *Miconic-STRIPS*, *Miconic-SIMPLE*, or *Miconic-ADL* collection. There was also a fourth group handling a domain

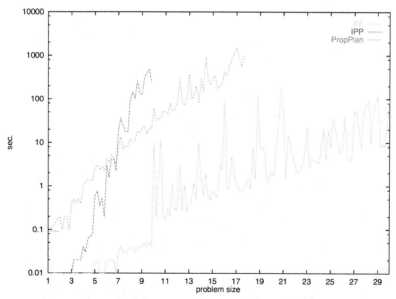

Fig. 6.5. Runtime curves for those planners that participated in *Miconic-ADL*. Time is shown on a logarithmic scale

version where numerical constraints (the number of passengers in the elevator at a time) needed to be considered. Figure 6.5 shows the runtime curves for the participants in the full ADL class.

FF outperforms the two other full ADL planners in terms of runtime. It should be noticed that IPP and PropPlan generate provably optimal plans here, so one needs to be careful when directly comparing those running times. On the other hand, FF's plans are rather close to optimal on these instances, being within in a range of maximally 1.33 times the optimal solution lengths to the instances solved by PropPlan, 1.11 on average.

Part III

Local Search Topology

7. Gathering Insights

We have seen in Part II, specifically in Chapter 3, that most of the planning benchmarks can very efficiently be solved by a rather simple algorithm: the FF base architecture, using an h^+ approximation in a greedy local search strategy, dramatically outperforms all previous approaches across almost all of our domains, c.f. Section 3.7. This opens up the question, *why* does such a simple approach work so well in so many domains? What are the underlying common patterns of structure to these domains? Can we find a characterization of the domains where the approach works well?

We now answer the above questions. We investigate the *local search topology* of the planning benchmarks. A state space with a heuristic function is, intuitively, a mountainous landscape where the heuristic function defines the height of the points in the landscape. A local search algorithm then wanders about the landscape in the search for a lowest point — a solution. The topology of the landscape determines the success of the algorithm. The effects of local search topology on local search performance have been studied in depth in the SAT community [20, 36, 51, 52]. We will see that, in the majority of our benchmark domains, the topology under FF's heuristic function provides an ideal basis for FF's search algorithm.

We start, in this chapter, by gathering insights through closely examining a collection of small example instances. Section 7.1 explains the empirical methodology. Section 7.2 looks at the h^+ function. We identify a number of characteristic topological phenomena, and hypothesize that these observations carry over to *all* instances in the respective domains. Section 7.3 then looks at FF's approximation h^{FF} of h^+, and we examine how the properties of h^+ carry over to h^{FF}. Section 7.4 shows some visualized examples to illustrate the results. Chapter 8 proves, analytically, that the hypotheses regarding the h^+ function do in fact hold true (with one exception). Chapter 9 verifies, empirically, that the properties of h^+ carry over to the approximation h^{FF} (with two exceptions). Throughout the investigation, we focus on solvable instances only. Our objective is to identify the reasons why FF's local search approach is so effective in *solving* many benchmarks, so unsolvable instances are irrelevant to the investigation.

First we need to define what exactly we mean with local search topology, i.e., which phenomena we are interested in. We adapt the definitions given for SAT by Frank et al. [36]. The difference between the SAT framework there and our planning formalism here is the *directedness of state transitions*. In the SAT

J. Hoffmann: Utilizing Problem Structure in Planning, LNAI 2854, pp. 115–134, 2003.
© Springer-Verlag Berlin Heidelberg 2003

search spaces considered by Frank et al., all state transitions can be traversed in both directions. This is in general not the case in planning, where it might be that an action can not be undone, resulting in a single-directed state transition. These directed transitions have an important impact on the topology, enabling for example the existence of dead ends which are not possible in the undirected case. Taking directed edges into consideration, our definitions are slightly more involved than the original ones by Frank et al., but move along the same lines of argumentation.

The base entity in the state space topology are what Frank et al. name *plateaus*. These are regions that are equivalent under reachability aspects, and look the same from the point of view of the heuristic function.

Definition 7.0.1. *Given a solvable task (A, I, G) with state space (S, E), and a completeness-preserving heuristic h. For $l \in \mathbf{N}_0 \cup \{\infty\}$, a plateau P of level l is a maximal subset of S for which the induced subgraph in (S, E) is strongly connected, and $h(s) = l$ for each $s \in P$.*

Remember that a completeness-preserving heuristic is one that returns ∞ only on dead end states, and that both h^+ and h^{FF} are completeness preserving, c.f. Propositions 4.0.1 and 4.0.2. The difference to the undirected case is that we require the states to be *strongly* connected, i.e., that each state is reachable from each other state — with undirected state transitions this is trivially fulfilled by any set of connected states.

Each state s lies on (is member of) exactly one plateau, which we denote by P_s. Following Frank et al. [36], we distinguish between plateaus in terms of the possibilities of leaving them without increasing the heuristic value.

Definition 7.0.2. *Given a solvable task (A, I, G) with state space (S, E), and a completeness-preserving heuristic h. Let $P \subseteq S$ be a plateau. The* border *of the plateau is*

$$B(P) := \bigcup_{s \in P} N(s) \setminus P$$

where $N(s) := \{s' | (s, s') \in E\}$ are the neighbors *of a state s. An* exit *of P is a state $s \in P$ with $s' \in N(s) \cap B(P), h(s') \leq h(s)$. s is an* improving exit *of P, if there is $s' \in N(s) \cap B(P), h(s') < h(s)$.*

Exits are states from which one can leave a plateau without increasing the value of the heuristic function. In the undirected case, all exits are improving: if s' is a neighbor of s but not on the same plateau then $h(s') \neq h(s)$. In the directed case this is not true as it might be that there is no transition from s' back to s.

Based on the behavior with respect to (improving) exits, Frank et al. distinguish between four different classes of plateaus: local minima (no exits at all), benches (at least one exit), contours (all states exits), and global minima (plateaus of minimal level). With our two different kinds of exits, we define the following six classes.

Definition 7.0.3. *Given a solvable task (A, I, G) with state space (S, E), and a completeness-preserving heuristic h.*

1. *A* recognized dead end *is a plateau P of level $h = \infty$.*
2. *A* local minimum *is a plateau P of level $0 < h < \infty$ that has no exits.*
3. *A* plain *is a plateau P of level $0 < h < \infty$ that has at least one exit, but no improving ones.*
4. *A* bench *is a plateau P of level $0 < h < \infty$ that has at least one improving exit, and at least one state that is not an improving exit.*
5. *A* contour *is a plateau P of level $0 < h < \infty$ that consists entirely of improving exits.*
6. *A* global minimum *is a plateau P of level 0.*

Each plateau belongs to exactly one of these classes. In solvable tasks, global minima are exactly the plateaus of level 0. Intuitively, the roles that the different kinds of plateaus play for local search are the following: recognized dead ends can be ignored with a completeness-preserving heuristic function; local minima are difficult for local search because all neighbors look worse so it is not clear in which direction to move next; benches are easier because one can step off them in the direction towards the goal; from contours, one can step off immediately.

It is at first sight not obvious what the role of plains is (if all edges are undirected, they do not exist). We view plains as a kind of entrance to either local minima or benches, depending on whether a bench is reachable from them without increasing the value of the heuristic function. More formally, this reads as follows. A *flat path* is a path where all states on the path have the same heuristic value. For a plateau P, the *flat region* $FR(P)$ from P is the set of all plateaus P' such that there is a flat path from some $s \in P$ to some $s' \in P'$ (if all edges are undirected, then $FR(P) = \{P\}$ holds). We say that a plain P *leads to benches* if there is at least one bench in $FR(P)$; otherwise, P *leads to local minima*. Note that a plain leads to benches if and only if one can, starting from the plain, reach a state with better evaluation without temporarily worsening the heuristic value. If a plateau is a bench or a plain leading to benches then we say that the plateau is *bench-related*. We will also use the concept of flat regions when we measure size and diameter of bench-related plateaus.

The above are our basic definitions of local search topology. We now introduce a few higher level concepts that we will need, and examine some of the relationships — those that are relevant to our investigation — between the different phenomena. We start by remarking that the existence of unrecognized dead ends implies the existence of local minima; this observation will be important for our characterization of different planning domains.

Theorem 7.0.1. *Given a solvable task (A, I, G) with state space (S, E), and a completeness-preserving heuristic h. If there exists an unrecognized dead end $s \in S$ then there exists a local minimum $P \subseteq S$.*

Proof. Let s be an unrecognized dead end, with minimal evaluation $h(s) > 0$. All states s' that are reachable from s are dead ends, and have therefore $h(s') \geq h(s)$.

In particular, $h(s') \geq h(s)$ for $s' \in B(P_s)$. Thus P_s is either a local minimum or a plain. In the first case, we are finished. In the second case, we step on to one adjacent same-level plateau P', and are in the same situation. Iterate. The process will terminate, as each encountered plateau P' is different from any seen before (otherwise, the plateaus would be strongly connected in contradiction), and as the state space is finite.

In general, a local minimum is only "the bottom of a valley". Imagine that the local minimum is surrounded by a number of neighboring plateaus which are benches. It might be that all exits from these benches lead back to the local minimum. In that case, the local minimum as well as the benches are part of the same "valley", and solving the task starting from one of the benches does not appear easier than solving it from the local minimum. The states in a valley are characterized by the property that one must temporarily increase the value of the heuristic function in order to reach the goal.

Definition 7.0.4. *Given a solvable task (A, I, G) with state space (S, E), and a completeness-preserving heuristic h. A state $s \in S$ has a full exit path if there is a path $\langle (s, s_1), \ldots, (s_n, s') \rangle$ from s to a goal state s' such that $h(s_1) \leq h(s)$, and $h(s_{i+1}) \leq h(s_i)$ for $1 \leq i < n$.*

Dead ends obviously do not have full exit paths. Neither do states on local minima: to leave a local minimum one must increase the heuristic value, so in particular there can not be a monotonically decreasing path to a goal state. One state on a plateau P has a full exit path if and only if all states on the plateau do so (the states are strongly connected and have the same heuristic value); in that case we say that P has *full exit paths*. Valleys are defined as follows.

Definition 7.0.5. *Given a solvable task (A, I, G) with state space (S, E), and a completeness-preserving heuristic h. A valley is a maximal set V of plateaus such that no $P \in V$ has full exit paths, no $P \in V$ is a recognized dead end, and for all $P, P' \in V$, P is strongly connected to P'.*

Note that we exclude (like in the definition of our plateau classes) recognized dead ends from valleys. Each plateau is contained in at most one valley. Like for plateaus, we are interested in the region that can be reached on a "flat" path; flat in this context means that the path moves only through (other) valleys. More formally: a *valley path* is a path where no state on the path has a full exit path; for a valley V, the *valley region* $VR(V)$ *from* V is the set of all valleys V' such that there is a valley path from some $P \in V$ to a plateau $P' \in V'$ (in the undirected case, $VR(V) = \{V\}$ holds).

Obviously, each local minimum is contained in a valley, as states on a local minimum do not have full exit paths, see above. The inverse direction holds in the following sense.

Theorem 7.0.2. *Given a solvable task (A, I, G) with state space (S, E), and a completeness-preserving heuristic h. If there exists a valley $V \subseteq 2^S$, then there exists a local minimum $P \in 2^S$.*

Proof. Let V be a valley. Let s be a state reachable from V without increasing the heuristic function, such that $h(s)$ is minimal. We have $h(s) < \infty$ and $h(s) > 0$. Also, $h(s') \geq h(s)$ for $s' \in B(P_s)$. Thus, P_s is either a local minimum, or a plain. In the first case, we are finished. In the second case, we step on to one adjacent same-level plateau P', and are in the same situation. Iterate. The process will terminate, as each encountered plateau P' is different from any seen before (otherwise, the plateaus would be strongly connected in contradiction), and as the state space is finite.

The existence of local minima is thus equivalent to the existence of valleys.[1]

Corollary 7.0.1. *Given a solvable task (A, I, G) with state space (S, E), and a completeness-preserving heuristic h. There exists a valley $V \subseteq 2^S$ if and only if there exists a local minimum $P \in 2^S$.*

Proof. Obvious with Theorem 7.0.2 and the fact that states on local minima do not have full exit paths.

Let us focus on benches. The problem with a bench, respectively a bench-related plateau, is that there are (improving) exits, but it may be difficult to figure out where. We will measure various parameters concerning bench-related plateaus, like size, diameter, and exit percentage. Of particular interest will be the parameter defined below. The *distance* $dist(s, s')$ between any two states $s, s' \in S$ is the usual graph distance: the length of a shortest path from s to s' in (S, E), or ∞ if there is no such path.

Definition 7.0.6. *Given a solvable task (A, I, G) with state space (S, E), and a completeness-preserving heuristic h. Let P be a bench-related plateau. For a state $s \in P$, the* exit distance *of s is*

$$ed(s) := min\{dist(s, s') \mid P_{s'} \in FR(P), s' \text{ is improving exit of } P_{s'}\}$$

The maximal exit distance *of P is $med(P) := max\{ed(s) \mid s \in P\}$. The maximal exit distance of (S, E) is the maximum over $med(P)$ for all bench-related plateaus P, or 0 if there is no such plateau.*

Note that, starting from a state on a bench-related plateau, one can always reach an improving exit on a flat path. Remember that what the maximal exit distance really means is the maximal distance to an *improving* exit. The distance to an improving exit is especially relevant for FF's search algorithm enforced hill-climbing as this algorithm performs repeated breadth first search for better states, so the exit distance determines the search depth. We will elaborate on this in Section 7.2.4. Let us first describe the methodology that we use for gathering insights into the local search topology of our benchmarks.

---

[1] In the undirected case, each valley V contains a local minimum. Let $P \in V$ be a plateau in the valley with minimal level. The states on the border of P are either in the valley, or not. In the former case their heuristic value is, with undirectedness, different from the level of P, i.e., greater. The heuristic value of a border state not in the valley is greater than the level of P as otherwise P would have full exit paths.

7.1 Methodology

Our methodology is the following.

1. Randomly generate collections of small example instances in our 20 domains.
2. Explicitly build the state spaces of all these examples, and compute h^+ respectively h^{FF} to all states.
3. Measure parameters of the resulting search space topologies, and summarize the results per domain.

As for the first point, the instances had to be small to make it possible to build the entire state space and to make it possible to do the NP-hard computation of h^+ for each single state. We have generated, following the randomization strategies described in Appendix B, at least 100 sufficiently small solvable random instances in each of our 20 domains, except six domains where this was not possible or necessary. These six domains are *Fridge*, *Gripper*, *Hanoi*, *Movie*, *Simple-Tsp*, and *Tireworld* — those domains in our collection where there is no random element and therefore only a single instance of each size. Of the smallest instances in these domains, in *Fridge* 12 (1 fridge and 1 to 9 screws, 2 fridges and 1 to 3 screws) were sufficiently small, in *Gripper* 7 (1 to 7 balls) were sufficiently small, in *Hanoi* 5 (3 to 7 discs) were sufficiently small, in *Simple-Tsp* 8 (2 to 9 locations) were sufficiently small, and in *Tireworld* only the single smallest instance (one wheel to be replaced) was sufficiently small. In *Movie* we have used the original AIPS-1998 collection as these 30 tasks were all small enough (remember that all *Movie* tasks do in fact share the same set of reachable states, c.f. Section 2.3.3). Let us briefly describe the collections in the other domains. Our terminology refers to the respective domain or generator parameters described in Appendix B. In both *Blocksworld* domains, we used 150 random instances with 2 to 5 blocks. In *Briefcaseworld*, there were 115 instances with 2 to 4 locations and 1 to 3 portables. In *Ferry*, there were 120 instances with 2 to 4 locations and 1 to 4 cars. In *Grid*, our 139 instances all used a 3×2 grid with a varying number of keys and locks, in sum between 2 and 6. In *Logistics*, we had 101 instances with 2 to 3 cities (all size 2), 1 airplane, and 1 to 2 objects. In *Miconic-SIMPLE* there were 113 instances with 1 to 4 passengers and 2 to 6 floors, in *Miconic-STRIPS* we had 101 instances with 1 to 4 passengers and 2 to 5 floors. In *Mprime*, we had 107 instances with 1 to 3 objects to be transported between 4 to 5 locations, each instance featuring 1 vehicle and a maximum space- or fuel-amount of 2; in *Mystery*, it were 112 instances with 1 to 3 objects and 4 to 6 locations, with 1 vehicle and a maximum space- or fuel-amount of 2. Our *Schedule* collection consisted of 191 instances with 1 to 2 parts and maximally 2 additional shapes, each instance featuring 1 color, 1 width, and 1 orientation. In *Freecell* and *Miconic-ADL* the instances had to be particularly small to make the computation of h^+ possible. Note in the following that, while the domain parameter values might not seem exceptionally small in comparison to what is described above, due to the specific semantics of the domains these values result in instances with very few reachable states (less than 200 in all our examples). The *Freecell* collection comprised 110 instances with each 2 suits of cards, 2 to 3 (non-home) cards per suit, 1 free cell, and 2 columns. In *Miconic-ADL* we had 107 instances with 1 to 4 passengers and 1 to 4 floors. For the other parameters (the ones that control the additional constraints) we used the default values (the same that were used for the AIPS-2000 competition collection, which was produced with the same generator, c.f. Section 2.3.1). Let us finally describe our *Assembly* collection. The generation parameters will be of interest when we analytically focus on *Assembly* in Section 8.5. We generated 135 instances with a *part-of* tree depth of 2, maximal number of sons 2 to 3, sons probability 70 to 90, and one resource (i.e., machine). In the AIPS-1998 competition collection, resource requirements and in particular constraints concerning transient parts as well as assemble and remove orders are very sparse. In coarse imitation of this, we set the probability of resource requirements to 25%, and those of transient part relations, assemble order relations, and remove order relations to 15%, 20% and 10%, respectively.

There is a technical subtlety as to what kind of pre-processing is done in the ADL case. The h^+ function is only defined for negation-free ADL (as the relaxation only makes sense if there are no negations), and the h^{FF} function is only defined for propositional ADL (as our implementation works on that language). When we built the state spaces, we used the standard FF pre-processing so what we built were the state spaces of the propositional compilations of the examples. By Proposition 3.1.6 and the fact that in none of our domains there are disjunctive goals, the results for h^+ are exactly the same as they would be for the negation-free compilation. The h^{FF} values were computed as usual. For h^+, we used a complete iterative deepening search algorithm, exploiting some simple symmetry properties that occur in relaxed planning tasks. We do not describe the symmetries and their exploitation as these techniques are not relevant for the rest of the investigation.

Measuring topological parameters in state space graphs with heuristic evaluation involves implementation work, but is conceptually trivial. Appropriately summarizing the results across a domain is more tricky. We have chosen the following method. Take the number of constants in an instance as the size parameter. Then group instances in a domain are then together according to their size, and average the topological parameters over the instances within a group. In the tables we show here, there are five groups in each domain. With min being the minimal size of any instance in the collection, and max being the maximal size, define five intervals $I_0, \ldots, I_4$ as $I_i := [min + i * \frac{max - min}{5}, min + (i+1) * \frac{max - min}{5}]$. Group together those instances whose size falls into the same interval (if the size of a task is exactly on the border between I_i and I_{i+1} then put the task into the group for I_i).

7.2 The Topology of h^+

We focus on topological phenomena concerning dead ends, local minima, and benches in turn. We summarize the results in a planning domain taxonomy which divides our domains with respect to the complexity that their state spaces (seem to) exhibit under h^+. We identify the consequences for the runtime behavior of FF's search algorithm.

7.2.1 Dead Ends

The first question to be answered with respect to dead ends is, of course, how many are there? And how many of them are recognized? We define the *relevant part* of the state space as $S^{N_0} := \{s \in S \mid h(s) < \infty\}$ — these are the states that might be considered by our search algorithm. Figure 7.1 summarizes the percentage of states in the relevant part for those domains where the relevant part is not the entire state space.

Domain	I_0	I_1	I_2	I_3	I_4
Assembly	100.0	99.8	99.5	99.0	99.9
Freecell	100.0			98.6	97.7
Miconic-ADL	100.0		88.5	90.9	84.7
Mprime	68.1	56.1	36.6	30.7	43.3
Mystery	52.7	36.3	28.8	21.4	14.1
Schedule	55.1	63.7	67.7	97.7	97.0

Fig. 7.1. Percentage of states with h^+ value less than infinity in the state space, i.e., relevant part percentage. Mean values for increasing number of constants in different domains

Only in six of our domains are there recognized dead ends. Note that, given the way we summarize our results, it does not make much sense to make inter-domain comparisons within the same column — apart from the semantical differences between domains, the intervals $I_0, \ldots, I_4$ are different for each domain. If a table entry is empty, this means that the respective group of instances of the respective domain is empty — there is no instance whose size falls into that interval. The sequence of table entries for each single domain can give an impression of how the values develop within the domain when size, i.e., number of constants, increases. In Figure 7.1, we see that there are particularly many recognized dead ends (few relevant states) in *Mprime* and *Mystery*. Also, in these domains, particularly *Mystery*, there is a tendency that the percentage of dead ends increases with instance size in our example collection.

Let us focus on *unrecognized* dead ends. We measure their percentage, not in the entire state space but in the relevant part of the state space. This parameter captures better the risk of getting trapped in an unrecognized dead end — after all, the non-relevant states will be ignored anyway. As it turns out, the domains with unrecognized dead ends are a subset of the domains with recognized dead ends (which is no generally true implication). See the data in Figure 7.2.

In the domains not shown in Figure 7.2, we did not find any unrecognized dead ends. There are particularly many unrecognized dead ends in our collections from the *Mprime* and *Mystery* domains, with a slight tendency to increase with instance size. In our collections from the *Freecell* and *Miconic-ADL* domains,

Domain	I_0	I_1	I_2	I_3	I_4
Freecell	0.0			0.4	2.8
Miconic-ADL	0.0		0.0	5.9	6.9
Mprime	13.3	37.9	55.5	41.5	58.8
Mystery	15.7	32.1	48.9	58.6	36.6

Fig. 7.2. Percentage of unrecognized dead ends in the relevant part of the state space under h^+. Mean values for increasing number of constants in different domains

there are only a few unrecognized dead ends, again with a tendency of growth with size.

Let us remark at this point that our measurements depend, of course, on the particular instances we used in the experiment. So the results must be interpreted with care. For example, as described above, in *Freecell* and *Miconic-ADL* the instances had to be extremely small in order to make the computation of h^+ possible. So the low percentage of unrecognized dead ends there is probably due to the size of the instances. Generally, the data allows us to draw existential conclusions like "there are unrecognized dead ends in the *Freecell*, *Miconic-ADL*, *Mprime*, and *Mystery* domains" but not universal conclusions like "there are only few unrecognized dead ends in the *Freecell* and *Miconic-ADL* domains".

We formulate our universal conclusions as hypotheses. Our first hypothesis concerns the dead end class of our domains. A domain belongs to dead end class i if all of its instances belong to a class $j \leq i$, and at least one instance belongs to class i, c.f. the definition of dead end classes in Definition 4.1.3. We have seen that only in four of our domains there are unrecognized dead ends, and that only in two more domains there are recognized dead ends. In many of the remaining domains, all of our instances are undirected. We hypothesize that each of our domains belongs to exactly the dead end class that our example collection suggests.

Hypothesis 7.2.1. *The state space to the propositional or negation free compilation of any solvable planning task (A, I, G) belonging to the*

1. *Blocksworld-arm, Blocksworld-no-arm, Briefcaseworld, Ferry, Fridge, Gripper, Hanoi, or Logistics domains is undirected,*
2. *Grid, Miconic-SIMPLE, Miconic-STRIPS, Movie, Simple-Tsp, or Tireworld domains is at most harmless,*
3. *Assembly or Schedule domains is at most recognized under evaluation with h^+.*

Remember that we obtain the results by looking at the propositional compilations of our examples, and that these results are by Proposition 3.1.6 exactly the same as they would be for the negation free compilations. By "at most" harmless (recognized), we mean that the task is either undirected or harmless (either undirected or harmless or recognized).

For the *Freecell*, *Miconic-ADL*, *Mprime*, and *Mystery* domains, we know for sure that unrecognized dead ends exist, so we know that their dead end class is 4.

For the *Blocksworld-arm*, *Blocksworld-no-arm*, *Ferry*, *Gripper*, *Hanoi*, and *Logistics* domains, Corollary 4.1.1 already tells us that all instances are undirected so there the hypothesis is right. For the *Movie*, *Simple-Tsp*, and *Tireworld* domains, Corollary 4.1.2 states that the instances are indeed harmless. In Chapter 8, we will focus on proving the rest of the hypothesis. Now, we gather data concerning the behavior of local minima in our example collections.

7.2.2 Local Minima

We measure parameters regarding the more general concept of valleys. Corollary 7.0.1 tells us that the existence of these is equivalent to the existence of local minima. Figure 7.3 summarizes the percentage of states on valleys in the relevant part of the state space for those of our domains where the percentage is non-zero.

Domain	I_0	I_1	I_2	I_3	I_4
Blocksworld-arm	0.0	21.0		31.1	47.5
Freecell	0.0			0.4	2.8
Miconic-ADL	0.0		0.0	5.9	6.9
Mprime	13.3	38.3	56.2	42.2	65.9
Mystery	15.7	32.6	49.6	60.9	37.0
Schedule	24.8	32.6	33.1	24.3	19.9

Fig. 7.3. Percentage of states on valleys in the relevant part of the state space under h^+. Mean values for increasing number of constants in different domains

There is a (more or less strong) tendency of growth with size in all domains pictured in Figure 7.3 except *Schedule*. In *Freecell* and *Miconic-ADL* the values are, like for unrecognized dead ends, rather low, which again is probably due to the size of our example instances. Remember that dead ends have no full exit paths, so unrecognized dead ends are valley states, and the values in Figure 7.3 are at least as high as those in Figure 7.2.

The most intriguing observation with respect to valleys is that in 14 out of our 20 domains there are none at all in our example collection. This leads us to our second hypothesis, conjecturing a most remarkable property of the majority of our benchmark domains under h^+.

Hypothesis 7.2.2. *Let* (A, I, G) *be the propositional or negation free compilation of a solvable planning task belonging to any of the Assembly, Blocksworld-no-arm, Briefcaseworld, Ferry, Fridge, Grid, Gripper, Hanoi, Logistics, Miconic-SIMPLE, Miconic-STRIPS, Movie, Simple-Tsp, or Tireworld domains. Then, the state space to* (A, I, G) *does not contain any local minima under evaluation with* h^+.

For those domains where there are valleys in our example collection, it is also interesting to see how large they are. For each instance, we measure the maximal size (number of states) of any valley region and the maximal diameter (highest finite distance between any two states) of any valley region. See the data in Figure 7.4.

Domain	I_0	I_1	I_2	I_3	I_4
Blocksworld-arm	0.0	7.0		33.4	315.0
Freecell	0.0			4.0	2.8
Miconic-ADL	0.0		0.0	7.8	8.5
Mprime	6.5	42.0	75.3	45.0	226.0
Mystery	6.5	8.1	34.1	88.4	4.3
Schedule	134.8	174.5	447.6	174.0	341.1
Blocksworld-arm	0.0	6.0		13.3	26.4
Freecell	0.0			3.0	1.8
Miconic-ADL	0.0		0.0	3.0	3.2
Mprime	2.1	5.0	6.1	4.3	8.0
Mystery	2.0	3.3	5.2	7.4	2.3
Schedule	7.6	8.4	11.6	11.5	12.6

Fig. 7.4. Maximal size (upper part) and diameter (lower part) of valley regions under h^+. Mean values for increasing number of constants in different domains

Once again, the values are particularly low in *Freecell* and *Miconic-ADL*. In all domains, there is a more or less strong tendency of growth in size. The values are particularly high in the *Blocksworld-arm* and *Schedule* domains. For *Blocksworld-arm*, we would have expected this — after all, this is one of the domains where FF (at least in the base architecture) does not work particularly well; in *Schedule*, however, FF works well. We observe the following. Although the size of the valleys in *Schedule* is greater than the size of those in *Blocksworld-arm*, their diameter is smaller. So it seems that it is easier to get out of the valleys in *Schedule*. To corroborate this, we have also measured the maximal distance to a state with better evaluation in our state spaces. For *Blocksworld-arm*, the average results in the five groups are $2.0, 4.5$, (empty) $, 6.8, 10.2$; for *Schedule*, the results are $2.7, 3.8, 4.3, 3.9, 3.6$. So though the valleys in *Schedule* seem to grow in diameter, from every point on them it is quite easy to get off: the next state with a better evaluation is always only few steps away. Remember that these observations are bound to the examples used in our experiment, so the above can serve as an intuition but not as a general explanation (whether the observation holds in general is an open question, see also Chapter 10).

7.2.3 Benches

We now focus on benches, or rather bench-related plateaus. To get started, let us examine how many states on such plateaus there are in our example collections, and how many states lie on plateaus of other kinds. We have measured the percentage of states on bench-related plateaus, on bench-related plateaus that are not part of a valley, on contours, on contours that are not part of a valley, and on global minima. We only show the data for the second criterion here, which is enough to get an impression of the results. Have a look at Figure 7.5.

Let us say some words on the data in Figure 7.5, and how they relate to our other measurements. First, one can identify a number of domains where there

Domain	I_0	I_1	I_2	I_3	I_4
Assembly	0.0	1.1	4.2	6.1	7.9
Blocksworld-arm	40.0	45.1		51.7	46.9
Blocksworld-no-arm	0.0	39.5		50.9	67.5
Briefcaseworld	0.0		37.7		28.7
Ferry	33.3	56.0	64.2	71.5	77.0
Freecell	0.0			2.1	0.5
Fridge	84.4	95.5	89.2	95.9	97.9
Grid	47.0	58.3			45.1
Gripper	23.2	29.5	39.8	48.6	57.8
Hanoi	88.9	96.3	98.8	99.6	99.9
Logistics	38.1	38.5	39.5		35.8
Miconic-ADL	33.3		24.9	35.5	34.9
Miconic-SIMPLE	33.3	31.1	30.3	31.0	33.5
Miconic-STRIPS	25.0	22.0	34.0	28.7	30.7
Movie	0.8	0.8	0.8	0.8	0.8
Mprime	11.5	7.1	3.6	2.0	2.3
Mystery	5.1	6.2	3.6	1.2	8.3
Schedule	11.1	13.5	10.1	14.5	16.8
Simple-Tsp	0.0	0.0	0.0	0.0	0.0
Tireworld	95.7				

Fig. 7.5. Percentage, under h^+, of states on bench-related plateaus that are not part of a valley. Mean values for increasing number of constants in different domains

are almost no benches. In *Assembly*, half of the relevant states lie on contours while the other half are goal states. In *Freecell*, more than 90% of the states lie on contours, in *Movie* the percentage is constantly 98.4%. In *Mprime* and *Mystery*, the states that are not on valleys are almost all on contours, a similar picture can be observed in *Schedule*. In *Simple-Tsp*, finally, the entire state spaces consist of contours and global minima. Next, there are some domains where almost all states lie on benches, with a growth in instance size: *Fridge*, *Hanoi*, and to some extent also *Blocksworld-no-arm*, *Ferry*, and *Tireworld* (remember that only a single instance of *Tireworld* was small enough for our investigation). In *Blocksworld-arm*, almost all states lie either on valleys or on benches. In the remaining domains, *Briefcaseworld*, *Grid*, *Gripper*, *Logistics*, and all *Miconic* variants, around 30% to 60% of the states lie on benches while most of the others lie on contours.

The difficulty, for local search, of escaping a bench is the difficulty of finding an improving exit. How difficult this is depends on a variety of parameters: the size of the bench, its diameter, the percentage of exits. We have measured all these parameters, i.e., for the flat regions from bench-related plateaus, the maximal size (number of states), maximal diameter (maximal finite distance between states), and minimal exit percentage (percentage of improving exits on the flat region). In both *Gripper* and *Movie*, the maximal size is constantly 2, the maximal diameter is constantly 1, and the minimal exit percentage is constantly 50%. In all other domains, the size and diameter values have a (more or less strong) tendency to increase with instance size, while the exit percentage values have a tendency to decrease. The size values are particularly high for the *Hanoi*, *Fridge*, *Blocksworld-arm*, and *Blocksworld-no-arm* domains, precisely 1458.0, 597.3, 131.3, respectively 111.1 on average in the group of largest instances. In the same four domains, the diameter values are particularly high, namely 127.0, 10.3, 25.8, respectively 9.9 on average in the largest group. As for the exit percentage values, they go down to 1% in *Hanoi* and *Fridge*, are around 10% in *Blocksworld-arm*, *Mprime*, and *Tireworld*, and range between 20% and 60% in the remaining domains.

By far the most interesting results were obtained for the maximal exit distance as introduced in Definition 7.0.6: the distance to an improving exit, maximized over all states on bench-related plateaus. We will see in the next section that this parameter is especially relevant for FF's search algorithm. See the data in Figure 7.6.

Domain	I_0	I_1	I_2	I_3	I_4
Assembly	0.0	1.7	1.9	2.0	2.3
Blocksworld-arm	1.0	3.0		3.5	4.9
Blocksworld-no-arm	0.0	1.0		1.5	2.4
Briefcaseworld	0.0		2.2		2.2
Ferry	1.0	1.0	1.0	1.0	1.0
Freecell	0.0			1.3	1.2
Fridge	2.5	4.5	4.0	6.0	7.7
Grid	3.0	3.4			3.3
Gripper	1.0	1.0	1.0	1.0	1.0
Hanoi	3.0	7.0	15.0	31.0	63.0
Logistics	1.0	1.0	1.0		1.0
Miconic-ADL	1.0		1.0	1.1	1.5
Miconic-SIMPLE	1.0	1.0	1.0	1.0	1.0
Miconic-STRIPS	1.0	1.0	1.0	1.0	1.0
Movie	1.0	1.0	1.0	1.0	1.0
Mprime	2.5	2.4	2.0	2.0	4.0
Mystery	1.2	1.7	1.3	1.5	2.3
Schedule	1.0	1.3	1.6	1.0	1.0
Simple-Tsp	0.0	0.0	0.0	0.0	0.0
Tireworld	6.0				

Fig. 7.6. Maximal exit distance under h^+. Mean values for increasing number of constants in different domains

There are seven domains, *Ferry*, *Gripper*, *Logistics*, *Miconic-SIMPLE*, *Miconic-STRIPS*, *Movie*, and *Simple-Tsp*, where the mean maximal exit distance is *constant* across our five groups of instances. In most of the other domains, there is a tendency of growth in instance size, exceptions being *Grid* and *Schedule*, where values first seem to grow slightly but then fall again, and *Tireworld*, where we have only a single instance. We hypothesize that, in the seven domains with constant mean values, there is a constant upper bound on the maximal exit distance across the whole domain.

Hypothesis 7.2.3. *To any of the Ferry, Gripper, Logistics, Miconic-SIMPLE, Miconic-STRIPS, Movie, or Simple-Tsp domains, there is a constant $c \in \mathbf{N}_0$, such that, for the propositional or negation free compilation (A, I, G) of any instance of the domain, the maximal exit distance in the state space to (A, I, G) is at most c under evaluation with h^+.*

7.2.4 A Planning Domain Taxonomy

Our most interesting observations are the following. In 16 of our domains all of our example instances are either undirected or harmless or recognized. In 14 of our domains there are no valleys respectively local minima at all. In 7 of our domains the maximal exit distance is constant across instance size. We have hypothesized that these observations carry over to *all* instances in the respective domains. The hypotheses can be viewed as dividing our domains into a taxonomy of different classes, different with respect to the complexity that their state spaces (seem to) exhibit under h^+. See Figure 7.7.

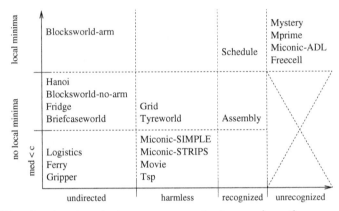

Fig. 7.7. The planning domain taxonomy, overviewing our hypotheses

The taxonomy, as we draw it in Figure 7.7, has two dimensions: the x-axis, corresponding to the four dead end classes, and the y-axis, corresponding to the existence or non-existence of local minima, and to the existence or non-existence of a constant upper bound on the maximal exit distance. The bottom right corner is crossed out because no domain can belong to the respective class: by Theorem 7.0.1, the existence of unrecognized dead ends implies the existence of local minima. Arranging the maximal exit distance property together with local minima on the y-axis is not generally justified. From our 20 domains, those where we hypothesize a constant upper bound on the maximal exit distance are a subset of those were we hypothesize the non-existence of local minima. In general, however, there can be such a constant upper bound in spite of the presence of local minima (imagine, for example, a domain with finitely many instances). Arranging the two properties on the same axis makes the taxonomy readable. Also, from the point of view of local search, if there are local minima then a bounded maximal exit distance is not generally of much use, as the exits might lead into nothing but a local minimum. In contrast, we will see below that without local minima a bounded maximal exit distance implies polynomiality of FF's search algorithm.

The intuition behind Figure 7.7 is that, from the point of view of a local search that approximates h^+, the "simple" domains are in the left bottom corner, while the "demanding" domains are in the top right corner. Now, FF's base search paradigm is a local search scheme with a heuristic function that approximates h^+. The runtime results of the FF base architecture coincide quite well with the picture in Figure 7.7. For example, the *Gripper* and *Logistics* domains constitute much less of a problem to FF than the *Mprime* and *Mystery* domains do. In fact, it is easy to see that FF's search algorithm is polynomial when given a heuristic function of the quality that corresponds to the left bottom side of our taxonomy.

Lemma 7.2.1. *Given a solvable task (A, I, G). Let h be a completeness-preserving heuristic function such that there are no local minima in the state space under h, and the maximal exit distance is $c \in \mathbf{N}_0$. Then, started on (A, I, G), enforced hill-climbing will find a goal state after considering at most $h(I) * (b^{c+1} + c)$ states, where b is the number of actions with different effects.*

Proof. By contra-position to Theorem 7.0.1, the non-existence of local minima implies the non-existence of unrecognized dead ends. By Theorem 4.0.1, enforced hill-climbing does therefore find a goal state to (A, I, G). Each iteration of enforced hill-climbing performs breadth first search for a state with better evaluation, starting at the initial state. As each iteration improves the heuristic value by at least one, after at most $h(I)$ iterations a goal state is reached. Without local minima, the entire relevant state space consists of bench-related plateaus, contours, and goal states. So from any non-goal point in the state space, a state with better evaluation has maximal distance $c + 1$: the distance to the nearest improving exit plus one step to find out that the state is in fact an improving exit. $c + 1$ is thus an upper bound on the depth that any breadth first search iteration encounters. The branching factor during breadth first search is bounded by the number b of actions with different effects. If $b = 1$ then the cost of reaching the exit is $c + 1$.

Lemma 7.2.1 gives us an upper bound on the number of states that are evaluated by enforced hill-climbing before it finds a goal state. The upper bound depends on $h(I)$, the number b of actions with different effects, and the maximal exit distance c. If, within a fixed domain without local minima, the first two values are polynomial and the third value is constant, then the number of evaluated states is polynomial. As there are always only polynomially many actions in an optimal relaxed plan, enforced hill-climbing, given h^+, has therefore the following property.

Theorem 7.2.1. *Given a fixed domain $\mathcal{D}$ such that, with $c \in \mathbf{N}_0$, in the propositional compilation of all instances of $\mathcal{D}$ there are no local minima in the state space under h^+ and the maximal exit distance is at most c. Let (C, I, G) be a solvable instance of $\mathcal{D}$. Then enforced hill-climbing, given h^+, solves the propositional compilation of the task to (C, I, G) after a number of state evaluations polynomial in $|C|$.*

Proof. For a fixed domain the number of actions, and the number of their effects, is polynomial in $|C|$ for STRIPS, c.f. Proposition 3.1.1. In the propositional compilation, the number of actions with different effects is polynomial in $|C|$, and the number of (conditional) effects with different add and delete lists is polynomial in $|C|$ for each action, c.f. Proposition 3.1.5. So in both cases the number of actions with different effects, and the total number of effects with different add and delete lists, is polynomial in $|C|$.

In a relaxed plan, where no facts are ever made false, each add list needs to become true at most once. As the total number of (effects with) different add lists is polynomial in $|C|$, the number of action applications in an optimal relaxed plan, and thus $h^+(I)$, is therefore polynomial in $|C|$.

We got no local minima, a constant upper bound on the maximal exit distance, and a number of actions with different effects that is polynomial in $|C|$. Finished with Lemma 7.2.1.

We remark that the argumentation in Theorem 7.2.1 also holds for negation free compilations: the only difference is that there, the total numbers of actions and their effects are polynomial in $|C|$, c.f. Proposition 3.1.4, not only the total numbers of *different* actions and *different* effects. The argumentation also remains valid when not h^+ but h^{FF} is the heuristic function in question.

Theorem 7.2.2. *Given a fixed domain $\mathcal{D}$ such that, with $c \in \mathbf{N}_0$, in the propositional compilation of all instances of $\mathcal{D}$ there are no local minima in the state space under h^{FF} and the maximal exit distance is at most c. Let (C, I, G) be a solvable instance of $\mathcal{D}$. Then enforced hill-climbing, given h^{FF}, solves the propositional compilation of the task to (C, I, G) after a number of state evaluations polynomial in $|C|$.*

Proof. Given the argumentation in the proof of Theorem 7.2.1, it suffices to show that h^{FF} always takes on values that are polynomial in $|C|$. This holds because the number of actions in Graphplan's respectively IPP's relaxed plans is polynomial in the number of (effects with) different add lists: even if not using the NOOPs-first strategy, c.f. Proposition 3.3.3, each effect (respectively the corresponding action) can be selected at most once at each graph layer, and the number of relaxed graph layers is bounded by the number of (effects with) different add lists.

For a brief summary, what we have seen so far is that FF's search algorithm is polynomial given a heuristic function with certain topological properties, and that there is a number of domains where h^+ seems to have these properties. This leaves us with the questions, does h^+ really have these properties, i.e., are our hypotheses true? And, as computing h^+ is NP-hard, in what sense do the properties of h^+ carry over to the approximation h^{FF}? We will deal with the first question in Chapter 8, and treat the second question in detail in Chapter 9. For now, we have a look at the topology of our example collection under evaluation with h^{FF}.

7.3 The Topology of h^{FF}

The behavior of h^{FF} with respect to dead ends is the same as the behavior of h^+: by Proposition 4.0.2, both functions have the value ∞ in exactly the same cases. In the following, we have a quick look at h^{FF}'s behavior with respect to local minima and benches in our example collection.

7.3.1 Local Minima

We first see how many states lie on valleys. The data is given in Figure 7.8.

Domain	I_0	I_1	I_2	I_3	I_4
Assembly	0.0	0.0	0.0	0.0	0.2
Blocksworld-arm	0.0	21.0		31.1	47.5
Briefcaseworld	0.0		0.3		0.9
Freecell	0.0			0.9	2.8
Grid	2.6	4.2			3.1
Hanoi	0.0	0.0	0.0	33.2	77.7
Miconic-ADL	0.0		0.2	6.5	8.7
Miconic-SIMPLE	0.0	0.3	2.9	0.6	0.4
Mprime	13.3	38.4	56.1	42.2	65.9
Mystery	15.7	32.5	49.4	60.5	37.0
Schedule	24.2	32.2	32.3	24.3	18.8

Fig. 7.8. Percentage of states on valleys in the relevant part of the state space under h^{FF}. Mean values for increasing number of constants in different domains

In difference to h^+, there are five "new" domains where local minima arise: *Assembly*, *Briefcaseworld*, *Grid*, *Hanoi*, and *Miconic-SIMPLE*. In the domains not shown in Figure 7.8, there are still no local minima at all. In the "old" domains where there are local minima under h^+, the valley percentage for h^{FF} is rather similar to the one for h^+, c.f. Figure 7.3. We observe that, for the "new" domains, the valley percentage is very low, with the exception of *Hanoi* and, to some extent, the *Grid* domain. This is in line with what we observed when measuring valley size and diameter: the values are extremely low for *Briefcaseworld* and *Miconic-SIMPLE*, a little higher for *Assembly*, still somewhat higher for *Grid*, and extremely high for *Hanoi*. More precisely, the average maximal values for the largest group of instances in *Briefcaseworld* and *Miconic-SIMPLE* are 2.0 respectively 1.5 for size, and 1.0 respectively 0.5 for diameter; in *Assembly*, these values are 9.0 and 6.0; in *Grid*, they are 46.0 and 14.0; in *Hanoi*, finally, they are 1700.0 and 131.0. So, with the exception of *Hanoi* and to some extent *Grid*, there are only few valleys in the "new" domains, and they tend to be small.

7.3.2 Benches

Like for h^+, we have measured the percentage of states on bench-related plateaus, on bench-related plateaus that are not part of a valley, on contours, on contours that are not part of a valley, and on global minima. We have also measured the size of (the flat regions from) bench-related plateaus, their diameter, their exit percentage, and the maximal exit distance. We only show the data regarding the maximal exit distance. For all the other parameters, the changes in comparison to the values for h^+ are marginal.

Domain	I_0	I_1	I_2	I_3	I_4
Assembly	0.0	1.7	2.0	2.1	2.6
Blocksworld-arm	1.0	3.0		3.5	4.9
Blocksworld-no-arm	0.0	1.0		1.3	2.4
Briefcaseworld	1.0		2.1		2.3
Ferry	1.0	1.0	1.0	1.0	1.0
Freecell	0.0			1.5	1.4
Fridge	2.5	4.5	4.0	6.0	7.7
Grid	3.0	4.0			4.3
Gripper	1.0	1.0	1.0	1.0	1.0
Hanoi	3.0	9.0	23.0	23.0	23.0
Logistics	1.0	1.0	1.0		1.0
Miconic-ADL	1.0		1.0	1.1	1.1
Miconic-SIMPLE	1.0	1.0	1.0	1.0	1.0
Miconic-STRIPS	1.0	1.0	1.0	1.0	1.0
Movie	1.0	1.0	1.0	1.0	1.0
Mprime	2.5	2.7	1.9	2.0	4.0
Mystery	1.2	1.8	1.5	1.8	2.0
Schedule	1.0	1.3	1.6	1.0	1.0
Simple-Tsp	0.0	0.0	0.0	0.0	0.0
Tireworld	6.0				

Fig. 7.9. Maximal exit distance under h^{FF}. Mean values for increasing number of constants in different domains

The observation to be made is that the properties of h^+ with respect to the maximal exit distance pretty much carry over to h^{FF} in our example collection: in the Ferry, Gripper, Logistics, Miconic-SIMPLE, Miconic-STRIPS, Movie, and Simple-Tsp domains, the average maximal exit distance is constant across instance size; in the other domains (except Schedule) there is a tendency of growth with instance size.

7.3.3 The Hypotheses

Our observations suggest that (except in the Hanoi and to some extent also the Grid domain) the properties of h^+ roughly carry over to h^{FF}. The author's intuition is that the overall topology of the state space under h^+ gets preserved when using h^{FF}, only the surface can become somewhat "crippled" — this intuition will be illustrated with a visualized example below. Our research hypotheses are the following.

1. In any instance of those domains where there are no local minima under h^+, there are no or only few states on valleys under evaluation with h^{FF}.
2. In any instance of those domains where there is a constant upper bound c on the maximal exit distance under h^+, the maximal exit distance under evaluation with h^{FF} is at most c or only a little higher than c.

Of course, "only few states on valleys" and "only a little higher than c" are rather imprecise formulations. The above statements are research hypotheses that can be empirically supported, or rejected. We will do that in Chapter 9. At this point, we shed some light on our results by giving a few visualized examples.

7.4 Visualization

In order to make the topological observations more palpable, a visualization tool was implemented. The work was carried out by the student Nils Weidmann under supervision by the author. A state space with heuristic function h is represented as a graph structure (nodes are states, edges are state transitions) in the 3-dimensional cube $[0;1] \times [0;1] \times [0;1]$: the x-axis corresponds to growing distance from the initial state (0 - initial state, 1 - states with maximal distance); states with identical such distance are arranged in equal intervals over the available space on the y-axis; the z-axis corresponds to goal distance as estimated by h (0 - goal states, 1 - states with maximal h value). The 3-dimensional visualization of such a graph can be arbitrarily rotated. Have a look at the examples depicted in Figures 7.10 (a) and 7.10 (b).

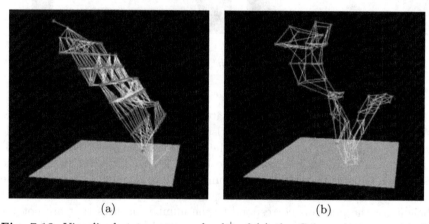

(a)   (b)

Fig. 7.10. Visualized state space under h^+ of (a) the *Gripper* instance with 4 balls and (b) a *Logistics* instance with 2 cities (each 3 locations and 1 truck), 1 object, and 1 airplane

The *Gripper* graph in Figure 7.10 (a) is easy to read. The initial state is (the right one of the two states) in the top left corner while the two goal states are in the right bottom corner. The state space forms an inclined plane that starts in the initial state and ends in a goal state. Viewing hill-climbing as the process of dropping a marble onto the surface of the search space, evidently what the marble in our *Gripper* task will do is roll straight down to a goal state. The *Logistics* graph in Figure 7.10 (b) is harder to read, but should still be understandable.

The initial state is the leftmost state in the picture. The goal states are somewhat to the right of the middle, forming the bottom of the valley. Thus starting in the initial state the gradient of the search space surface again leads straight down to a goal state. Expressed in the topological terms defined above, there are no local minima in the graphs shown in Figure 7.10 because one never needs to go upwards when moving towards the goal. As for the maximal exit distance, there are some points where the step towards the goal is a horizontal one (e.g., just above the middle of the *Gripper* state space), but at no point more than one such horizontal step is necessary.

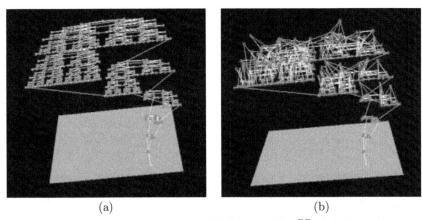

(a)   (b)

Fig. 7.11. Visualized state space under (a) h^+ and (b) h^{FF} of the *Hanoi* instance with 6 discs

Figure 7.11 gives an example to illustrate the relation of the h^+ and h^{FF} functions. While in most of the examples we visualized there was no easily discernible difference at all between both pictures, the intuition given above (Section 7.3.3) can nicely be observed in instances of the *Hanoi* domain. Figure 7.11 shows the instance with 6 discs. The state space is, under h^+, arranged in 6 plateaus whose size decreases exponentially with their height (we will see in Section 8.3.6 that the heights of the plateaus correspond to the number of discs that are not yet in their goal position). Figure 7.11 (b) shows how this carries over to evaluation with h^{FF}. The overall arrangement of the state space into the 6 plateaus is still the same, only their surface is rather crippled. Note also that the nearer one gets to the goal, the less crippled does the surface get — the nearer to the goal, the more closely does h^{FF} resemble h^+.

8. Verifying the h^+ Hypotheses

We now verify the hypotheses we stated in Section 7.2, i.e., we determine what exactly the local search topology under h^+ is in our domains. It turns out that all the hypotheses are true except those about the *Assembly* domain. As a side effect of the proofs we also determine what the structural reasons are behind the topological phenomena, on the level of the planning tasks' specifications. The investigation proceeds as follows.

The topological properties are proved for each single domain in turn. We order the domains by decreasing number of hypotheses we need to verify, which coincides pretty much with increasing difficulty of verification — the domains in the lower parts of our taxonomy are generally rather simple in structure, which makes the proofs simple, too. Note that our hypotheses really concern the propositional or negation-free compilations of the instances. Here, we will focus on the negation-free compilations. The original instances and their negation-free compilations are semantically the same, c.f. Section 3.1. Also, as we have already argued in Chapter 7, the results carry directly over to the propositional compilations, with Proposition 3.1.6 and the fact that in none of our domains there are disjunctive goals.

The investigation starts with a section summing up the core of the theory, i.e., the structural properties underlying most of the proofs (Section 8.1). Apart from simplifying the subsequent investigation, this identifies the relevant patterns of structure in a manner that generalizes above single domains. The first specific domains investigated are then those where the non-existence of local minima and a bounded maximal exit distance are hypothesized (Section 8.2). Afterwards we focus on the domains where the hypotheses only concern the non-existence of local minima (Section 8.3). Then we deal with the domains where only the dead end class needs to be verified (Section 8.4), and finally we deal with the *Assembly* domain (Section 8.5), where the situation is rather complex. We close the chapter by overviewing the results in terms of the planning domain taxonomy they determine (Section 8.6).

For those domains where we find that there are no local minima, but for which there is no hypothesis concerning the maximal exit distance, we also determine the maximal exit distance behavior: we either prove that there is a constant upper bound, or give an example sequence of instances where the maximal exit distance grows arbitrarily high. Remember that, given the non-existence of local

J. Hoffmann: Utilizing Problem Structure in Planning, LNAI 2854, pp. 135–180, 2003.
© Springer-Verlag Berlin Heidelberg 2003

minima, the maximal exit distance is very relevant for FF's search algorithm, c.f. Theorem 7.2.1.

It had to be decided what exactly the instances of our 20 domains are. As mentioned at the beginning of the book, this was done by abstracting from the published benchmark collections. The formal definitions can be looked up in Appendix A. We include more informal descriptions as preludes to the sections about single domains. These descriptions capture the properties that are relevant for the subsequent proofs. The definitions in Appendix A are negation-free, i.e., in those domains where the negation-free compilations are different from the original instances, the domains are not formulated according to the original definitions, but so that the instances defined are those that result from negation-free compilation. This provides a more direct connection to the investigation. Like in Chapter 7, we are only interested in solvable instances.

8.1 A Structural Core

In many of our domains, similar patterns of structure — on the level of the planning task *specifications* — cause the topological phenomena we have observed in Chapter 7. These patterns of structure thus form the core of the theory behind the high quality of h^+. We capture this structural core in the form of a number of definitions and implications. The first half has already been presented in Section 4.1, when we introduced sufficient criteria for the state space of a planning task to be undirected or at most harmless. The same patterns of structure that cause the non-existence of dead ends are responsible, in combination with others, for the non-existence of local minima and to some extent also for bounds on the maximal exit distance.

Let us briefly repeat the relevant parts of Section 4.1. The first half of the core theory is formed by Definition 4.1.5 and Theorem 4.1.2, as well as Definition 4.1.6, Definition 4.1.7, and Theorem 4.1.3. Theorem 4.1.2 proves that a planning task is undirected if all actions are *invertible* according to Definition 4.1.5. An action a is invertible if its effects always appear $(del(a) \subseteq pre(a)$, and $add(a)$ is inconsistent with $pre(a))$, and if there is an action $\bar{a}$ that is always applicable after execution of a $(pre(\bar{a}) \subseteq (pre(a) \cup add(a)) \setminus del(a))$ and that undoes a's effects $(add(\bar{a}) = del(a)$, and $del(\bar{a}) = add(a))$. Theorem 4.1.3 proves that a planning task is at most harmless if all actions are either *at least invertible* according to Definition 4.1.6, or have *static add effects* and *irrelevant delete effects* according to Definition 4.1.7. An action a is at least invertible if there is an action $\bar{a}$ that is always applicable after execution of a $(pre(\bar{a}) \subseteq (pre(a) \cup add(a)) \setminus del(a))$ and that re-achieves a's delete effects and deletes no propositions that have been true before $(add(\bar{a}) \supseteq del(a)$, and $del(\bar{a})$ is inconsistent with $pre(a))$. Note that an invertible action is also at least invertible $(del(\bar{a}) = add(a)$, and $add(a)$ is inconsistent with $pre(a))$. An action a has static add effects if these are not deleted by any action $(add(a) \cap \bigcup_{a' \in A} del(a') = \emptyset)$, and it has irrelevant delete effects if these are not needed for any other action or the goal $(del(a) \cap (G \cup \bigcup_{a \neq a' \in A} pre(a')) = \emptyset)$.

In this section, we formulate the second half of the structural core. We define a yet weaker notion of invertibility (invertibility in the relaxation), and an important kind of relationship between the role of an action in the real task and its role in the relaxed task. Combining these definitions with the notion of irrelevant delete effects yields a criterion that is sufficient for the non-existence of local minima under h^+. The criterion can be directly applied in 7 of our 20 domains, and can be applied with slight modifications in 3 more domains. We do not come up with a general sufficient criterion to determine an upper bound on the maximal exit distance. Nevertheless, the respective proofs all use very similar arguments. We will give an outline of these. For the sake of notational simplicity, the following definitions are for STRIPS tasks only. The proofs for ADL tasks will proceed along the same lines of argumentation. We start with the following simple technical observation.

Lemma 8.1.1. *Given a STRIPS task (A, I, G), a state s, and an action a that is applicable in s yielding the state s'. If P^+ is a relaxed plan for (A, s, G) that contains a, and $\overline{a} \in A$ is an action that is applicable in s' and for which $add(\overline{a}) \supseteq del(a)$ holds, then a relaxed plan for (A, s', G) can be constructed by removing a from P^+, and adding $\langle \overline{a} \rangle$ as a prefix.*

Proof. Without loss of generality, a starts the relaxed plan P^+ (a is applicable so one can execute its relaxed version immediately). After executing the relaxed version of $\overline{a}$ in s', all propositions are true that were true in s, plus the propositions that were made true by a. Thus, P^+ without a is a relaxed plan from there.

The importance of Lemma 8.1.1 is that (with the Lemma's terminology) there is a relaxed plan starting in s' that *has the same length* as the one for s. So if the relaxed plan for s was optimal, we can conclude that $h^+(s') \leq h^+(s)$ holds.

Examples of actions that qualify for the role of $\overline{a}$ in Lemma 8.1.1 are the inverse, and at least inverse, actions $\overline{a}$ in Definitions 4.1.5 and 4.1.6. These actions are always applicable in the state where a has been executed. Moreover, the add effects of an inverse action are exactly a's delete effects, and the add effects of an at least inverse action are a superset of a's delete effects. To fulfill the prerequisites of Lemma 8.1.1 the following weaker requirement is already sufficient.

Definition 8.1.1. *Given a STRIPS task (A, I, G). An action $a \in A$ is at least relaxed invertible, if there is an action $\overline{a} \in A$ such that $pre(\overline{a}) \subseteq (pre(a) \cup add(a)) \setminus del(a)$, and $add(\overline{a}) \supseteq del(a)$.*

The delete effects need not be mentioned in the above definition because $\overline{a}$, in the context of Lemma 8.1.1, is only used within the relaxation anyway. As indicated above, Definitions 4.1.5 and 4.1.6 are stronger than Definition 8.1.1, i.e., both invertible and at least invertible actions are also at least relaxed invertible.

Apart from (at least relaxed) invertible actions, the key property behind the lack of local minima under h^+ is, in most of our domains, that every action that is good for solving the real task is also good for solving the relaxed task.

Definition 8.1.2. *Given a task (A, I, G). An action $a \in A$ is respected by the relaxation if, for any reachable state $s \in S$ such that a starts an optimal plan for (A, s, G), there is an optimal relaxed plan for (A, s, G) that also starts with a.*

Note that this definition is not restricted to STRIPS tasks, as the same terminology will be used in ADL tasks. As a simple example for an action that is respected by the relaxation, consider loading (unloading) a car onto (from) the ferry in *Ferry*: the only means of transporting a car is by using the ferry, so *all* plans, real or relaxed, must use the respective action if the car is not already at its goal position. We will say more on that topic below.

We now combine actions that are respected by the relaxation (Definition 8.1.2), the existence of actions that at least invert an action's effects in the relaxation (Definition 8.1.1), and irrelevant delete effects (Definition 4.1.7), to obtain our main tool for identifying planning tasks where h^+ does not yield any local minima.

Lemma 8.1.2. *Given a solvable STRIPS task (A, I, G), such that the state space (S, E) does not contain unrecognized dead ends. If each action $a \in A$*

1. *is respected by the relaxation, and*
2. *is at least relaxed invertible or has irrelevant delete effects,*

then there are no local minima in (S, E) under evaluation with h^+.

Proof. The states with $gd(s) = \infty$ are not on local minima by prerequisite, with $h^+(s) = \infty$. We will prove that, in each reachable state s with $gd(s) \neq \infty$, if an action a starts an optimal plan for (A, s, G) then $h^+(Result(s, \langle a \rangle)) \leq h^+(s)$. This proves the lemma: iterating the argument, we obtain a path to a goal state on which the value of h^+ decreases monotonically, i.e., a full exit path.

Let s be a reachable state with $gd(s) \neq \infty$. Let a be an action that starts an optimal plan for (A, s, G). We denote $s' := Result(s, \langle a \rangle)$. The action is respected by the relaxation so there is an optimal relaxed plan P^+ for (A, s, G) that starts with a. First case, removing a from P^+ yields a relaxed plan for (A, s', G). Then $h^+(s') < h^+(s)$ follows and we are finished. This is the case, in particular, if a has irrelevant delete effects: the propositions that a deletes are not needed by any other action nor by the goal, so P^+ without a achieves the goal starting from s' (where a has already been applied). Second case, assume removing a from P^+ does *not* yield a relaxed plan for s'. Then, with what was said before, a does not have irrelevant delete effects and must thus be at least relaxed invertible: there is an action $\bar{a} \in A$ with $pre(\bar{a}) \subseteq (pre(a) \cup add(a)) \setminus del(a)$ and $add(\bar{a}) \supseteq del(a)$. Applying Lemma 8.1.1 finishes the argument: the action $\bar{a}$ is guaranteed to be applicable in s', and re-achieves a's delete effects, so we can replace a in P^+ with $\bar{a}$ to obtain a relaxed plan for (A, s', G), yielding $h^+(s') \leq h^+(s)$.

As the argument in the proof only applies to solvable states, we must postulate that there are no or only recognized dead ends, like when the task at hand is undirected or harmless. Note that the second prerequisite of Lemma 8.1.2 is already fulfilled by planning tasks qualifying for the undirectedness or harmlessness criteria given by Theorems 4.1.2 and 4.1.3. The missing bit that implies the non-existence of local minima under h^+ is then the first prerequisite, all actions being respected by the relaxation. The reason why this half of the lemma's prerequisites holds true in many of our domains is that, intuitively, if an action a is needed for an optimal solution, then this action either

− achieves some proposition that is needed by *all* solutions from the current state, no matter if relaxed or not, and that can not be achieved in a better way (there is no action achieving strictly more propositions than a); or
− achieves some proposition representing one way to get closer to the goals, where no other way is better, relaxed or not.

A typical (with respect to our benchmark collection) example for actions of the first kind are the *Ferry* actions mentioned above, loading (unloading) a car onto (from) the ferry — one has no other choice. A typical example for an action of the second kind is picking up a ball from room A in *Gripper*, when both hands are empty: the ball must be transported, and it does not matter at all which hand is used for that.

Let us focus on the maximal exit distance. As said, we do not have a general sufficient criterion. We do however have a proving technique that works in all the domains where there is an upper bound. In planning tasks that fulfill the requirements for Lemma 8.1.2, optimal solution paths are flat in the sense that h^+ does not increase when one moves along them. So one can move along an optimal solution path from any reachable state s, and identify at which point, at the latest, a strictly shorter relaxed plan than the optimal one for s can be constructed. Relaxed plans here will be constructed along the path according to the proof of Lemma 8.1.2: we either replace an applied action a with its inverse counterpart $\bar{a}$ (if its delete effects are still needed), or remove it completely (if its delete effects are irrelevant upon application). In the latter case, we are finished.

Proposition 8.1.1. *Given a planning task (A, I, G), a reachable state s, and an action a that starts an optimal relaxed plan P^+ for (A, s, G). If removing a from P^+ yields a relaxed plan for $(A, Result(s, a), G)$, then $h^+(Result(s, a)) < h^+(s)$, i.e., s is an exit state under h^+.*

Proof. Obvious.

We remark that this proposition corresponds to the first case in the proof of Lemma 8.1.2. Note also that the proposition's prerequisites are fulfilled if the action a is respected by the relaxation and has irrelevant delete effects.

Before we start the investigation, the reader is invited to recollect the introductory example from Section 1.2. We observed that, in a simple transportation task, relaxed plan length along a solution path decreased monotonically. Starting in a location L_1, a vehicle needed to transport object O_1 from L_1 to location L_2, and to transport object O_2 from L_2 to L_1. Actions were to move the vehicle, or to load/unload an object. The (optimal) solution path we considered was to load O_1, move to L_2, unload O_1, load O_2, move back to L_1, and unload O_2. Initially, the (optimal) relaxed plan was identical to the real plan except that it did not contain the action moving back to L_1. At all points on the solution path the relaxed plan could be obtained by skipping the last action executed on the path, and in a single case (the move to L_2) additionally inserting the inverse action (the move back to L_1). We have now formalized the reasons for the observed phenomena. All actions are invertible in the sense of Definition 4.1.5, and respected by the relaxation in the sense of Definition 8.1.2 (the actions are all of the first kind described above, i.e., if they start an optimal plan then they achieve a needed proposition that can not be achieved in any other way). The heuristic value on the solution path decreases monotonically according to Lemma 8.1.2, the updates of the relaxed plans along the solution path correspond to the updates described in that lemma's proof. At all points on the solution path, except when moving away from L_1, the delete effects are not needed anymore (neither in the real nor in the relaxed task) after application of the action, so Lemma 8.1.1 applies and the heuristic value decreases immediately. As announced in Section 1.2, we will now see that the same patterns of structure appear across a wide range of more general situations.

8.2 No Local Minima and Bounded Maximal Exit Distance

As said, we first look at the domains where both a bounded maximal exit distance and the non-existence of local minima are hypothesized. These are the *Simple-Tsp*, *Movie*, *Gripper*, *Ferry*, *Logistics*, *Miconic-STRIPS*, and *Miconic-SIMPLE* domains. We focus on them in that order. The proofs become gradually more difficult — though most of them are very simple anyway.

8.2.1 Simple-Tsp

In *Simple-Tsp*, there is a single operator to move between locations. The precondition states that the locations must be different (which condition we have inserted to avoid absurd actions), and as an effect the destination location is visited. The instances specify a number of locations that must be visited, starting in one of them.

All instances of *Simple-Tsp* are solvable. We consider the tasks that result when removing static predicates. This is necessary in order to directly apply the sufficient criteria we have presented earlier. Considering the tasks after removing static predicates is justified by Proposition 3.1.3 (stating semantic identity of a task with or without static predicates). Removing static predicates in a *Simple-Tsp* task yields only actions that move between different locations, getting rid of the non-equality precondition. The actions are all at least invertible in the sense of Definition 4.1.6 (by moving back), implying that the state space is at most harmless, as stated in Corollary 4.1.2 (because visiting a location can not be undone, the state space is not undirected).

Generally, we need to take care of the technical subtlety concerning negation-free and propositional compilations as can be distinct from the original tasks. As *Simple-Tsp* is a STRIPS domain, the compilations do nothing so there is no difference.

Theorem 8.2.1. *Given an instance (C, I, G) of the Simple-Tsp domain, the corresponding state space does not contain local minima under h^+.*

Proof. As all actions are at least invertible, with Lemma 8.1.2 it suffices to show that all actions are respected by the relaxation. If a move(x, y) starts an optimal plan, then y has not yet been visited, so one optimal relaxed plan starts with the same action.

Let us introduce an abbreviation. Henceforth, if s is a reachable state in a task (A, I, G), and P^+ is a relaxed plan for (A, s, G), then we also denote this by saying P^+ *is a relaxed plan for* s.

Theorem 8.2.2. *Given an instance (C, I, G) of the Simple-Tsp domain, the maximal exit distance in the corresponding state space is 0 under h^+.*

Proof. By the argumentation in the proof of Theorem 8.2.1, all actions are respected by the relaxation. In any non-goal state s, an optimal plan starts by visiting one yet unvisited location, move(x, y). Let P^+ be an optimal relaxed plan for s that starts with a. We can assume that a is the only moving action in P^+ that starts in x: else, the actions of the form move(x, y') can be replaced by move(y, y'). Thus, removing a from P^+ yields a relaxed plan for $Result(s, \langle a \rangle)$, and s is an exit by Proposition 8.1.1.

We remark that, trivially, in *Simple-Tsp* every optimal plan is also an optimal relaxed plan, implying $h^+ \equiv gd$, from which the two above claims follow immediately. We have chosen the formulation above to demonstrate that *Simple-Tsp* exhibits similar structural patterns like the other domains where we prove the non-existence of local minima and an upper bound on the exit distance.

8.2.2 Movie

In *Movie*, there are seven different operators: one to rewind the tape, whose delete effect is that the counter is no longer at zero; one to reset the counter, whose only effect is that the counter is at zero; five to get different kinds of snacks, whose only effect is that one has the respective snack. Instances differ only in terms of the number of items that there are of each sort of snacks. The goal is always to have one snack of each sort, to have the tape rewound, and to have the counter at zero.

All instances of *Movie* are solvable. The actions that get snacks all have irrelevant delete effects (namely none at all) and static add effects in the sense of Definition 4.1.7, while rewinding the movie and resetting the counter are at least invertible in the sense of Definition 4.1.6 (by resetting the counter). So the state space is at most harmless, as stated in Corollary 4.1.2 (because getting a snack can not be undone, the state space is not undirected). As *Movie* is a STRIPS domain the original and the compiled tasks are identical.

Theorem 8.2.3. *Given an instance (C, I, G) of the Movie domain, the corresponding state space does not contain local minima under h^+.*

Proof. All actions produced by one of the getting snacks operators, and the reset-counter() action, have irrelevant delete effects (none at all), and the rewind-movie() action is at least relaxed invertible. With Lemma 8.1.2 it suffices to show that all actions are respected by the relaxation. This is trivial: if a snack is not yet there, one must get it; if the counter is not at zero, one must reset it; if the tape is not yet rewound, one must rewind it.

Theorem 8.2.4. *Given an instance (C, I, G) of the Movie domain, the maximal exit distance in the corresponding state space is 1 under h^+.*

Proof. By the argumentation in the proof of Theorem 8.2.3, all actions are respected by the relaxation, and h^+ never increases on optimal solution paths. All actions except rewind-movie() have irrelevant delete effects, so states s where they start an optimal plan are exits by Proposition 8.1.1. Assume the only action starting an optimal plan for the state s is rewind-movie(), meaning that one has all snacks already. Then, applying rewind-movie() to s yields a successor state s' where reset-counter() starts an optimal plan (in fact, reset-counter() achieves the goal from s'), so an upper bound on the exit distance is 1. In the state s where one has got all snacks and the counter is at zero, but the movie is not rewound, no action except rewind-movie() can change s at all, and $h^+(s) = h^+(s') = 1$, so then the exit distance is exactly 1.

8.2.3 Gripper

In *Gripper*, there is the operator move(x, y) to move between locations, the operator pick(x, y, z) to pick up a ball (at a location with a hand), and the operator drop(x, y, z) to drop a ball (at a location from a hand). There are always exactly two locations, room a and room b, and a number of balls shall be transported from a into b by using two gripper hands l and r that can each carry one ball at a time (we use the notation for instances as given in Appendix A). Instances differ only in terms of the number of balls. The moves are constrained to be between different rooms, and all operator parameters are constrained to be of the appropriate types, i.e., for example, in a move both parameters must fulfill a (room, x) predicate.

All instances of *Gripper* are solvable. Removing static predicates gets rid of the type information and of actions that try to move within the same room. As is justified by Proposition 3.1.3, we assume in the following that static predicates have been removed. The actions are invertible in the sense of Definition 4.1.5, implying that the state space is undirected, as stated in Corollary 4.1.1. In a

STRIPS domain there is no difference between the original tasks and their compilations. The notational details used in the proofs can be found in Appendix A.

Theorem 8.2.5. *Given an instance (C, I, G) of the Gripper domain, the corresponding state space does not contain local minima under h^+.*

Proof. All actions are invertible, so with Lemma 8.1.2 it suffices to show that all actions are respected by the relaxation. If the optimal starting action in a reachable state s is a pick(x, y, z) or a drop(x, y, z), this holds because then the ball x is not yet in room b, and must be transported. If the optimal starting action is a move(x, y), then there are either balls left to pick in $y = a$, or balls left to drop in $y = b$, so a relaxed plan from s has no choice but applying the respective move action.

Theorem 8.2.6. *Given an instance (C, I, G) of the Gripper domain, the maximal exit distance in the corresponding state space is at most 1 under h^+.*

Proof. By the argumentation in the proof of Theorem 8.2.5, all actions are respected by the relaxation; the instance fulfills the requirements for Lemma 8.1.2, so h^+ never increases on optimal solution paths. Assume we have a reachable state s and an optimal starting action act (we use that name to avoid confusion with the *room a* used in the instance), yielding the successor state s'. Assume also that act starts the optimal relaxed plan P^+ for s. If $act = \text{drop}(x, y, z)$ then $y = b$, and removing act from P^+ yields a relaxed plan for s' as x is in its goal position and (carry, x, z) is not needed anymore; thus in that case s is an exit. If $act = \text{pick}(x, y, z)$ then $y = a$, and P^+ also contains the actions move(a, b) and drop(x, b, z). A relaxed plan for s' can be constructed by removing act from P^+ and placing the two other actions up front: that way, (free, z) is re-achieved before any other action is applied; the deletion of (at, x, a) does not matter as x is picked up only once due to the optimality of P^+. So in that case, s is also an exit. Finally, consider the case where $act = \text{move}(x, y)$. Then, the successor state s' falls into one of the two above cases, so an upper bound on the exit distance is 1.

If, in the situation described at the end of the proof to Theorem 8.2.6, *picks* or *drops* are left to do in room x, then the relaxed plan from s' must contain the inverse action move(y, x), so then the exit distance is exactly 1.

8.2.4 Ferry

Ferry is very closely related to *Gripper*. There are three operators, one to sail a ferry between two locations, one to board a car onto the ferry, and one to debark a car from the ferry. The ferry can transport only one car at a time, which is realized by an (empty-ferry) predicate. The goal is to have a subset of the cars at their goal locations. The sailing actions are constrained to be between different locations, and all operator parameters are constrained to be of the appropriate types, i.e., for example, in a debark(x, y) action x must fulfill a (car, x) predicate while y must fulfill a (location, y) predicate.

All instances of *Ferry* are solvable. Removing static predicates gets rid of the type information and of actions that try to move within the same location. As is justified by Proposition 3.1.3, we assume in the following that static predicates have been removed. The actions are invertible in the sense of Definition 4.1.5, implying that the state space is undirected, as stated in Corollary 4.1.1. In a STRIPS domain there is no difference between the original tasks and their compilations. The proofs are similar to *Gripper*. Notational details are in Appendix A.

Theorem 8.2.7. *Given an instance (C, I, G) of the Ferry domain, the corresponding state space does not contain local minima under h^+.*

Proof. All actions are invertible, so with Lemma 8.1.2 it suffices to show that all actions are respected by the relaxation. If the optimal starting action in a reachable state s is a board(x, y) or a debark(x, y), this holds because then the car x is not yet at its goal location, and must be transported. If the optimal starting action is a sail(x, y), then at location y there is either a car to board, or a car to debark, so a relaxed plan from s will have to visit that location. When this is done does not matter in the relaxation, as the (at-ferry, y) proposition remains true throughout relaxed plan execution. So one can start an optimal relaxed plan from s by sailing the ferry to y.

Theorem 8.2.8. *Given an instance (C, I, G) of the Ferry domain, the maximal exit distance in the corresponding state space is at most 1 under h^+.*

Proof. By the argumentation in the proof of Theorem 8.2.7, all actions are respected by the relaxation; the instance fulfills the prerequisites of Lemma 8.1.2, so h^+ never increases on optimal solution paths. Assume we have a reachable state s and an optimal starting action a, yielding the successor state s'. Assume also that a starts the optimal relaxed plan P^+ for s. If $a = $ debark(x, y) then either y is the goal location of x, or x has no goal location, so removing a from P^+ yields a relaxed plan for s' as (on, x) is not needed anymore; thus in that case s is an exit. If $a = $ board(x, y) then x must be transported, and P^+ also contains the actions sail(y, y') and debark(x, y'), where y' is the goal location of x; a relaxed plan for s' can be constructed by removing a from P^+ and placing the two other actions up front: that way, (empty-ferry) is re-achieved before any other action is applied; the deletion of (at, x, y) does not matter as x is boarded only once due to the optimality of P^+. So in that case, s is also an exit. Finally, consider the case where the optimal starting action is $a = $ sail(x, y). Then, the successor state s' falls into one of the two above cases — some car is boarded or debarked — so an upper bound on the exit distance is 1.

If, in the situation described at the end of the proof to Theorem 8.2.8, a car is left at x which must be boarded later, or some other car must still be transported to x, then the relaxed plan from s' must contain the inverse action sail(y, x), so then the exit distance is exactly 1.

8.2.5 Logistics

In *Logistics*, there are six operators to drive a truck between two locations within a city, to fly an airplane between two airports, to load (unload) an object onto (from) a truck at a location, and to load (unload) an object onto (from) an airplane at an airport. There is always at least one city, and each city has a non-zero number of locations one of which is an airport. There is an arbitrary number of airplanes (which are located at airports) and of objects. The goal is to have a subset of the objects at their goal locations. The moves are constrained to be between different locations, and all operator parameters are constrained to be of the appropriate types.

An instance of *Logistics* can be unsolvable when there is an object that must be transported, but there is no adequate vehicle for doing so. Removing static predicates gets rid of the type information and of actions that try to move within the same location. As is justified by Proposition 3.1.3, we assume in the following that static predicates have been removed. The actions are invertible in the sense of Definition 4.1.5, implying that the state space is undirected, as stated in Corollary 4.1.1. In a STRIPS domain there is no difference between the original tasks and their compilations.

Theorem 8.2.9. *Given a solvable instance (C, I, G) of the Logistics domain, the corresponding state space does not contain local minima under h^+.*

Proof. As all actions are invertible, with solvability (implying the non-existence of dead ends) and Lemma 8.1.2 it suffices to show that all actions are respected by the relaxation. If the optimal starting action a in a reachable state s is any loading or unloading action, then a is respected by the relaxation because in that case the respective package is not yet at its goal location, so it must be transported, and it is best — for relaxed as well as for real plans — to do that when an adequate vehicle is already at the respective location. If the optimal starting action a is a driving or flying action to some location z, then some package must either be loaded or unloaded at z, so a relaxed plan from s has no choice but applying some action moving a transportation vehicle (of a's kind) there. All vehicles are equally good, except when there is a clever choice, i.e., a vehicle that already carries packages to be unloaded at z; but then, a will move one of those vehicles just like an optimal relaxed plan will, and all such vehicles are equally good in the relaxation.

Theorem 8.2.10. *Given a solvable instance (C, I, G) of the Logistics domain, the maximal exit distance in the corresponding state space is at most 1 under h^+.*

Proof. By the argumentation in the proof of Theorem 8.2.9, all actions are respected by the relaxation; the instance fulfills the prerequisites of Lemma 8.1.2, so h^+ monotonically decreases on optimal solution paths. Assume we have a reachable state s and an optimal starting action a, yielding the successor state s'. Assume also that a starts the optimal relaxed plan P^+ for s. If a is a loading (unloading) action, its only delete is the at (in) relation of the transported object; as the object is loaded from the respective location (unloaded from the respective vehicle) only once in P^+, removing a from P^+ yields a relaxed plan for s', so s is an exit. Otherwise, consider the case where a drives or flies some vehicle x from y to z. Then s' is an exit: no optimal plan moves the same vehicle twice in a row — all locations are immediately accessible, if accessible at all — so one optimal plan for s' starts by loading (unloading) some package to (from) x. Thus an upper bound on the exit distance is 1.

If, for example, in the situation described at the end of the proof to Theorem 8.2.10, x is a truck, y is the airport, and the package must be transported to a different city, then the relaxed plan from s' must include the action driving x back from z to y, so then the exit distance is exactly 1.

8.2.6 Miconic-STRIPS

In *Miconic-STRIPS*, there are four operators to move the lift up from one floor to another floor, to move the lift down from one floor to another floor, to board a passenger at a floor (the precondition being that the floor is the passenger's origin, and the only effect being that the passenger is boarded), and to let a passenger depart at a floor (the preconditions being that the floor is the passenger's destination and that the passenger is boarded, and the effects being that the passenger is served but no longer boarded). There is always at least one floor, and an arbitrary number of passengers each of which is given an origin and a destination floor. The goal is to serve all passengers. Lift moves are constrained so that the floors stand in the appropriate relation to each other (i.e., one can only move up from x to y if y is indeed above x, and vice versa), and all operator parameters are constrained to be of the appropriate types.

All instances of *Miconic-STRIPS* are solvable. Removing static predicates gets rid of the type information, of actions that try to move between inappropriate (in particular identical) locations, and of actions that board or depart a passenger at a location other than its origin respectively destination. As is justified by Proposition 3.1.3, we assume in the following that static predicates have been removed. The lift move actions are invertible in the sense of Definition 4.1.5, the boarding actions are at least invertible in the sense of Definition 4.1.6, and the departing actions have irrelevant delete effects and static add effects in the sense of Definition 4.1.7. So the state space is at most harmless, as stated in Corollary 4.1.2 (because boarding and departing can not be undone, the state space is not undirected if there is at least one passenger). In a STRIPS domain there is no difference between the original tasks and their compilations.

Theorem 8.2.11. *Given an instance (C, I, G) of the Miconic-STRIPS domain, the corresponding state space does not contain local minima under h^+.*

Proof. All actions are either at least invertible or have irrelevant delete effects. Therefore, with Lemma 8.1.2 it suffices to show that all actions are respected by the relaxation. For boarding and departing actions, this is obvious. For up(x, y)

and down(x, y) actions, if an optimal plan starts with such an action, then at least one passenger must board or depart at floor y, so any relaxed plan will have to visit that floor. When this is done does not matter in the relaxation — the (lift-at, y) proposition remains true throughout relaxed plan execution — so one can start an optimal relaxed plan by moving the lift to y.

Theorem 8.2.12. *Given an instance (C, I, G) of the Miconic-STRIPS domain, the maximal exit distance in the corresponding state space is at most 1 under h^+.*

Proof. By the argumentation in the proof of Theorem 8.2.11, all actions are respected by the relaxation; the instance fulfills the requirements for Lemma 8.1.2, so h^+ never increases on optimal solution paths. Assume we have a reachable state s and an optimal starting action a, yielding the successor state s'. The boarding and departing actions have irrelevant delete effects (boarding has no delete effects at all), so if a is one of those actions, then s is an exit by Proposition 8.1.1. In the other case, if a is an up or down action, then s' falls into the first case because no optimal plan moves the lift twice in a row (all floors are directly accessible from each other). So an upper bound on the exit distance is 1.

If, for example, in the situation described at the end of the proof of Theorem 8.2.12, there are two floors, the lift is in the bottom floor in s, and the single passenger wants to travel from the top to the bottom floor, then the relaxed plan from s' must include the action moving the lift back from the top to the bottom floor, so then the exit distance is exactly 1.

8.2.7 Miconic-SIMPLE

The *Miconic-SIMPLE* domain is semantically rather similar to the *Miconic-STRIPS* domain we have discussed above. The difference is that boarding and departing passengers is not done by separate actions, but by conditional effects that can appear when the lift *stops*. Once the lift is stopped, all boarded passengers that have their destination at the respective floor depart, and all passengers still waiting at the respective floor are boarded. The former conditional effects add that the respective passengers are served, and delete that they are boarded. The latter conditional effects require that the respective passengers are not served (on top of having their origin at the respective floor), and add that they are boarded. The lift move operators are identical to those in *Miconic-STRIPS*. The instances are also the same. All operator and effect parameters are constrained to be of the appropriate types.

All instances of *Miconic-SIMPLE* are solvable. Removing static predicates gets rid of the type information, of actions that try to move between identical locations, and of conditional effects that board or depart a passenger at a location other than its origin respectively destination. As is justified by Proposition 3.1.3, we assume in the following that static predicates have been removed. The boarding effect has a negative condition (the passenger not being served) which is compiled into a not-served condition which holds in the initial state and is deleted by the conditional effect that lets the respective passenger depart. There are no disjunctive goals so the properties of the propositional and of the negation-free compilations are the same, c.f. Proposition 3.1.6. Our sufficient criteria for the non-existence of dead ends are not directly applicable to *Miconic-SIMPLE* instances, so we insert a short proof.

Proposition 8.2.1. *Given the propositional or negation-free compilation of an instance (C, I, G) of the Miconic-SIMPLE domain, the corresponding state space is at most harmless.*

Proof. The floors are all directly accessible from each other. The deletes of the stopping effects are all irrelevant in the sense that they are not needed anymore once those effects have occured. One can thus, from any reachable state s, construct a plan by moving the lift back to the floor where it was in the initial state, and thereafter executing a plan for the task.

If there is at least one passenger, the instance is not undirected, as the effects of the stop actions can not be undone. Let us focus on local minima and the maximal exit distance.

Theorem 8.2.13. *Given the propositional or negation-free compilation of an instance (C, I, G) of the Miconic-SIMPLE domain, the corresponding state space does not contain local minima under h^+.*

Proof. We show that all actions are respected by the relaxation. This suffices with the following slight extension of Lemma 8.1.2. The $\text{up}(x, y)$ and $\text{down}(x, y)$ actions are invertible in the sense of Definition 4.1.5. The delete effects of the $\text{stop}(x)$ actions are conditional and thus are not irrelevant in the strict syntactical sense of Definition 4.1.7. They do, however, have the same semantics — the only delete effects are that a passenger reaching the destination is no longer boarded and no longer not-served. These propositions are irrelevant upon execution of the action. If the actions are respected by the relaxation, one can thus construct a full exit path from any state in parallel to the proof of Lemma 8.1.2.

The $\text{up}(x, y)$ and $\text{down}(x, y)$ actions are respected by the relaxation due to the same reasons as given for *Miconic-STRIPS* in the proof of Theorem 8.2.11. Assume $a = \text{stop}(x)$ starts an optimal plan for some reachable state s. Then a also starts an optimal relaxed plan for s. We prove that by contradiction. Assume that no optimal relaxed plan for s starts with $\text{stop}(x)$, although the lift is already located at x. Then the following must hold. First, there is a different floor x' where another passenger with destination x is waiting; second, there is no passenger for x' waiting at x. But in this situation, executing the stop at x' first would also yield a shorter real solution plan.

Theorem 8.2.14. *Given the propositional or negation-free compilation of an instance (C, I, G) of the Miconic-SIMPLE domain, the maximal exit distance in the corresponding state space is at most 1 under h^+.*

Proof. By the argumentation in the proof of Theorem 8.2.13 all actions are respected by the relaxation, h^+ never increases on optimal solution paths, and the stop(x) actions have delete effects that are irrelevant once they have appeared. Assume we have a reachable state s and an optimal starting action a, yielding the successor state s'. If a is a stop(x) action, then s is an exit by Proposition 8.1.1. In the other case, if a is an up or down action, then s' falls into the first case because no optimal plan moves the lift twice in a row (all floors are directly accessible from each other). So an upper bound on the exit distance is 1.

In the same situation that is described for the *Miconic-STRIPS* domain in Section 8.2.6 below Theorem 8.2.12, the exit distance is exactly 1.

8.3 No Local Minima

We now consider those domains where only the non-existence of local minima is hypothesized — which gives us less things to verify for each single domain. The domains in question are the *Tireworld, Briefcaseworld, Fridge, Blocksworld-no-arm, Grid,* and *Hanoi* domains, on which we focus in that order. The proofs become gradually more difficult (except in *Hanoi*, which comes in last place because it is just hilarious). As it turns out, in the first of these domains the maximal exit distance is, in fact, bounded by a constant (we did not have a hypothesis about that because only a single *Tireworld* instance was sufficiently small for the experiment in Chapter 7). In all the other domains, we will see that there is no constant upper bound on the maximal exit distance.

8.3.1 Tireworld

In *Tireworld*, one must replace a number of flat tires. This involves a collection of objects that must be used in the appropriate working steps. The details are in Appendix A. Briefly summarized for the proofs below, the situation is as follows. There is a boot that can be either opened or closed; it is initially closed and shall be so in the end. There are a pump, a wrench, and a jack which can be fetched or put away (from/into the boot); they are initially in the boot and shall be put back in the end. The spare wheels are initially not inflated, and can be inflated using the pump (the add effect is that the wheel is inflated, the delete effect is that it is no longer not-inflated). Each hub is fastened with nuts; these can be loosened or tightened, using the wrench, while the respective hub is on ground. The jack can be used to either jack up or jack down a hub. Once a hub is jacked up, one can undo the (loose) nuts, or do them up; if the nuts are undone, one can remove the respective wheel, or put on one. An optimal solution plan is this: open the boot; fetch the tools; inflate all spare wheels; loosen all nuts; in turn jack up each hub, undo the nuts, remove the flat wheel, put on the spare wheel, do up the nuts, and jack the hub down again; tighten all nuts; put away the tools; and close the boot.

All instances of *Tireworld* are solvable. All actions are invertible in the sense of Definition 4.1.5, except inflating a wheel which has irrelevant delete effects and static add effects in the sense of Definition 4.1.7. So the state space is at most harmless, as stated in Corollary 4.1.2 (as a wheel can not be "de-flated", the state space is not undirected). In a STRIPS domain there is no difference between the compilations and the original tasks. Before we start the proofs, one technical remark on the notation: in our formal definition of the domain, see Appendix A, some operators have a parameter — the tool used — that must always be grounded with the same constant — the one representing the respective tool. These parameters serve to replace the domain constants that are used in the original formulation. We omit these parameters here to improve readability (as an example, we write inflate(x...) instead of inflate(x, y) where y must always be the pump for the action to be applicable).

Theorem 8.3.1. *Given an instance (C, I, G) of the Tireworld domain, the corresponding state space does not contain local minima under h^+.*

Proof. The inflate(x...) actions have irrelevant delete effects, and all other actions are invertible, so with Lemma 8.1.2 it suffices to show that all actions are respected by the relaxation. This is obvious: if any action a starts an optimal plan from a reachable state, then that action adds a proposition that must be achieved, and that can only be achieved by a. As an example, consider the actions that open/close the boot, or loosen/tighten nuts. If those actions are needed to achieve the goal, they can not be avoided by the relaxation: as for opening (closing) the boot, this is necessary to fetch tools (achieve the respective goal); as for loosening (tightening) the nuts, this is necessary for removing the respective flat wheel (achieving the respective goal).

As said above, the maximal exit distance in *Tireworld* is bounded by a constant. The proof is simple but a bit difficult to formulate in detail, due to the large number of different working steps. For notation details, consider Appendix A (flat wheels are w_i, spare wheels are s_i, hubs are h_i, and nuts are n_i). The maximal exit distance is, in difference to the other domains where the constant is either 0 or 1, bounded by 6. Roughly, this is the "depth" of the working process, i.e., the maximum number of working steps we need to take before we can apply an action that does not need to be undone later on.

Theorem 8.3.2. *Given an instance (C, I, G) of the Tireworld domain, the maximal exit distance in the corresponding state space is at most 6 under h^+.*

Proof. By the argumentation in the proof of Theorem 8.3.1, all actions are respected by the relaxation; the instance fulfills the requirements for Lemma 8.1.2, so h^+ never increases on optimal solution paths. It now suffices to show that a state s' with a better evaluated neighbor can be reached on an optimal solution path from any reachable state s in at most 6 steps. We will use the fact that a state s' is an exit if there is an action a starting an optimal plan for (A, s', G), such that removing a from an optimal relaxed plan P^+ for (A, s', G) yields a relaxed plan for $(A, Result(s', \langle a \rangle), G)$, c.f. Proposition 8.1.1.

Consider the actions close-boot(), put-away(x), inflate($x \ldots$), tighten ($x, y \ldots$), do-up($x, y \ldots$), remove-wheel(x, y), and put-on-wheel(x, y). For all these actions it holds that when they start an optimal plan for a state, then the propositions that they delete are not needed anymore after applying them, neither by a real nor by a relaxed plan: a do-up($x, y \ldots$) action, for example, deletes (have, x) and (not-fastened, y) for nuts x and hub y; if do-up($x, y \ldots$) starts an optimal plan, then this means that the spare wheel has been put on the hub y already and that the nuts belong to the respective hub, so neither of both propositions will be needed for achieving the goals. Our proof thus comes down to identifying in at most how many steps on an optimal path a state s' can be reached from which one of the above actions starts an optimal plan. We distinguish the following cases.

1. There is a spare wheel that is not inflated, (not-inflated, s_i) $\in s$ for some s_i. The wheel must be inflated, for which one must at most open the boot and fetch the pump, yielding the distance 2.

2. The above case 1 does not hold, and there is a flat wheel that is still on, or a spare wheel that is on the wrong hub, i.e., (on, w, h_j) $\in s$, (on, w, h_j) $\notin G$ for some w and h_j. We identify an optimal path to a state where remove-wheel(w, h_j) can be applied (and thus starts an optimal plan). First, one must at most open the boot and fetch the wrench (maximal 2 steps). If nuts are tightened to h_j and h_j is jacked up, then h_j must be jacked down; if some other hub with a flat or wrong wheel on is already jacked up, one must at most jack down that hub (which is necessary anyway in order to loosen the nuts on the respective hub); if a hub with a good wheel is jacked up, one can jack down that hub, yielding a better state; else, the jack must at most be fetched from the boot (maximal 1 more step in all four cases). Loosening the nuts tightened to h_j, jacking up h_j, and undoing the respective nuts takes at most another 3 steps, so our path is at most 6 steps long. Note that all steps on the path are unavoidable implying that the path is an optimal solution path from s.

3. The above cases do not hold, and there is a hub that is free, (free, h_i) $\in s$ for some h_i. One must put on the respective spare. If the spare is in the boot, then fetching it yields a state with better h^+. Else, one has the spare already (otherwise case 2 would hold). One must at most perform the same steps as in case 2 (note that nuts can be done up and tightened to h_i even if there is no wheel on it), yielding again an unavoidable path of maximal length 6.

4. The above cases do not hold, and some nuts are still not done up to the correct hub, (loose, n_i, h_i) $\notin s$ for some n_i and h_i with (tight, n_i, h_i) $\in G$. If the nuts are in the boot, fetching them yields a better state. If some hub is jacked up, we can assume that either the correct nuts are fastened to that hub, or that the hub is h_i. Therefore, if some other nuts are fastened to h_i, maximal 5 unavoidable steps similar as above lead to a state where those other nuts can be undone, yielding a better state; otherwise maximal 4 unavoidable steps lead to a state where do-up($n_i, h_i \ldots$) can be applied.

5. The above cases do not hold, and a hub is jacked up, (not-on-ground, h_i) ∈ s for some h_i. The hub can immediately be jacked down, improving the h^+ value.
6. The above cases do not hold, and some nuts are still loose, (loose, n_i, h_i) ∈ s for some n_i and h_i. The nuts must be tightened which involves at most opening the boot and fetching the wrench.
7. If none of the above cases holds, then there is either a tool or a flat wheel that can be put away, or one can close the boot.

The cases are exhaustive, and in none of them does one need more than 6 steps in order to reach an exit.

The maximal exit distance is exactly 6 for all *Tireworld* instances. Consider the state where all hubs except one have already been processed completely (spare wheel inflated and on, nuts tight, flat wheel in boot), the boot is closed, the wrench and the jack are in the boot, the last spare wheel is already inflated, and nothing has yet been done about the last flat wheel. We are in the second case of the list given in the above proof of Theorem 8.3.2, and we require the whole sequence of opening the boot, fetching the wrench and the jack, loosing the nuts, jacking up the hub, and undoing the nuts in order to get to a state where the flat wheel can be removed. All the actions in the sequence must be inverted later on, and there is no other way of improving the h^+ value, so there the exit distance is exactly 6.

8.3.2 Briefcaseworld

In *Briefcaseworld*, a number of portables must be transported, where the transportation is done via conditional effects of the move actions. There are three operators: putting in a portable at a location can be done if the portable and the briefcase are at the respective location, and the portable is not yet inside; taking a portable out can be done if it is inside; a move can be applied between two locations, and achieves, beside the is-at relation for the briefcase, the respective at relations for all portables that are inside (i.e., the portables inside are moved along by conditional effects). The goal is to have a subset of the portables, and the briefcase, at their goal locations. The move actions are constrained to be between different locations, and all operator parameters are constrained to be of the appropriate types.

All instances of *Briefcaseworld* are solvable. Removing static predicates gets rid of the type information and of actions that try to move within the same location. With Proposition 3.1.3, we assume in the following that static predicates have been removed. There are no negations, so the negation-free and propositional compilations are identical to the original tasks (putting in a portable requires that it is not inside, but this negation is originally formulated in exactly the way that negation-free compilation would come up with, i.e., by a not-in predicate).

Proposition 8.3.1. *Given an instance (C, I, G) of the Briefcaseworld domain. The corresponding state space is undirected.*

Proof. Though none of the actions is invertible in the strict syntactical sense of Definition 4.1.5, to each reachable state and applicable action a yielding the successor state s' there is an action $\bar{a}$ leading back to s from s'. If a is a move(x, y), it can be undone by move(y, x). If a is a put-in(x, y), it can be undone by take-out(x). If a is a take-out(x), it can be undone by put-in(x, y) where y is the current location of the briefcase and x (with x being inside prior to the application of take-out(x), it is at the same location as the briefcase in s).

Theorem 8.3.3. *Given an instance (C, I, G) of the Briefcaseworld domain, the corresponding state space does not contain local minima under h^+.*

Proof. We prove that the heuristic value does not increase on optimal solution paths. The put-in(x, y) action is respected by the relaxation, because if such an action starts an optimal plan, then x is not at its goal location, so it must be put in. Also, as seen in the proof to Proposition 8.3.1, the action can be inverted. Now assume we got a reachable state s, and an optimal plan for (A, s, G) starting with a take-out(x) action. Assume P^+ is an optimal relaxed plan for (A, s, G). Then P^+ is also an optimal relaxed plan for (A, s', G), where s' is the state that results from applying take-out(x) to s: x is already at its goal location, so P^+ does not do anything with it (x can be kept inside the briefcase in the relaxation, as moving away does not delete its current location there). Finally, assume we got a reachable state s and an optimal plan for (A, s, G) starting with a move(x, y) action. Assume P^+ is an optimal relaxed plan for (A, s, G), and s' is the state that results from applying move(x, y) to s. If P^+ starts with move(x, y), then we can replace move(x, y) in P^+ with move(y, x) to form a relaxed plan for (A, s', G), so we are finished then. In the other case, P^+ starts with some other move action move(x, z) (because moving away starts an optimal real plan, no portables must be put in at the current location). We construct a relaxed plan for (A, s', G) from P^+ by: replacing move(x, y), if it is contained in P^+, with move(z, y) (so the at relations that were achieved by move(x, y) in P^+ are now achieved by move(z, y); note that (is-at, z) is achieved by move(x, z)); and replacing all other move(x, y'), $y' \neq y$, actions in P^+ with move(y, y') (so the respective at relations are achieved; note that (is-at, y) is fulfilled in s').

The shortest path to an exit can be arbitrarily long in the *Briefcaseworld* domain because taking out a portable is not necessary in a relaxed plan. Consider the following instances. There are two locations l_1 and l_2 and n portables $p_1, \ldots, p_n$. The briefcase is initially at l_1 and shall be at l_1 for the goal. The portable p_1 must be transported from l_2 to l_1, and the portables $p_2, \ldots, p_n$ must be transported from l_1 to l_2. An optimal plan puts in all of $p_2, \ldots, p_n$, moves to l_2, and puts in p_1; it then takes out all of $p_2, \ldots, p_n$, and moves back to l_1. Consider the state s where the briefcase is in l_2, and all portables are inside. $h^+(s) = 1$, as moving to l_1 does the job in the relaxation. However, the nearest state s' with $h^+(s') < h^+(s)$ is the nearest goal state, which is n steps away.

8.3.3 Fridge

In *Fridge*, one must replace the broken compressor in a fridge. To do this, one must remove the compressor; this involves unfastening the screws that hold the compressor, which in turn involves first switching the fridge off. The goal is to have the new compressor attached to the fridge, all screws fastened, and the fridge switched back on. The origin of this domain is a STRIPS formulation. Our adaption allows for an arbitrary number of fridges and screws, where each compressor is fastened by the same (arbitrary, at least one) number of screws. The adaption involves introducing a complex precondition: a compressor can only be removed if *all* screws are unfastened.

The discussion is probably easier to understand after a look at the formal definition of the domain in the respective section of Appendix A. A brief summary is this. There are six operators. One can stop (start) a fridge, which exchanges the respective (fridge-on, x) with the respective (not-fridge-on, x) proposition (vice versa). One can unfasten (fasten) a screw from (to) a compressor attached to a fridge, which exchanges the respective (screwed, x) with the respective (not-screwed, x) proposition (vice versa). To do that, the fridge needs to be turned off, the compressor needs to be attached, and the screw must fit the compressor (each screw fits only the compressor it is originally fastened to, and that compressor's replacement). Finally, one can remove (attach) a compressor from (to) a fridge, which exchanges the respective (attached, x, y) proposition with the respective (free, x) and (free, y) propositions for the fridge and the compressor. Removing a compressor requires that the fridge is turned off, and that none of the screws that fit the compressor are fastened. Attaching a compressor requires that the fridge is turned off, and that the compressor fits the fridge (for each fridge, only the initial compressor and its replacement fit). All operator parameters are constrained to be of the appropriate types.

All instances of *Fridge* are solvable (by in turn stopping a fridge, unfastening the screws, exchanging the compressors, fastening the screws, and starting the fridge again). There are various negations that are compiled away by negation-free compilation. There are no disjunctive goals so the properties of the propositional and of the negation-free compilations are the same, c.f. Proposition 3.1.6.

Proposition 8.3.2. *Given the propositional or negation-free compilation of an instance (C, I, G) of the Fridge domain, the corresponding state space is undirected.*

Proof. After removing static predicates, the stop-fridge(x) and start-fridge(x) actions as well as the fasten(x, y, z) and unfasten(x, y, z) actions are invertible in the sense of Definition 4.1.5 (by each other, respectively). For remove-compressor(x, y) and attach-compressor(x, y), matters are a bit more complicated. While they obviously undo each other's effects, applicability is slightly less obvious. Assume a compressor c has just been removed from a fridge f in a reachable state s. Then, c fits f — otherwise it couldn't have been attached in s — so one can attach c back onto f. Now assume a compressor c has just been attached to a fridge f in a reachable state s. The question is, are the screws all unscrewed? If not, then they must have been fastened (and not unfastened afterwards) to a matching compressor that is already attached to a fridge. However, both matching compressors can be attached only to the same fridge f, and f has been free in s.

Theorem 8.3.4. *Given the propositional or negation-free compilation of an instance (C, I, G) of the Fridge domain, the corresponding state space does not contain local minima under h^+.*

Proof. We show that all actions are respected by the relaxation. With the argumentation given above in the proof to Proposition 8.3.2, this suffices by a slight extension of Lemma 8.1.2, allowing for the inverse relation between remove-compressor(x, y) and attach-compressor(x, y). This does not syntactically follow Definition 4.1.5, but has the same consequences semantically.

It is obvious that start-fridge(x) and attach-compressor(x, y) actions are respected by the relaxation: such actions can only start an optimal plan if they add the respective goal, which can not be added by any other action. So those actions are then contained in any optimal relaxed plan P^+, and can be used to start P^+ because they are applicable. If fasten(x, y, z) starts an optimal plan, then this means that y is the new compressor for z, so that action is also part of an optimal relaxed plan (the relaxed plan could also achieve the goal (screwed, x) by fastening x to the broken compressor for z, but this involves more steps). If stop-fridge(x) starts an optimal plan, then this means that either the broken compressor is attached to x, or that one of the screws is still unfastened. In both cases a relaxed plan must also stop x in order to apply the respective actions: the first case is obvious, the second case follows because the screws can only be fastened to a matching compressor, which in turn can only be attached to x. If unfasten(x, y, z) starts an optimal plan, then y is the broken compressor for z, so unfastening x prior to removing y from z can not be avoided in a relaxed plan. Similarly, remove-compressor(x, y) starting an optimal plan means that x is the broken compressor for y, removing which can not be avoided.

The maximal exit distance in *Fridge* is not bounded because there can be an arbitrary number of screws for each compressor. Consider the instances with a single fridge and n screws. From the initial state, an optimal relaxed plan stops the fridge, unfastens all screws, removes the broken compressor, and attaches the new one, so $h^+(I) = n + 3$. The nearest better state is the one where the broken compressor has been removed already: in all states where that has not been done, one must in the relaxed plan always do the removing and attaching action, either start or stop the fridge, and either fasten or unfasten each screw, depending on the current state of the fridge or screw (if a screw is unfastened, it needs to be fastened for achieving the respective goal, and if a screw is fastened, it needs to be unfastened in order to remove the broken compressor; similarly for the fridge). So h^+ is constantly $h^+(s) = n + 3$ for all states s where the broken compressor is attached to the fridge. Getting from the initial state to a state where the broken compressor can be removed requires $n + 1$ steps, which is a lower bound on the maximal exit distance.

As a matter of fact, with arbitrarily many fridges and n screws, $n + 1$ is exactly the maximal exit distance. From a state where an old compressor is attached one can, like described above, get to a better state by at most stopping that fridge, unfastening all screws, and removing the compressor. From a state where no compressor is attached, one can get to a better state by attaching a new compressor, first stopping the respective fridge. From a state where a new compressor is attached one gets to a better state by stopping the respective fridge if it's on, and fastening one more of the compressor's screws. Therefore, restricting the maximal number of screws per compressor would yield a domain with a constant upper bound on the maximal exit distance under h^+.

8.3.4 Blocksworld-no-arm

In *Blocksworld-no-arm*, there are three operators: move a block x from the table to a block y (which exchanges (clear, y) and (on-table, x) with (on, x, y)); move a block x from a block y to the table (which does the above exchange the other way round); finally, move a block x from a block y to a block z, which exchanges (on, x, z) and (clear, y) with (on, x, y) and (clear, z). The initial state of an instance specifies the initial positions of the blocks, the goal state specifies a (consistent, i.e., cycle-free) set of (on, x, y) propositions. In the operators that move a block onto another block, it is required that the two blocks are different (which does not follow from the other preconditions, so must be postulated to avoid absurd actions).

All instances of *Blocksworld-no-arm* are solvable (by moving all blocks to the table and thereafter building the goal stacks from bottom to top). Removing static predicates gets rid of actions that try to move a block onto itself. With Proposition 3.1.3, we assume in the following that static predicates have been removed. The actions are invertible in the sense of Definition 4.1.5, implying that the state space is undirected, as stated in Corollary 4.1.1. In a STRIPS domain there is no difference between the original tasks and their compilations. Proving the non-existence of local minima under h^+ is more complicated than in the domains we have seen so far.

Theorem 8.3.5. *Given an instance (C, I, G) of the Blocksworld-no-arm domain, the corresponding state space does not contain local minima under h^+.*

Proof. We prove that there is always at least one optimal solution path on which the heuristic value does not increase. Let $s \in S$ be a reachable state with $gd(s) > 0$. We distinguish the following two cases:

1. There is an optimal plan for (A, s, G) starting with an action a that puts some block x into its goal position on block y.
2. No optimal plan for (A, s, G) starts with such an action.

In the first case, we will see that there is an optimal relaxed plan for (A, s, G) containing a. In the second case, we will identify an optimal plan P_s for (A, s, G) starting with an action a that moves a block x onto the table, and an optimal relaxed plan P_s^+ for (A, s, G) containing an action a' that moves x. In both cases, we prove that $h^+(Result(s, \langle a \rangle)) \le h^+(s)$, which finishes the argumentation.

Assume there is an optimal plan for (A, s, G) starting with a, putting block x into its goal position on block y, $(on, x, y) \in G$, i.e., $a = $ move-table-to-block(x, y) or $a = $ move-block-to-block(x, z, y) for some third block z. Obviously, all relaxed plans for (A, s, G) must also at some point move x onto y. If this is done in a different way than by a, then x must first be moved to a different position, involving one more step. Moreover, moving x to a different position can achieve — apart from the $(clear, z)$ proposition that is then also achieved by a — only an $(on-table, x)$ or (on, x, u) proposition. Those propositions are of no other use than for moving around x. It follows that all optimal relaxed plans for (A, s, G) use a for achieving (on, x, y). With invertibility, we are finished.

Now assume that there is no optimal plan for (A, s, G) that starts by putting some block into its goal position. We have a closer look at the situation. The blocks are arranged on the table in stacks — a bottom block directly on the table, a sequence of blocks transitively on that block, a clear top block. The *trivial* stack contains only a single block that is bottom and top at once. We say that a stack is a *good* stack, if it is consistent with the goal conditions, i.e., if $(on, x, y) \in G$ and x or y are in the stack, then x is located on y (implying that both blocks are in the stack). Obviously, optimal plans leave good stacks unchanged — blocks in these stacks are either not mentioned in the goal, or already in their final position. Focusing on the stacks in s that are *not* good, we observe the following:

1. Any plan for (A, s, G), relaxed or real, will need to move the top blocks x of all stacks in s that are not good: either x itself is not in its goal position, or some block y below isn't, in which case x must be moved away for clearing y.

2. Let a be an action that moves a block x to the table where x is top of a non-trivial stack that is not good. Then a starts an optimal plan for (A, s, G): the blocks x must be moved, but by prerequisite no such block x can be optimally moved into its goal position right away; moving x to the table can only be better than moving it onto some block where it does not need to be finally.

Moreover, we observe that there is at least one non-trivial non-good stack in s: otherwise, all non-good stacks would consist of a single block, implying that some block *could* be put into its goal position right away. Let x be the top block of a non-trivial non-good stack in s, located on y, and $a := $ move-block-to-table(x, y). By the above second observation, a starts an optimal plan P_s for (A, s, G), and by the above first observation, an arbitrary optimal relaxed plan P_s^+ for (A, s, G) contains an action moving x away from y; let a' be the first such action. If $a' = $ move-block-to-table(x, y), we are finished with invertibility. Assume $a' = $ move-block-to-block(x, y, z). Denote by $s' := Result(s, \langle a \rangle)$ the result of applying a in s. We distinguish two cases:

1. $(on, x, y) \in G$: Construct an action sequence $P_{s'}^+$ by replacing a' in P_s^+ with move-table-to-block(x, y). $P_{s'}^+$ is a relaxed plan for (A, s', G): no action

before a' needs (on, x, y) as precondition (by prerequisite, a' is the first action moving x away from y); executing the relaxed version of move-block-to-block(x, y, z) in P_s^+ achieves one more proposition, (on, x, z), but x is already in its goal position, so the optimal relaxed plan P_s^+ moves x only once, thus (on, x, z) is not needed by any other action.

2. (on, x, y) $\notin G$: Construct an action sequence $P_{s'}^+$ by replacing a' in P_s^+ with move-table-to-block(x, z). Now, $P_{s'}^+$ is a relaxed plan for (A, s', G) unless there is some action that needs (on, x, y) as precondition, which must be a move-block-to-block(x, y, u) (moving x to the table is useless after applying the relaxed version of a'). Such an action comes after a' in P_s^+ (remember that a' is the first action moving x away from y), so it can be replaced by move-block-to-block(x, z, u) in $P_{s'}^+$. This replacement does not achieve (clear, y), but that proposition has already been true in s' anyway.

In both cases, we have a relaxed plan $P_{s'}^+$ for (A, s', G) with $|P_{s'}^+| = |P_s^+|$, which concludes our argumentation.

The maximal exit distance in *Blocksworld-no-arm* is not bounded. Consider an instance with $n + 1$ blocks $\{b_1, \ldots, b_{n+1}\}$, initial state $I = \{(\text{clear}, b_1),$ (on, b_1, b_2), ..., (on, b_{n-1}, b_n), (on-table, b_n), (clear, b_{n+1}), (on-table, b_{n+1})$\}$ and goal state $G = \{(\text{on}, b_1, b_2), \ldots, (\text{on}, b_n, b_{n+1})\}$. Here, the stack $b_1, \ldots, b_n$ needs to be disassembled, and rebuilt on top of b_{n+1}. An optimal relaxed plan for I has length n, by moving $b_1 \ldots b_{n-1}$ to the table, and moving b_n on top of b_{n+1}. Now, $h^+(s') \geq n$ for all reachable states s' where b_n is not on top of b_{n+1}: b_n must be moved to b_{n+1}; to make this possible, b_{n-1} must be moved away from b_n if it is currently on top of it, and otherwise it must be moved to b_n for achieving the goal; the same argument can iteratively applied upwards to b_1. Now consider again the initial state. Reaching, from there, the nearest state s' where b_n is on top of b_{n+1} involves n steps moving $b_1 \ldots b_{n-1}$ away, and moving b_n onto b_{n+1}. Thus the maximal exit distance in the instance is at least n.

8.3.5 Grid

In *Grid*, a robot must move along places that are arranged in a grid-like reachability relation; the places can be locked and there are keys of different shapes to open them; the goal is to have some keys at their goal places. More explicitly, there are five operators: one can move from place x to place y, which requires (apart from the obvious preconditions) that x and y are connected and that y is open (not locked); one can pick up a key y at a place x, which requires that the arm is empty (one can only hold one key at a time), and has as effects that one holds the key, that the arm is no longer empty, and that the key is no longer at x; one can put a key y down at a place x, which inverts the effects of picking y up at x; one can abbreviate the two previous actions by doing a pickup-and-lose of keys y and z at a place x; to do this, one must hold y, which is directly exchanged for z, i.e., the effects are that one holds z and that y is located at x; finally, one can unlock a place y when one is at a place x that is connected to y, and holds a key z that has the same shape v as the locked place y; the add effect of that is that the place x is open, the delete effect is that the place is no longer locked. The instances specify the initial locations of all keys, locked places, and of the robot, as well as the shapes of the keys and the locked places; the goal specifies places for a subset of the keys. The robot always starts on an *open* place. This does make a significant difference: if the robot is allowed to start on a locked place, there can be local minima under h^+ while otherwise, as we prove below, there are none. Intuitively, it makes more sense to let the robot be located only in open places; this is also the case in the published benchmark examples.

A *Grid* instance can be unsolvable if, for example, some important place is locked with a shape for which there is no matching key. In a STRIPS domain there is no difference between the original tasks and their compilations. Proving the non-existence of dead ends is easy; proving the non-existence of local minima under h^+ is rather tricky.

Proposition 8.3.3. *Given a solvable instance (C, I, G) of the Grid domain, the corresponding state space is at most harmless.*

Proof. As the robot can only *open* locks, one possible solution plan for any reachable state s is this: re-establish the initial situation as far as possible, i.e., put all keys that have been moved back to their initial places, and move back to the initial place of the robot (this is possible because to all these places there must be a path on which all places are open — otherwise the keys, respectively the robot, could not have been moved). Afterwards, execute an arbitrary solution plan for the initial state, omitting actions that try to unlock a place that is already open.

As unlocking a place can not be undone, a *Grid* instance is not undirected if there is at least one locked place that can be opened. Let us focus on local minima.

Theorem 8.3.6. *Given a solvable instance (C, I, G) of the Grid domain, the corresponding state space does not contain local minima under h^+.*

Proof. Let $s \in S$ be a reachable state with $gd(s) > 0$. We identify a flat path to an exit, i.e., a path on which h^+ does not increase.

Let p be the current position of the robot, $(\text{at-robot}, p) \in s$. Let P_s^+ be an optimal relaxed plan for (A, s, G) (with solvability and Proposition 8.3.3, there is at least one such P_s^+). We focus in the following on one action a in P_s^+ that makes use of a key k at place p'. If there is an unlock action in P_s^+, then we select the first such action $a = \text{unlock}(p', y, k, v)$. If there is no single unlock, then we select an arbitrary putdown action $a = \text{putdown}(p', k)$; without loss of generality, there is at least one such action because we can assume that the last action in P_s^+ is a putdown (remember that the only goals are to have some keys at their goal places). We distinguish between three cases:

1. The robot is holding k in s, $(\text{holding}, k) \in s$.
2. The arm is empty in s, $(\text{arm-empty}) \in s$.
3. The robot is holding $k' \neq k$ in s, $(\text{holding}, k') \in s, k' \neq k$.

In the first case, we identify a flat path to an exit state s'. In the second and third cases, we identify a flat path to a state s' where the robot is holding k, i.e., where the first case holds.

Assume the robot is holding key k. The action a we have selected is either the first unlock in P_s^+, or a putdown, using k. In both cases, a could be executed given the robot was at place p', and in both cases, P_s^+ contains what we will call an *open path from p to p'* in the following: P_s^+ contains, preceding a, a subsequence $\langle \text{move}(p = p_1, p_2), \ldots, \text{move}(p_{n-1}, p_n = p') \rangle$ of moving actions connecting p to p', such that $(\text{open}, p_i) \in s$ for $1 \le i \le n$; the moving actions are there because otherwise a could not be applied at the point in P_s^+ where it appears; p_1 is open because the robot can only be at open places in all reachable states by definition (note that at this point we need the restriction that the robot is not allowed to start at locked places), and $p_2, \ldots, p_n$ are open because we selected a to be the *first* unlock in P_s^+. Let $s_i := Result(s, \langle \text{move}(p_1, p_2), \ldots, \text{move}(p_{i-1}, p_i) \rangle)$. Our flat path is the above open path, and our exit state s' is $s' := s_n$. It suffices to show that $h^+(s_i) \le h^+(s)$ for $1 \le i \le n$, and that there is a state s'', $(s', s'') \in E$, $h^+(s'') < h^+(s)$. Consider s_2, resulting from s by executing $\text{move}(p, p_2)$. As that action is contained in P_s^+, Lemma 8.1.1 allows us to construct a relaxed plan $P_{s_2}^+$ for (A, s_2, G) by removing $\text{move}(p, p_2)$, and adding $\langle \text{move}(p_2, p) \rangle$ as a prefix. Therefore, $h^+(s_2) \le h^+(s)$. Now, the next action $\text{move}(p_2, p_3)$ on our open path is still contained in $P_{s_2}^+$, so the same argument applies to s_3, and so forth. Let $P_{s'}^+$ be the thus constructed relaxed plan for $s' = s_n$. Our action a is applicable in s', and it is contained in $P_{s'}^+$. Let $s'' := Result(s', a)$. We construct a relaxed plan for s'' as follows. First, we remove a from $P_{s'}^+$. If $a = \text{unlock}(p', y, k, v)$, that does the job: the single delete is (locked, y), which is only needed for actions that unlock y. Now, the optimal relaxed plan P_s^+ for (A, s, G) does of course not open y twice, and we did not add new unlock actions when constructing $P_{s'}^+$. If $a = \text{putdown}(p', k)$, the delete is $(\text{holding}, k)$. No unlock actions are contained in $P_{s'}^+$, but $(\text{holding}, k)$ might be needed by pickup-and-lose(x, k, z) actions contained in $P_{s'}^+$. These can, however, be replaced by pickup(x, z) actions when the relaxed plan starts out in s''. In both cases for the selection of a, the resulting relaxed plan for (A, s'', G) is one step shorter than that for (A, s', G), which concludes the argument.

We still need to deal with the cases where the arm is empty in s, or where the robot is holding some different key $k' \ne k$. In both cases, we can move along open paths in P_s^+ to end up in a state s' where the robot holds k. Consider the case where $(\text{arm-empty}) \in s$. At the point in P_s^+ where a is applied, $(\text{holding}, k)$ has been achieved. This was done via a pickup(p', k) or a pickup-and-lose(p', k'', k) action preceding a in P_s^+. In the first case, we stop, in the second case, we apply the same argument to k'', i.e., before pickup-and-lose(p', k'', k) is applied in P_s^+ there must be some action achieving $(\text{holding}, k'')$. At some point, a key must be picked up, as initially in s no key is held. So we end up with a list $k_1, \ldots, k_n = k$ of keys such that $\langle \text{pickup}(p_1, k_1), \text{pickup-and-lose}(p_2, k_1, k_2), \ldots, \text{pickup-and-}$lose$(p_n, k_{n-1}, k_n = k) \rangle$ is a subsequence of P_s^+ for certain places $p_1, \ldots, p_n$. P_s^+ contains open paths from p to all p_i, $1 \le i \le n$ (remember that either our selected action a using k is the very first unlock in P_s^+, or there are no unlocks needed at all). We move along the path from p to p_1, execute pickup(p_1, k_1), and move back from p_1 to p. At all points on this path we can use, like above, Lemma 8.1.1 to construct a relaxed plan for the new state that has the same number of steps like P_s^+: putdown(p_1, k_1) inverts pickup(p_1, k_1), and the actions moving back from p_1 to p are all contained in the relaxed plan constructed when moving to p_1. Moving back to p constructs a relaxed plan that contains exactly the same move actions as P_s^+. We can thus in the same fashion move from p to p_i, $2 \leq i \leq n-1$, execute pickup-and-lose(p_i, k_{i-1}, k_i) (inverted by pickup-and-lose(p_i, k_i, k_{i-1})), and move back to p. We finally move from p to p_n and execute pickup-and-lose($p_n, k_{n-1}, k_n = k$) which brings us to the desired state s' where the robot is holding the key k.

Finally, consider the case where (holding, k') $\in s, k' \neq k$. Like in the above case, at the point in P_s^+ where a is applied, (holding, k) has been achieved. So, like above, there is either a pickup(p', k) or a pickup-and-lose(p', k'', k) action preceding a in P_s^+, the same holding for k'' unless $k'' = k'$. Iterating the argument gives us a key list $k_1, \ldots, k_n = k$ such that either $\langle$pickup(p_1, k_1), pickup-and-lose(p_2, k_1, k_2), $\ldots$, pickup-and-lose($p_n, k_{n-1}, k_n = k$)$\rangle$ or $\langle$pickup-and-lose(p_1, k' $= k_1, k_2$), $\ldots$, pickup-and-lose($p_n, k_{n-1}, k_n = k$)$\rangle$ is a subsequence of P_s^+. The first case can be reduced to the second case by replacing pickup(p_1, k_1) with pickup-and-lose(p_1, k', k_1) in P_s^+, and adding k' as the front member of the key list. Just like we did above, we can then move along the open paths from p to p_i, execute the adequate pickup-and-lose(p_i, k_{i-1}, k_i) action, and move back to p, finally ending up in the state s' where pickup-and-lose($p_n, k_{n-1}, k_n = k$) has been executed, and the robot is thus holding the correct key, which case we have treated earlier.

We remark two things about the above argumentation. First, Theorem 8.3.6 also holds when there is no pickup-and-lose operator (in fact, the proof is a lot easier in this case). Second, the identified flat paths can be arbitrarily long and the maximal exit distance in *Grid* is thus *not* proved to be bounded by a constant. Consider the simple example where the robot and one key k have initially n moving steps distance, and k shall be put to the robot's starting place. The h^+ value for the initial state is $n + 2$: walk over to the key, pick it up, and drop it at the starting place (remember that the at-robot propositions are not deleted). The nearest state with better h^+ value is the state where k has been picked up, which is $n + 1$ steps away.

8.3.6 Hanoi

The *Hanoi* domain is a STRIPS encoding of the classical *Towers of Hanoi* problem. There are n discs $d_1, \ldots, d_n$, and three pegs p_1, p_2, and p_3. There is a single operator that moves a constant x from a constant y onto a constant z (note that the operator parameters can be grounded with discs as well as pegs). The preconditions of the move are that x is on y, x is clear, z is clear, and x *is smaller than z*; the effects are that x is on z and y is clear, while x is no longer on y

and z is no longer clear. The semantics of *Towers of Hanoi* are encoded via the *smaller* relation. This relation holds in the obvious way between the discs, and all discs are smaller than the pegs (the pegs are not smaller than anything so can not be moved). The instances differ in terms of the number n of discs that must be transferred from p_1 to p_3.

All instances of *Hanoi* are solvable. After removing static predicates (i.e., the smaller relations), all actions are invertible in the sense of Definition 4.1.5. So the state space is undirected, as stated in Corollary 4.1.1. There is no difference between the original tasks and their compilations. We prove the non-existence of local minima by first giving an exact measure of what $h^+(s)$ is for any reachable state s: as it turns out, h^+ is always equal to the number of discs that are not yet in their goal position. This suffices because an optimal plan does not move discs that are already where they should be.

Lemma 8.3.1. *Given an instance (C, I, G) of the Hanoi domain, and a reachable state $s \in S$. Denote p_3 by d_{n+1}, and let $sg(s)$ be defined as follows:*

$$sg(s) := min\{m \mid 1 \leq m \leq n+1, (on, d_m, d_{m+1}), \ldots, (on, d_n, d_{n+1}) \in s\}$$

Then $h^+(s) = sg(s) - 1$ holds.

Proof. $sg(s)$ is the number of the smallest disc that is already in its goal position in s, with all discs below it also being in their goal position ($sg(s) = n+1$ if no disc, or only p_3, is already in its goal position). If $sg(s) = 1$, the goal is achieved and there is nothing to show. Else, we show by induction over i, $i \leq n$, that i relaxed steps can get us to a state s' where $(on, d_1, d_2), \ldots$, $(on, d_i, d_{i+1}) \in s'$. With that, the lemma follows: after $sg(s) - 1$ steps, (on, d_1, d_2), $\ldots$, $(on, d_{sg(s)-1}, d_{sg(s)}) \in s'$, which gives us $G \subseteq s'$ as $(on, d_{sg(s)}, d_{sg(s)+1})$, $\ldots$, $(on, d_n, d_{n+1} = p_3)$ are true in s already (also, at least $sg(s) - 1$ relaxed steps are necessary as that many (on, d_i, d_{i+1}) propositions from G are missing in s, and each action achieves at most one such proposition).

We prove the stronger result that, after i relaxed steps, we can get to a state s' where $(on, d_1, d_2), \ldots, (on, d_i, d_{i+1}) \in s'$, $(clear, d_1), \ldots, (clear, d_{i+1}) \in s'$, and $(clear, d) \in s'$ for all discs or pegs d such that $(on, d_j, d) \in s$ for some $j \leq i$.

Base case $i = 1$: $(clear, d_1) \in s$ simply because s is reachable and no disc can be placed onto the smallest disc d_1. Either d_1 is on d_2 in s, or d_1 is on some other disc or peg d. In the first case, we execute the relaxed step $move(d_1, d_2, z)^+$ for some z that is clear in s; in the second case, d_2 is clear (no disc other than d_1 can be on d_2), so we can execute $move(d_1, d, d_2)^+$. In both cases, $(clear, d_1)$, $(clear, d_2)$, and (on, d_1, d_2) are contained in the resulting state s', and also $(clear, d)$ holds for the disc or peg d on which d_1 is in s.

Inductive case $i \longrightarrow i+1, i+1 \leq n$: let s' be the state reached after i relaxed steps, with the required properties. Either d_{i+1} is on d_{i+2} in s (remember that we denote $d_{n+1} := p_3$), or d_{i+1} is on some other disc or peg d. In both cases there is an action applicable to s' which yields, in its relaxed version, a state that satisfies the requirements. Consider the second case. We can apply $move(d_{i+1}, d, d_{i+2})^+$: $(clear, d_{i+1}) \in s'$ by induction hypothesis; if d_{i+2} was not clear, this would be due to a smaller disc d_j, $j < i + 1$, being on d_{i+2} in s, so again (clear, d_{i+2}) $\in s'$ per induction hypothesis. The resulting state has d clear, and d_{i+1} on d_{i+2}, so it fulfills the requirements. Consider now the first case, where d_{i+1} is on d_{i+2} in s. Applying move$(d_{i+1}, d_{i+2}, z)^+$ for some z would obviously yield a state satisfying the requirements (the only proposition that must be achieved is (clear, d_{i+2})). Concerning the applicability of move$(d_{i+1}, d_{i+2}, z)^+$ in s', (clear, d_{i+1}) $\in s'$ per induction hypothesis. It remains to find a disc or peg z with (smaller, d_{i+1}, z) $\in s'$ and (clear, z) $\in s'$. Let p be a peg such that d_{i+1} is not transitively on p in s, and z be the topmost disc transitively on p in s such that (smaller, d_{i+1}, z) $\in s'$, or $z := p$ if there is no such disc. z is clear: if not, (on, d_j, z) $\in s$ would hold for some disc $j \leq i$ smaller than d_{i+1}, so (clear, z) $\in s'$ per induction hypothesis.

Theorem 8.3.7. *Given an instance (C, I, G) of the Hanoi domain, the corresponding state space does not contain local minima under h^+.*

Proof. Follows from Lemma 8.3.1 and the fact that an optimal plan does not move around the discs that are already in their goal position. In a reachable non-goal state s, with $sg(s) > 1$ being the number of the smallest disc that is already in its goal position in s (all discs below it also being in their goal position), the optimal plan from s moves around smaller discs until the next smaller disc is in its goal position. Lemma 8.3.1 proves that, before this is achieved, h^+ remains $sg(s) - 1$ constantly, and that, when this is achieved, h^+ goes down to $sg(s) - 2$. Iterating the argument, h^+ does not increase on the optimal solution path from s.

We remark that the length of the flat paths is not bounded by a constant. Quite differently, their length is exponential in the number of discs: from the initial state of an instance with n discs, the nearest state where the largest disc d_n is in its goal position is 2^{n-1} steps away.

8.4 No Unrecognized Dead Ends

There are two domains where our hypotheses concern only the dead end class of the instances. They are the *Blocksworld-arm* and *Schedule* domains. The former domain has already been dealt with in Chapter 4.

8.4.1 Blocksworld-arm

The instances of *Blocksworld-arm* are the same as those of *Blocksworld-no-arm*. The difference is that blocks are moved via an arm, so that there are four operators to pickup a block, put a block down, stack a block onto some other block, or unstack a block from some other block. The empirical investigation in Chapter 7 has shown that — in difference to the *Blocksworld-no-arm* domain, c.f. Theorem 8.3.5 — there can be local minima under h^+. As for the dead end class, this has already been proven in Corollary 4.1.1: all actions are invertible in the sense of Definition 4.1.5.

8.4.2 Schedule

In *Schedule*, a collection of parts must be processed with a number of working steps changing their shape, surface, or color; one can also drill holes of varying widths in varying orientations. Our hypothesis is that all dead ends are recognized by h^+. The full domain description is rather lengthy, with nine large operators that make use of a simple form of conditional effects (for example, painting an object results in the object being painted in the new color, and not any longer being painted in any other color it was painted in before). The full details are in Appendix A. The details that are important for the proof below are the following. Initially, any part can have an arbitrary shape, one of three surface conditions, an arbitrary color, and arbitrarily many holes in arbitrary widths and orientations. For the goal, a part can be required to be of cylindrical shape, and to have arbitrary other properties. A part p is made cylindrical, with a rough surface, by applying the do-lathe($p\ldots$) action.[1] Polished (smooth) surfaces are achieved via the do-polish($p\ldots$) (do-grind($p\ldots$)) action. A hole of width w and orientation o is made by do-drill-press($p, w, o\ldots$). Finally, painting p in a color c is done by do-immersion-paint($p, c\ldots$). All operators require that the respective machine is not busy, and that the part is not currently processed elsewhere. These propositions are achieved (for all machines and parts) by do-time-step(). There are other operators, but as we will see the above operators suffice for solving the tasks. The do-polish($p\ldots$) and do-drill-press($p, w, o\ldots$) actions require that the part is cold; do-drill-press($p, w, o\ldots$) also requires that there is not already a hole in p of width w and orientation o. Apart from some static propositions like type information or the existence of the appropriate drill, none of those six operators has other preconditions. All parts p are cold initially and the only action that makes them hot is do-roll($p\ldots$) (which is not needed to achieve the goal). All operators that can make a part polished or drill a hole (apart from the two operators above, there is one more for each of these two jobs) require that the part is cold. There is no way of making a part cold. This can lead into dead ends.

There are various negations, for example the requirement that a machine is not already busy at the time when it is assigned a job. There are no disjunctive goals, so the negation-free and propositional compilations have the same properties, c.f. Proposition 3.1.6. We prove that all instances are solvable, and that, if there is no real plan from a state, then neither is there a relaxed plan.

Theorem 8.4.1. *Given the propositional or negation-free compilation of an instance (C, I, G) of the Schedule domain, the corresponding planning task is solvable, and the corresponding state space is at most recognized under h^+.*

Proof. We must show solvability, and that $h^+(s) = \infty$ for all $s \in S$ with $gd(s) = \infty$. For the initial state I of the task, a solution plan can be constructed as follows. Look at each part p in turn. If (shape, p, cylindrical) $\in G$

---

[1] In our formal definition, see Appendix A, most operators have parameters, like the machine, that must always be grounded with the same constant. These parameters serve to replace the domain constants that are used in the original formulation. We omit these parameters here to improve readability.

or (surface-condition, p, rough) $\in$ G, and the respective proposition is not true in I, then apply do-lathe($p\ldots$), and afterwards do-time-step() (applying do-lathe($p\ldots$) for (surface-condition, p, rough) deletes all other shapes than (shape, p, cylindrical); this does not matter as being cylindrical is the only shape that is allowed to be required for the goal). If (surface-condition, p, polished) $\in$ G or (surface-condition, p, smooth) $\in$ G, and the respective proposition is not currently true, then apply do-polish(p) or do-grind($p\ldots$), respectively, and afterwards do-time-step() (note that p has temperature cold initially, so do-polish($p\ldots$) can be applied). Next step, all still required holes (has-hole, p, w, o) $\in$ G can be achieved by iteratively applying do-drill-press(p, w, $o\ldots$) and do-time-step() (p is still cold). Finally, if (painted, p, c) $\in$ G for some c, and (painted, p, c) is not currently true, we can apply do-immersion-paint(p, $c\ldots$), and are finished. After another application of do-time-step(), the same process can be iterated for the next part until all parts are processed.

The same algorithm to construct a solution plan can be applied for every reachable state s $\in$ S unless there is some part p with (surface-condition, p, polished) $\in$ G or (has-hole, p, w, o) $\in$ G for some w and o, such that (temperature, p, cold) $\notin$ s: all other preconditions of the required actions are obviously fulfilled at the point where they are needed — except the temperature, required non-static propositions are only those concerning busy machines, scheduled objects, or p not having a certain hole. The first two are achieved by doing time steps, the third one is only required by do-drill-press(p, w, $o\ldots$). If that precondition is not true, this means that there already is an appropriate hole, so the action does not need to be applied at all. It can be that a part p has (temperature, p, cold) $\notin$ s when, on the path from the initial state to s, do-roll($p\ldots$) has been applied at some point. As there is no way of re-achieving (temperature, p, cold), s is then a dead end, $gd(s) = \infty$, if p needs to be polished or get holes made to achieve the goal: all actions that can achieve (surface-condition, p, polished) or (has-hole, p, w, o) for some w and o need (temperature, p, cold) as a precondition, which is not contained in s, and is not added by any action. But then, (A^+, s, G) is also unsolvable, $h^+(s) = \infty$.

Note that the above proof also proves that there can be dead ends. Also, the *Schedule* instances are not undirected: in each instance there is at least one part p; the effects of do-roll(p) can not be undone; the precondition requires merely that the respective machine is not busy and that the part is not processed elsewhere, so do-roll(p) can be applied, for example, in the initial state.

8.5 Assembly

We finally consider the *Assembly* domain, where a complex object must be constructed by assembling its parts — other objects which stand in a *part-of* relation to it — together, obeying certain ordering constraints. The parts themselves might need to be assembled in the same way beforehand. *Assembly* is the only domain where it turns out that our hypotheses are false. The situation is way more complex than in the domains we have seen before.

We give an example of an unrecognized dead end state, which falsifies both the hypothesis that all dead ends are recognized, and the hypothesis that there are no local minima (as their existence is implied by the existence of unrecognized dead ends, c.f. Theorem 7.0.1). From a pure verification point of view, this would suffice. It is however an interesting question *why* the small example instances used to come up with the hypotheses, c.f. Chapter 7, do not contain the more complex structures that can in principle be present in *Assembly* — especially as there is no such discrepancy in any other of our domains, and as FF demonstrates excellent behavior in the AIPS-1998 *Assembly* collection, c.f. Section 3.7. So, instead of leaving it at the counter-example, we perform a detailed investigation of the topological properties of *Assembly* instances, depending on their part-of relations and ordering constraints. While the results do not provide a fully satisfactory explanation as to why our small examples do not contain any unrecognized dead ends or local minima under h^+, we do identify a number of interesting implications. We prove under exactly which circumstances an *Assembly* instance is solvable; we prove a sufficient criterion for the non-existence of dead ends; we finally prove a sufficient criterion for the initial state (amongst other states) having a full exit path under h^+. We will see that these results are relevant for our randomly generated small examples, and particularly relevant for the AIPS-1998 benchmark collection.

The investigation involves a lot of details from the formal definition of the *Assembly* domain, and is probably hard to understand without first having a look at that definition in Appendix A. Nevertheless, we give a short summary of the crucial points and of the notation. In any instance, the goal is to have some assembly g completed. The set of all assemblies is denoted by As. Each assembly $y \in As$ has a (possibly empty) set of *parts* $pa(y) \subseteq As$, so that the relations (x, y) where $x \in pa(y)$ form a tree with root g (the tree specifying which assembly "consists" of which other ones). Each assembly $y \in As$ has a set of *transient parts* $tr(y) \subseteq As$, where $pa(y) \cap tr(y) = \emptyset$ and $y \notin tr(y)$, and $pa(y) = \emptyset \Rightarrow tr(y) = \emptyset$ (i.e., the leafs of the tree, the "atomic" assemblies, have no transient parts either). One can assemble x into y if either x is a part of y, $x \in pa(y)$, or x is a transient part of y, $x \in tr(y)$. To execute such an assembling action x must be available, and all assemblies z that have an *assemble order* before x in y, $(z, x) \in ao(y)$, must already have been assembled into y. Upon execution of the assembling action x is incorporated into y, and y is complete and available if no transient part is incorporated into it, and $x \in pa(y)$ is the only part of y that was not yet incorporated. A transient part $x \in tr(y)$ can be removed from y if it is incorporated into y, and all z that have a *remove order* before x in y, $(z, x) \in ro(y)$, are already incorporated into y. In effect, x is available and no longer incorporated into y. If all parts $z \in pa(y)$ are incorporated into y, and x is the last transient part that is removed, then the removing action makes y complete and available. One can also remove a part $x \in pa(y)$ from y, under the condition that it is incorporated, and that all z which have an assemble order before x in y, $(z,x) \in ao(y)$, are *not* incorporated into y (in difference to transient parts, where the assemblies with remove orders must be incorporated for removal). Removing x does *not* delete the completeness or availability of y, in fact there is no operator at all that can delete completeness (which appears to be a domain bug, but after all what we want to look at are the properties of the domain as it is used in the planning community). In the initial state, all assemblies y are available (but not complete) that have no parts, $pa(y) = \emptyset$ (i.e., the leafs of the tree given by the $x \in pa(y)$ relations, the "atomic" assemblies, are initially available). The assemble and remove orders are consistent, i.e., $ao(y)$ respectively $ro(y)$ is cycle-free for all assemblies y. Furthermore, if $(x,z) \in ao(y)$ and $z \in pa(y) \cup tr(y)$ then $x \in pa(y) \cup tr(y)$. Similarly, if $(x,z) \in ro(y)$ and $z \in tr(y)$ then $x \in pa(y) \cup tr(y)$ (we say some words below on the restrictions we make). Assembling x into y or removing x from y can require an arbitrary amount of resources (i.e., machines) to be committed to y. All resources are available in the initial state. A resource r can be committed to (released from) an assembly y simply by applying the commit(r,y) (release(r,y)) action, which exchanges availability of r for its being committed to y (vice versa). There are no additional constraints on the application of these actions.

The set of instances makes (on top of the pa relation being a tree and the obvious constraints on transient parts) the following restrictions. The assemble and remove orders are consistent. If $(x,z) \in ao(y)$ and $z \in pa(y) \cup tr(y)$ (z might have to be incorporated into y) then $x \in pa(y) \cup tr(y)$ (one has the chance to incorporate x into y). Similarly, if $(x,z) \in ro(y)$ and $z \in tr(y)$ then $x \in pa(y) \cup tr(y)$. These restrictions are fulfilled in the AIPS-1998 example collection, with the following exceptions. There are three examples with syntax errors (the initial states use undeclared constants). Furthermore, in two examples there are x, z, and y with $(x,z) \in ro(y)$, $z \in tr(y)$, and $x \notin pa(y) \cup tr(y)$. As, additionally, in both tasks z must at some point be assembled into y, these two tasks are trivially unsolvable — x must be assembled into y in order to remove z, but cannot be because it is neither a part nor a transient part of y. We assume that these tasks' specifications are flawed. The remaining 25 tasks adhere to the restrictions of our formal definition described above. One could define the set of instances more generously, and include all of the AIPS-1998 examples (except the ones with syntax errors, of course). This would not offer new insights as the restrictions only exclude cases that trivially imply unsolvability if at least one of the affected assembling or removing actions is required for solving the task. Including all the special cases in the subsequent discussion would make some of the claims rather unreadable. We thus settle for the (intuitively reasonable) set of instances specified above.

Our random generator, c.f. Appendix B, imposes more restrictions on the instances. The following two will play a role in what is to come.

1. Each assembly is only transient part of assemblies at a higher tree level (in the tree given by the $x \in pa(y)$ relations).
2. No transient parts are needed for removing other transients, i.e., if $(x,z) \in ro(y)$ and $z \in tr(y)$ then $x \in pa(y)$.

We remark that these restrictions also hold true in the AIPS-1998 instances except the flawed ones. The restrictions do *not* imply the non-existence of unrecognized dead ends or local minima. We will see below, however, that the first restriction implies solvability of the instance. The second restriction is among the prerequisites of both the sufficient criterion for the non-existence of dead ends and the sufficient criterion for the existence of a full exit path to the initial state.

Assembly is an ADL domain and makes extensive use of complex preconditions and conditional effects. There are various negations but no disjunctive goals, so the negation-free and propositional compilations behave identically, c.f. Proposition 3.1.6. We start the investigation by looking at conditions for solvability, then we focus on dead ends, finally we focus on local minima.

8.5.1 Solvability

The following definition will be important throughout the subsequent investigation. It specifies, for a reachable state in an *Assembly* task, exactly which assemblies must still be assembled into which other ones.

Definition 8.5.1. *Given the propositional or negation-free compilation of an instance (C, I, G) of the Assembly domain, and a reachable state $s \in S$. We define*

$$NA_0(s) := \{(x, y) \mid (complete, y) \notin s, x \in pa(y), (incorporated, x, y) \notin s\} \cup$$
$$\{(x, y) \mid (complete, y) \notin s, x \in tr(y), (incorporated, x, y) \notin s,$$
$$\exists z : z \in tr(y), (x, z) \in ro(y), (incorporated, z, y) \in s\}$$
$$NA_{i+1}(s) := \{(x, y) \mid (complete, y) \notin s, x \in tr(y), (incorporated, x, y) \notin s,$$
$$\exists z : (z, y) \in NA_i(s), (x, z) \in ao(y)\} \cup$$
$$\{(x, y) \mid (complete, y) \notin s, x \in tr(y), (incorporated, x, y) \notin s,$$
$$\exists z : (z, y) \in NA_i(s), z \in tr(y), (x, z) \in ro(y)\}$$
$$NA(s) := \bigcup_{i=0}^{\infty} NA_i(s)$$

We call $NAG(s) := (As, NA(s))$ the needed assembles graph to s, *and $NAG(I)$ the* needed assembles graph to the instance.

$NA_0(s)$ captures all pairs (x, y) where x must still be assembled into y because it is either a part of y, or a transient part that must be incorporated in order to remove some other transient part. $NA_{i+1}(s)$ captures all pairs (x, y) where x must still be assembled into y because either it is needed due to an assemble order before some other needed part or transient part, or due to a remove order before some other needed transient part.

In the rest of the investigation, a *leaf* in a graph will denote a node that has no ingoing edges, and a *relevant leaf* will denote a leaf that has at least one outgoing edge. The following is a sufficient condition for a state s to be no dead end.

Lemma 8.5.1. *Given the propositional or negation-free compilation of an instance (C, I, G) of the Assembly domain, with action set A. Let $s \in S$ be a* *reachable state such that $NAG(s)$ is cycle-free. If, for all relevant leafs x in $NAG(s)$, $(available, x) \in s$, then (A, s, G) is solvable.*

Proof. If $(complete, g) \in s$, we have nothing to prove. Else, as $NAG(s)$ is cycle-free, there are either no relevant leafs at all, or there is at least one non-leaf node y such that all sons of y are leafs. Assume there are no relevant leafs at all. It follows that all parts, and transient parts needed for removing other transient parts, are incorporated into g already (because there are no ingoing edges to g), so one can remove the transient parts in an order obeying $ro(g)$ (note that $ro(g)$ is cycle-free by definition), after committing (and beforehand releasing, if necessary) the resources required by g.

In the other case, select a node y that is not a leaf, but for which all sons are leafs. Let us focus on y's ingoing edges $(x, y) \in NA(s)$. All x are available by prerequisite. Also, from the definition of $NA(s)$, the set of those x is all we need for assembling y: all parts of y, all transient parts needed for assembling that parts, all transient parts needed to remove other transient parts again, and all transient parts needed for assembling those, have an edge to y if they are not yet assembled. Assume we commit (and beforehand release) all resources required by y, and carry out the respective sequence of assemble(x, y) actions (which can be applied in some order because $ao(y)$ is cycle-free by definition). We can then remove all transient parts from y by a remove(x, y) sequence (which can be applied because all parts with a remove order have been assembled). This gets us to a state s' where $(complete, y) \in s'$. Afterwards, we can also remove all parts of y again in a bottom-to-top order regarding $ao(y)$; remember that this does not delete $(complete, y)$. We then have a state s'' where all assemblies that have been available in s are again available, and where there is one more complete assembly, namely y. The new assembles graph $NAG(s'')$ differs from $NAG(s)$ only in the sense that all edges (x, y) have been removed. The new graph is therefore again cycle-free; the only node that might be a new leaf is y, and $(available, y) \in s''$. We can thus iterate the argument and are finished with the monotonicity of completeness.

The opposite implication holds in the following sense.

Lemma 8.5.2. *Given the propositional or negation-free compilation of an instance (C, I, G) of the Assembly domain, with action set A. Let $s \in S$ be a reachable state. If $NAG(s)$ contains a cycle, then (A, s, G) is unsolvable.*

Proof. With $(x, y) \in NA(s)$, we know that y is not complete in s; this either means that y is not available (both properties are achieved together, and completeness is never deleted), or that y was already available initially; the latter can not be as otherwise there would be no edge $(x, y) \in NA(s)$ (as then $pa(y) = tr(y) = \emptyset$). Further, all such assemblies y must be made complete (and with that available) at some point because the pa relation is a tree with root g that includes all non-atomic assemblies. Finally, $(x, y) \in NA(s)$ implies that, in any solution plan from s, x must be available at some point before y can be made available. Putting all of this together, a cycle in $NAG(s)$ gives us a sequence $y_0, \ldots, y_{n-1}, y_n = y_0$ of assemblies such that y_i must in any solution from s be made available before y_{i+1} is made available, which is a contradiction.

With Lemmata 8.5.1 and 8.5.2, we get an exact classification of solvability of the *initial state*.

Theorem 8.5.1. *Given the propositional or negation-free compilation of an instance (C, I, G) of the Assembly domain. The instance is solvable if and only if the needed assembles graph $NAG(I)$ to the instance is cycle-free.*

Proof. Consequence of Lemmata 8.5.1 and 8.5.2 and the fact that initially the leafs of the needed assemble graph are exactly the atomic assemblies x for which $pa(x) = \emptyset$. Those are available.

Note that, if each assembly is transient part only of assemblies at a higher level in the tree given by the $x \in pa(y)$ relations (i.e., if the first restriction of our generator is met), then the needed assembles graph to the instance is cycle free (because $(x, y) \in NAG(I)$ implies that either $x \in pa(y)$ or $x \in tr(y)$). Thus by Theorem 8.5.1 all instances that can be generated according to the strategy described in Appendix B are solvable. Likewise, it is implied that the AIPS-1998 benchmark examples are all solvable, except the flawed ones.

8.5.2 Some Observations Concerning Dead Ends

We now focus on the role of dead ends in the *Assembly* domain. As said, the hypothesis that all dead ends are recognized under h^+ is not correct: there can be unrecognized dead ends, which immediately also falsifies the other hypothesis that there are no local minima under h^+. Have a look at Figure 8.1, where the part-of relations are depicted by dotted arrows, the transient part relations are depicted by dashed arrows, and the ordering relations are full arrows; for ordering relations, the kind of ordering and the respective higher level assembly are written at the left hand side of the relation, i.e., the beginning of the arrow.

The situation s where G is incorporated into D and I is incorporated into C is an unrecognized dead end: either G or I must be removed first; say one tries G. This requires assembling E into D, in order to assemble H. But once E is assembled into D, one must assemble I to get it out again; this is, however, impossible, as I is at that point still assembled into C, and needs E to be assembled in the first place for being removed. A symmetrical situation arises when one tries to remove I from C first, starting from s. On the other hand, a relaxed plan for (A, s, G) can be constructed by assembling E into both C and D (the availability of E remains undeleted), then assembling F and H, then removing G and I, and so on.

The instance depicted in Figure 8.1 adheres to all restrictions applied by our random generator, c.f. Appendix B, and could thus have been produced by that generator. One wonders why among more than a hundred random instances there was no single unrecognized dead end when there could have been theoretically. It is important to note here the role of *how* the instances are generated, i.e., how

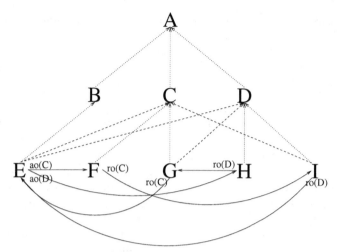

Fig. 8.1. An *Assembly* instance where an unrecognized dead end arises in the situation where G is incorporated into D, and I is incorporated into C

frequently assemble and remove orders appear. Imitating the published benchmark collection, the random instances were generated such that assemble orders and in particular remove orders are rather seldom, c.f. Section 7.1. We will prove below that unless an instance contains a quite complex structure of remove order constraints there are no dead ends at all.

The following definition formalizes the situation where some incorporated assembly needs other assemblies to be incorporated in order to be removed — this plays a key role in states where some parts that are needed elsewhere are "stuck" somewhere.

Definition 8.5.2. *Given the propositional or negation-free compilation of an instance (C, I, G) of the Assembly domain, and a reachable state $s \in S$. For assemblies x such that $(incorporated, x, y) \in s$ for some y, we define the needed removers $NR(x, s)$ for x in s as:*

1. *if $x \in tr(y)$: those $z \in As$, $(incorporated, z, y) \notin s$ with $(z, x) \in ro(y)$, and*
2. *if $x \in pa(y)$: those $z \in As$, $(incorporated, z, y) \notin s$ such that there is some $z' \in tr(y), (z, z') \in ro(y)$ so that ex. $z' = z_0, \ldots, z_n = x$ with $(z_i, z_{i+1}) \in ao(y), (incorporated, z_i, y) \in s$ for $i \geq 0$ and $z_i \in pa(y)$ for $i \geq 1$.*

The first case, that of a transient part of y to be removed, is obvious. In the second case, a part x of y to be removed, all z_i must be removed before one can remove x, and z must be incorporated in order to remove z_0 (remember that all parts with an assemble order before x must not be incorporated when removing x). As we show now, if the needed removers for a number of assemblies that are incorporated into an assembly y are all empty, then one can remove all these assemblies.

Lemma 8.5.3. *Given the propositional or negation-free compilation of an instance* (C, I, G) *of the Assembly domain, and a reachable state* $s \in S$. *If* $x_1, \ldots x_n$ *are assemblies such that, for some* y, $(incorporated, x_i, y) \in s$ *for* $1 \leq i \leq n$, *and* $NR(x_i, s) = \emptyset$ *for all* i, *then there is an action sequence that, when applied to* s, *yields a state* s' *where* $(available, x_i) \in s'$ *for all* i.

Proof. First of all, one can commit (and beforehand, if necessary, release) the resources required by y. Then collect together as the relevant transients all $x_i \in tr(y)$, and all $z \in tr(y)$ that are transitively ordered before some $x_i \in pa(y)$ regarding $ao(y)$. As $NR(x_i, s) = \emptyset$, all parts that have a remove order before a relevant transient are incorporated into y. Thus, one can apply a sequence of actions removing all relevant transients, in some order respecting $ro(y)$ (this is possible because $ro(y)$ is cycle-free by definition). Afterwards, all relevant parts — the $x_i \in pa(y)$ together with all $z \in pa(y)$ that are transitively ordered before some $x_i \in pa(y)$ regarding $ao(y)$ — can be removed in some order respecting inverse $ao(y)$ (which is, again, cycle-free by definition).

If a part x is incorporated in y', but needed in y, and can not be removed (and thus made available) easily, then there is a constraint between y' and y in the sense that y' must be disassembled before one assemble y. The following definition formalizes that situation.

Definition 8.5.3. *Given the propositional or negation-free compilation of an instance* (C, I, G) *of the Assembly domain, and a reachable state* $s \in S$. *The remove conflicts* $RC(s)$ *of* s *are defined as*

$$RC(s) := \{(y', y) \mid (complete, y) \notin s, \\ \exists x : (x, y) \in NA(s), (incorporated, x, y') \in s, \\ NR(x, s) \neq \emptyset\}$$

The next is the core lemma of this section. We will later identify a situation — occurring, e.g., in all but the flawed AIPS-1998 examples — where the seemingly very strong prerequisite of the lemma is fulfilled. The proof is an extension of the proof to Lemma 8.5.1.

Lemma 8.5.4. *Given the propositional or negation-free compilation of an instance* (C, I, G) *of the Assembly domain, with action set* A. *If, for all reachable states* $s \in S$, *the graph* $(As, NA(s) \cup RC(s))$ *is cycle-free, then* (A, s, G) *is solvable for all such* s, *i.e., the instance is dead-end free.*

Proof. If all $a \in As$ have $(complete, a) \in s$, then we are finished. If all nodes in $(As, NA(s) \cup RC(s))$ are leafs, then in particular the goal assembly g has no ingoing edges in $NA(s)$, so we can make it complete by committing the required resources, and removing all transient parts.

In the non-trivial case, let y be a node in $(As, NA(s) \cup RC(s))$ that is not a leaf, but for which all sons are leafs. In particular, $(complete, y) \notin s$. We construct an action sequence leading to a state s' where $(complete, y) \in s'$. Iterating the argument proves the lemma with the monotonicity of completeness. The construction proceeds as follows.

1. Process all sons y', $(y', y) \in RC(s)$: let, for such a y', $x \in pa(y) \cup tr(y)$, $(x, y) \in NA(s)$ be incorporated into y'. If y' was not complete, then $NR(x, s) \neq \emptyset$ would imply an ingoing edge to y' in $NA(s)$ (obvious if $x \in tr(y')$; if $x \in pa(y')$, there is an incorporated transient part z' for which a remover z must be incorporated). Thus, y' is complete in s, and thus, all $z \in pa(y') \cup tr(y')$ are complete in s or initially available. As y' has no ingoing edges in $RC(s)$, all such z that are incorporated into some y'' have $NR(z, s) = \emptyset$. We can thus apply the following action sequence:
   a) remove, using Lemma 8.5.3, all $z \in pa(y') \cup tr(y')$ from those y'' were they are incorporated (if they are);
   b) commit the resources required by y', and assemble all $z \in pa(y') \cup tr(y')$ into y' in some order respecting $ao(y')$;
   c) completely disassemble y', by first removing all transients in an order respecting $ro(y')$, then removing all parts in an order respecting $ao(y')$ (note that this does not delete the completeness of y').
2. Process all sons x, $(x, y) \in NA(s)$, $(\text{complete}, x) \notin s, pa(x) \neq \emptyset$: as such x have no ingoing edges in $NA(s)$ — remember that they are leafs in $(As, NA(s) \cup RC(s))$ — all parts $z \in pa(x)$ are incorporated, and all parts needed for removing transients are incorporated, too. So x can be made complete by committing the resources, and removing all transients in an order respecting $ro(x)$.
3. Process all sons x, $(x, y) \in NA(s)$, $(\text{incorporated}, x, y') \in s$, and there is no remove conflict between y' and y, i.e., $NR(x, s) = \emptyset$: with Lemma 8.5.3, all those x can be removed from the assemblies y'.

After the above steps have been carried out, it holds that all x with $(x, y) \in NA(s)$ are available. If, in s, they have been incorporated into some y' with $NR(x, s) \neq \emptyset$, then they have been removed from y' in the first process. If they have not been complete, they have been made so, and available, in process two. If they have been incorporated into some y' with $NR(x, s) = \emptyset$, then they have been removed from y' in the third process. We can therefore get to our desired state s' by committing the resources required by y, assembling all x with $(x, y) \in NA(s)$ into y in an order respecting $ao(y)$, and afterwards removing the transient parts in an order respecting $ro(y)$, making y complete.

We now identify cases where Lemma 8.5.4 can be applied. Our first observation is this. If the remove orders behave in the manner imposed by our generator (and present in the AIPS-1998 benchmarks except the flawed ones), then the needed assembles graph is monotonic in the following sense.

Lemma 8.5.5. *Given the propositional or negation-free compilation of an instance (C, I, G) of the Assembly domain, such that $\forall y \in As : (x, z) \in ro(y) \wedge z \in tr(y) \Rightarrow x \in pa(y)$. Then, for all reachable states $s \in S$, $NA(s) \subseteq NA(I)$ holds.*

Proof. With $\forall y \in As : (x, z) \in ro(y) \wedge z \in tr(y) \Rightarrow x \in pa(y)$, the role of incorporated transients in a state is diminished to the effect that all removers are parts and must therefore be incorporated anyway. The lemma then follows because in the initial state, both the set of parts that are not complete is maximal (all parts), and the set of pairs (x, y) where x is not incorporated into y is maximal (no part is incorporated into any other part). The other constituents of Definition 8.5.1 are static (the pa, tr, ao and ro functions). The proof proceeds by induction.

$NA_0(s) \subseteq NA_0(I)$ follows from the above, with the observation that the second set in the definition of $NA_0(s)$ always yields the empty set because of our prerequisite $\forall y \in As : (x, z) \in ro(y) \wedge z \in tr(y) \Rightarrow x \in pa(y)$: for a pair (x, y) in the second set, $x \in tr(y)$, $z \in tr(y)$ and $(x, z) \in ro(y)$ hold for some z, in contradiction. The induction step from $NA_i \longrightarrow NA_{i+1}$ is straightforward: in addition to I's maximality properties, we know from the induction hypothesis that each $(z, y) \in NA_i(s)$ is also contained in $NA_i(I)$. This gives us $NA_{i+1}(s) \subseteq NA_{i+1}(I)$, and consequently $NA(s) \subseteq NA(I)$.

Our second observation is that a remove conflict between y' and y implies the presence of the respective ordering constraints between y' and y in the instance, i.e., there must be a potential remove conflict between those two in the following sense.

Definition 8.5.4. *Given the propositional or negation-free compilation of an instance (C, I, G) of the Assembly domain. The potential remove conflicts pRC of the instance are defined as*

$$pRC := \{(y', y) \mid y \neq y', \exists x \in (pa(y) \cup tr(y)) \cap tr(y') : \exists z : (z, x) \in ro(y')\} \cup$$
$$\{(y', y) \mid \exists \, x \in tr(y) \cap pa(y') :$$
$$\exists \, z' \in tr(y'), z_1, \ldots, z_n \in pa(y') :$$
$$(z', z_1) \in ao(y'), (z_i, z_{i+1}) \in ao(y') \text{ for all } i,$$
$$(z_n, x) \in ao(y'), \exists z : (z, z') \in ro(y')\}$$

Reconsider Definitions 8.5.2 and 8.5.3. Imagine a remove conflict that is due to a transient part $x \in tr(y')$ that is incorporated into y' and needs some z to be incorporated for its removal. Such a conflict demands the existence of a potential remove conflict according to the first set in Definition 8.5.4 (remember that $(x, y) \in NA(s)$ for a state s implies $x \in pa(y) \cup tr(y)$). Slightly more complicated, say the conflict is due to a part $x \in pa(y')$ that is incorporated into y' such that removing x first involves removing all of $z_1, \ldots, z_n \in pa(y')$ (due to assemble orders), but removing z_1 requires incorporating z' (due to a remove order). That situation demands the existence of a potential remove conflict according to the second set in Definition 8.5.4. So in any state the remove conflicts are a subset of the potential remove conflicts of the instance, i.e., $RC(s) \subseteq pRC$ holds for all $s \in S$.

The set in the first line of the above definition has not many members if remove orders are seldom. Even more so for the second set, where there must be a complex construct of assemble orders in addition to the remove order. We will now see that, if the potential remove conflicts are cycle-free together with the needed assembles of an instance adhering to the restriction that $\forall y \in As : (x, z) \in ro(y) \wedge z \in tr(y) \Rightarrow x \in pa(y)$, then the instance is dead-end free.

Theorem 8.5.2. *Given the propositional or negation-free compilation of an instance (C, I, G) of the Assembly domain, with action set A. If $\forall y \in As : (x, z) \in ro(y) \wedge z \in tr(y) \Rightarrow x \in pa(y)$, and $(As, NA(I) \cup pRC)$ is cycle-free, then (A, I, G) is dead-end free.*

Proof. With Lemma 8.5.4, it suffices to show that $(As, NA(s) \cup RC(s))$ is cycle-free for all $s \in S$. With Lemma 8.5.5 and $\forall y \in As : (x, z) \in ro(y) \wedge z \in tr(y) \Rightarrow x \in pa(y)$, we have $NA(s) \subseteq NA(I)$ for all states $s \in S$. Furthermore, we got $RC(s) \subseteq pRC$. Finished with the prerequisite that $(As, NA(I) \cup pRC)$ is cycle-free.

As an example, reconsider Figure 8.1. There is a cycle in (As, pRC): we have a potential remove conflict between C and D because $I \in pa(D)$, $I \in tr(C)$, and $(F, I) \in ro(C)$. The other way round, we have a potential remove conflict between D and C because $G \in pa(C)$, $G \in tr(D)$, and $(H, G) \in ro(D)$.

Theorem 8.5.2 proves that there are no dead ends in 24 of the 25 unflawed AIPS-1998 benchmark examples. All the unflawed examples fulfill $\forall y \in As : (x, z) \in ro(y) \wedge z \in tr(y) \Rightarrow x \in pa(y)$, and in all but one of them $(As, NA(I) \cup pRC)$ is cycle-free. Theorem 8.5.2 also explains, to some extent, our observations in Chapter 7. From the 135 random instances used there, no dead ends occur in 103 examples. In 93 of these examples, the prerequisites of Theorem 8.5.2 are fulfilled. What the theorem does *not* explain is why the dead ends are all recognized in the 32 examples where they occur. This is a topic for future work.

8.5.3 Some Observations Concerning Local Minima

There is more to be said, except their existence, about local minima in the *Assembly* domain. First, let us state that there can be local minima under h^+ even if there are no unrecognized dead ends. An example, adhering to the restrictions of our random generator, is depicted in Figure 8.2. The meaning of the arrows is the same as in Figure 8.1.

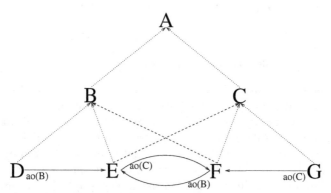

Fig. 8.2. An *Assembly* instance where a local minimum arises when D is incorporated into B, and G is incorporated into C

The phenomenon here is the following. With D and G incorporated, $h^+(s) = 6$: an optimal relaxed plan is to assemble E into C, assemble F into C, assemble F into B, assemble E into B, and assemble B and C into A. Note here that we must assemble the transient part E into C (F into B) before we can assemble F into C (E into B), but — in the relaxed plan — do not need to remove E from C (F from B) again. One must either first assemble E into C or F into B (the two other applicable actions are removing D from B or G from C but that does open up no new options except assembling them back). Say we decide to assemble E into C. In the resulting state s', we get, again, $h^+(s') = 6$ (like above, but remove E from C instead of assembling it). Assembling F into C afterwards, however, worsens the situation to $h^+(s'') = 7$ (where s'' is the respective resulting state): in addition to the above steps, one must remove G from C due to its assemble order before F. In more detail, an optimal relaxed plan from s'' is to remove E from C, remove G from C, remove F from C (which can not be done if G is incorporated into C, as $(G, F) \in ao(C)$), assemble F into B, assemble E into B (which can not be done unless F is incorporated into B), and assemble B and C into A. A symmetrical situation arises if we decide to go the other way round, i.e., to assemble F into B first.

Once again, one wonders why no local minima occured in more than a hundred random instances. While we have no fully satisfactory answer to that, we do make an interesting observation concerning the behavior of local minima under h^+ in *Assembly* instances, and the ease of solving such instances using that heuristic. Unless there are complex structures concerning assemble orders, the *initial state* of an *Assembly* instance has a full exit path.

In the instance from Figure 8.2, the initial state does not have a full exit path. This is because there is a circle between B and C in the sense that they are conflicted (B, C) and (C, B) as follows.

Definition 8.5.5. *Given the propositional or negation-free compilation of an instance (C, I, G) of the Assembly domain, and a reachable state $s \in S$. The assemble conflicts $AC(s)$ of s are defined as*

$$AC(s) := \{(y', y) \mid y \neq y', \exists x, z \in pa(y) : (x, y) \in NA(s),$$
$$(z, x) \in ao(y),$$
$$(x, y') \in NA(s)\}$$

$AC(I)$ *are the* assemble conflicts *of the instance.*

The difficulty with an assemble conflict between y' and y with regards to an assembly x is that x is needed for both y' and y, but once x is incorporated into y we will have trouble removing it because there is another part z with an assemble order before it. So one should care about y' first. This is not always possible in the example Figure 8.2 because that kind of conflict appears between B and C in both directions. If one can always care about y' first then states where all relevant leafs (in the needed assembles graph) are available have a monotonically decreasing path to the goal, under the additional condition that no needed assemble constraint is due only to a remove order.

Lemma 8.5.6. *Given the propositional or negation-free compilation of an in-stance (C, I, G) of the Assembly domain with action set A, and a reachable state $s \in S$, such that for all relevant leafs x in $NAG(s)$, $(available, x) \in s$. If it holds that*

1. *$(As, NA(s) \cup AC(s))$ is cycle-free, and*
2. *for all $(x, y) \in NA(s)$, there is a sequence $x = x_0, x_1, \ldots, x_n$ such that $x_n \in pa(y)$, $(x_{i-1}, x_i) \in ao(y)$ and $(x_i, y) \in NA(s)$ for $1 \le i \le n$,*

then s has a full exit path under h^+.

Proof. We prove that h^+ decreases monotonically on a solution path that can be obtained by Lemma 8.5.1 ($NAG(s)$ is cycle-free by the first prerequisite). This iteratively processes an arbitrary non-leaf assembly y where all sons x are leafs in $NAG(s)$; if all assemblies are leafs in $NAG(s)$, achieving the goal can be done by committing (and beforehand releasing) the resources required by the goal assembly g, and then removing the transient parts from g, all of which actions are contained in an optimal relaxed solution, and delete only propositions that are not needed anymore. We change the algorithm from Lemma 8.5.1 to iteratively process nodes y where all sons are leafs in $(As, NA(s) \cup AC(s))$ (i.e., we additionally consider the edges in $AC(s)$). If a node has no ingoing edges in $NA(s)$, then it has no outgoing edges in $AC(s)$ ($(y', y) \in AC(s)$ implies, by definition, $(x, y') \in NA(s)$ for some x), so the only ingoing edges (x, y) of y are such that $(x, y) \in NA(s)$. The solution algorithm first releases and commits all resources required by y, then assembles all x with $(x, y) \in NA(s)$ into y in an appropriate order, and afterwards removes all transient parts and parts of y in an appropriate order. The process ends up in a state where prerequisites 1 and 2 are again fulfilled; for prerequisite 2, this is obvious (all edges (x, y) are removed from $NA(s)$, and the edges (x, y') for other assemblies y' remain unchanged), and for prerequisite 1 it holds because no new edges are introduced into $NA(s)$, which implies that no new edges are introduced into $AC(s)$. So let us consider the optimal relaxed solution lengths on the constructed path. Removing an assembly x from y only deletes $(incorporated, x, y)$, which is not needed anymore once $(complete, y)$ has been achieved; it is also not needed anymore when all parts of y have been incorporated and x is a transient which is not needed for removing any other transient, both of which conditions are fulfilled when the algorithm removes a transient part x from y. As y is not complete, the required resources must be released and committed to y at some point in an optimal relaxed solution from s; as releasing and committing actions are invertible, those actions do therefore not increase optimal relaxed solution length. Thus, the only actions left to take care of are the assemble(x, y) parts of the process, transforming a state s' into another state s''. It suffices to show that there is a relaxed solution to s'' that is at most as long as an optimal relaxed solution to s'. Assume $P_{s'}^+$ is an optimal relaxed solution to (A, s', G). x may be a part, or a transient part of y.

In the first case, assemble(x, y) is contained in $P_{s'}^+$ simply because x must be incorporated into y at some point. If there is no $z \in pa(y)$, $(z, x) \in ao(y)$, then a relaxed plan $P_{s''}^+$ for (A, s'', G) can be constructed by removing assemble(x, y)

from $P_{s'}^+$, and placing remove(x, y) up front. If there is such a z, then, because y has no ingoing edges from $AC(s)$, it follows that there is no edge (x, y') in $NA(s)$ (otherwise, $(y', y) \in AC(s)$ would hold), so (available, x) is not needed anymore; neither do we need (not-incorporated, x, y) when x is a part (not a transient part) of y, so we can construct $P_{s''}^+$ by removing assemble(x, y) from $P_{s'}^+$ and are finished.

In the second case, x being a transient part of y, assemble(x, y) is contained in $P_{s'}^+$ because by prerequisite 2 x must be assembled into y at some point for the integration of all parts, due to assemble orders (none of $x_1, \ldots, x_n$ can already be integrated into y in s', due to the assemble orders and $(x_i, y) \in NA(s)$ for all i). So our first step in the construction of a relaxed plan $P_{s''}^+$ for (A, s'', G) is to remove assemble(x, y) from $P_{s'}^+$. It then suffices to show that remove(x, y) can be applied at some point in the resulting relaxed plan before (available, x) or (not-incorporated, x, y) are needed. This follows again from prerequisite 2: remove(x, y) can be applied in $P_{s''}^+$ as soon as all z with $(z, x) \in ro(y)$ have been incorporated into y. With prerequisite 2, all z that have this property must either already be incorporated, or assembled into y at some point. All these actions — and the actions assembling their necessary (transient) parts $(z', z) \in ao(y)$ — can be moved to the front of $P_{s''}^+$ in the appropriate order. We insert remove(x, y) directly after those actions. This is early enough: obviously, none of the assemble(z, y) actions needs (available, x) as prerequisite; for (not-incorporated, x, y), matters are a bit more complicated, as the last of the assemble(z, y) actions might have been responsible for adding (complete, y); but in that case, all parts of y are incorporated at that point, and all transient parts except x have not been incorporated in s', so remove(x, y) achieves (complete, y) at that point of $P_{s''}^+$ starting from s''. Our construction $P_{s''}^+$ is therefore a relaxed plan for (A, s'', G), which concludes the argument.

Let us identify situations where the prerequisites of Lemma 8.5.6 are fulfilled. First observe that with $\forall y \in As : (x, z) \in ro(y) \wedge z \in tr(y) \Rightarrow x \in pa(y)$ the assemble conflicts are monotonic, simply because the needed assembles are.

Lemma 8.5.7. *Given the propositional or negation-free compilation of an instance (C, I, G) of the Assembly domain, such that $\forall y \in As : (x, z) \in ro(y) \wedge z \in tr(y) \Rightarrow x \in pa(y)$. Then, for all reachable states $s \in S$, $AC(s) \subseteq AC(I)$ holds.*

Proof. Follows directly from Lemma 8.5.5 and the definition of assemble conflicts.

It is easy to see that the same restriction on remove orders implies the second prerequisite of Lemma 8.5.6 (no needed assembles due only to remove orders). So we know that, under the restriction, the initial state has a full exit path unless there is a cycle in the assemble conflicts with the needed assembles.

Theorem 8.5.3. *Given the propositional or negation-free compilation of an instance (C, I, G) of the Assembly domain, such that*

1. *$(As, NA(I) \cup AC(I))$ is cycle-free, and*
2. *$\forall y \in As : (x, z) \in ro(y) \wedge z \in tr(y) \Rightarrow x \in pa(y)$.*

Then, any reachable state $s \in S$ where all relevant leafs in $NAG(s)$ are available, in particular the initial state, has a full exit path under h^+.

Proof. The prerequisites 1 and 2 are sufficient for prerequisites 1 and 2 of Lemma 8.5.6, respectively. As for prerequisite 2, with $\forall y \in As : (x,z) \in ro(y) \wedge z \in tr(y) \Rightarrow x \in pa(y)$, the only edges (x,y) in $NA(s)$ inserted due to a remove order are such that $x \in pa(y)$, implying that x must be incorporated anyway (in the terminology of the second prerequisite of Lemma 8.5.6, the trivial sequence $x = x_0 = x_n \in pa(y)$ suffices). The other implication follows directly from Lemmata 8.5.5 and 8.5.7: as there is no cycle in $(As, NA(I) \cup AC(I))$, and for all states s we got $NA(s) \subseteq NA(I)$ and $AC(s) \subseteq AC(I))$, there can not be a cycle in $(As, NA(s) \cup AC(s))$ for any s.

Theorem 8.5.3 proves that the initial states of all unflawed AIPS-1998 instances have full exit paths under h^+: all these instances fulfill the theorem's prerequisites. Assuming that FF's search mechanism does stick to the full exit paths, this result explains the excellent runtime performance of the system in the AIPS-1998 collection. As for the random instances from Chapter 7, these, too, all fulfill the prerequisites of Theorem 8.5.3. They thus contain many states with full exit paths. It is an open question why *all* the reachable states have full exit paths in these instances.

8.6 The Taxonomy

After these our adventures in the *Assembly* domain, let us get back to the main line of argumentation. The purpose of the chapter was to verify the hypotheses that Chapter 7 made about the topological properties of h^+ in our domains. Figure 8.3 overviews our results.

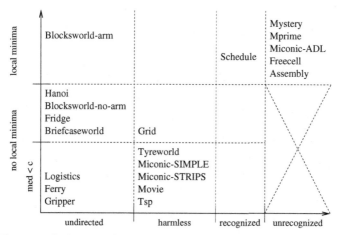

Fig. 8.3. The proved planning domain taxonomy, overviewing our results

The picture is pretty much the same as the one in Figure 7.7, telling us that our hypotheses are for the most part in fact true. In particular, there are eight domains where FF's search algorithm enforced hill-climbing is polynomial, c.f. Theorem 7.2.1, assuming h^+ is given. The only case where our hypotheses were wrong is *Assembly*, where there can be unrecognized dead ends in contrary to what our collection of small example instances suggested. As another (positive) difference to our hypotheses, we have found out that there is a constant upper bound ($c = 6$, namely) on the maximal exit distance under h^+ in the *Tireworld* domain (where the single small enough instance did not give us much reason to speculate about this property).

To summarize the results: in 15 of our benchmark domains there are no unrecognized dead ends, in 13 of them there are no local minima, and in 8 of them there even is a constant upper bound on the maximal exit distance. We have also determined what the most common patterns of structure are that cause the topological phenomena. At the level of the planning tasks' specifications, the most common pattern of structure causing the non-existence of dead ends is that all actions are (at least) invertible or need not be inverted (like when their adds are static and their deletes are irrelevant). Together with that, the most common reason for the non-existence of local minima is that the actions are respected by the relaxation, i.e., often there is simply no other way to achieve the goal than by applying them. As for those of our domains with bounded maximal exit distance, the bounds are all caused by the following phenomenon: many of the actions have delete effects that are not needed anymore once they have been applied, while the other actions need not be applied more than a constant number of times in a row.

In Chapter 10, we will discuss the consequences that these results have for AI planning research. Right now, it remains to verify in what sense the topological properties of h^+ carry over to FF's approximation h^{FF}. This is the duty of the next chapter.

9. Supporting the h^{FF} Hypotheses

As the final investigation in this book, we examine in what sense the topological properties of h^+ carry over to the approximation h^{FF}. We need only concentrate on local minima and the maximal exit distance: h^+ and h^{FF} have the value ∞ in exactly the same cases, c.f. Proposition 4.0.2, so the behavior with respect to dead ends is provably identical. Reiterating what has been said in Section 7.3.3, our hypotheses are that the topological properties of h^+ roughly carry over to h^{FF} — this is what the data for our collection of small example instances suggests. The intuition is that the overall topology of the state space under h^+ gets preserved when using h^{FF}, only the surface might become somewhat more "crippled", c.f. the visualized *Hanoi* example in Section 7.4. More explicitly, the hypotheses are the following.

1. In any instance of those domains where there are no local minima under h^+, there are no or only few states on valleys under evaluation with h^{FF}.[1]
2. In any instance of those domains where there is a constant upper bound c on the maximal exit distance under h^+, the maximal exit distance under evaluation with h^{FF} is at most c or only a little higher than c.

These are not formal statements. They are research hypotheses that we will either support or reject by empirical observation. We will do that by taking samples from the state spaces of large planning tasks from the respective domains, and looking at parameters of the distribution of sample states on valleys, as well as of the sample states' exit distances.

We start the investigation by explaining our empirical methodology in detail (Section 9.1). Then there are three sections each of which shows our results for a number of domains (Sections 9.2, 9.3, and 9.4). The sections are ordered by increasing amount of effort involved to obtain and present the results, as is determined by the number of *domain parameters* that the respective domains have. We conclude the chapter with a brief results overview (Section 9.5).

9.1 Methodology

As said, we take samples from the state spaces of large planning tasks. That is, given an example task, we repeatedly walk randomly into the state space to

---

[1] Remember that it are the states on valleys, not only those on local minima, that hinder local search; any local minimum is contained in a valley, c.f. Chapter 7.

J. Hoffmann: Utilizing Problem Structure in Planning, LNAI 2854, pp. 181–197, 2003.

some state s, then measure topological parameters of that state's surroundings, and finally we summarize our observations for the states we have looked at. This approach has been applied to SAT by Frank et al. [36]. The investigation at hand is inspired by this work in that it uses the same base idea; the details are rather different due to the circumstances in our planning context. The questions to be answered are, how exactly do we do this "random walk"? What exactly are the topological parameters we measure? How many states do we look at, and how do we summarize our observations? And what exactly are these "large example tasks" going to be?

Let us answer these questions in reverse order. To elaborate some more on what we mean by "large", the tasks that we will look at still adhere to the restrictions that FF must be able to solve them, and that we must be able to measure the desired topological parameters (more on these issues below). At least, the examples are a lot larger than the instances that we used in Chapter 7. We will include precise descriptions of our example collections. The more interesting question is which examples we choose to look at in each domain. Our intention is to obtain a picture of what the behavior is across *all* instances. There are infinitely many of them. The key concept helping us out here is that of a *domain parameter* (not to be confused with the *topological parameters* that we are going to measure). Domain parameters have first been mentioned in Section 2.3. Let us elaborate on what they are, and what their role in the investigation at hand is.

In each domain, the instances are characterized in terms of a number of domain parameters modulo randomization. As an example, consider the *Miconic-STRIPS* domain where an instance is determined by the two parameters "number of floors" and "number of passengers", modulo the random origin and destination floors of all passengers, and the initial location of the elevator. Technically, a set of domain parameters is *exhaustive* for a domain if the Cartesian product of the possible values of all parameters contains all instances of the domain modulo random elements (and constant names), the set of all instances (in the case of our domains here) being given by the formal definitions in Appendix A. Note that, looking at a specific domain, there can be a choice about what exactly one assumes as the borderline between "domain parameters" and "random elements". We do not fully formalize the concept of exhaustive sets of domain parameters, but settle for the intuitively clear interpretation, which is appropriate for the empirical purposes pursued here. If we have an exhaustive set of domain parameters, we can empirically reason about the structure of all instances of the domain by looking at (random) example instances for all possible combinations of domain parameter values. Of course, there can still be infinitely many combinations of domain parameter values, so one needs to restrict oneself to a finite subset of them. What we do is this. We let the domain parameters range within large intervals, and determine whether there are any discernible tendencies of co-development for the topological parameters we are interested in. If there are none, then it is reasonable to assume that the topological parameters will neither develop when the domain parameters range further — at least if the example intervals are sufficiently large.[2]

Precisely, the experimental method is this. We keep, in each experiment, all but at most two of the domain parameters fixed, and determine how the topological parameters develop when the variable domain parameters change (using at most two variable domain parameters at a time makes it feasible to visualize the results). For each experiment we thus generate — using the respective automated generation strategy, c.f. Appendix B — an example collection where at most two domain parameters vary within intervals that yield tasks of appropriate size. If a domain has only one or two domain parameters, a single such experiment suffices. If there are more than two domain parameters, we perform several separate experiments. We order the domains by their number of domain parameters, and thus by the number of experiments and the difficulty of presenting the results. For each experiment we will state exactly what the example collection looked at is. On all examples, we ran FF and accepted them only if they were solved — like in the previous chapters, we are only interested in solvable instances. Note that this determines an (rather generous) upper limit to the size of the tasks.

Let us answer the questions which topological parameters we are going to measure, and how we are going to summarize the observations. We are interested in the behavior with regards to local minima respectively valleys, and the maximal exit distance. It is thus simple to come up with the topological parameters: given a random state s, we determine whether that state has a full exit path under h^{FF}, and what its exit distance under that heuristic function is. Note that determining states on local minima rather than on valleys does not appear to make much sense as there can be huge valleys but still only few states on local minima, so that hitting one at random is not particularly likely. As for computation time, note that the decision about the existence of a full exit path can be costly: to find out that there is no such path, one must explore all paths from s on which the heuristic value decreases monotonically. So the need to decide about the existence of full exit paths determines another upper limit to the size of the tasks looked at, in addition to their being solvable by FF; in practice, deciding about full exit paths was a much stronger restriction to the size of the examples. To complete the experiments in a reasonable amount of time, we set the number of samples per example task, i.e., of random states looked at, to 100. We summarize the observations for each task by computing the percentage of sample states on valleys, and the maximum over the exit distances of the sample states that lie on bench-related plateaus. Across a domain, i.e., in each of our experiments, we summarize the observations in a manner similar to what we have done in Chapter 7: the example tasks are arranged in groups, and we show

---

[2] We sometimes relax the exhaustiveness condition somewhat in order to make the experiments more feasible. We justify these simplifications at the points where they are applied — mostly, the justification is that the published benchmark collections do not explore the full variability as is allowed by the formal definitions in Appendix A.

values that are averaged over all tasks within a group. Tasks are in the same group if they were generated according to the same domain parameter values.[3]

Let us finally focus on how exactly we do the random walk to our sample states. The obvious idea is to repeatedly apply an action drawn randomly from the set of applicable actions. One must decide how many action applications are to be done. We have done a little experimentation with different strategies, and evaluated them by running them on the collection of small examples from Chapter 7 — for these tasks, we knew the precise values of the topological parameters so we could see how close our sampled values were to these. The different strategies did generally not make much difference. We have chosen to do a random number of action applications, between 0 and 2 times the plan length that FF returned when solving the task — the length of a plan can be taken as a rough indication of how "deep" the state space is (different strategies were to use different products of FF's plan length as the lower and upper bounds on the number of action applications).

To give an impression of how precise the values obtained by sampling can be, let us consider the values for the example collection from Chapter 7. The topological parameters we consider are valley percentage and maximal exit distance. As for valleys, remember that in this investigation we are interested in those domains where h^+ does not yield local minima, and want to check the valley behavior of h^{FF}. There are four domains where h^+ does (provably) not yield local minima, but h^{FF} does yield some in the example collection from Chapter 7. The four domains are *Briefcaseworld*, *Grid*, *Hanoi*, and *Miconic-SIMPLE*. They are shown in Figure 9.1, providing the sampled percentage of states on valleys against the real percentage of these states (in parentheses).

Domain	I_0	I_1	I_2	I_3	I_4
Briefcaseworld	0.0 (0.0)		0.0 (0.3)		3.4 (0.9)
Grid	4.4 (2.6)	4.8 (4.2)			0.3 (3.1)
Hanoi	0.0 (0.0)	0.0 (0.0)	0.0 (0.0)	81.0 (33.2)	100.0 (77.7)
Miconic-SIMPLE	0.0 (0.0)	1.4 (0.3)	5.7 (2.9)	3.4 (0.6)	2.3 (0.4)

Fig. 9.1. Percentage of sample states on valleys. Mean values for increasing number of constants in different domains, in the example collection from Chapter 7. Real values are in parentheses

Let us compare the values approximated by sampling to the real values. Generally, the sampled values are roughly within the same range as the real values, and somewhat higher. There are a few exceptions, two cases (in the middle group of *Briefcaseworld* and the last group of *Grid*) where the sampled values are a little lower than the real values, and at least one case (in the second last group of *Hanoi*) where the sampled value is a lot higher than the real value.

---

[3] An exception are the experiments for domains with only a single domain parameter: there, we simply group tasks according to the number of constants, as is explained below.

The overall picture seems to be adequate for the purposes of our investigation: the values are most of the time not too far away from the real values, and a little overestimation makes the data more conservative if anything — after all, our hypothesis is that there are only few valley states in those domains where there are none under h^+.

As for the maximal exit distance values, there are eight domains where h^+ yields a constant upper bound: *Ferry, Gripper, Logistics, Miconic-SIMPLE, Miconic-STRIPS, Movie, Simple-Tsp,* and *Tireworld.* In all these domains, the sampled values are exactly the same as the real values — 6 in the single instance of *Tireworld*, constantly 0 in *Simple-Tsp*, and constantly 1 in the other domains.

Before we start the investigation, let us make one more technical remark. The domain parameters we use to generate our example collections coincide with the input parameters to the automated generation strategies described in Appendix B. The chapter is self-contained in that we include the most important information about the domains and their domain parameters. In Appendix B, one can look up additional background information on what exhaustive sets of domain parameters would be, on which sets of domain parameters we use, and how randomization is done.

9.2 Domains with a Single Parameter

We first focus on those domains whose instances are determined by a single domain parameter. In these cases, a single experiment suffices, and it is very easy to present the data. Those single-parameter domains where we must verify properties of h^{FF} are *Blocksworld-no-arm, Gripper, Hanoi, Movie, Simple-Tsp,* and *Tireworld.* The respective domain parameters and example collections used are the following.

- *Blocksworld-no-arm* — Domain parameter: number of blocks; example collection interval: $2 \ldots 11$; number of random examples per domain parameter value: 10.
- *Gripper* — Domain parameter: number of balls; example collection interval: $1 \ldots 100$.
- *Hanoi* — Domain parameter: number of discs; example collection interval: $3 \ldots 10$.
- *Movie* — Domain parameter: number of snacks of each sort; example collection interval: $1 \ldots 100$.
- *Simple-Tsp* — Domain parameter: number of locations; example collection interval: $1 \ldots 100$.
- *Tireworld* — Domain parameter: number of flat tires; example collection interval: $1 \ldots 5$.

In all these domains except *Blocksworld-no-arm,* there is only a single instance per domain parameter value. In all domains except *Movie,* it is clear that the single domain parameter is exhaustive. In *Movie* we have simplified the situation in that we assume that each sort of snacks contains the same number of items. This holds true in the AIPS-1998 benchmark collection, Also, as was said in Section 2.3 already, all *Movie* instances share the same set of reachable states so the domain parameter does not seem to matter much.

Note that, across all of the domains, the number of constants in an instance is linearly dependent on the respective domain parameter. We utilize this property to simplify the presentation of the results. We use the same presentation as in Chapter 7, where two instances within a domain are grouped together if their size, i.e., their number of constants, falls into the same interval. There are five intervals $I_0, \ldots, I_4$, which divide the size range within each domain into 5 equally large parts. The data for topological parameters is averaged over the instances within a group. As in the domains looked at the number of constants is linearly dependent on the domain parameter, the resulting data shows the development of the respective topological parameter when the respective domain parameter undergoes a linear increase. We start with the local minima behavior. See the data in Figure 9.2.

Domain	I_0	I_1	I_2	I_3	I_4
Blocksworld-no-arm	0.0	0.0	0.0	0.1	0.0
Gripper	0.0	0.0	0.0	0.0	0.0
Hanoi	0.0	0.0	96.0	100.0	100.0
Movie	0.0	0.0	0.0	0.0	0.0
Simple-Tsp	0.0	0.0	0.0	0.0	0.0
Tireworld	0.0	0.0	0.0	0.0	0.0

Fig. 9.2. Percentage of sample states on valleys. Mean values for increasing number of constants in different domains

Clearly, the data strongly support our hypothesis that in the domains in question there are only few states on valleys under h^{FF}. The single exception is the *Hanoi* domain where, like in our experiments on the smaller instances, the valley states seem to dominate as the number of discs increases.

Domain	I_0	I_1	I_2	I_3	I_4
Gripper	1.0	1.0	1.0	1.0	1.0
Movie	1.0	0.9	0.6	0.4	0.6
Simple-Tsp	0.0	0.0	0.0	0.0	0.0
Tireworld	6.0	6.0	6.0	6.0	2.0
Blocksworld-no-arm	0.3	1.8	2.8	3.8	3.7
Hanoi	6.0	23.0	12.0	2.0	2.0

Fig. 9.3. Maximal exit distance. Mean values for increasing number of constants in different domains

Let us focus on the maximal exit distance. Figure 9.3 shows the data. The four domains (of those we consider here) with a constant upper bound on the maximal exit distance under h^+ are *Gripper*, *Movie*, *Simple-Tsp*, and *Tireworld*. For interest, we also show the values that we obtained in *Blocksworld-no-arm* and *Hanoi*. For *Gripper* and *Simple-Tsp*, the data clearly supports the hypothesized upper bounds 1 and 0, respectively. The same holds for the hypothesized upper bounds 1 and 6 to *Movie* respectively *Tireworld*. A bit strange it might seem that the maximal exit distance appears to decrease as the value of the domain parameter increases. This is probably due to the sampling method: the larger the state spaces become (like in *Tireworld*), or the more applicable actions there are (like in *Movie*, though they all have the same effects), the more unlikely it seems to get that applying a number of random actions ends up in one of the states where the exit distance is maximal. The reason why this does not happen in *Gripper* could be that in this domain there are more states (than in *Movie*, for example) where the exit distance is 1. We will observe similar phenomena in the domains below. In *Blocksworld-no-arm*, the maximal exit distance values increase rather clearly with the domain parameter, i.e., with the number of blocks. In *Hanoi*, like we observed in Figure 7.9 for the small examples, there is first an increase, but then the large benches appear to vanish.

9.3 Domains with Two Parameters

We now focus on those domains whose instances are determined by two domain parameters. There are five such domains where we must verify properties of h^{FF}: *Briefcaseworld*, *Ferry*, *Fridge*, *Miconic-SIMPLE*, and *Miconic-STRIPS*. In each domain, a single experiment suffices. We present the data in terms of 3-dimensional diagrams, showing the development of a topological parameter against the development of both domain parameters in their given intervals. We focus on the domains in one subsection each, ordered alphabetically.

9.3.1 Briefcaseworld

Briefcaseworld instances are determined by the number of locations, the total number of portables, and the number of portables that must be transported, modulo the random distribution of initial and goal locations. We make the slightly simplifying assumption that all portables must be transported (which is true in the published benchmarks). We obtained the example collection by letting the number of locations take on the values 2, 5, 8, 11, and 14, and letting the number of portables take on the values 1, 4, 7, 10, and 13. For each combination of these domain parameter values we generated a group of 5 random instances. So we have a total number of 25 groups of randomized examples, 5 instances per group.

Under h^+, there are no local minima in *Briefcaseworld*. We need to verify how many states on valleys there are under h^{FF}. Figure 9.4 shows the average percentage of sample states on valleys across our 25 domain parameter settings.

The data supports our hypothesis: the maximum valley percentage we have obtained by sampling is 5.0% (the maximum value 15% on the z-axis has merely

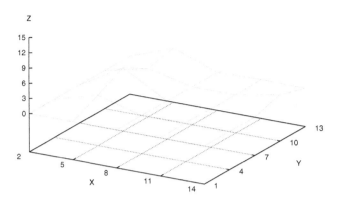

Fig. 9.4. Valley percentage (z-axis) in *Briefcaseworld* instances, scaling locations (x-axis) against portables (y-axis)

been chosen to improve readability). The number of valley states appears to be highest if there are few locations (but more than two) and a lot of portables to be transported, but still there is no clear tendency of growth in that direction.

There is no upper bound on the maximal exit distance under h^+ so we do not need to verify a hypothesis and thus do not include a figure. The observation is that the values strongly increase with the number of portables but decrease with the number of locations. This is in line with our theoretical observations concerning h^+: the exit distance can be high when one must take a lot of portables out of the briefcase before one can move on, c.f. Section 8.3.2.

9.3.2 Ferry

Ferry instances are determined by the number of locations, the total number of cars, and the number of cars that must be transported, modulo the random distribution of initial and goal locations. We make the slightly simplifying assumption that all cars must be transported (which is true in the published benchmarks). We obtained our example collection by letting (each of) the domain parameters take on the values 4, 8, 12, 16, and 20. For each combination of the values, we generated a group of 5 random instances, giving us, again, a total number of 25 groups of randomized examples, 5 instances per group.

Under h^+, there are no local minima in *Ferry*, and $c = 1$ is an upper bound on the maximal exit distance. Our data strongly supports our hypotheses that both properties carry over to h^{FF}: not a single sample state is on a valley, and the average maximal exit distance is constantly 1 across all 25 groups.

9.3.3 Fridge

The *Fridge* instances are determined by the number of fridges and the number of screws. There is only a single instance per domain parameter setting, and thus no random element. Our example collection contains instances with 1 to 12 fridges and 1 to 12 screws. Those instances where both the number of fridges and the number of screws is high were too large to look at in our experiment, so we used less screws with increasing number of fridges.

As shown in Section 8.3.3, the properties of h^+ are that there are no local minima, and that the maximal exit distance is $n + 1$ if there are n screws. Our sampling data convincingly confirms that these properties carry directly over to h^{FF}. No single sample state is on a valley. Have a look at the maximal exit distance data in Figure 9.5.

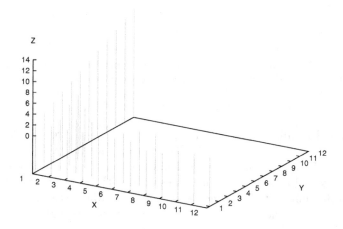

Fig. 9.5. Maximal exit distance (z-axis) in *Fridge* instances, scaling fridges (x-axis) against screws (y-axis)

The sampled maximal exit distance is exactly $n + 1$ in all our examples with n screws, with two exceptions: in the instances with 8 respectively 9 fridges and a single screw, the maximum exit distance of the sampled states is 1 instead of its ideal value 2.

9.3.4 Miconic-SIMPLE

Miconic-SIMPLE instances are determined by the number of floors and the number of passengers, modulo the random distribution of origin- and destination-floors of all passengers, and the initial location of the elevator. We obtained our example collection by letting the domain parameters take on the values 1, 5, 9, 13, and 17. For each combination of the values, we generated a group of 5 random instances, giving us a total number of 25 groups of randomized examples, 5 instances per group.

The properties of h^+ are that there are no local minima, and that $c = 1$ is an upper bound on the maximal exit distance. Figure 9.6 shows, for both topological parameters, the data we have obtained by sampling.

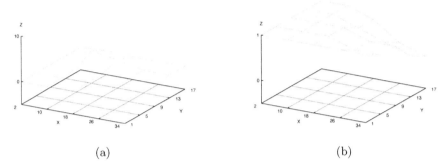

(a)   (b)

Fig. 9.6. Sampled average valley percentage (a) and maximal exit distance (b) in *Miconic-SIMPLE*. Data is shown on the z-axis, scaling floors (x-axis) against passengers (y-axis)

The sampled valley percentage is equal to 0 in all but three of our groups, and takes on a maximum value of 2.2%. The sampled maximal exit distance is equal to 1 in most of our groups, and below 1 in the others. The observation is that the sampled maximal exit distance decreases both with increasing number of floors and increasing number of passengers. It seems that the states with maximal exit distance 1 are rare when the domain parameter values are high, similarly to what we have observed above in the *Movie* domain.

9.3.5 Miconic-STRIPS

The domain parameters in *Miconic-STRIPS* are exactly the same as in *Miconic-SIMPLE*. Also, we have used the same value settings in our example collection, generating 5 random instances for each combination of 1, 5, 9, 13, or 17 floors respectively passengers.

Sampling yields exactly the same strong confirmation of our hypotheses like we have seen above in the *Ferry* domain: again, not a single sample state is on a valley, and the average maximal exit distance is constantly 1 across all 25 groups.

9.4 Domains with Multiple Parameters

There are two domains in which we need to verify properties of h^{FF}, and which have more than two domain parameters. These domains are *Logistics* and *Grid*. We start with the *Logistics* domain, which is somewhat simpler.

9.4.1 Logistics

In *Logistics*, instances are determined by: the number of cities; the number of objects; the numbers of trucks and airplanes; the sizes (number of locations) of the cities; the number of objects that must be transported. The random elements are the initial locations of all objects, trucks, and airplanes, as well as the goal locations of those objects that must be transported. Our random generation method, c.f. Appendix B, simplifies the situation in that all cities are of the same size, that all objects must be transported, and that there is exactly one truck in each city (which restrictions are true in the AIPS-2000 benchmark collection). So the method uses the four domain parameters "number of cities", "number of objects", "number of airplanes", and "size of cities".

To reduce the number of experiments, we fix one of the domain parameters, city size, to 3. This is justified in that, in the published benchmark collections, there is only little variation in the city size. There are thus three experimental settings to explore: scaling the number of cities against the number of objects; scaling the number of cities against the number of airplanes; and scaling the number of objects against the number of airplanes. In all experiments, we let the number of cities or objects range over the values 1, 3, 5, 7, and 9; the number of airplanes ranged over the values 1, 2, 3, 4, and 5. If a parameter was fixed, we set it to the middle value of its range. For each parameter combination, we generated 5 random instances.

The properties of h^+ in *Logistics* are that there are no local minima, and that $c = 1$ is an upper bound on the maximal exit distance. In all our experiments, the data we obtained by sampling confirmed that these properties carry over to h^{FF} in the sense of our respective hypotheses. See the diagrams in Figure 9.7.

In all of the diagrams regarding valley percentage in Figure 9.7, the maximum value on the z-axis is set to 1%; in the diagrams regarding maximal exit distance, the maximum value on the z-axis is set to 2. In the experiment scaling cities against objects, all sampled valley percentages are 0 except one case where it is 0.2%; the sampled maximal exit distance is 1 or below 1 except in one case where it is 1.2; with many cities and objects, the states with high exit distance seem to be hard to find by sampling. A similar picture is obtained in the experiment that scales cities against airplanes: there is a single case where the valley percentage is non-zero, precisely 0.4%; the maximal exit distance is at most equal to 1 across all groups, and decreases (probably due to the sampling method, as above) when there are both many cities and many airplanes. When scaling objects against airplanes, there are no sample states on valleys at all, and the maximal exit distance is always at most 1, varying with no discernible tendency.

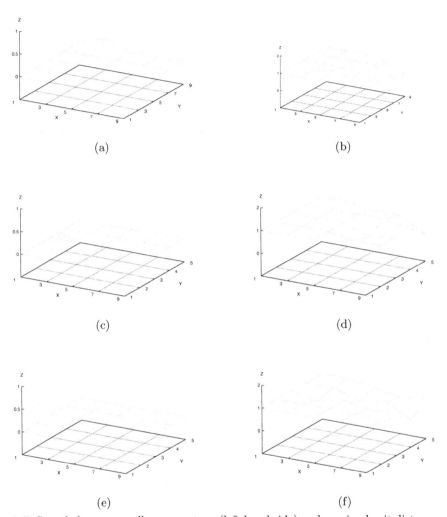

Fig. 9.7. Sampled average valley percentage (left hand side) and maximal exit distance (right hand side) in *Logistics*, when scaling cities against objects (a and b), cities against airplanes (c and d), and objects against airplanes (e and f). Data is shown on the z-axis; when scaling domain parameter A against domain parameter B, the value of A is depicted on the x-axis, and the value of B is depicted on the y-axis

9.4.2 Grid

In *Grid*, the instances depend on rather a lot of parameters: the x and y extension of the grid; the number of different key and lock shapes; the number of keys and the number of locked places (of each shape); the number of keys (of each shape) that must be transported. The random elements are the locations of the locked places, the initial locations of the robot and the keys, as well as the goal locations of those keys that must be transported. We make the following simplifications to reduce the number of experiments: all keys must be transported; there are exactly two different key and lock shapes; the y extension is fixed to 3. This leaves us with the domain parameters "x-extension", "number of keys", and "number of locks". The first simplification is justified in that it does not seem to change much intuitively. As for the second simplification, a low number of different shapes was necessary to enable our experiments, at least if there is going to be at least one key or lock of each shape — the necessary computations could only be done for very low numbers of keys and locks. The simplification is justified in that with two different shapes, it can still happen that a key does not match a lock. As for the third simplification, what we want to scale is the size of the grid, for which it is enough if we scale one (the x-) extension. Altogether, it can be hoped that the simplified domain can still give a picture of what happens in *Grid*, though one must be careful with the interpretation of the results. Anyway, it turns out that our data does *not* support our hypothesis about the *Grid* domain (as was already indicated by the data gathered in our collection of small examples, c.f. Section 7.3.1). So our experiments give a counter-example and it does not matter much that one must be careful in interpreting them as representative for the whole domain.

We have three varying domain parameters so, like in *Logistics* above, there are three experiments to be made. We generated our example collections as follows. We let the x-extension take on the values 4, 5, 6, 7, and 8, and we let the number of keys or locks take on the values $2|1$, $2|2$, $3|2$, $3|3$, and $4|3$. By $a|b$ here we denote that there are a many keys or locks of the first shape, and b many of the second shape (remember that there are exactly two different key and lock shapes). In each experiment, we set the fixed parameter to the middle value of its range. As we found that there was a lot of variance between different random instances, we generated 100 solvable random instances for each combination of the domain parameter values (giving us a total of 2500 instances, or 250000 sample states, per experiment). Under evaluation with h^+, there are no local minima in *Grid*. The hypothesis is that this property roughly carries over to h^{FF}. We focus on the three experiments in turn.

In the first experiment, diagram shown in Figure 9.8, we scale x-extension against number of keys. Note that this is the first valley percentage diagram where the maximum value on the z-axis is given by the full 100%. It can be observed that the valley percentage grows with both domain parameters. With x-extension 4, the average values are all around 20%. With x-extension 8 and $2|1$ keys, there are 44.9% valley states on average, with x-extension 8 and $4|3$ keys the percentage goes up to 62.4%. So the experiment falsifies the hypothesis

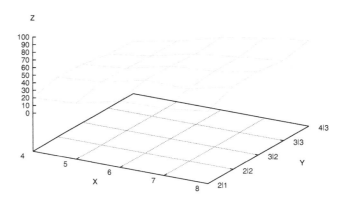

Fig. 9.8. Valley percentage in *Grid* instances, scaling x-extension (x-axis) against keys (y-axis). There are two different key and lock shapes, y-extension is fixed to 3, number of locks is fixed to 3|2

that the no-valley property of h^+ carries over to h^{FF}, even in a rough sense. As for the maximal exit distance, there is no hypothesis about that; it turns out that the average values vary between 4 and 5 in this experiment, without any discernible tendency.

In the second experiment, diagram shown in Figure 9.9, we scale x-extension against number of locks. Again, it can be observed that the average valley percentage grows with x extension (from around 20% with x-extension 4 to around 60% with x-extension 8). As for the number of locks, there is a slight tendency of decrease with their number: across all values of the x-extension, the valley percentage is maximal with 2|1 locks, and goes down by roughly 10% when increasing the number of locks to 4|3. The maximal exit distance varies, like above, between 4 and 5 without a discernible tendency.

The third experiment scaled keys against locks, keeping the x-extension fixed to 6. We do not include a diagram. The valley percentage varies between 30% and 50%, without any discernible tendency. We have done the same experiment but with less space on the grid, x-extension fixed to 4 (so the keys and locks are distributed more densely across the available space). The resulting valley percentage values are considerably lower, between 10% and 30%, and again there is no tendency of increase or decrease with the domain parameters — this being a bit puzzling as one would have expected that the many valley states have something to do with the interplay between keys and locks. We do not have a good explanation. Concerning the maximal exit distance, this varied inconclusively between 4 and 5 in both experiments.

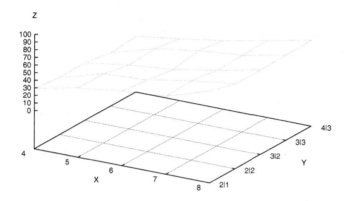

Fig. 9.9. Valley percentage in *Grid* instances, scaling x-extension (x-axis) against locks (y-axis). There are two different key and lock shapes, y-extension is fixed to 3, number of keys is fixed to 3/2

Altogether, the experiments demonstrate that there can indeed be many valley states in *Grid* instances under evaluation with h^{FF} — though we do not have a good explanation for the specific interplay between the parameters. It seems a bit strange that the maximal exit distance does not show any clear tendencies in any of our experiments. Consider what has been demonstrated in Section 8.3.5: imagine the set of *Grid* instances where the y-extension is 1, there are no locks and exactly one key, the robot starts on the leftmost place and the key starts on the rightmost place, and the goal is to transport the key to the leftmost place. The maximal exit distance under h^+ grows arbitrarily high with increasing x-extension (in fact, the maximal exit distance is equal to the x-extension). Thus, one would have expected that the sampled maximal exit distance under h^{FF} grows with this domain parameter. We can only speculate that this phenomenon gets "drowned" by the other ingredients of the above example collections. To corroborate this, we conducted an experiment with a very sparse set of *Grid* instances. The set was identical to the one above, except that the start and goal places of the robot and the key were assigned randomly. We let the x-extension take on the values 5, 10, 15, 20, and 25, and generated 100 instances for each of these settings. The resulting sampled average maximal exit distance values were 2.9, 5.6, 6.7, 9.9, and 13.1. This clearly demonstrates that the maximal exit distance can get arbitrarily high in *Grid* under h^{FF}. We remark that in this example collection there were no states on valleys, so it seems that the presence of more or differently shaped keys and locks is necessary for those to appear.

9.5 Results Overview

Let us summarize our observations. For convenience, we overview the results of this chapter in terms of the familiar taxonomy paradigm. See Figure 9.10. Note, however, that this time the border lines concerning local minima and the maximal exit distance are not strict. We have indicated this by drawing them as dotted lines, and specifying the domains in the lower part of the picture as those with "hardly any local minima".

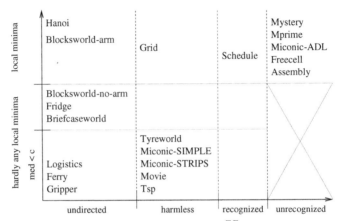

Fig. 9.10. How the h^+ properties carry over to h^{FF}, summarized in terms of the taxonomy paradigm

The properties of h^{FF} with regards to dead ends are provably the same as those of h^+ so the domains in the top right corner are classified correctly. Also, for *Blocksworld-arm* and *Schedule* we have found a lot of states on valleys in the small example collection from Chapter 7 already, c.f. Figure 7.8. We have seen that many valley states can arise under h^{FF} in the *Grid* and *Hanoi* domains, in difference to h^+. Concerning all the other domains where there are no local minima under h^+, our data strongly indicates that this property is largely preserved: we found sample states on valleys only in some example groups of the *Briefcaseworld* (maximum 5.0%), *Miconic-SIMPLE* (maximum 2.2%), *Logistics* (maximum 0.4%), and *Blocksworld-no-arm* (maximum 0.1%) domains. In all these domains, the sampled data for the large majority of our example instances does not contain any states on valleys at all. As for the maximal exit distance, our sampled data convincingly confirms all the upper bounds for h^+ in the sense that they also hold for h^{FF}. Only in a single case, a group of 5 example instances of the *Logistics* domain, is the average sampled maximal exit distance above the respective constant, namely 1.2 instead of 1 (so in a single example instance there was at least one sample state with exit distance 2).

We conclude that the properties of h^+ get largely preserved in all of our domains except *Grid* and *Assembly*. In particular, consider enforced hill-climbing using h^{FF}, i.e., the FF base architecture without helpful actions. Theorem 3.3.1 tells us that h^{FF} can be computed in polynomial time (in the STRIPS case, and trivially also in the propositional ADL case). Theorem 7.2.2 tells us that enforced hill-climbing does, in a fixed domain, polynomially many heuristic evaluations if h^{FF} yields no local minima and a bounded maximal exit distance. The empirical data gathered in this chapter gives strong evidence that in the *Ferry*, *Gripper*, *Logistics*, *Miconic-SIMPLE*, *Miconic-STRIPS*, *Movie*, *Simple-Tsp*, and *Tireworld* domains h^{FF} does in fact largely, or "approximatively", have this quality. So we can conclude that enforced hill-climbing using h^{FF} is "approximatively" polynomial in these eight domains.

10. Discussion

A single-line summary of the results in this book is the following:

Most of the current planning benchmarks share certain patterns of structure that can efficiently be utilized by a certain local search approach.

Filling in a bit more details, the 20 benchmark domains we considered here exhibit the following patterns of structure. First, in almost all of the domains all actions are either (at least) invertible or need not be inverted (like when their adds are static and their deletes are irrelevant). Second, in half of the domains all actions are respected by the relaxation, i.e., often there is simply no other way to achieve the goal than by applying them. Third, in almost half of the domains many actions have delete effects that are not needed anymore once they have been applied, while the other actions need not be applied more than a constant number of times in a row. The first pattern of structure implies that there are no dead ends. The first and second pattern together imply that there are no local minima under evaluation with h^+. The third pattern on top of that implies that there is a constant upper bound on the maximal exit distance under h^+. The patterns of structure can thus efficiently be utilized by approximating h^+, and using the resulting estimates in a local search strategy. Specifically, the proposed search strategy enforced hill-climbing is polynomial in domains where the heuristic function yields no local minima and a bounded maximal exit distance. In those eight of our domains where all three patterns of structure occur, h^+ has this quality. We have seen that the h^{FF} approximation preserves the quality of h^+ well.

Let us discuss the results, and some questions that are left to answer. We start with a number of open research topics. They fall, roughly, into the following two areas:

1. Improving planning algorithms; and
2. Explaining planning algorithm behavior.

One important research topic that falls into the first of these areas is the extension of FF's techniques to new, more expressive, formalisms. To some extent, this has already been done. Do and Kambhampati [22] have adapted the FF heuristic for use in a temporal metric framework, i.e., in a framework that allows durative actions and numeric state variables. Concerning the numeric variables, Do and Kambhampati's approach is somewhat unsatisfying in that

J. Hoffmann: Utilizing Problem Structure in Planning, LNAI 2854, pp. 199–202, 2003.
© Springer-Verlag Berlin Heidelberg 2003

the heuristic function ignores these variables completely when extracting the relaxed plan, and later uses some rather ad hoc heuristics to estimate their impact on plan length. The author himself has developed a more natural extension of FF's heuristic function to numeric state variables, treating them as part of the relaxed planning process [46, 47].

Another interesting topic is trying to improve (the performance of) FF's algorithms. An ideal basis for this is provided by Part III: knowing about the strengths and weaknesses of FF's heuristic function, one can focus research by concentrating on the weaknesses. An interesting direction here is trying to recognize dead ends that go unrecognized by h^{FF}, i.e., to find sufficient criteria for unsolvability that are weaker than relaxed planning but can be computed reasonably fast, namely in each single search state. One can also try to avoid large benches that stem from specific properties of relaxed plans in certain situations. In a way this has been done, for the case of transportation domains, in work by Fox and Long [34]. They inform the heuristic function about the fact that a vehicle can only be in one place at a time (which knowledge is extracted automatically from the domain description) and thereby improve performance — presumably by reducing the size of benches, though there is yet no explicit data to confirm that. One might also try to improve on the heuristic function by getting rid of local minima, for example by attempting to generalize from the way in which they arise, under h^+, in *Blocksworld-arm*, but don't arise in *Blocksworld-no-arm*.

One can also venture to improve not the quality of the heuristic function, but the *speed* of its computation. This is an important topic because that computation is the main bottleneck in FF (and other systems such as HSP and Mips). The author has approached the topic by automatically identifying and removing actions that are irrelevant for the function's computation — actions that will never be needed for a relaxed plan [49]. The results are yet unsatisfying in that speedups are obtained in only 3 out of the 20 domains in this book; it is an open question how one can improve on that. Liu et al. [68] have developed a different approach, speeding up HSP's heuristic function by re-using information from previous computations as well as optimizing the order of action applications. The obtained speedups are as yet moderate, around a constant factor of 2 to 5 in the AIPS-2000 benchmarks. An interesting third option to speed up the heuristic computation is to *not* perform it on the grounded task representation, i.e., to implement it using the parameterized operators rather than the grounded actions. While this does not per se avoid the number of parameter groundings that need to be considered, it may inspire new code optimizations: for example, one might think about utilizing symmetries between objects and treat *sets* of them as equivalent parameter instantiations during the relaxed planning process. Implementing the heuristic this way would also avoid the potentially exponential blow up inherent in the grounding process.

There are some questions left open by the investigation of the properties of h^+. For instance, FF is extremely efficient in *Schedule* though there can be local minima under h^+. The question is if these local minima – and those in other domains – are restricted in any way. This and other issues, including the h^+ topology of the benchmark domains used in the AIPS-2002 competition, have been clarified by the author in work yet only available as a technical report [48]. As for *Schedule*, it turns out that, from a state on a local minimum, the distance to the nearest state with a strictly better evaluation is always at most 6. Another interesting research topic would be to try and prove properties of h^+ for domain *classes* rather than for single domains. This might be possible along the lines of work by Malte Helmert on the complexity of planning in transportation and construction domains [42, 43]. With Helmert's terminology, in our results from Chapter 8 it is the case that h^+ does not yield local minima in any transportation domain where there is unlimited fuel. One could try to verify this observation in general. The main problem to be overcome in such a research effort would be that, while Helmert focuses on the semantics of the domains, we need to deal with their syntax: after all, h^+ depends directly on the syntax of the operators.

Apart from the above, there is the question whether the classes of the taxonomy stand in any provable relation to the computational complexity of deciding plan existence in the respective domains. An obvious positive result is that deciding plan existence in domains that belong to the lower most part of the taxonomy is in NP — there is a polynomial upper bound on plan length (given by $h^+(I) * (c + 1)$ where c is the upper bound on the exit distance). The other already known results are negative: there are polynomially decidable domains (domains in which deciding plan existence is in P) in which unrecognized dead ends occur, and there are NP-hard domains which do not exhibit local minima under h^+. An open question is, e.g., whether there is an NP-hard domain with no local minima and bounded maximal exit distance.

Let us close the book by discussing one of the most pressing questions opened up by this work. The main result is that most of the current planning benchmarks share a structure that makes h^+ a very high quality heuristic. Now:

Is this a good or a bad result for AI planning? Does it mean that we have identified widely spread patterns of structure that can make planning feasible, or does it only mean that the benchmarks are superficial?

Formulated less dramatically, the question is whether the current benchmarks are an adequate means of evaluation in the sense that they capture the structures that are important in the envisioned applications. This is not a question one can answer just like that. There is not even a clear picture in the community of what the "envisioned applications" are. While domains like *Simple-Tsp*, *Movie*, or *Gripper* are so trivial they seem highly unlikely to contain any structures relevant in reality,[1] it is much harder to assess the relevance of domains like *Tireworld*, *Grid*, or *Blocksworld-arm*. The author personally believes that, at this point in time, there are the following two things to do about the benchmarks/about evaluation in planning:

---

[1] Indeed, these domains have been designed with the intention to highlight certain characteristic shortcomings of certain planning systems, rather than with the intention to model realistic problems.

1. Design new benchmark domains and example suits that are as close as possible to existing real-world applications of planning. To name a few, examples for such applications are Jana Koehler's Miconic domain [65], Sylvie Thiebaux's PSR domain [4, 14], and Stefan Edelkamp's software verification domain [25]. The use of more such domains will hopefully yield a more conclusive picture of how efficient the current planning technology can be expected to be in reality, and provide a testbed suitable for steering the field into a fruitful direction.

2. Avoid the repeated use of structurally similar benchmark domains. It has been no exception in the past to see papers evaluate planners in test beds including, e.g., all of the *Gripper*, *Logistics*, and *Miconic-STRIPS* domains. This obviously does not make much sense, at least if the performance of (one of) the tested planner(s) depends a lot on the quality of h^+ – polemically put, the only thing that changes are the names of the predicates. What a good testbed should do is, test the planners on a variety of different problem structures. A criterion for a good testbed could be to cover the relevant complexity classes (at least P, NP, and PSPACE) for the complexity of deciding (bounded) plan existence within the domains; or, at least for planners that use relaxed plan based heuristics, to cover all the relevant distinctions in the planning domain taxonomy provided herein.

While the above two directives are basically common sense, a better thought through choice of benchmark examples, and interpretation of results obtained that way, would certainly do good to the AI planning community.[2] Together with Stefan Edelkamp, the author intends to promote just this, by applying the above directives in the next international planning competition alongside ICAPS-2004.

---

[2] While there have traditionally been a lot of complaints about the *Blocksworld* domain, there has rarely been an argument against *Blocksworld* except that it intuitively is a "toy" domain. But that's a property that most STRIPS domains are likely to share, and it does not exclude their potential ability to capture *structures* that are relevant in the real world. With respect to the topology under h^+, the investigation at hand indeed proves that *Blocksworld-arm* is one of the domains with a more interesting structure.

A. Formalized Benchmark Domains

This appendix contains the formal definitions of all benchmark domains in our collection. These formalities are needed as the background to the investigation in Chapter 8, proving topological properties of h^+ across all instances of domains. The formal details also supplement the intuitive descriptions of the domains given in Section 2.3.

As said at the beginning of Chapter 8, to ease the connection to that chapter the formalizations we present here are made such that the domains are negation-free, which is in some ADL domains slightly different (syntactically, but not semantically) from the original formulation used in the planning community. We state the differences explicitly. As has also been mentioned before, the decisions about what exactly the instances of the domains are have been made by abstracting from the published benchmarks. In most cases, this is obvious. In the less obvious cases, we add a few comments. Generally, this appendix contains only the formal definitions and some explanation of the formal means involved. More intuitive descriptions of the domains are, as said, in Section 2.3.

We list the 20 domains in alphabetical order. For getting used to the notation, it is probably better to proceed in the order given by Chapter 8, i.e., to start with simple examples like *Simple-Tsp*, *Movie*, *Gripper*, and *Logistics*.

A.1 Assembly

Definition A.1.1. *Assembly is the ADL domain* $(\mathcal{P}, \mathcal{O}, \mathcal{I})$ *where the set of predicates is*

$$
\begin{aligned}
\mathcal{P} = \{ \ & (equal, 2), (assembly, 1), (not\text{-}assembly, 1), (resource, 1), \\
& (not\text{-}resource, 1), (requires, 2), (not\text{-}requires, 2), (part\text{-}of, 2), \\
& (not\text{-}part\text{-}of, 2), (transient\text{-}part, 2), (not\text{-}transient\text{-}part, 2), \\
& (assemble\text{-}order, 3), (not\text{-}assemble\text{-}order, 3), (remove\text{-}order, 3), \\
& (not\text{-}remove\text{-}order, 3), (commited, 2), (available, 1), \\
& (incorporated, 2), (not\text{-}incorporated, 2), (complete, 1) \}
\end{aligned}
$$

J. Hoffmann: Utilizing Problem Structure in Planning, LNAI 2854, pp. 203–233, 2003.
© Springer-Verlag Berlin Heidelberg 2003

$\mathcal{O}$ *consists of the operators*

− *commit:*

$(\ (x,y),$
$\ \ \{(resource, x), (assembly, y), (available, x)\},$
$\ \ \{(committed, x, y)\},$
$\ \ \{(available, x)\})$

− *release:*

$(\ (x,y),$
$\ \ \{(resource, x), (assembly, y), (commited, x, y)\},$
$\ \ \{(available, x)\},$
$\ \ \{(committed, x, y)\})$

− *assemble:*

$(\ (x,y),$
$\ \ (assembly, x) \wedge (assembly, y) \wedge (available, x)\wedge$
$\ \ (\forall z : (not\text{-}resource, z) \vee (not\text{-}requires, y, z) \vee (committed, z, y))\wedge$
$\ \ ((part\text{-}of, x, y) \vee (transient\text{-}part, x, y))\wedge$
$\ \ (\forall z : (not\text{-}assembly, z) \vee (not\text{-}assemble\text{-}order, z, x, y)\vee$
$\ \ \ \ \ \ \ (incorporated, z, y)),$
$\ \ \{\ ((), \top, \{(incorporated, x, y)\}, \{(available, x), (not\text{-}incorporated, x, y)\}),$
$\ \ \ \ (\ (),$
$\ \ \ \ \ \ (part\text{-}of, x, y)\wedge$
$\ \ \ \ \ \ (\forall z : (not\text{-}assembly, z) \vee (not\text{-}part\text{-}of, z, y) \vee (equal, z, x)\vee$
$\ \ \ \ \ \ \ \ \ \ (incorporated, z, y))\wedge$
$\ \ \ \ \ \ (\forall z : (not\text{-}assembly, z) \vee (not\text{-}transient\text{-}part, z, y)\vee$
$\ \ \ \ \ \ \ \ \ \ (not\text{-}incorporated, z, y)),$
$\ \ \ \ \ \ \{(complete, y), (available, y)\},$
$\ \ \ \ \ \ \emptyset)\})$

− *remove:*

$(\ (x,y),$
$\ \ (assembly, x) \wedge (assembly, y) \wedge (incorporated, x, y)\wedge$
$\ \ (\forall z : (not\text{-}resource, z) \vee (not\text{-}requires, y, z) \vee (committed, z, y))\wedge$
$\ \ (\ (transient\text{-}part, x, y)\wedge$
$\ \ \ \ (\forall z : (not\text{-}assembly, z) \vee (not\text{-}remove\text{-}order, z, x, y)\vee$
$\ \ \ \ (incorporated, z, y)) \vee (part\text{-}of, x, y)\wedge$
$\ \ \ \ (\forall z : (not\text{-}assembly, z) \vee (not\text{-}assemble\text{-}order, z, x, y)\vee$
$\ \ \ \ \ \ \ \ (not\text{-}incorporated, z, y))),$
$\ \ \{\ ((), \top, \{(available, x), (not\text{-}incorporated, x, y)\}, \{(incorporated, x, y)\}),$
$\ \ \ \ (\ (),$
$\ \ \ \ \ \ (transient\text{-}part, x, y)\wedge$
$\ \ \ \ \ \ (\forall z \in C : (not\text{-}assembly, z) \vee (not\text{-}part\text{-}of, z, y)\vee$

$(incorporated, z, y)) \wedge$
$(\forall z \in C : (not\text{-}assembly, z) \vee (not\text{-}transient\text{-}part, z, y) \vee (equal, z, x) \vee$
$(not\text{-}incorporated, z, y)),$
$\{(complete, y), (available, y)\},$
$\emptyset)\})$

and the set of instances is

$\mathcal{I} = \{\ (\ As \cup R,$
$\quad \{(equal, x, x) \mid x \in As \cup R\} \cup$
$\quad \{(assembly, x) \mid x \in As\} \cup \{(not\text{-}assembly, x) \mid x \in R\} \cup$
$\quad \{(resource, x) \mid x \in R\} \cup \{(not\text{-}resource, x) \mid x \in As\} \cup$
$\quad \{(requires, x, y) \mid x \in As, y \in re(x)\} \cup$
$\quad \{(not\text{-}requires, x, y) \mid x \in As, y \in R \setminus re(x)\} \cup$
$\quad \{(part\text{-}of, x, y) \mid y \in As, x \in pa(y)\} \cup$
$\quad \{(not\text{-}part\text{-}of, x, y) \mid y \in As, x \in As \setminus pa(y)\} \cup$
$\quad \{(transient\text{-}part, x, y) \mid y \in As, x \in tr(y)\} \cup$
$\quad \{(not\text{-}transient\text{-}part, x, y) \mid y \in As, x \in As \setminus tr(y)\} \cup$
$\quad \{(assemble\text{-}order, x, z, y) \mid y \in As, (x, z) \in ao(y)\} \cup$
$\quad \{(not\text{-}assemble\text{-}order, x, z, y) \mid y \in As, (x, z) \in (As \times As) \setminus ao(y)\} \cup$
$\quad \{(remove\text{-}order, x, z, y) \mid y \in As, (x, z) \in ro(y)\} \cup$
$\quad \{(not\text{-}remove\text{-}order, x, z, y) \mid y \in As, (x, z) \in (As \times As) \setminus ro(y)\} \cup$
$\quad \{(available, x) \mid x \in As, pa(x) = \emptyset\}\ \cup$
$\quad \{(not\text{-}incorporated, x, y) \mid y \in As, x \in pa(y) \cup tr(y)\},$
$\quad \{(complete, g)\})$
$\mid As \cup R \subseteq \Sigma^+, As \cap R = \emptyset, |As| \geq 2$
$pa : As \mapsto 2^{As}, (As, \{(x, y) \mid y \in As, x \in pa(y)\})$ *is tree with root* $g,$
$tr : As \mapsto 2^{As},$
$\forall y \in As : pa(y) = \emptyset \Rightarrow tr(y) = \emptyset \wedge tr(y) \cap pa(y) = \emptyset \wedge y \notin tr(y),$
$re : As \mapsto 2^R,$
$ao : As \mapsto 2^{(As \times As)}, (As, ao(y))$ *is cycle-free for* $y \in As,$
$\forall y \in As : (x, z) \in ao(y) \wedge z \in pa(y) \cup tr(y) \Rightarrow x \in pa(y) \cup tr(y)$
$ro : As \mapsto 2^{(As \times As)}, (As, ro(y))$ *is cycle-free for* $y \in As,$
$\forall y \in As : (x, z) \in ro(y) \wedge z \in tr(y) \Rightarrow x \in pa(y) \cup tr(y)\}$

Remember that we allow ADL domains also to comprise STRIPS operators, c.f. Section 2.2.5. The *commit* and *release* operators are STRIPS formulations; *assemble* and *remove* are ADL operators, with complex preconditions and complex effect conditions but with empty effect parameters. In the instances, the *pa* function defines the part-of relation, which forms a tree where the root node is the goal assembly. Each non-leaf node of the tree $(pa(y) \neq \emptyset)$ can have arbitrary transient parts except its own parts, given by the *tr* function, and each non-leaf node can require an arbitrary amount of resources specified via the *re* function. The assemble order $ao(y)$ is a consistent partial ordering between parts and transient parts of an assembly y, and the remove order $ro(y)$ is a consistent partial ordering between (transient) parts and transient parts of an assembly *y*. In the original domain there are a lot of negations, which are formulated by the extra predicates *not-assembly*, *not-resource*, *not-requires*, *not-part-of*, *not-transient-part*, *not-assemble-order*, *not-remove-order*, and *not-incorporated*.

The set of instances makes a number of restrictions excluding cases that are obvious nonsense. The restrictions are the following. The *pa* relation forms a tree — otherwise one part would need to be incorporated into several others simultaneously, or similar nonsense. There are no transient parts in the atomic assemblies (the leafs of the *pa*-tree), no assembly is transient part and part (of the same higher-level assembly) simultaneously, and no assembly is transient part of itself. The assemble and remove orders are consistent. Given an assemble order $(x, z) \in ao(y)$ where it might be that z must be incorporated into y at some point (as $z \in pa(y) \cup tr(y)$) we postulate that x can in principle be incorporated into y, $x \in pa(y) \cup tr(y)$. Similarly, given a remove order $(x, z) \in ro(y)$ where it might be that x must be incorporated into y at some point in order to get z out (which can only happen if $z \in tr(y)$) we postulate that this can in principle be done, $x \in pa(y) \cup tr(y)$.

The tasks produced by our generator, c.f. Appendix B, all adhere to the above restrictions. In the AIPS-1998 benchmark collection, the situation is as follows. There are three tasks where the initial state uses undeclared constants, which is a violation of the ADL language. There are furthermore two tasks that do not adhere to the last of the restrictions described above, i.e., where there are x, z, and y with $(x, z) \in ro(y)$, $z \in tr(y)$, and $x \notin pa(y) \cup tr(y)$. These two tasks are trivially unsolvable, and we assume that their specification is flawed. The remaining 25 tasks adhere to the restrictions of our definition.

A.2 Blocksworld-arm

Definition A.2.1. *Blocksworld-arm is the STRIPS domain* $(\mathcal{P}, \mathcal{O}, \mathcal{I})$ *where the set of predicates is*

$$\mathcal{P} = \{(clear, 1), (holding, 1), (arm\text{-}empty, 0), (on\text{-}table, 1), (on, 2)\}$$

$\mathcal{O}$ *consists of the operators*

– *pickup:*

> ((x),
> $\{(clear, x), (on\text{-}table, x), (arm\text{-}empty)\}$,
> $\{(holding, x)\}$,
> $\{(clear, x), (on\text{-}table, x), (arm\text{-}empty)\}$)

– *putdown:*

> ((x),
> $\{(holding, x)\}$,
> $\{(clear, x), (on\text{-}table, x), (arm\text{-}empty)\}$,
> $\{(holding, x)\}$)

− *unstack:*

$$(\ (x, y),$$
$$\{(clear, x), (on, x, y), (arm\text{-}empty)\},$$
$$\{(holding, x), (clear, y)\},$$
$$\{(clear, x), (on, x, y), (arm\text{-}empty)\})$$

− *stack:*

$$(\ (x, y),$$
$$\{(holding, x), (clear, y)\},$$
$$\{(clear, x), (on, x, y), (arm\text{-}empty)\},$$
$$\{(holding, x), (clear, y)\})$$

and the set of instances is

$$\mathcal{I} = \{ \ (\ B,$$
$$\{(arm\text{-}empty)\} \cup \{(on\text{-}table, x) \mid x \in B, \forall y : (x, y) \notin I\} \cup$$
$$\{(on, x, y) \mid (x, y) \in I\} \cup \{(clear, x) \mid x \in B, \forall y : (y, x) \notin I\},$$
$$\{(on, x, y) \mid (x, y) \in G\})$$
$$\mid B \subseteq \Sigma^+, |B| \geq 1,$$
$$I \subseteq B \times B, (B, I) \text{ is cycle-free graph with in- and out-degree 1},$$
$$G \subseteq B \times B, (B, G) \text{ is cycle-free graph with in- and out-degree 1}\}$$

In the instances, the edge sets I and G represent the initial and goal states, respectively, by the semantics that $(x, y) \in I$ ($\in G$) if and only if x is initially (shall be finally) located on y. Note that an edge set represents a legal state iff there are no cycles in the corresponding on relation, each block has at most one block located on top of it, and each block is located on top of at most one other block.

A.3 Blocksworld-no-arm

Definition A.3.1. *Blocksworld-no-arm is the STRIPS domain* $(\mathcal{P}, \mathcal{O}, \mathcal{I})$ *where the set of predicates is*

$$\mathcal{P} = \{(not\text{-}eq, 2), (clear, 1), (on\text{-}table, 1), (on, 2)\}$$

$\mathcal{O}$ *consists of the operators*

− *move-table-to-block:*

$$(\ (x, y),$$
$$\{(not\text{-}eq, x, y), (clear, x), (clear, y), (on\text{-}table, x)\},$$
$$\{(on, x, y)\},$$
$$\{(clear, y), (on\text{-}table, x)\})$$

− *move-block-to-table:*

$$((x, y), \{(clear, x), (on, x, y)\}, \{(on\text{-}table, x), (clear, y)\}, \{(on, x, y)\}$$

$-$ *move-block-to-block:*

$(\ (x, y, z),$
$\{(not\text{-}eq, x, z), (clear, x), (on, x, y), (clear, z)\},$
$\{(on, x, z), (clear, y)\},$
$\{(on, x, y), (clear, z)\})$

and the set of instances is

$\mathcal{I} = \{\ (\ B,$
$\{(not\text{-}eq, x, y) \mid x, y \in B, x \neq y\}\ \cup$
$\{(on\text{-}table, x) \mid x \in B, \forall y : (x, y) \notin I\}\ \cup$
$\{(on, x, y) \mid (x, y) \in I\} \cup \{(clear, x) \mid x \in B, \forall y : (y, x) \notin I\},$
$\{(on, x, y) \mid (x, y) \in G\})$
$\mid\ B \subseteq \Sigma^{+}, |B| \geq 1,$
$I \subseteq B \times B, (B, I)$ *is cycle-free graph with in- and out-degree 1,*
$G \subseteq B \times B, (B, G)$ *is cycle-free graph with in- and out-degree 1*\}

The instances are exactly the same as for *Blocksworld-arm*, see above. We have introduced non-equality to get rid of actions that try to move a block on top of itself.

A.4 Briefcaseworld

Definition A.4.1. *Briefcaseworld is the ADL domain* $(\mathcal{P}, \mathcal{O}, \mathcal{I})$ *where the set of predicates is*

$$\mathcal{P} = \{(not\text{-}eq, 2), (location, 1), (portable, 1), (at, 2), (in, 1), (not\text{-}in, 1), (is\text{-}at, 1)\}$$

$\mathcal{O}$ *consists of the operators*

$-$ *move:*

$(\ (x, y),$
$(not\text{-}eq, x, y) \wedge (location, x) \wedge (location, y) \wedge (is\text{-}at, x),$
$\{\ ((), \top, \{(is\text{-}at, y)\}, \{(is\text{-}at, x)\}),$
$((z), (portable, z) \wedge (in, z), \{(at, z, y)\}, \{(at, z, x)\})\})$

$-$ *take-out:* $((x), \{(portable, x)\}, \{(not\text{-}in, x)\}, \{(in, x)\})$
$-$ *put-in:*

$(\ (x, y, z),$
$\{(portable, x), (location, y), (not\text{-}in, x), (at, x, y), (is\text{-}at, y)\},$
$\{(in, x)\},$
$\{(not\text{-}in, x)\})$

and the set of instances is

$\mathcal{I} = \{ \ (\ L \cup P,$
$\{(not\text{-}eq, x, y) \mid x, y \in L, x \neq y\} \cup \{(location, x) \mid x \in L\} \cup$
$\{(portable, x) \mid x \in P\} \cup \{(is\text{-}at, il)\} \cup \{(at, x, pil(x)) \mid x \in P\},$
$(is\text{-}at, gl) \wedge \bigwedge\{(at, x, pgl(x)) \mid x \in P'\})$
$\mid (L \cup P) \subseteq \Sigma^+, L \cap P = \emptyset, |L| \geq 1,$
$il \in L, pil : P \mapsto L, gl \in L, P' \subseteq P, pgl : P' \mapsto L\}$

Note that we have a mixture between STRIPS and ADL operators, the only ADL element being the conditional effect of the *move* operator (which has one effect parameter). In the definition of the instances, *il* and *gl* are the initial and goal locations of the briefcase, while *pil* and *pgl* are the initial and goal location functions for portables. $P' \subseteq P$ is the subset of portables that must be transported, i.e., that are mentioned in the goal specification. We have introduced non-equality to get rid of actions that try to move within a location. The *not-in* predicate is part of the original domain formulation.

A.5 Ferry

Definition A.5.1. *Ferry is the STRIPS domain* $(\mathcal{P}, \mathcal{O}, \mathcal{I})$ *where the set of predicates is*

$\mathcal{P} = \{ \ (not\text{-}eq, 2), (car, 1), (location, 1), (at\text{-}ferry, 1),$
$(at, 2), (empty\text{-}ferry, 0), (on, 1)\}$

$\mathcal{O}$ *consists of the operators*

− *sail:*

$(\ (x, y),$
$\{(not\text{-}eq, x, y), (location, x), (location, y), (at\text{-}ferry, x)\},$
$\{(at\text{-}ferry, y)\},$
$\{(at\text{-}ferry, x)\})$

− *board:*

$(\ (x, y),$
$\{(car, x), (location, y), (at, x, y), (at\text{-}ferry, y), (empty\text{-}ferry)\},$
$\{(on, x)\},$
$\{(at, x, y), (empty\text{-}ferry)\})$

− *debark:*

$(\ (x, y),$
$\{(car, x), (location, y), (on, x), (at\text{-}ferry, y)\},$
$\{(at, x, y), (empty\text{-}ferry)\},$
$\{(on, x)\})$

and the set of instances is

$\mathcal{I} = \{\ (\ C \cup L,$
$\{(not\text{-}eq, x, y) \mid x, y \in L, x \neq y\} \cup \{(car, x) \mid x \in C\} \cup$
$\{(location, x) \mid x \in L\} \cup \{(at\text{-}ferry, il)\} \cup \{(at, x, cil(x)) \mid x \in C\},$
$\{(at, x, cgl(x)) \mid x \in C'\})$
$\mid (C \cup L) \subseteq \Sigma^+, C \cap L = \emptyset, |L| \geq 1,$
$il \in L, cil : C \mapsto L, C' \subseteq C, cgl : C' \mapsto L\}$

In the instances, il is the initial location of the ferry, and cil is the car initial location function mapping the cars to their respective initial locations. Likewise, cgl maps cars to their goal locations, where only the subset C' of all cars is required to be at a specific location to fulfill the goal. We have introduced non-equality to get rid of actions that try to sail within a location.

A.6 Freecell

Definition A.6.1. *Freecell is the STRIPS domain* $(\mathcal{P}, \mathcal{O}, \mathcal{I})$ *where the set of predicates is*

$\mathcal{P} = \{\ (card, 1), (suit\text{-}type, 1), (num, 1), (successor, 2), (suit, 1),$
$(value, 2), (canstack, 2), (home, 1), (bottomcol, 1), (on, 2),$
$(clear, 1), (incell, 1), (cellspace, 1), (colspace, 1)\}$

$\mathcal{O}$ *consists of the operators*

– *move:*

$(\ (x, y, z),$
$\{\ (card, x), (card, y), (card, z), (clear, x), (clear, z),$
$(on, x, y), (canstack, x, z)\},$
$\{(on, x, z), (clear, y)\},$
$\{(on, x, y), (clear, z)\})$

– *move-b:*

$(\ (x, y, z, u),$
$\{\ (card, x), (card, y), (num, z), (num, u), (clear, x), (bottomcol, x),$
$(clear, y), (canstack, x, y), (colspace, z), (successor, u, z)\},$
$\{(on, x, y), (colspace, u)\},$
$\{(bottomcol, x), (clear, y), (colspace, z)\})$

– *sendtofree:*

$(\ (x, y, z, u),$
$\{\ (card, x), (card, y), (num, z), (num, u),$
$(clear, x), (on, x, y), (cellspace, z), (successor, z, u)\},$
$\{(incell, x), (clear, y), (cellspace, u)\},$
$\{(on, x, y), (clear, x), (cellspace, z)\})$

− sendtofree-b:

((x, y, z, u, v),
{ $(card, x), (num, y), (num, z), (num, u), (num, v)$,
$(clear, x), (bottomcol, x), (cellspace, y)$,
$(successor, y, z), (colspace, u), (successor, v, u)$},
{$(incell, x), (cellspace, z), (colspace, v)$},
{$(bottomcol, x), (clear, x), (cellspace, y), (colspace, u)$})

− sendtonewcol:

((x, y, z, u),
{ $(card, x), (card, y), (num, z), (num, u)$,
$(clear, x), (on, x, y), (colspace, z), (successor, z, u)$},
{$(bottomcol, x), (clear, y), (colspace, u)$},
{$(on, x, y), (colspace, z)$})

− sendtohome:

((x, y, z, u, v, w),
{ $(card, x), (card, y), (suit\text{-}type, z), (num, u), (card, v)$,
$(num, w), (on, x, y), (clear, x), (home, v), (suit, x, z)$,
$(suit, v, z), (value, x, u), (value, v, w), (successor, u, w)$},
{$(home, x), (clear, y)$},
{$(on, x, y), (clear, x), (home, v)$})

− sendtohome-b:

((x, y, z, u, v, w, q),
{ $(card, x), (suit\text{-}type, y), (num, z), (card, u)$,
$(num, v), (num, w), (num, q)$,
$(bottomcol, x), (clear, x), (home, u)$,
$(suit, x, y), (suit, u, y), (value, x, z)$,
$(value, u, v), (successor, z, v), (colspace, w), (successor, q, w)$},
{$(home, x), (colspace, q)$},
{$(bottomcol, x), (clear, x), (home, u), (colspace, w)$})

− homefromfreecell:

((x, y, z, u, v, w, q),
{ $(card, x), (suit\text{-}type, y), (num, z), (card, u)$,
$(num, v), (num, w), (num, q)$,
$(incell, x), (home, u), (suit, x, y)$,
$(suit, u, y), (value, x, z), (value, u, v)$,
$(successor, z, v), (cellspace, w), (successor, q, w)$},
{$(home, x), (cellspace, q)$},
{$(incell, x), (home, u), (cellspace, w)$})

− *colfromfreecell:*

$$(\ (x, y, z, u),$$
$$\{ \ (card, x), (card, y), (num, z), (num, u), (incell, x), (clear, y),$$
$$(canstack, x, y), (cellspace, z), (successor, u, z)\},$$
$$\{(on, x, y), (clear, x), (cellspace, u)\},$$
$$\{(incell, x), (clear, y), (cellspace, z)\})$$

− *newcolfromfreecell:*

$$(\ (x, y, z, u, v),$$
$$\{ \ (card, x), (num, y), (num, z), (num, u), (num, v), (incell, x),$$
$$(cellspace, y), (successor, z, y), (colspace, u), (successor, u, v)\},$$
$$\{(bottomcol, x), (clear, x), (cellspace, z), (colspace, v)\},$$
$$\{(incell, x), (cellspace, y), (colspace, u)\})$$

and the set of instances is

$$\mathcal{I} = \{ \ (\ C \cup S \cup N, where \ \ C = \{c_{10}, \ldots, c_{1m_1}, \ldots, c_{n0}, \ldots, c_{nm_n}\},$$
$$S = \{s_1, \ldots, s_n\}, N = \{n_0, \ldots, n_m\},$$
$$\{(card, x) \mid x \in C\} \cup \{(suit, x) \mid x \in S\} \cup \{(num, x) \mid x \in N\} \cup$$
$$\{(successor, n_{i+1}, n_i) \mid 0 \le i < m\} \cup$$
$$\{(suit, c_{ij}, s_i) \mid 1 \le i \le n, 0 \le j \le m_i\} \cup$$
$$\{(value, c_{ij}, n_j) \mid 1 \le i \le n, 0 \le j \le m_i\} \cup$$
$$\{(canstack, c_{ij}, c_{i'j'}) \mid co(i) \ne co(i'), j = j' - 1\} \cup$$
$$\{(home, c_{i0}) \mid 1 \le i \le n\} \cup \{(bottomcol, x) \mid x \in C, \forall y : (x, y) \notin I\} \cup$$
$$\{(on, x, y) \mid (x, y) \in I\} \cup \{(clear, x) \mid x \in C, \forall y : (y, x) \notin I\} \cup$$
$$\{(cellspace, n_{nce})\} \cup$$
$$\{(colspace, n_{nrco}) \mid nrco = nco - |\{x \in C \mid \forall y : (x, y) \notin I\}|\},$$
$$\{(home, c_{im_i}) \mid 1 \le i \le n\})$$
$$\mid (S \cup C \cup N) \subseteq \Sigma^+, S, C, \ and \ N \ are \ pairwise \ disjoint,$$
$$|S| \ge 1, m_i \in \mathbf{N}_0 \ for \ 1 \le i \le n, nce \in \mathbf{N}_0, nco \in \mathbf{N}_0,$$
$$m \ge max\{m_1, \ldots, m_n, nce, nco\}, co : S \mapsto \{0, 1\},$$
$$I \subseteq C \times C, (C, I) \ is \ cycle\text{-}free \ graph \ with \ in\text{-} \ and \ out\text{-}degree \ 1,$$
$$|\{x \in C \mid \forall y : (x, y) \notin I\}| \le nco\}$$

The different operators express different ways of changing the position of a card. Options are to move a card on top of another card if the respective cards can be stacked, to move a card to a free column or a free cell, or to move a card home. The operators keep track of the respective numbers of free columns or free cells left, and of the appropriate informations about the current configuration of the cards. In the instances, there are n suits of cards each of which has at least one element: the one that is initially home already. The cards within a suit have different values, encoded by numbers. There are at least as many numbers as are needed to account for all given items. Each suit has one of two colors given by the co function, and a card can be stacked on top of another one if and only if its color (the one of its suit) is different, and its value is one less than the one of the destination card. The total number of free cells is nce, the total number of columns is *nco*. The initial configuration of the cards is given by the edge set I, specifying which cards are on top of other ones. The edge set represents a legal state as there are no cycles, each card has at most one card located on top of it, and each card is located on top of at most one other card; also, the number of bottom cards — those that are placed directly on a column — is at most as high as the number of columns *nco*, such that the difference between both numbers, the number of (initially) remaining free columns, is $nrco \geq 0$.

A.7 Fridge

Definition A.7.1. *Fridge is the ADL domain* $(\mathcal{P}, \mathcal{O}, \mathcal{I})$ *where the set of predicates is*

$$\mathcal{P} = \{ \ (fridge, 1), (compressor, 1), (fits, 2), (not\text{-}fits, 2),$$
$$(screwed, 1), (not\text{-}screwed, 1), (fridge\text{-}on, 1), (not\text{-}fridge\text{-}on, 1),$$
$$(screw, 1), (not\text{-}screw, 1), (attached, 1), (free, 1)\}$$

$\mathcal{O}$ *consists of the operators*

— *stop-fridge:*

$$((x), \{(fridge, x), (fridge\text{-}on, x)\}, \{(not\text{-}fridge\text{-}on, x)\}, \{(fridge\text{-}on, x)\})$$

— *start-fridge:*

$$((x), \{(fridge, x), (not\text{-}fridge\text{-}on, x)\}, \{(fridge\text{-}on, x)\}, \{(not\text{-}fridge\text{-}on, x)\})$$

— *unfasten:*

$$(\ (x, y, z),$$
$$\{ \ (screw, x), (compressor, y), (fridge, z),$$
$$(screwed, x), (fits, x, y), (attached, y, z), (not\text{-}fridge\text{-}on, z)\},$$
$$\{(not\text{-}screwed, x)\},$$
$$\{(screwed, x)\})$$

— *fasten:*

$$(\ (x, y, z),$$
$$\{ \ (screw, x), (compressor, y), (fridge, z),$$
$$(not\text{-}screwed, x), (fits, x, y), (attached, y, z), (not\text{-}fridge\text{-}on, z)\},$$
$$\{(screwed, x)\},$$
$$\{(not\text{-}screwed, x)\})$$

— *remove-compressor:*

$$(\ (x, y),$$
$$(compressor, x) \wedge (fridge, y) \wedge (attached, x, y) \wedge (not\text{-}fridge\text{-}on, y) \wedge$$
$$\forall z : (not\text{-}screw, z) \vee (not\text{-}fits, z, x) \vee (not\text{-}screwed, z),$$
$$\{((), \top, \{(free, x), (free, y)\}, \{(attached, x, y)\})\})$$

− *attach-compressor:*

$((x, y),$
$\quad \{ (compressor, x), (fridge, y),$
$\qquad (free, x), (free, y), (fits, x, y), (not\text{-}fridge\text{-}on, y)\},$
$\quad \{(attached, x, y)\},$
$\quad \{(free, x), (free, y)\})$

and the set of instances is

$\mathcal{I} = \{ (F \cup C \cup S, where \;\; F = \{f_1, \ldots, f_n\}, C = \{b_1, n_1, \ldots, b_n, n_n\},$
$\qquad\qquad\qquad S = \{s_{11}, \ldots s_{1m}, \ldots, s_{n1}, \ldots, s_{nm}\},$
$\qquad \{(fridge, x) \mid x \in F\}\cup$
$\qquad \{(compressor, x) \mid x \in C\}\cup$
$\qquad \{(screw, x) \mid x \in S\}\cup$
$\qquad \{(not\text{-}screw, x) \mid x \in F \cup C\}\cup$
$\qquad \{(fits, b_i, f_i), (fits, n_i, f_i) \mid 1 \le i \le n\}\cup$
$\qquad \{(fits, s_{ij}, b_i), (fits, s_{ij}, n_i) \mid 1 \le i \le n, 1 \le j \le m\}\cup$
$\qquad \{(not\text{-}fits, s_{ij}, b_{i'}) \mid 1 \le i \ne i' \le n, 1 \le j \le m\}\cup$
$\qquad \{(not\text{-}fits, s_{ij}, n_{i'}) \mid 1 \le i \ne i' \le n, 1 \le j \le m\}\cup$
$\qquad \{(fridge\text{-}on, x) \mid x \in F\} \cup \{(screwed, s_{ij}) \mid 1 \le i \le n, 1 \le j \le m\}\cup$
$\qquad \{(attached, b_i, f_i) \mid 1 \le i \le n\} \cup \{(free, n_i) \mid 1 \le i \le n\},$
$\qquad \bigwedge\{(fridge\text{-}on, x) \mid x \in F\}\wedge$
$\qquad \bigwedge\{(screwed, s_{ij}) \mid 1 \le i \le n, 1 \le j \le m\}\wedge$
$\qquad \bigwedge\{(attached, n_i, f_i) \mid 1 \le i \le n\})$
$\quad \mid (F \cup C \cup S) \subseteq \Sigma^+, F, C, \;\; and \;\; S \;\; are \;\; pairwise \;\; disjoint,$
$\quad n \ge 1, m \ge 1\}$

Note that we have a mixture between STRIPS and ADL operators, the only ADL element being the complex precondition of the *remove* operator. In the instances, F is the set of fridges, C the set of compressors, and S the set of screws. For each fridge f_i, there is the broken compressor b_i that is initially attached, and the new compressor n_i that shall be mounted. For each compressor b_i or n_i, there are the m screws $s_{i1}, \ldots, s_{im}$ that fit for the compressor. In the original formulation there are various negations, which are formulated by the extra predicates *not-screw*, *not-fits*, *not-fridge-on*, and *not-screwed*.

A.8 Grid

Definition A.8.1. *Grid is the STRIPS domain* $(\mathcal{P}, \mathcal{O}, \mathcal{I})$ *where the set of predicates is*

$\mathcal{P} = \{ (place, 1), (key, 1), (shape, 1), (conn, 2), (holding, 1), (arm\text{-}empty, 1),$
$\qquad (key\text{-}shape, 2), (lock\text{-}shape, 2), (open, 1), (locked, 1), (at, 2), (at\text{-}robot, 1)\}$

$\mathcal{O}$ *consists of the operators*

- *move:*

  ((x, y),
    $\{(place, x), (place, y), (conn, x, y), (at\text{-}robot, x), (open, y)\}$,
    $\{(at\text{-}robby, y)\}$,
    $\{(at\text{-}robby, x)\}$)

- *pickup:*

  ((x, y),
    $\{(place, x), (key, y), (at\text{-}robot, x), (at, y, x), (arm\text{-}empty)\}$,
    $\{(holding, y)\}$,
    $\{(at, y, x), (arm\text{-}empty)\}$)

- *pickup-and-lose:*

  ((x, y, z),
    $\{(place, x), (key, y), (key, z), (at\text{-}robot, x), (holding, y), (at, z, x)\}$,
    $\{(holding, z), (at, y, x)\}$,
    $\{(holding, y), (at, z, x)\}$)

- *putdown:*

  ((x, y),
    $\{(place, x), (key, y), (at\text{-}robot, x), (holding, y)\}$,
    $\{(at, y, x), (arm\text{-}empty)\}$,
    $\{(holding, y)\}$)

- *unlock:*

  ((x, y, z, v),
    $\{$ $(place, x), (place, y), (key, z), (shape, v), (conn, x, y), (at\text{-}robot, x)$,
        $(holding, z), (key\text{-}shape, z, v), (lock\text{-}shape, y, v), (locked, y)\}$,
    $\{(open, y)\}$,
    $\{(locked, y)\}$)

and the set of instances is

$\mathcal{I} = \{$ ($P \cup S \cup K$, *where* $P = \{p_{11}, \ldots, p_{nm}\}$,
    $\{(place, x) \mid x \in P\} \cup \{(shape, x) \mid x \in S\} \cup \{(key, x) \mid x \in K\} \cup$
    $\{(conn, p_{ij}, p_{i'j'}) \mid p_{ij}, p_{i'j'} \in P,\ i = i', |j - j'| = 1$ *or*
    $\qquad\qquad\qquad\qquad\qquad j = j', |i - i'| = 1\} \cup$
    $\{(open, x) \mid x \in P'\} \cup \{(locked, x) \mid x \in P \setminus P'\} \cup$
    $\{(lock\text{-}shape, x, ls(x)) \mid x \in P \setminus P'\} \cup$
    $\{(key\text{-}shape, x, ks(x)) \mid x \in K\} \cup$
    $\{(at\text{-}robot, ip) \cup \{(at, x, kip(x)) \mid x \in K\} \cup \{(arm\text{-}empty)\}$,
    $\{(at, x, kgp(x)) \mid x \in K'\}$)
    $\mid (P \cup S \cup K) \subseteq \Sigma^+, P, S,$ *and* K *are pairwise disjoint,* $|P| \geq 1$,
    $P' \subseteq P, ls : P \setminus P' \mapsto S, ks : K \mapsto S$,
    $ip \in P', kip : K \mapsto P, K' \subseteq K, kgp : K' \mapsto P\}$

In the instances, P' is the set of places that are initially already open. The ls function assigns to the other, locked, places, their lock shape, and ks assigns to all keys their shape. The initial place of the robot is $ip \in P'$, which *must be open*. This is an intuitively justified restriction (after all the robot is supposed to only be standing at unlocked places), and holds in the published benchmarks. The restriction is necessary to prove the non-existence of local minima under h^+, c.f. Section 8.3.5. The kip function assigns the initial key places, and kgp assigns the goal key places for those keys that must be transported, i.e., that are in $K' \subseteq K$.

A.9 Gripper

Definition A.9.1. *Gripper is the STRIPS domain* $(\mathcal{P}, \mathcal{O}, \mathcal{I})$ *where the set of predicates is*

$$\mathcal{P} = \{ \ (not\text{-}eq, 2), (room, 1), (ball, 1), (gripper, 1),$$
$$(at\text{-}robby, 1), (at, 2), (free, 1), (carry, 2)\}$$

$\mathcal{O}$ *consists of the operators*

– *move:*

$(\ (x, y),$
$\quad \{(not\text{-}eq, x, y), (room, x), (room, y), (at\text{-}robby, x)\},$
$\quad \{(at\text{-}robby, y)\},$
$\quad \{(at\text{-}robby, x)\})$

– *pick:*

$(\ (x, y, z),$
$\quad \{(ball, x), (room, y), (gripper, z), (at, x, y), (at\text{-}robby, y), (free, z)\},$
$\quad \{(carry, x, z)\},$
$\quad \{(at, x, y), (free, z)\})$

– *drop:*

$(\ (x, y, z),$
$\quad \{(ball, x), (room, y), (gripper, z), (carry, x, z), (at\text{-}robby, y)\},$
$\quad \{(at, x, y), (free, z)\},$
$\quad \{(carry, x, z)\})$

and the set of instances is

$$\mathcal{I} = \{ \ (\ \{a, b, l, r\} \cup B,$$
$$\{(not\text{-}eq, a, b), (not\text{-}eq, b, a)\}\cup$$
$$\{(room, a), (room, b), (gripper, l), (gripper, r)\}\cup$$
$$\{(ball, x), (at, x, a) \mid x \in B\} \cup \{(free, l), (free, r), (at\text{-}robby, a)\},$$
$$\{(at, x, b) \mid x \in B\})$$
$$\mid (\{a, b, l, r\} \cup B) \subseteq \Sigma^+, \{a, b, l, r\} \cap B = \emptyset,$$
$$a, b, l, \text{ and } r \text{ are pairwise different}, |B| \geq 1\}$$

We have introduced non-equality to get rid of actions that try to move within a room.

A.10 Hanoi

Definition A.10.1. *Hanoi is the STRIPS domain* $(\mathcal{P}, \mathcal{O}, \mathcal{I})$ *where the set of predicates is*

$$\mathcal{P} = \{(smaller, 2), (clear, 1), (on, 2)\}$$

$\mathcal{O}$ *consists of the single operator*

– *move:*

$$((x, y, z),$$
$$\{(on, x, y), (clear, x), (clear, z), (smaller, x, z)\},$$
$$\{(on, x, z), (clear, y)\},$$
$$\{(on, x, y), (clear, z)\})$$

and the set of instances is

$$\mathcal{I} = \{ (\{p_1, p_2, p_3, d_1, \ldots, d_n\},$$
$$\{(smaller, d_i, p_1), (smaller, d_i, p_2), (smaller, d_i, p_3) \mid 1 \le i \le n\} \cup$$
$$\{(smaller, d_i, d_j) \mid 1 \le i < j \le n\} \cup$$
$$\{(on, d_n, p_1)\} \cup \{(on, d_i, d_{i+1}) \mid 1 \le i \le n - 1\} \cup$$
$$\{(clear, d_1), (clear, p_2), (clear, p_3)\},$$
$$\{(on, d_n, p_3)\} \cup \{(on, d_i, d_{i+1}) \mid 1 \le i \le n - 1\})$$
$$\mid \{p_1, p_2, p_3, d_1, \ldots, d_n\} \subseteq \Sigma^+,$$
$$p_1, p_2, p_3, d_1, \ldots, d_n \text{ are pairwise different}, n \ge 1\}$$

In the instance encodings, p_1, p_2, and p_3 are the three pegs, while $d_1, \ldots, d_n$ are the discs in increasing order of size. A move(x, y, z) action moves disc x from disc (or peg) y to disc (or peg) z.

A.11 Logistics

Definition A.11.1. *Logistics is the STRIPS domain* $(\mathcal{P}, \mathcal{O}, \mathcal{I})$ *where the set of predicates is*

$$\mathcal{P} = \{ (not\text{-}eq, 2), (obj, 1), (truck, 1), (location, 1), (airplane, 1), (city, 1),$$
$$(airport, 1), (at, 2), (in, 2), (in\text{-}city, 2)\}$$

$\mathcal{O}$ *consists of the operators*

− *drive-truck:*

$$((x, y, z, v),$$
$$\{ (truck, x), (not\text{-}eq, y, z), (location, y), (location, z), (city, v),$$
$$(in\text{-}city, y, v), (in\text{-}city, z, v), (at, x, y)\},$$
$$\{(at, x, z)\},$$
$$\{(at, x, y)\})$$

− *fly-airplane:*

$$((x, y, z),$$
$$\{(airplane, x), (not\text{-}eq, y, z), (airport, y), (airport, z), (at, x, y)\},$$
$$\{(at, x, z)\},$$
$$\{(at, x, y)\})$$

− *load-truck:*

$$((x, y, z),$$
$$\{(obj, x), (truck, y), (location, z), (at, x, z), (at, y, z)\},$$
$$\{(in, x, y)\},$$
$$\{(at, x, z)\})$$

− *load-airplane:*

$$((x, y, z),$$
$$\{(obj, x), (airplane, y), (location, z), (at, x, z), (at, y, z)\},$$
$$\{(in, x, y)\},$$
$$\{(at, x, z)\})$$

− *unload-truck:*

$$((x, y, z),$$
$$\{(obj, x), (truck, y), (location, z), (in, x, y), (at, y, z)\},$$
$$\{(at, x, z)\},$$
$$\{(in, x, y)\})$$

− *unload-airplane:*

$$((x, y, z),$$
$$\{(obj, x), (airplane, y), (location, z), (in, x, y), (at, y, z)\},$$
$$\{(at, x, z)\},$$
$$\{(in, x, y)\})$$

and the set of instances is

$$\mathcal{I} = \{ (O \cup T \cup A \cup C \cup L_1 \cup \ldots \cup L_n, \text{ where } C = \{c_1, \ldots, c_n\},$$
$$\{(not\text{-}eq, x, y) \mid x, y \in L_1 \cup \ldots \cup L_n, x \neq y\} \cup$$
$$\{(obj, x) \mid x \in O\} \cup \{(truck, x) \mid x \in T\} \cup \{(airplane, x) \mid x \in A\} \cup$$
$$\{(city, x) \mid x \in C\} \cup \{(location, x) \mid x \in L_1 \cup \ldots \cup L_n\} \cup$$
$$\{(in\text{-}city, x, c_i) \mid x \in L_i\} \cup \{(airport, l_1), \ldots, (airport, l_n)\} \cup$$

$\{(at, x, il(x)) \mid x \in O \cup T \cup A\},$
$\{(at, x, gl(x)) \mid x \in O'\})$
$\mid (O \cup T \cup A \cup C \cup L_1 \cup \ldots \cup L_n) \subseteq \Sigma^+,$
$O, T, A, C, L_1, \ldots, L_n$ *pairwise disjoint,*
$n \geq 1, |L_i| \geq 1, l_i \in L_i$ *for* $1 \leq i \leq n,$
$il : O \cup T \cup A \mapsto L_1 \cup \ldots \cup L_n, \forall x \in A : il(x) \in \{l_1, \ldots, l_n\},$
$O' \subseteq O, gl : O' \mapsto L_1 \cup \ldots \cup L_n\}$

In the definition of the instances, *il* and *gl* are the initial location and goal location functions, respectively. There is at least one city, each city has at least one location, airplanes are only allowed at airports (of which each city has exactly one), and only a subset of the transportable objects need to have goal locations specified. We have introduced non-equality to get rid of actions that try to drive a truck, or fly an airplane, within a single location.

A.12 Miconic-ADL

Definition A.12.1. *Miconic-ADL is the ADL domain* $(\mathcal{P}, \mathcal{O}, \mathcal{I})$ *where the set of predicates is*

$\mathcal{P} = \{$ $(passenger, 1), (not\text{-}passenger, 1), (floor, 1), (origin, 2), (not\text{-}origin, 2),$
$(above, 2), (destin, 2), (not\text{-}destin, 2), (not\text{-}no\text{-}access, 2), (attendant, 1),$
$(not\text{-}going\text{-}up, 1), (not\text{-}going\text{-}down, 1), (not\text{-}going\text{-}nonstop, 1),$
$(not\text{-}never\text{-}alone, 1), (vip, 1), (not\text{-}vip, 1), (not\text{-}conflict\text{-}A, 1),$
$(not\text{-}conflict\text{-}B, 1), (boarded, 1), (not\text{-}boarded, 1),$
$(served, 1), (not\text{-}served, 1), (lift\text{-}at, 1)\}$

$\mathcal{O}$ *consists of the operators*

− *stop:*

$((x),$
$(floor, x) \wedge (lift\text{-}at, x) \wedge$
$(\forall y : (not\text{-}passenger, y) \vee (not\text{-}no\text{-}access, y, x) \vee (not\text{-}boarded, y)) \wedge$
$(\forall y : ((not\text{-}vip, y) \vee (served, y)) \vee$
$\exists y : (vip, y) \wedge ((origin, y, x) \vee (destin, y, x))) \wedge$
$(\forall y : (not\text{-}going\text{-}nonstop, y) \vee (not\text{-}boarded, y) \vee (destin, y, x)) \wedge$
$(\forall y : (not\text{-}never\text{-}alone, y) \vee$
$\quad (((not\text{-}boarded, y) \vee (destin, y, x)) \wedge$
$\quad ((served, y) \vee (not\text{-}origin, y, x))) \vee$
$\exists z : (attendant, z) \wedge$
$\quad (((boarded, z) \wedge (not\text{-}destin, z, x)) \vee$
$\quad ((not\text{-}served, z) \wedge (origin, z, x)))) \wedge$
$(\forall y : (not\text{-}conflict\text{-}A, y) \vee$
$\quad (((not\text{-}boarded, y) \vee (destin, y, x)) \wedge$
$\quad ((served, y) \vee (not\text{-}origin, y, x))) \vee$

$$\forall y : (\text{not-conflict-B}, y) \vee$$
$$(((\text{not-boarded}, y) \vee (\text{destin}, y, x)) \wedge$$
$$((\text{served, } y) \vee (\text{not-origin}, y, x)))),$$
$$\{ ((y),$$
$$(\text{passenger}, y) \wedge (\text{boarded}, y) \wedge (\text{destin}, y, x),$$
$$\{(\text{served}, y), (\text{not-boarded}, y)\},$$
$$\{(\text{boarded}, y), (\text{not-served}, y)\}),$$
$$((y),$$
$$(\text{passenger}, y) \wedge (\text{not-served}, y) \wedge (\text{origin}, y, x),$$
$$\{(\text{boarded}, y)\},$$
$$\{(\text{not-boarded}, y)\})\}\})$$

− up:

$$((x, y),$$
$$(\text{floor}, x) \wedge (\text{floor}, y) \wedge (\text{lift-at}, x) \wedge (\text{above}, y, x) \wedge$$
$$\forall z : (\text{not-going-down}, z) \vee (\text{not-boarded}, z),$$
$$\{((), \top, \{(\text{lift-at}, y)\}, \{(\text{lift-at}, x)\})\})$$

− down:

$$((x, y),$$
$$(\text{floor}, x) \wedge (\text{floor}, y) \wedge (\text{lift-at}, x) \wedge (\text{above}, x, y) \wedge$$
$$\forall z : (\text{not-going-up}, z) \vee (\text{not-boarded}, z),$$
$$\{((), \top, \{(\text{lift-at}, y)\}, \{(\text{lift-at}, x)\})\})$$

and the set of instances is

$$\mathcal{I} = \{ (P \cup F, \text{where } F = \{f_1, \ldots, f_n\},$$
$$\{(\text{passenger}, x) \mid x \in P\} \cup$$
$$\{(\text{not-passenger}, x) \mid x \in F\} \cup \{(\text{floor}, x) \mid x \in F\} \cup$$
$$\{(\text{origin}, x, \text{of}(x)) \mid x \in P\} \cup \{(\text{not-origin}, x, y) \mid x \in P, y \neq \text{of}(x)\} \cup$$
$$\{(\text{destin}, x, \text{df}(x)) \mid x \in P\} \cup \{(\text{not-destin}, x, y) \mid x \in P, y \neq \text{df}(x)\} \cup$$
$$\{(\text{above}, f_i, f_j) \mid i < j\} \cup$$
$$\{(\text{not-no-access}, x, y) \mid x \in P, y \in F, y \notin \text{na}(x)\} \cup$$
$$\{(\text{not-going-up}, x) \mid x \in (F \cup P) \setminus GU\} \cup$$
$$\{(\text{not-going-down}, x) \mid x \in (F \cup P) \setminus GD\} \cup$$
$$\{(\text{not-going-nonstop}, x) \mid x \in (F \cup P) \setminus GN\} \cup$$
$$\{(\text{attendant}, x) \mid x \in AT\} \cup$$
$$\{(\text{not-never-alone}, x) \mid x \in (F \cup P) \setminus NA\} \cup$$
$$\{(\text{vip}, x) \mid x \in VI\} \cup \{(\text{not-vip}, x) \mid x \in (F \cup P) \setminus VI\} \cup$$
$$\{(\text{not-conflict-A}, x) \mid x \in (F \cup P) \setminus CA\} \cup$$
$$\{(\text{not-conflict-B}, x) \mid x \in (F \cup P) \setminus CB\} \cup$$
$$\{(\text{not-boarded}, x), (\text{not-served}, x) \mid x \in P\} \cup \{(\text{lift-at}, \text{if})\},$$
$$\bigwedge \{(\text{served}, x) \mid x \in P\})$$
$$\mid (P \cup F) \subseteq \Sigma^+, P \cap F = \emptyset, |F| \geq 1,$$
$$\text{of} : P \mapsto F, \text{df} : P \mapsto F, \text{if} \in F, \text{na} : P \mapsto 2^F,$$
$$GU \subseteq P, GD \subseteq P, GN \subseteq P, AT \subseteq P, NA \subseteq P,$$
$$VI \subseteq P, CA \subseteq P, CB \subseteq P\}$$

All operators are ADL operators, making use of complex preconditions to formulate the constraints concerning different types of passengers. The *move* operator has two conditional effects with one effect parameter each. The *up* and *down* operators each have a single unconditional effect. One help in understanding the rather complicated precondition of *stop*: there often appears a sub-expression of the form $((\text{boarded}, y) \wedge (\text{not-destin}, y, x)) \vee ((\text{not-served}, y) \wedge (\text{origin}, y, x))$, or the respective negated version, for a floor x and a passenger y; the expression is true if and only if y will be boarded during the next lift move, after stopping at x. In the definition of the instances, *of* and *df* are the origin and destination floors of the passengers, and *if* is the floor where the elevator (the lift) is initially positioned. The *na* function specifies, for each passenger, the set of floors he does not have access to. The sets GU, GD, GN, AT, NA, VI, CA, and CB specify the different types of passengers. In the original domain there are a lot of negations, which are formulated by the extra predicates *not-passenger*, *not-origin*, *not-destin*, *not-going-up*, *not-going-down*, *not-going-nonstop*, *not-never-alone*, *not-vip*, *non-conflict-A*, *non-conflict-B*, *not-boarded*, and *not-served*.

A.13 Miconic-SIMPLE

Definition A.13.1. *Miconic-SIMPLE is the ADL domain* $(\mathcal{P}, \mathcal{O}, \mathcal{I})$ *where the set of predicates is*

$$\mathcal{P} = \{ \ (\textit{passenger}, 1), (\textit{floor}, 1), (\textit{origin}, 2), (\textit{destin}, 2),$$
$$(\textit{above}, 2), (\textit{boarded}, 1), (\textit{served}, 1), (\textit{not-served}, 1), (\textit{lift-at}, 1)\}$$

$\mathcal{O}$ *consists of the operators*

– *stop:*

$(\ (x),$
$\quad (\textit{floor}, x) \wedge (\textit{lift-at}, x),$
$\quad \{ \ (\ (y),$
$\qquad (\textit{passenger}, y) \wedge (\textit{boarded}, y) \wedge (\textit{destin}, y, x),$
$\qquad \{(\textit{served}, y)\},$
$\qquad \{(\textit{boarded}, y), (\textit{not-served}, y)\}),$
$\qquad ((y), (\textit{passenger}, y) \wedge (\textit{not-served}, y) \wedge (\textit{origin}, y, x), \{(\textit{boarded}, y)\}, \emptyset)\})$

– *up:*

$(\ (x, y),$
$\quad \{(\textit{floor}, x), (\textit{floor}, y), (\textit{lift-at}, x), (\textit{above}, y, x)\},$
$\quad \{(\textit{lift-at}, y)\},$
$\quad \{(\textit{lift-at}, x)\})$

– *down:*

$$((x, y),$$
$$\{(\mathit{floor}, x), (\mathit{floor}, y), (\mathit{lift\text{-}at}, x), (\mathit{above}, x, y)\},$$
$$\{(\mathit{lift\text{-}at}, y)\},$$
$$\{(\mathit{lift\text{-}at}, x)\})$$

and the set of instances is

$$\mathcal{I} = \{ \ (\ P \cup F, \mathit{where} \ F = \{f_1, \ldots, f_n\},$$
$$\{(\mathit{passenger}, x) \mid x \in P\} \cup \{(\mathit{floor}, x) \mid x \in F\} \cup$$
$$\{(\mathit{above}, f_i, f_j) \mid i < j\} \cup \{(\mathit{not\text{-}served}, x) \mid x \in P\} \cup$$
$$\{(\mathit{origin}, x, \mathit{of}(x)), (\mathit{destin}, x, \mathit{df}(x)) \mid x \in P\} \cup \{(\mathit{lift\text{-}at}, \mathit{if})\},$$
$$\bigwedge\{(\mathit{served}, x) \mid x \in P\})$$
$$| \ (P \cup F) \subseteq \Sigma^+, P \cap F = \emptyset, |F| \geq 1, \mathit{of} : P \mapsto F, \mathit{df} : P \mapsto F, \mathit{if} \in F\}$$

The only ADL element are the two conditional effects of the *move* operator, both of which have one effect parameter. In the definition of the instances, *of* and *df* are the origin and destination floors of the passengers, and *if* is the floor where the elevator (the "lift") is initially positioned. The second conditional effect of the *stop* operator requires the respective passengers not to be served already. This negative condition is formulated by the *not-served* predicate.

A.14 Miconic-STRIPS

Definition A.14.1. *Miconic-STRIPS is the STRIPS domain* $(\mathcal{P}, \mathcal{O}, \mathcal{I})$ *where the set of predicates is*

$$\mathcal{P} = \{ \ (\mathit{passenger}, 1), (\mathit{floor}, 1), (\mathit{origin}, 2), (\mathit{destin}, 2), (\mathit{above}, 2), (\mathit{boarded}, 1),$$
$$(\mathit{served}, 1), (\mathit{lift\text{-}at}, 1)\}$$

$\mathcal{O}$ *consists of the operators*

– *board:*

$$((x, y), \{(\mathit{floor}, x), (\mathit{passenger}, y), (\mathit{lift\text{-}at}, x), (\mathit{origin}, y, x)\}, \{(\mathit{boarded}, y)\}, \emptyset)$$

– *depart:*

$$((x, y),$$
$$\{(\mathit{floor}, x), (\mathit{passenger}, y), (\mathit{lift\text{-}at}, x), (\mathit{destin}, y, x), (\mathit{boarded}, y)\},$$
$$\{(\mathit{served}, y)\},$$
$$\{(\mathit{boarded}, y)\})$$

– *up:*

((x, y),
    $\{(floor, x), (floor, y), (lift\text{-}at, x), (above, y, x)\}$,
    $\{(lift\text{-}at, y)\}$,
    $\{(lift\text{-}at, x)\})$

– *down:*

((x, y),
    $\{(floor, x), (floor, y), (lift\text{-}at, x), (above, x, y)\}$,
    $\{(lift\text{-}at, y)\}$,
    $\{(lift\text{-}at, x)\})$

and the set of instances is

$\mathcal{I} = \{$ ($P \cup F$, *where* $F = \{f_1, \ldots, f_n\}$,
        $\{(passenger, x) \mid x \in P\} \cup \{(floor, x) \mid x \in F\} \cup$
        $\{(above, f_i, f_j) \mid i < j\} \cup$
        $\{(origin, x, of(x)), (destin, x, df(x)) \mid x \in P\} \cup \{(lift\text{-}at, if)\}$,
        $\{(served, x) \mid x \in P\})$
    $\mid (P \cup F) \subseteq \Sigma^+, P \cap F = \emptyset, |F| \geq 1, of\colon P \mapsto F, df\colon P \mapsto F, if \in F\}$

In the definition of the instances, *of* and *df* are the origin and destination floors of the passengers, and *if* is the floor where the elevator (the "lift") is initially positioned.

A.15 Movie

Definition A.15.1. *Movie is the STRIPS domain* $(\mathcal{P}, \mathcal{O}, \mathcal{I})$ *where the set of predicates is*

$\mathcal{P} = \{$ ($movie\text{-}rewound$, 0), ($counter\text{-}at\text{-}other\text{-}than\text{-}two\text{-}hours$, 0),
        ($counter\text{-}at\text{-}zero$, 0), ($have\text{-}chips$, 0), ($have\text{-}dip$, 0), ($have\text{-}pop$, 0),
        ($have\text{-}cheese$, 0), ($have\text{-}crackers$, 0), ($chips$, 1),
        (dip, 1), (pop, 1), ($cheese$, 1), ($crackers$, 1)$\}$

$\mathcal{O}$ *consists of the operators*

– *rewind-movie:*

((),
    $\{(counter\text{-}at\text{-}other\text{-}than\text{-}two\text{-}hours)\}$,
    $\{(movie\text{-}rewound)\}$,
    $\{(counter\text{-}at\text{-}zero)\})$

– *reset-counter:* $((), \emptyset, \{(counter\text{-}at\text{-}zero)\}, \emptyset)$
– *get-chips:* $((x), \{(chips, x)\}, \{(have\text{-}chips)\}, \emptyset)$

- *get-dip:* $((x), \{(dip, x)\}, \{(have\text{-}dip)\}, \emptyset)$
- *get-pop:* $((x), \{(pop, x)\}, \{(have\text{-}pop)\}, \emptyset)$
- *get-cheese:* $((x), \{(cheese, x)\}, \{(have\text{-}cheese)\}, \emptyset)$
- *get-crackers:* $((x), \{(crackers, x)\}, \{(have\text{-}crackers)\}, \emptyset)$

and the set of instances is

$$\mathcal{I} = \{ \ (\ C \cup D \cup P \cup Z \cup K,$$
$$\{(chips, x) \mid x \in C\} \cup \{(dip, x) \mid x \in D\} \cup \{(pop, x) \mid x \in P\} \cup$$
$$\{(cheese, x) \mid x \in Z\} \cup \{(crackers, x) \mid x \in K\} \cup$$
$$\{(counter\text{-}at\text{-}other\text{-}than\text{-}two\text{-}hours)\},$$
$$\{ \ (movie\text{-}rewound), (counter\text{-}at\text{-}zero), (have\text{-}chips),$$
$$(have\text{-}dip), (have\text{-}pop), (have\text{-}cheese), (have\text{-}crackers)\})$$
$$\mid (C \cup D \cup P \cup Z \cup K) \subseteq \Sigma^+, C, D, P, Z, \text{ and } K \text{ are pairwise disjoint,}$$
$$|C| \geq 1, |D| \geq 1, |P| \geq 1, |Z| \geq 1, |K| \geq 1\}$$

Note that none of the effects contains an operator parameter, implying that the set of reachable states is, as said in Section 2.3, essentially the same across instances.

A.16 Mprime

Definition A.16.1. *Mprime is the STRIPS domain* $(\mathcal{P}, \mathcal{O}, \mathcal{I})$ *where the set of predicates is*

$$\mathcal{P} = \{ \ (location, 1), (vehicle, 1), (object, 1), (fuel, 1), (space, 1),$$
$$(conn, 2), (has\text{-}fuel, 2), (at, 2), (fuel\text{-}nextlower, 2),$$
$$(in, 2), (has\text{-}space, 2), (space\text{-}nextlower, 2)\}$$

$\mathcal{O}$ *consists of the operators*

- move:

$$(\ (x, y, z, u, v),$$
$$\{ \ (vehicle, x), (location, y), (location, z), (fuel, u), (fuel, v),$$
$$(at, x, y), (conn, y, z), (has\text{-}fuel, y, u), (fuel\text{-}nextlower, v, u)\},$$
$$\{(at, x, z), (has\text{-}fuel, y, v)\},$$
$$\{(at, x, y), (has\text{-}fuel, y, u)\})$$

- load:

$$(\ (x, y, z, u, v),$$
$$\{ \ (object, x), (vehicle, y), (location, z), (space, u), (space, v),$$
$$(at, x, z), (at, y, z), (has\text{-}space, x, u), (space\text{-}nextlower, v, u)\},$$
$$\{(in, x, y), (has\text{-}space, y, v)\},$$
$$\{(at, x, z), (has\text{-}space, y, u)\})$$

— *unload:*

$(\ (x, y, z, u, v),$
$\quad \{\ (object, x), (vehicle, y), (location, z), (space, u), (space, v),$
$\qquad (in, x, y), (at, y, z), (has\text{-}space, x, u), (space\text{-}nextlower, u, v)\},$
$\quad \{(at, x, z), (has\text{-}space, y, u)\},$
$\quad \{(in, x, y), (has\text{-}space, y, v)\})$

— *transfer:*

$(\ (x, y, z, u, v, w, q),$
$\quad \{\ (location, x), (location, y), (fuel, z), (fuel, u), (fuel, v), (fuel, w), (fuel, q),$
$\qquad (conn, x, y), (has\text{-}fuel, x, z), (fuel\text{-}nextlower, u, z), (fuel\text{-}nextlower, v, u),$
$\qquad (has\text{-}fuel, y, w), (fuel\text{-}nextlower, w, q)\},$
$\quad \{(has\text{-}fuel, x, u), (has\text{-}fuel, y, q)\},$
$\quad \{(has\text{-}fuel, x, z), (has\text{-}fuel, y, w)\})$

and the set of instances is

$\mathcal{I} = \{\ (\ L \cup V \cup O \cup F \cup S,$
$\qquad where\ F = \{f_0, \ldots, f_n\}, S = \{s_0, \ldots, s_m\}$
$\qquad \{(location, x) \mid x \in L\} \cup \{(vehicle, x) \mid x \in V\}\cup$
$\qquad \{(object, x) \mid x \in O\}\cup$
$\qquad \{(fuel, x) \mid x \in F\} \cup \{(space, x) \mid x \in S\}\cup$
$\qquad \{(fuel\text{-}nextlower, f_i, f_{i+1}) \mid 0 \le i < n\}\cup$
$\qquad \{(space\text{-}nextlower, s_i, s_{i+1}) \mid 0 \le i < m\}\cup$
$\qquad \{(conn, x, y) \mid (x, y) \in M\} \cup \{(has\text{-}fuel, x, f(x)) \mid x \in L\}\cup$
$\qquad \{(has\text{-}space, x, s(x)) \mid x \in V\}\cup$
$\qquad \{(at, x, il(x)) \mid x \in V\} \cup \{(at, x, il(x)) \mid x \in O\},$
$\qquad \{(at, x, gl(x)) \mid x \in O'\})$
$\qquad \mid (L \cup V \cup O \cup F \cup S) \subseteq \Sigma^+, L, V, O, F,\ and\ S\ are\ pairwise\ disjoint,$
$\qquad |L| \ge 2, |F| \ge 1, |S| \ge 1,$
$\qquad M \subseteq L \times L, f : L \mapsto F, s : V \mapsto S,$
$\qquad il : V \cup O \mapsto L, O' \subseteq O, gl : O' \mapsto L\}$

Varying fuel and space is realized by the objects in F and S, which are ordered via the (fuel-nextlower, 2) and (space-nextlower, 2) predicates: the left hand side is the next lower fuel or space amount; f_0 respectively s_0 are the zero-amounts, having no lower neighbor. The transfer operator transfers one fuel unit from location x to a connected location y, as long as x has still at least one fuel unit left after the transaction. The locations are connected according to the edge set M, f and g determine the initial fuel and space amounts for locations and vehicles, il specifies the initial positions of vehicles and objects, finally gl are the goal locations for the subset O' of objects. We remark that in the version of the domain used at AIPS-1998 all predicates were given counter-intuitive names to conceal the nature of the domain. We have translated all names back to ease readability.

A.17 Mystery

The *Mystery* domain is exactly identical with *Mprime*, see above, except that there is no *transfer* operator.

A.18 Schedule

Definition A.18.1. *Schedule is the ADL domain* $(\mathcal{P}, \mathcal{O}, \mathcal{I})$ *where the set of predicates is*

$\mathcal{P} = \{$ *(not-equal, 2), (p-cylindrical, 1), (p-cold, 1), (p-hot, 1), (p-polished, 1),*
(p-rough, 1), (p-smooth, 1), (p-roller, 1), (p-lathe, 1), (p-polisher, 1),
(p-grinder, 1), (p-punch, 1), (p-drill-press, 1), (p-spray-painter, 1),
(p-immersion-painter, 1), (part, 1), (ashape, 1), (atemperature, 1),
(surface, 1), (color, 1), (width, 1), (anorient, 1), (machine, 1),
(shape, 2), (temperature, 2), (surface-condition, 2), (painted, 2),
(has-hole, 3), (not-has-hole, 3), (busy, 1), (not-busy, 1),
(scheduled, 1), (not-scheduled, 1), (objscheduled, 1),
(not-objscheduled, 1), (has-paint, 2), (has-bit, 2), (can-orient, 2)$\}$

$\mathcal{O}$ *consists of the operators*

– do-roll:
$(\ (x, y, z, u),$
$(part, x) \wedge (p\text{-}roller, y) \wedge (p\text{-}hot, z) \wedge$
$(p\text{-}cylindrical, u) \wedge (not\text{-}busy, roller) \wedge (not\text{-}scheduled, x),$
$\{\ (\ (),$
$\top,$
$\{(busy, y), (scheduled, x), (temperature, x, z), (shape, x, u)\},$
$\{(not\text{-}busy, roller), (not\text{-}scheduled, x)\}),$
$((), (not\text{-}objscheduled), \{(objscheduled)\}, \{(not\text{-}objscheduled)\}),$
$(\ (v),$
$(surface, v) \wedge (surface\text{-}condition, x, v),$
$\emptyset,$
$\{(surface\text{-}condition, x, v)\}),$
$((v), (color, v) \wedge (painted, x, v), \emptyset, \{(painted, x, v)\}),$
$((v), (ashape, v) \wedge (shape, x, v) \wedge (not\text{-}equal, v, u), \emptyset, \{(shape, x, v)\}),$
$(\ (v),$
$(atemperature, v) \wedge (temperature, x, v) \wedge (not\text{-}equal, y, z),$
$\emptyset,$
$\{(temperature, x, v)\}),$
$(\ (v, w),$
$(width, v) \wedge (anorient, w) \wedge (has\text{-}hole, x, v, w),$
$\{(not\text{-}has\text{-}hole, x, v, w)\},$
$\{(has\text{-}hole, x, v, w)\})\})$

− do-lathe:

((x, y, z, u),
  $(part, x) \wedge (p\text{-}lathe, y) \wedge (p\text{-}rough, z) \wedge (p\text{-}cylindrical, u) \wedge$
  $(not\text{-}busy, lathe) \wedge (not\text{-}scheduled, x)$,
  { ((),
      $\top$,
      $\{(busy, y), (scheduled, x), (surface\text{-}condition, x, z), (shape, x, u)\}$,
      $\{(not\text{-}busy, y), (not\text{-}scheduled, x)\}$),
    $((), (not\text{-}objscheduled), \{(objscheduled)\}, \{(not\text{-}objscheduled)\})$,
    $((v), (color, v) \wedge (painted, x, v), \emptyset, \{(painted, x, v)\})$,
    $((v), (ashape, v) \wedge (shape, x, v) \wedge (not\text{-}equal, v, u), \emptyset, \{(shape, x, v)\})$,
    ((v),
      $(surface, v) \wedge (surface\text{-}condition, x, v) \wedge (not\text{-}equal, v, z)$,
      $\emptyset$,
      $\{(surface\text{-}condition, x, v)\})\})$

− do-polish:

((x, y, z, u),
  $(part, x) \wedge (p\text{-}polisher, y) \wedge (p\text{-}polished, z) \wedge (p\text{-}cold, u) \wedge$
  $(not\text{-}busy, y) \wedge (not\text{-}scheduled, x) \wedge (temperature, x, u)$,
  { ((),
      $\top$,
      $\{(busy, y), (scheduled, x), (surface\text{-}condition, x, z)\}$,
      $\{(not\text{-}busy, y), (not\text{-}scheduled, x)\}$),
    $((), (not\text{-}objscheduled), \{(objscheduled)\}, \{(not\text{-}objscheduled)\})$,
    ((v),
      $(surface, v) \wedge (surface\text{-}condition, x, v) \wedge (not\text{-}equal, v, polished)$,
      $\emptyset$,
      $\{(surface\text{-}condition, x, v)\})\})$

− do-grind:

((x, y, z),
  $(part, x) \wedge (p\text{-}grinder, y) \wedge (p\text{-}smooth, z) \wedge$
  $(not\text{-}busy, y) \wedge (not\text{-}scheduled, x)$,
  { ((),
      $\top$,
      $\{(busy, y), (scheduled, x), (surface\text{-}condition, x, z)\}$,
      $\{(not\text{-}busy, y), (not\text{-}scheduled, x)\}$),
    $((), (not\text{-}objscheduled), \{(objscheduled)\}, \{(not\text{-}objscheduled)\})$,
    $((u), (color, u) \wedge (painted, x, u), \emptyset, \{(painted, x, u)\})$,
    ((u),
      $(surface, u) \wedge (surface\text{-}condition, x, u) \wedge (not\text{-}equal, y, z)$,
      $\emptyset$,
      $\{(surface\text{-}condition, x, u)\})\})$

– do-punch:

$(\ (x, y, z, u, v, w),$
$(part, x) \wedge (width, y) \wedge (anorient, z) \wedge (p\text{-}punch, u) \wedge$
$(p\text{-}cold, v) \wedge (p\text{-}rough, w) \wedge (not\text{-}busy, u) \wedge (not\text{-}scheduled, x) \wedge$
$(not\text{-}has\text{-}hole, x, y, z) \wedge (has\text{-}bit, u, y) \wedge$
$(can\text{-}orient, u, z) \wedge (temperature, x, v),$
$\{\ (\ (),$
    $\top,$
    $\{\ (busy, u), (scheduled, x), (has\text{-}hole, x, y, z),$
       $(surface\text{-}condition, x, w)\},$
    $\{(not\text{-}busy, u), (not\text{-}scheduled, x), (not\text{-}has\text{-}hole, x, y, z)\}),$
  $((), (not\text{-}objscheduled), \{(objscheduled)\}, \{(not\text{-}objscheduled)\}),$
  $(\ (t),$
    $(surface, t) \wedge (surface\text{-}condition, x, t) \wedge (not\text{-}equal, t, w),$
    $\emptyset,$
    $\{(surface\text{-}condition, x, t)\})\})$

– do-drill-press:

$(\ (x, y, z, u, v),$
$(part, x) \wedge (width, y) \wedge (anorient, z) \wedge (p\text{-}drill\text{-}press, u) \wedge (p\text{-}cold, v) \wedge$
$(not\text{-}busy, u) \wedge (not\text{-}scheduled, x) \wedge (not\text{-}has\text{-}hole, x, y, z) \wedge$
$(has\text{-}bit, u, y) \wedge (can\text{-}orient, u, z) \wedge (temperature, x, v),$
$\{\ (\ (),$
    $\top,$
    $\{(busy, u), (scheduled, x), (has\text{-}hole, x, y, z)\},$
    $\{(not\text{-}busy, u), (not\text{-}scheduled, x), (not\text{-}has\text{-}hole, x, y, z)\}),$
  $((), (not\text{-}objscheduled), \{(objscheduled)\}, \{(not\text{-}objscheduled)\})\})$

– do-spray-paint:

$(\ (x, y, z, u),$
$(part, x) \wedge (color, y) \wedge (p\text{-}spray\text{-}painter, z) \wedge (p\text{-}cold, u) \wedge$
$(not\text{-}busy, z) \wedge (not\text{-}scheduled, x) \wedge$
$(has\text{-}paint, z, y) \wedge (temperature, x, u),$
$\{\ (\ (),$
    $\top,$
    $\{(busy, z), (scheduled, x), (painted, x, y)\},$
    $\{(not\text{-}busy, z), (not\text{-}scheduled, x)\}),$
  $((), (not\text{-}objscheduled), \{(objscheduled)\}, \{(not\text{-}objscheduled)\}),$
  $(\ (v),$
    $(color, v) \wedge (painted, x, v) \wedge (not\text{-}equal, v, y),$
    $\emptyset,$
    $\{(painted, x, v)\}),$
  $(\ (v),$

$$(surface, v) \wedge (surface\text{-}condition, x, v),$$
$$\emptyset,$$
$$\{(surface\text{-}condition, x, v)\})\})$$

− do-immersion-paint:

$$(\ (x, y, z),$$
$$(part, x) \wedge (color, y) \wedge (p\text{-}immersion\text{-}painter, z) \wedge$$
$$(not\text{-}busy, z) \wedge (not\text{-}scheduled, x) \wedge (has\text{-}paint, z, y),$$
$$\{ \ (\ (),$$
$$\top,$$
$$\{(busy, z), (scheduled, x), (painted, x, y)\},$$
$$\{(not\text{-}busy, z), (not\text{-}scheduled, x)\}),$$
$$((), (not\text{-}objscheduled), \{(objscheduled)\}, \{(not\text{-}objscheduled)\}),$$
$$(\ (u),$$
$$(color, u) \wedge (painted, x, u) \wedge (not\text{-}equal, u, y),$$
$$\emptyset,$$
$$\{(painted, x, u)\})\})$$

− do-time-step:

$$(\ (),$$
$$(objscheduled),$$
$$\{ \ ((x), (part, x) \wedge (scheduled, x), \emptyset, \{(scheduled, x)\}),$$
$$((x), (machine, x) \wedge (busy, x), \emptyset, \{(busy, x)\})\})$$

and the set of instances is

$$\mathcal{I} = \{ \ (\ \{ \ cylindrical, cold, hot, polished, rough,$$
$$smooth, roller, lathe, polisher, grinder,$$
$$punch, drill\text{-}press, spray\text{-}painter, immersion\text{-}painter\} = C' \cup$$
$$P \cup S \cup L \cup W \cup O,$$
$$\{(not\text{-}equal, x, y) \mid x, y \in C, x \neq y\} \cup$$
$$\{ \ (p\text{-}cylindrical, cylindrical), (p\text{-}cold, cold), (p\text{-}hot, hot),$$
$$(p\text{-}polished, polished), (p\text{-}rough, rough), (p\text{-}smooth, smooth),$$
$$(p\text{-}roller, roller), (p\text{-}lathe, lathe), (p\text{-}polisher, polisher),$$
$$(p\text{-}grinder, grinder), (p\text{-}punch, punch),$$
$$(p\text{-}drill\text{-}press, drill - press),$$
$$(p\text{-}spray\text{-}painter, spray - painter),$$
$$(p\text{-}immersion\text{-}painter, immersion - painter)\} \cup$$
$$\{(part, x) \mid x \in P\} \cup \{(ashape, cylindrical)\} \cup$$
$$\{(ashape, x) \mid x \in S\} \cup$$
$$\{(atemperature, cold), (atemperature, hot)\} \cup$$
$$\{(surface, polished), (surface, rough), (surface, smooth)\} \cup$$
$$\{(color, x) \mid x \in L\} \cup \{(width, x) \mid x \in W\} \cup$$

$\{(anorient, x) \mid x \in O\} \cup$
$\{ \ (machine, polisher), (machine, roller), (machine, lathe),$
$\quad (machine, grinder), (machine, punch), (machine, drill\text{-}press),$
$\quad ((machine, spray\text{-}painter), (machine, immersion\text{-}painter)\} \cup$
$\{(has\text{-}paint, spray\text{-}painter, x) \mid x \in L\} \cup$
$\{(has\text{-}paint, immersion\text{-}painter, x) \mid x \in L\} \cup$
$\{(has\text{-}bit, punch, x), (has\text{-}bit, drill\text{-}press, x) \mid x \in W\} \cup$
$\{(can\text{-}orient, punch, x), (can\text{-}orient, drill\text{-}press, x) \mid x \in O\} \cup$
$\{(temperature, x, cold) \mid x \in P\} \cup \{(shape, x, is(x)) \mid x \in P\} \cup$
$\{(surface\text{-}condition, x, ic(x)) \mid x \in P\} \cup$
$\{(painted, x, ip(x)) \mid x \in P^{ip}\} \cup \{(has\text{-}hole, x, y, z) \mid (y, z) \in ih(x)\},$
$\bigwedge \{(shape, x, cylindrical) \mid x \in P^{gs}\} \wedge$
$\bigwedge \{(has\text{-}hole, x, y, z) \mid (y, z) \in gh(x)\} \wedge$
$\bigwedge \{(painted, x, gp(x)) \mid x \in P^{gp}\} \wedge$
$\bigwedge \{(surface\text{-}condition, x, gc(x)) \mid x \in P^{gc}\})$
$\mid (C' \cup P \cup S \cup L \cup W \cup O) \subseteq \Sigma,$
$C', P, S, L, W, \ and \ O \ are \ pairwise \ disjoint,$
$|P| \geq 1, |L| \geq 1, |W| \geq 1, |O| \geq 1, is : P \mapsto \{cylindrical\} \cup S,$
$ic : P \mapsto \{polished, rough, smooth\},$
$P^{ip} \subseteq P, ip : P^{ip} \mapsto L, ih : P \mapsto 2^{(W \times O)},$
$P^{gs} \subseteq P, P^{gc} \subseteq P, gc : P^{gc} \mapsto \{polished, rough, smooth\},$
$P^{gp} \subseteq P, gp : P^{gp} \mapsto L, gh : P \mapsto 2^{(W \times O)}\}$

All *Schedule* operators are ADL operators, and make use of conditional effects, sometimes with effect parameters, sometimes without effect parameters; complex conditions are not used. All instances share the constants *cylindrical, cold, hot, polished, rough, smooth, roller, lathe, polisher, grinder, punch, drillpress, spray-painter,* and *immersion-painter*: the relevant shape, temperatures, surface conditions, and machines. In the operators, these are all encoded via specific predicates, which deviates slightly from the original operators that explicitly refer to these constants. We have avoided such "domain constants" in order to keep our formal framework (i.e., the framework for ADL) as simple as possible. After removing static predicates, there is no difference at all.

Initially, all parts are cold, and have a shape and a surface condition specified. Some of the parts are also painted initially, and a part can have none or several holes. In the goal condition, some of the parts can be required to have cylindrical shape (the only shape that can be produced by the machines), some need an arbitrary surface condition (note that only the three given surface conditions can be produced by the machines), some must be painted, and each part can be required to have an arbitrary number of holes (note here that the parts can not be required to have *no* holes). In the original domain there are various negations, which are formulated by the extra predicates *not-equal* (the original formulation makes use of an *equality* predicate which is negated in all its appearances), *not-has-hole, not-busy, not-scheduled,* and *not-objscheduled*. It might seem restrictive that all appropriate machines can achieve all the respective goal conditions (like both painting machines having access to all colors), but that's what's the case in the published benchmarks.

A.19 Simple-Tsp

Definition A.19.1. *Simple-Tsp is the STRIPS domain* $(\mathcal{P}, \mathcal{O}, \mathcal{I})$ *where the set of predicates is*

$$\mathcal{P} = \{(not\text{-}eq, 2), (at, 1), (visited, 1)\}$$

$\mathcal{O}$ *consists of the single operator*

– *move:* $((x, y), \{(not\text{-}eq, x, y), (at, x)\}, \{(at, y), (visited, y)\}, \{(at, x)\})$

and the set of instances is

$$\mathcal{I} = \{ (L,$$
$$\{(not\text{-}eq, x, y) \mid x, y \in L, x \neq y\} \cup \{(at, l_0)\},$$
$$\{(visited, x) \mid x \in L\})$$
$$\mid L \subseteq \Sigma^+, |L| \geq 2, l_0 \in L\}$$

We have introduced non-equality to get rid of actions that try to move within a location.

A.20 Tireworld

Definition A.20.1. *Tireworld is the STRIPS domain* $(\mathcal{P}, \mathcal{O}, \mathcal{I})$ *where the set of predicates is*

$$\mathcal{P} = \{ (wheel, 1), (nut, 1), (obj, 1), (hub, 1), (ppump, 1), (pwrench, 1), (pjack, 1),$$
$$(open\text{-}boot, 0), (closed\text{-}boot, 0), (in\text{-}boot, 1), (have, 1), (intact, 1),$$
$$(inflated, 1), (not\text{-}inflated, 1), (loose, 2), (tight, 2), (on\text{-}ground, 1),$$
$$(not\text{-}on\text{-}ground, 1), (fastened, 1), (not\text{-}fastened, 1), (free, 1), (on, 2)\}$$

$\mathcal{O}$ *consists of the operators*

– *open-boot:* $((), \{(closed\text{-}boot)\}, \{(open\text{-}boot)\}, \{(closed\text{-}boot)\})$
– *close-boot:* $((), \{(open\text{-}boot)\}, \{(closed\text{-}boot)\}, \{(open\text{-}boot)\})$
– *fetch:* $((x), \{(obj, x), (in\text{-}boot, x), (open\text{-}boot)\}, \{(have, x)\}, \{(in\text{-}boot, x)\})$
– *put-away:* $((x), \{(obj, x), (have, x), (open\text{-}boot)\}, \{(in\text{-}boot, x)\}, \{(have, x)\})$
– *inflate:*

$$((x, y),$$
$$\{(wheel, x), (ppump, y), (have, y), (not\text{-}inflated, x), (intact, x)\},$$
$$\{(inflated, x)\},$$
$$\{(not\text{-}inflated, x)\})$$

– *loosen:*

$((x, y, z),$
$\{(nut, x), (hub, y), (pwrench, z), (have, z), (tight, x, y), (on\text{-}ground, y)\},$
$\{(loose, x, y)\},$
$\{(tight, x, y)\})$

– *tighten:*

$((x, y, z),$
$\{(nut, x), (hub, y), (pwrench, z), (have, z), (loose, x, y), (on\text{-}ground, y)\},$
$\{(tight, x, y)\},$
$\{(loose, x, y)\})$

– jack-up:

$((x, y),$
$\{(hub, x), (pjack, y), (have, y), (on\text{-}ground, x)\},$
$\{(not\text{-}on\text{-}ground, x)\},$
$\{(have, y), (on\text{-}ground, x)\})$

– *jack-down:*

$((x, y),$
$\{(hub, x), (pjack, y), (not\text{-}on\text{-}ground, x)\},$
$\{(have, y), (on\text{-}ground, x)\},$
$\{(not\text{-}on\text{-}ground, x)\})$

– undo:

$((x, y, z),$
$\{ (nut, x), (hub, y), (pwrench, z),$
$(have, z), (fastened, y), (loose, x, y), (not\text{-}on\text{-}ground, y)\},$
$\{(have, x), (not\text{-}fastened, y)\},$
$\{(fastened, y), (loose, x, y)\})$

– do-up:

$((x, y, z),$
$\{ (nut, x), (hub, y), (pwrench, z),$
$(have, z), (have, x), (not\text{-}fastened, y), (not\text{-}on\text{-}ground, y)\},$
$\{(fastened, y), (loose, x, y)\},$
$\{(have, x), (not\text{-}fastened, y)\})$

– remove-wheel:

$((x, y),$
$\{(wheel, x), (hub, y), (on, x, y), (not\text{-}on\text{-}ground, y), (not\text{-}fastened, y)\},$
$\{(have, x), (free, y)\},$
$\{(on, x, y)\})$

$-$ *put-on-wheel:*

$((x, y),$
$\quad \{ (wheel, x), (hub, y), (have, x), (free, y),$
$\quad\quad (not\text{-}on\text{-}ground, y), (not\text{-}fastened, y)\},$
$\quad \{(on, x, y)\},$
$\quad \{(have, x), (free, y)\})$

and the set of instances is

$\mathcal{I} = \{ \ (\ \{pump, wrench, jack\} \cup N \cup H \cup W,$
$\quad\quad where \ \ N = \{n_1, \ldots, n_n\}, H = \{h_1, \ldots, h_n\},$
$\quad\quad\quad W = \{w_1, s_1, \ldots, w_n, s_n\},$
$\quad\quad \{(obj, pump), (obj, wrench), (obj, jack)\} \cup \{(nut, x) \mid x \in N\} \cup$
$\quad\quad \{(hub, x) \mid x \in H\} \cup \{(wheel, x) \mid x \in W\} \cup$
$\quad\quad \{(obj, x) \mid x \in N \cup W\} \cup$
$\quad\quad \{(ppump, pump), (pwrench, wrench), (pjack, jack)\} \cup$
$\quad\quad \{(on, w_i, h_i), (on\text{-}ground, h_i), (tight, n_i, h_i) \mid 1 \leq i \leq n\} \cup$
$\quad\quad \{(fastened, h_i), (intact, s_i) \mid 1 \leq i \leq n\} \cup$
$\quad\quad \{(in\text{-}boot, s_i), (not\text{-}inflated, s_i) \mid 1 \leq i \leq n\} \cup$
$\quad\quad \{(in\text{-}boot, pump), (in\text{-}boot, wrench), \} \cup$
$\quad\quad \{(in\text{-}boot, jack), (closed\text{-}boot)\},$
$\quad\quad \{(on, s_i, h_i), (inflated, s_i), (tight, n_i, h_i), (in\text{-}boot, w_i) \mid 1 \leq i \leq n\} \cup$
$\quad\quad \{(in\text{-}boot, pump), (in\text{-}boot, wrench), (in\text{-}boot, jack), (closed\text{-}boot)\})$
$\quad \mid \{pump, wrench, jack\} \cup N \cup H \cup W \subseteq \Sigma^+,$
$\quad\quad \{pump, wrench, jack\}, N, H, \ and \ W \ are \ pairwise \ disjoint, n \geq 1\}$

All instances share the constants *pump*, *wrench*, and *jack*, i.e., the tools required for performing the different working steps. These are encoded in the operators by using a specific predicate for each tool. We remark that the original operators directly refer to the tools as constants. We have avoided such "domain constants" in order to keep our formal framework (i.e., the framework for ADL) as simple as possible. After removing static predicates, there is no difference at all.

B. Automated Instance Generation

In this appendix, we list the automated instance generation strategies we use in all domains. This information forms the background for all points in the text where we describe how a collection of example instances was generated. The information is especially relevant for the investigation in Chapter 9, which aims at empirically identifying, for a number of domains, properties that hold across all instances, i.e., more practically, properties that hold across all instances as can be generated with the generation strategies described below.

In all of our domains, the instances are determined by a set of *domain parameters* (like the numbers of floors and passengers in *Miconic-STRIPS*), usually modulo a *random element* (like the distribution of origin- and destination-floors in *Miconic-STRIPS*). The domain parameter values, roughly, form the input parameters of our generation strategies, which output a (randomized, if necessary) instance according to these parameter values. Technically, a set of domain parameters is *exhaustive* if the Cartesian product of the possible values of all parameters contains all instances of the domain modulo random elements (and constant names). The set of all instances, in our cases here, is given by the formal definitions in Appendix A. Note that there can be a choice about what exactly one assumes as the borderline between "domain parameters" and "random elements". We do not fully formalize the concept of exhaustive sets of domain parameters, but settle for the intuitively clear interpretation: the only point in the book where the domain parameter concept is crucial is the empirical investigation in Chapter 9, and for this an intuitive interpretation seems sufficient.

Ideally, and as a necessary prerequisite (only) for the experiments in Chapter 9, the input parameters of our generation strategies each should form an exhaustive set of parameters for the respective domain. While this is in fact true in most of the domains, in some cases we apply simplifications to make automated generation more feasible. Mostly, the simplifications are justified in that the published benchmark collections are more restrictive than the formal definitions in Appendix A. Some domains are not investigated in Chapter 9 at all so we do not necessarily need an exhaustive generation method.

For intuitive descriptions of the domains, see Section 2.3. For formal definitions, see Appendix A. We use the notation given in Appendix A for the sets of instances, and include short explanations. We list the 20 domains in alphabetical order.

J. Hoffmann: Utilizing Problem Structure in Planning, LNAI 2854, pp. 235–241, 2003.
© Springer-Verlag Berlin Heidelberg 2003

B.1 Assembly

In *Assembly*, an exhaustive set of domain parameters is the following. The number $|R|$ of resources; the depth and maximal branching factor of the tree defined by the part-of relation; the number of resources that each assembly requires; the number of transient-part relations (x, y) for each assembly y; the number of assemble-order relations $(x, z) \in ao(y)$ for each assembly y; finally the number of remove-order relations $(x, z) \in ro(y)$ for each assembly y. The random elements are then the exact shape of the part-of tree, as well as the specific resource requirements, transient-part relations, assemble-order relations, and remove-order relations.

Our generator realizes a simplified version of the above domain parameters. There are parameters for the part-of tree structure, and probabilities that control the frequency of resource requirements, transient-part relations, assemble-order relations, and remove-order relations. The simplifications are these. First, each assembly is only transient part of assemblies at a higher tree level. Second, there are no remove orders $(x, z) \in ro(y)$ where x is a transient part, precisely $ro(y) \subseteq pa(y) \times tr(y)$ for all $y \in As$ (remember that As denotes the set of all assemblies). Third, each assembly requires at most one resource. The first and third properties are fulfilled by all examples in the AIPS-1998 benchmark collection except the 5 flawed ones (c.f. the discussion of the AIPS-1998 *Assembly* collection in Section 8.5). The second simplifying property holds in 24 of the 25 unflawed benchmark examples.[1] We need the generator only for the experiment in Chapter 7, for which exhaustiveness is no necessary prerequisite.

Precisely, the generator parameters that control the part-of tree structure are the depth of the tree, the maximal branching factor (sons of any node), and additionally a probability specifying the likelihood with which a node in the tree has any sons at all (the last parameter serves as a means of restricting the sizes of trees with large depths). The part-of tree is generated by starting with g, inserting sons to a node with the given probability, and choosing the number of sons — if any — as uniformly drawn between 1 and the maximal branching factor. To control the remaining properties of the instance, the parameters are $|R|$, and four probabilities for the insertion of resource requirements, transient-part relations, assemble-order relations, and remove-order relations. All non-leaf nodes in the tree are given a uniformly drawn resource requirement with the respective probability. The transient-part relation $x \in tr(y)$ is inserted with the respective probability between any pair x and y of assemblies where y is in a higher tree level than x. An assemble-order relation $(x, z) \in ao(y)$ is inserted with the respective probability between pairs x and z of assemblies where x and z are parts or transient parts of y. A remove-order relation $(x, z) \in ro(y)$ is inserted with the respective probability between pairs x and z of assemblies where x is a part and z is a transient part of y. In the assemble-order and remove-

---

[1] Note that $\forall y \in As : ao(y) \subseteq pa(y) \times tr(y)$ is slightly stronger than $\forall y \in As : (x, z) \in ro(y) \wedge z \in tr(y) \Rightarrow x \in pa(y)$, the latter of which we use in Section 8.5. The weaker restriction holds across all unflawed AIPS-1998 instances.

order constraints, cycles are avoided by arbitrarily arranging the assemblies in question and only allow pairs x and z where x is arranged prior to z.

B.2 Blocksworld-arm

In *Blocksworld-arm* there is only one domain parameter: the number of blocks. Random element is the initial and goal configuration of the blocks. Our generator takes in the single parameter, and creates initial and goal configurations using the random Blocksworld state generator by John Slaney and Sylvie Thiebaux [93].

B.3 Blocksworld-no-arm

Identical to *Blocksworld-arm*, see above.

B.4 Briefcaseworld

In *Briefcaseworld*, exhaustive domain parameters are $|L|$, $|P|$, and $|P'|$: the numbers of locations, of portables, and of portables that must be transported, respectively. Random element is the distribution of initial and goal locations. Our generation method simplifies that by assuming $P = P'$ (which is true in the published benchmarks). The generator takes in $|L|$ and $|P|$, and uniformly draws the initial and goal locations for all portables and the briefcase.

B.5 Ferry

In *Ferry*, exhaustive domain parameters are $|L|$, $|C|$, and $|C'|$: the numbers of locations, of cars, and of cars that must be transported, respectively, with the random element being the distribution of initial and goal locations. Our generation method simplifies that slightly by assuming $C = C'$ (all portables are mentioned in the goal, which is true in the published benchmarks as far as the author is aware of them). The generator takes in $|L|$ and $|C|$, and uniformly draws the initial and goal locations for all cars, as well as the initial location of the ferry.

B.6 Freecell

In *Freecell*, an exhaustive set of domain parameters is this: the number n of suits, the numbers $m_1, \ldots, m_n$ of cards in each suit, the numbers nce of free cells and nco of columns, and finally the colors (0 or 1) of all suits; the random element then is the initial distribution I of the cards over the columns.

Our generator implements a slightly simplified version of these parameters, where there are at most four suits of cards, and their colors are alternatively black and red (i.e., 0 or 1) like in every real-world card game. These simplifications are naturally fulfilled by the examples in the published benchmark collection, which contains only real-world instances and some smaller versions thereof (in any case, we need the generator only for the experiment in Chapter 7, for which exhaustiveness is no necessary prerequisite). The parameters of the generator are $n \leq 4$, $m_1, \ldots, m_n$, nce, and nco. Instances, i.e., the initial distribution I of the cards, are generated by repeatedly uniformly drawing a card from the set of all cards until a card is drawn that has not yet been placed in I; the card is then placed on top of (the stack in) a uniformly drawn column. The goal is always to have the highest-valued card of each suit home.

B.7 Fridge

In *Fridge*, exhaustive domain parameters are n and m: the numbers of fridges, and of screws per compressor. There is no random element.

B.8 Grid

In *Grid*, an exhaustive set of domain parameters is as follows: n and m, the x- and y-extensions of the grid; $|S|$, the number of different shapes; $|K|$, the number of keys; $|P'|$, the number of locked places; $|K'|$, the number of keys that must be transported; assuming that the shapes of the keys and of the locked places are also given as parameters, the random elements are then all initial and goal places.

Our generation method realizes the above domain parameters as follows. The parameters of the generator are n, m, $|S|$, the number of keys and locks for each shape (i.e., two $|S|$-vectors of numbers), and the probability that a key is mentioned in the goal. The initial locations of the locked places, the keys, and the robot are drawn uniformly from the set of all places on the grid. Each key is inserted into the goal with the given probability. The specific goal places are drawn uniformly from the grid.

B.9 Gripper

In *Gripper*, the only domain parameter is $|B|$: the number of balls to be transported. There is no random element.

B.10 Hanoi

In *Hanoi*, the only domain parameter is n: the number of discs. There is no random element.

B.11 Logistics

In *Logistics*, the instances are exhaustively determined by: the number $|C| = n$ of cities; the sizes $|L_1|, \ldots, |L_n|$ (number of locations) of the cities; the number $|O|$ of objects; the numbers $|T|$ of trucks and $|A|$ of airplanes; and the number $|O'|$ of objects that must be transported. The random element is the distribution of initial and goal locations. Our generation method simplifies the situation in that $|L_1| = \ldots = |L_n|$, that $O = O'$, and that $|T| = |C|$ where each truck is located in a different city (which restrictions are true in the AIPS-2000 benchmark collection). The parameters of the generation strategy are thus $|C|$, $|O|$, $|A|$, and $|L_i|$. The generator takes in the values, and uniformly draws the initial locations for all objects, airplanes, and trucks (the latter with the restriction that no two trucks are in the same city), as well as the goal locations for all objects.

B.12 Miconic-ADL

In *Miconic-ADL*, an exhaustive set of domain parameters are the numbers $|F|$ of floors and $|P|$ of passengers, together with all the additional constraints: the number $|GU|$ of passengers that can only ever be transported upwards, the number $|GD|$ of passengers with the same constraint downwards, the number $|GN|$ of passengers that must go non-stop, the number $|AT|$ of attendants, the number $|NA|$ of passengers that must never be alone, the number $|VI|$ of VIPs, the number $|CA|$ of passengers in conflict group A, the number $|CB|$ of passengers in conflict group B; finally, the number of passengers for whom an access restriction applies, and for each of them the number of floors to which they have no access. The random elements here are the origin and destination floors of the passengers, as well as the distribution of all the constraints.

Our generator takes in $|F|$ and $|P|$, as well as all the above values in terms of percentages of total, i.e., for example $\frac{|VI|}{|P|} * 100$, the percentage of passengers that are VIPs. The origin and destination floors are drawn uniformly from the available set of floors. To create the appropriate number of passengers of a certain type, one passenger is iteratively uniformly chosen until the required number of passengers is selected; similarly for the floors to which a passenger has no access. The generator excludes some obvious cases implying unsolvability, like when passengers of both conflict groups are waiting at the same origin floor, or a passenger has no access to her own destination floor. The default values of the parameters that control the constraints (the default values have been used both for the AIPS-2000 competition collection and for the collection that we use in Chapter 7) are: 20% passengers that can only travel in their own direction (corresponding to $|GU| + |GD|$), 5% non-stop passengers, 60% attendants and 10% passengers that can not travel alone, 5% VIPs, as well as 20% passengers in conflict group A and 80% in conflict group B.

B.13 Miconic-SIMPLE

In *Miconic-SIMPLE*, exhaustive domain parameters are $|P|$ and $|F|$: the numbers of passengers, and of floors. The random element is the distribution of origin and destination floors. The generator takes in $|P|$ and $|F|$, and uniformly draws the origin and destination floors of all passengers.

B.14 Miconic-STRIPS

Identical to *Miconic-SIMPLE*, see above.

B.15 Movie

In *Movie*, the exhaustive domain parameters are the numbers of items in each type of snacks, $|C|$, $|D|$, $|P|$, $|Z|$, and $|K|$. There is no random element. Our generation method simplifies the situation in that it assumes $|C| = |D| = |P| = |Z| = |K|$, i.e., we assume the number of items is constant across snack types. This holds true in the AIPS-1998 competition collection. Our generator takes in the single parameter value, and outputs the respective instance.

B.16 Mprime

In *Mprime*, an exhaustive set of domain parameters are the number $|L|$ of locations, the number $|M|$ of edges between locations, the number $|V|$ of vehicles, the number $|O|$ of objects, the number $|O'|$ of objects that must be transported, as well as the numbers $|F|$ and $|S|$ of different fuel and space amounts. The random elements here are the distribution of the edges, the initial and goal locations, and the assignment of fuel (space) units to locations (vehicles).

Our generator simplifies the situation in that the edge set M forms a bi-directional cycle together with the locations L, i.e., if $L = \{l_1, \ldots, l_n\}$ then $M = \{(l_1, l_2), (l_2, l_1), \ldots, (l_{n-1}, l_n), (l_n, l_{n-1}), (l_n, l_1), (l_1, l_n)\}$. This simplification is not justified by the published benchmarks, but we need the generator only for the experiment in Chapter 7, for which exhaustiveness is no necessary prerequisite. We additionally assume that all objects must be transported, $O = O'$. The parameters of our generation strategy are $|L|$, $|V|$, $|O|$, $|F|$, and $|S|$. Appropriate initial and goal locations are created by uniformly drawing from L. Fuel amounts are assigned to locations by uniformly drawing from F. Space amounts are assigned by uniformly drawing from $S \setminus \{s_0\}$, i.e., each vehicle has at least one transport space.

B.17 Mystery

Identical to *Mprime*, see above.

B.18 Schedule

In *Schedule*, an exhaustive set of domain parameters is this: the number $|P|$ of parts to be processed, the number $|S|$ of additional shapes (except cylindrical), the number $|L|$ of colors, the number $|W|$ of hole widths, the number $|O|$ of hole orientations, the number $|P^{ip}|$ of initially painted parts, the number $|P^{gs}|$ of parts that have to be cylindrical for the goal, the number $|P^{gc}|$ of parts that have to have a certain surface condition for the goal, the number $|P^{gp}|$ of parts that must be colored for the goal; finally, the numbers (for each part) of holes in the initial and goal states. The random elements here are the specific initial shapes, surface conditions, colors, and holes, as well as the specific goal surface conditions, colors, and holes.

Our generator realizes a slightly simplified version of the above domain parameters, in terms of probabilities for all the initial and goal conditions. The parameters of the generator are $|P|$, $|S|$, $|L|$, $|W|$, and $|O|$, as well as probabilities that any part is initially colored or has a hole, and that any part must be cylindrical, have a surface condition, be colored, or have a hole for the goal. The simplification is that each part has at most one hole in (each of) the initial and goal states. While this simplification is not justified by the published benchmarks, we need the generator only for the experiment in Chapter 7, for which exhaustiveness is no necessary prerequisite. The generator creates the initial state by assigning a uniformly drawn shape and surface condition to each part, and additionally with the respective probabilities a uniformly drawn color and a uniformly drawn (from all combinations of widths and orientations) hole. The goal state is created similarly by introducing with the respective probabilities for each part the constraint that the part must be cylindrical in the end, have a uniformly drawn surface condition, a uniformly drawn color, or a uniformly drawn hole.

B.19 Simple-Tsp

In *Simple-Tsp*, the only domain parameter is $|L|$: the number of locations to be visited. There is no random element.

B.20 Tireworld

In *Tireworld*, the only domain parameter is n: the number of flat tires to be replaced. There is no random element.

References

1. *Proceedings of the 17th National Conference of the American Association for Artificial Intelligence (AAAI-00)*, Austin, TX, July 2000. MIT Press.
2. Corin R. Anderson, David E. Smith, and Daniel S. Weld. Conditional effects in Graphplan. In Simmons et al. [92], pages 44–53.
3. Fahiem Bacchus. The AIPS'00 planning competition. *The AI Magazine*, 22(3):47–56, 2001.
4. Piergioirgio Bertoli, Alessandro Cimatti, John Slaney, and Sylvie Thiebaux. Solving power supply restoration problems with planning via symbolic model checking. In ECAI-02 [23], pages 576–80.
5. Piergiorgio Bertoli, Alessandro Cimatti, Marco Roveri, and Paolo Traverso. Planning in nondeterministic domains under partial observability via symbolic model checking. In Nebel [75], pages 473–478.
6. S. Biundo and M. Fox, editors. *Recent Advances in AI Planning. 5th European Conference on Planning (ECP'99)*, Durham, UK, September 1999. Springer-Verlag.
7. Avrim L. Blum and Merrick L. Furst. Fast planning through planning graph analysis. In *Proceedings of the 14th International Joint Conference on Artificial Intelligence (IJCAI-95)*, pages 1636–1642, Montreal, Canada, August 1995. Morgan Kaufmann.
8. Avrim L. Blum and Merrick L. Furst. Fast planning through planning graph analysis. *Artificial Intelligence*, 90(1-2):279–298, 1997.
9. Blai Bonet and Héctor Geffner. HSP: Heuristic search planner. In *AIPS-98 Planning Competition*, Pittsburgh, PA, 1998.
10. Blai Bonet and Héctor Geffner. Planning as heuristic search: New results. In Biundo and Fox [6], pages 60–72.
11. Blai Bonet and Héctor Geffner. Heuristic search planner 2.0. *The AI Magazine*, 22(3):77–80, 2001.
12. Blai Bonet and Héctor Geffner. Planning as heuristic search. *Artificial Intelligence*, 129(1–2):5–33, 2001.
13. Blai Bonet, Gábor Loerincs, and Héctor Geffner. A robust and fast action selection mechanism for planning. In *Proceedings of the 14th National Conference of the American Association for Artificial Intelligence (AAAI-97)*, pages 714–719. MIT Press, July 1997.
14. Blai Bonet and Sylvie Thiebaux. GPT meets PSR. In *Proceedings of the 13th International Conference on Automated Planning and Scheduling (ICAPS-03)*, pages 102–111, Trento, Italy, 2003. Morgan Kaufmann.
15. Tom Bylander. The computational complexity of propositional STRIPS planning. *Artificial Intelligence*, 69(1–2):165–204, 1994.
16. A. Cesta and D. Borrajo, editors. *Recent Advances in AI Planning. 6th European Conference on Planning (ECP'01)*, Toledo, Spain, September 2001. Springer-Verlag.
17. A. K. Chandra and D. Harel. Structure and complexity of relational queries. *Journal of Computer and System Sciences*, 25(1):99–128, 1982.

18. Jie Cheng and Keki B. Irani. Ordering problem subgoals. In N. S. Sridharan, editor, *Proceedings of the 11th International Joint Conference on Artificial Intelligence (IJCAI-89)*, pages 931–936, Detroit, MI, August 1989. Morgan Kaufmann.

19. S. Chien, R. Kambhampati, and C. Knoblock, editors. *Proceedings of the 5th International Conference on Artificial Intelligence Planning Systems (AIPS-00)*. AAAI Press, Menlo Park, 2000.

20. D. Clark, J. Frank, I. Gent, E. MacIntyre, N. Tomov, and T. Walsh. Local search and the number of solutions. In *Proceedings of the 3rd International Conference on Principles and Practice of Constraint Programming*, pages 119–133, Cambridge, Massachusetts, 1996.

21. J. Crawford and L. Auton. Experimental results on the cross-over point in satisfiability problems. In *Proceedings of the 11th National Conference of the American Association for Artificial Intelligence (AAAI-93)*, pages 21–27, Washington, DC, July 1993. MIT Press.

22. Minh. B. Do and Subbarao Kambhampati. Sapa: A domain-independent heuristic metric temporal planner. In Cesta and Borrajo [16], pages 109–120.

23. *Proceedings of the 15th European Conference on Artificial Intelligence (ECAI-02)*, Lyon, France, July 2002. Wiley.

24. S. Edelkamp. Heuristic search planning with BDDs. In *ECAI-Workshop: PuK*, 2000.

25. Stefan Edelkamp. Promela planning. In *Proceedings SPIN-03*, 2003. Accepted for publication.

26. Stefan Edelkamp and Malte Helmert. Exhibiting knowledge in planning problems to minimize state encoding length. In Biundo and Fox [6], pages 135–147.

27. Stefan Edelkamp and Malte Helmert. MIPS: The model checking integrated planning system. *AI Magazine*, 22(3):67–71, 2001.

28. George W. Ernst and Allen Newell. *GPS: A Case Study in Generality and Problem-Solving*. Academic Press, New York, NY, 1969.

29. Kutluhan Erol, Dana S. Nau, and James A. Hendler. UMCP: A sound and complete planning procedure for hierarchical task-network planning. In *Proceedings of the 2nd International Conference on Artificial Intelligence Planning Systems (AIPS-94)*, pages 249–254, Chicago, IL, 1994. AAAI Press, Menlo Park.

30. Shimon Even and Yossi Shiloach. NP-completeness of several arrangement problems. Technical Report 43, Department of Computer Science, Haifa, Israel, 1975.

31. Richard E. Fikes and Nils Nilsson. STRIPS: A new approach to the application of theorem proving to problem solving. *Artificial Intelligence*, 2:189–208, 1971.

32. Maria Fox and Derek Long. The automatic inference of state invariants in TIM. *Journal of Artificial Intelligence Research*, 9:367–421, 1998.

33. Maria Fox and Derek Long. The detection and exploitation of symmetry in planning problems. In IJCAI-96 [53], pages 956–961.

34. Maria Fox and Derek Long. Hybrid STAN: Identifying and managing combinatorial optimisation sub-problems in planning. In Nebel [75], pages 445–450.

35. Maria Fox and Derek Long. STAN4: A hybrid planning strategy based on subproblem abstraction. *The AI Magazine*, 22(3):81–84, 2001.

36. Jeremy Frank, Peter Cheeseman, and John Stutz. When gravity fails: Local search topology. *Journal of Artificial Intelligence Research*, 7:249–281, 1997.

37. B. Cenk Gazen and Craig Knoblock. Combining the expressiveness of UCPOP with the efficiency of Graphplan. In Steel and Alami [95], pages 221–233.

38. A. Gerevini and L. Schubert. Inferring state constraints in DISCOPLAN: Some new results. In AAAI-00 [1], pages 761–767.

39. Alfonso Gerevini and Len Schubert. Accelerating partial-order planners: Some techniques for effective search control and pruning. *Journal of Artificial Intelligence Research*, 5:95–137, 1996.

40. Enrico Giunchiglia, Alessandro Massarotto, and Roberto Sebastiani. Act, and the rest will follow: Exploiting determinism in planning as satisfiability. In *Proceedings of the 15th National Conference of the American Association for Artificial Intelligence (AAAI-98)*, pages 948–953, Madison, WI, July 1998. MIT Press.

41. Patrick Haslum and Hector Geffner. Admissible heuristics for optimal planning. In Chien et al. [19], pages 140–149.

42. Malte Helmert. On the complexity of planning in transportation domains. In Cesta and Borrajo [16], pages 349–360.

43. Malte Helmert. Complexity results for standard benchmark domains in planning. *Artificial Intelligence*, 143:219–262, 2003.

44. Jörg Hoffmann. A heuristic for domain independent planning and its use in an enforced hill-climbing algorithm. In *Proceedings of the 12th International Symposium on Methodologies for Intelligent Systems (ISMIS-00)*, pages 216–227. Springer-Verlag, October 2000.

45. Jörg Hoffmann. FF: The fast-forward planning system. *The AI Magazine*, 22(3):57–62, 2001.

46. Jörg Hoffmann. Extending FF to numerical state variables. In ECAI-02 [23], pages 571–575.

47. Jörg Hoffmann. The Metric-FF planning system: Translating "ignoring delete lists" to numerical state variables. *Journal of Artificial Intelligence Research*, 2003. Special issue on the 3rd International Planning Competition, to appear.

48. Jörg Hoffmann. Where ignoring delete lists works: Local search topology in planning benchmarks. Technical Report 185, Albert-Ludwigs-Universität, Institut für Informatik, Freiburg, Germany, 2003. available at http://www.informatik.uni-freiburg.de/~hoffmann/papers/ai03report.ps.gz.

49. Jörg Hoffmann and Bernhard Nebel. RIFO revisited: Detecting relaxed irrelevance. In Cesta and Borrajo [16], pages 325–336.

50. Steffen Hölldobler and Hans-Peter Störr. Solving the entailment problem in the fluent calculus using binary decision diagrams. In *Proceedings of the First International Conference on Computational Logic (CL)*, 2000. To appear.

51. Holger Hoos. SAT-encodings, search space structure, and local search performance. In IJCAI-96 [53], pages 296–302.

52. Holger Hoos and Thomas Stuetzle. Towards a characterisation of the behaviour of stochastic local search algorithms for sat. *Artificial Intelligence*, 112:213–232, 1999.

53. *Proceedings of the 16th International Joint Conference on Artificial Intelligence (IJCAI-99)*, Stockholm, Sweden, August 1999. Morgan Kaufmann.

54. Keki B. Irani and Jie Cheng. Subgoal ordering and goal augmentation for heuristic problem solving. In J. McDermott, editor, *Proceedings of the 10th International Joint Conference on Artificial Intelligence (IJCAI-87)*, pages 1018–1024, Milan, Italy, August 1987. Morgan Kaufmann.

55. David Joslin and John W. Roach. A theoretical analysis of conjunctive-goal problems. *Artificial Intelligence*, 41:97–106, 1990.

56. Subbarao Kambhampati, Eric Parker, and Eric Lambrecht. Understanding and extending Graphplan. In Steel and Alami [95], pages 260–272.

57. Henry Kautz and Bart Selman. The role of domain-specific knowledge in the planning as satisfiability framework. In Simmons et al. [92], pages 181–189.

58. Henry Kautz and Bart Selman. Unifying SAT-based and graph-based planning. In IJCAI-96 [53], pages 318–325.

59. Henry A. Kautz and Bart Selman. Planning as satisfiability. In *Proceedings of the 10th European Conference on Artificial Intelligence (ECAI-92)*, pages 359–363, Vienna, Austria, August 1992. Wiley.

60. Henry A. Kautz and Bart Selman. Pushing the envelope: Planning, propositional logic, and stochastic search. In *Proceedings of the 13th National Conference of the American Association for Artificial Intelligence (AAAI-96)*, pages 1194–1201. MIT Press, July 1996.

61. Jana Koehler. Solving complex planning tasks through extraction of subproblems. In Simmons et al. [92], pages 62–69.

62. Jana Koehler and Jörg Hoffmann. On reasonable and forced goal orderings and their use in an agenda-driven planning algorithm. *Journal of Artificial Intelligence Research*, 12:338–386, 2000.

63. Jana Koehler and Jörg Hoffmann. On the instantiation of ADL operators involving arbitrary first-order formulas. In *Proceedings ECAI-00 Workshop on New Results in Planning, Scheduling and Design*, 2000.

64. Jana Koehler, Bernhard Nebel, Jörg Hoffmann, and Yannis Dimopoulos. Extending planning graphs to an ADL subset. In Steel and Alami [95], pages 273–285.

65. Jana Koehler and Kilian Schuster. Elevator control as a planning problem. In Chien et al. [19], pages 331–338.

66. Vladimir Lifschitz. On the semantics of STRIPS. In M. P. Georgeff and A. Lansky, editors, *Reasoning about Actions and Plans: Proceedings of the 1986 Workshop*, pages 1–9, Timberline, OR, June 1986. Morgan Kaufmann.

67. Fangzhen Lin. A planner called R. *The AI Magazine*, 22(3):73–76, 2001.

68. Y. Liu, S. Koenig, and D. Furcy. Speeding up the calculation of the heuristics for heuristic search-based planning. In *Proceedings of the 18th National Conference of the American Association for Artificial Intelligence (AAAI-02)*, pages 484–491, Edmonton, AL, July 2002. MIT Press.

69. David A. McAllester and David Rosenblitt. Systematic nonlinear planning. In *Proceedings of the 9th National Conference of the American Association for Artificial Intelligence (AAAI-91)*, pages 634–639, Anaheim, CA, July 1991. MIT Press.

70. John McCarthy. Programs with common sense. In *Proceedings of the Symposium on Mechanisation of the Thought Process I*, 1959.

71. John McCarthy and Patrick J. Hayes. Some philosophical problems from the standpoint of artificial intelligence. In B. Meltzer and D. Michie, editors, *Machine Intelligence*, volume 4, pages 463–502. Edinburgh University Press, Edinburgh, UK, 1969. Also published in [99].

72. Drew McDermott. A heuristic estimator for means-ends analysis in planning. In *Proceedings of the 3rd International Conference on Artificial Intelligence Planning Systems (AIPS-96)*, pages 142–149. AAAI Press, Menlo Park, 1996.

73. Drew McDermott. The 1998 AI planning systems competition. *The AI Magazine*, 21(2):35–55, 2000.

74. Drew V. McDermott. Using regression-match graphs to control search in planning. *Artificial Intelligence*, 109(1-2):111–159, 1999.

75. B. Nebel, editor. *Proceedings of the 17th International Joint Conference on Artificial Intelligence (IJCAI-01)*, Seattle, Washington, USA, August 2001. Morgan Kaufmann.

76. Bernhard Nebel. On the compilability and expressive power of propositional planning formalisms. *Journal of Artificial Intelligence Research*, 12:271–315, 2000.

77. Bernhard Nebel, Yannis Dimopoulos, and Jana Koehler. Ignoring irrelevant facts and operators in plan generation. In Steel and Alami [95], pages 338–350.

78. Allen Newell and Herbert Simon. GPS, a program that simulates human thought. In E. Feigenbaum and J. Feldman, editors, *Computers and Thought*, pages 279–293. McGraw-Hill, 1963.

79. XuanLong Nguyen and Subbarao Kambhampati. Reviving partial order planning. In Nebel [75], pages 459–464.

80. Judea Pearl. *Heuristics*. Morgan Kaufmann, 1983.

81. Edwin P.D. Pednault. ADL: Exploring the middle ground between STRIPS and the situation calculus. In R. Brachman, H. J. Levesque, and R. Reiter, editors, *Principles of Knowledge Representation and Reasoning: Proceedings of the 1st International Conference (KR-89)*, pages 324–331, Toronto, ON, May 1989. Morgan Kaufmann.

82. J. Scott Penberthy and Daniel S. Weld. UCPOP: A sound, complete, partial order planner for ADL. In B. Nebel, W. Swartout, and C. Rich, editors, *Principles of Knowledge Representation and Reasoning: Proceedings of the 3rd International Conference (KR-92)*, pages 103–114, Cambridge, MA, October 1992. Morgan Kaufmann.

83. Martha E. Pollack, David Joslin, and Massimo Paolucci. Flaw selection strategies for partial-order planning. *Journal of Artificial Intelligence Research*, 6:1–34, 1997.

84. Julie Porteous and Laura Sebastia. Extracting and ordering landmarks for planning. In *Proceedings UK Planning and Scheduling SIG Workshop*, 2000.

85. Ioannis Refanidis and Ioannis Vlahavas. GRT: a domain independent heuristic for STRIPS worlds based on greedy regression tables. In Biundo and Fox [6], pages 47–59.

86. Ioannis Refanidis and Ioannis Vlahavas. The GRT planner. *The AI Magazine*, 22(3):63–65, 2001.

87. Jussi Rintanen. An iterative algorithm for synthesizing invariants. In AAAI-00 [1], pages 806–811.

88. Stuart Russell and Peter Norvig. *Artificial Intelligence: A Modern Approach*. Prentice-Hall, Englewood Cliffs, NJ, 1995.

89. E. Sacerdoti. *A Structure for Plans and Behavior*. North-Holland, Amsterdam, Holland, 1977.

90. Bart Selman, Hector J. Levesque, and David Mitchell. A new method for solving hard satisfiability problems. In *Proceedings of the 10th National Conference of the American Association for Artificial Intelligence (AAAI-92)*, pages 440–446, San Jose, CA, July 1992. MIT Press.

91. S. Siegel and Jr. N. J. Castellan. *Nonparametric Statistics for the Behavioral Sciences*. McGraw-Hill, 2nd edition, 1988.

92. R. Simmons, M. Veloso, and S. Smith, editors. *Proceedings of the 4th International Conference on Artificial Intelligence Planning Systems (AIPS-98)*. AAAI Press, Menlo Park, 1998.

93. John Slaney and Sylvie Thiebaux. Blocks world revisited. *Artificial Intelligence*, 125:119–153, 2001.

94. David E. Smith and Daniel S. Weld. Temporal planning with mutual exclusion reasoning. In IJCAI-96 [53], pages 326–337.

95. S. Steel and R. Alami, editors. *Recent Advances in AI Planning. 4th European Conference on Planning (ECP'97)*, volume 1348 of *Lecture Notes in Artificial Intelligence*, Toulouse, France, September 1997. Springer-Verlag.

96. L. J. Stockmeyer and A. R. Meyer. Word problems requiring exponential time. In *Proceedings of the 5th Annual ACM Symposium on Theory of Computing*, pages 1–9. ACM Press, 1983.

97. Hans-Peter Stoerr. Planning in the fluent calculus using binary decision diagrams. *The AI Magazine*, 22(3):103–105, 2001.

98. Moshe Y. Vardi. The complexity of relational query languages. In *Proceedings of the 14th ACM Symposium on the Theory of Computation*, pages 137–146, 1982.

99. Bonnie Lynn Webber and Nils J. Nilsson, editors. *Readings in Artificial Intelligence*. Tioga, Palo Alto, CA, 1981.

Index